# STRUGGLES
# FOR SOCIAL
# RIGHTS IN
# LATIN AMERICA

# STRUGGLES FOR SOCIAL RIGHTS IN LATIN AMERICA

Edited by

Susan Eva Eckstein

and Timothy P. Wickham-Crowley

Routledge

NEW YORK AND LONDON

Published in 2003 by
Routledge
29 West 35th Street
New York, NY 10001
www.routledge-ny.com

Published in Great Britain by
Routledge
11 New Fetter Lane
London EC4P 4EE
www.routledge.co.uk

Routledge is an imprint of the Taylor & Francis Group.
Printed in the United States of America on acid-free paper.

A different version of chapter 12: "Under the Shadows of Yaruquíes: Gaining Indigenous Autonomy in Cacha, Ecuador" by Amalia Pallares appears also in *From Peasant Struggles to Indian Resistance: The Ecuadorian Andes in the Late Twentieth Century*, by Amalia Pallares. Copyright © 2002 by the University of Oklahoma Press, Norman.

10 9 8 7 6 5 4 3 2 1

Library of Congress Cataloging-in-Publication Data

Struggles for social rights in Latin America / edited by Susan Eva Eckstein and Timothy P. Wickham-Crowley.
    p.   cm.
  ISBN 0-415-93527-X (hardback) — ISBN 0-415-93528-8 (pbk.)
  1. Social rights—Latin America. 2. Social justice—Latin America. 3. Basic needs—Latin America. I. Eckstein, Susan, 1942– II. Wickham-Crowley, Timothy P., 1951–
  HM671 .S77 2002
  303.3'72'098—dc21
                        2002004514

*This book is dedicated to our spouses,*
*Paul Osterman and Kelley Wickham-Crowley,*
*who endured trials of their own*
*while we brought this book to fruition.*

# Contents

## part III: *Gender, Sexuality, and Social Rights*

## part IV: *Racial and Ethnic Rights*

# Illustrations

**Tables**

**Figure**

# Preface

This book explores how, when, and why the rural and urban poor, wage-workers, and the more marginal middle classes have been denied social rights, struggled to claim and reclaim them, and redefined such rights. Recognizing that such class differences and material inequities do not come close to exhausting highly pertinent social inequalities and rights-violations, we also closely address issues arising from differences in gender, sexuality, race, and ethnicity.

Our focus is on Latin America, past and present, from Mexico through the Southern Cone of South America. In that region of the world the historical extension and contemporary enjoyment of social and economic rights only partly resembles the American and European experiences, even as we acknowledge that the struggle for social rights south of the Rio Grande has been *partly* shaped by norms and social forces emanating from the industrial world. Certainly many more Latin Americans than their northern counterparts have been and are still denied rights to which they feel entitled. Yet have they also conceived those rights differently, and increasingly we see evidence that they value the right to be different (and in different ways).

This book is designed to deepen our understanding of Latin Americans' views of rights and their ability and inability to enjoy those rights. We know too little of their views and lived experiences, whether unique to them or shared with the Western world. Such themes loom more important each and every day as Latin America and the United States become ever more intertwined *economically*, as trade, international finance, and investment levels soar; *socially*, as the United States becomes increasingly populated by Latin American immigrants (legal and otherwise) and as transhemispheric communications grow by leaps and bounds, fed by our web-linked existences; *culturally*, as the global impact of the mass media and popular culture of the United States are perhaps felt most acutely to our south; and *politically*, not only because of a number of policy initiatives that our governments currently pursue, but also as we react to the tragic killings by terrorists on September 11, 2001, which sensitize us to the need to understand Third World peoples' deprivations and desires, including those that may result from the imposition of Western ways.

Given that need to avoid the ethnocentric, we thus stress that our conception of social rights differs from the typical concern with human rights, since that latter term connotes universality, not to mention both ethnic and ethical invariability. We contend rather that people within and among different societies may conceive their rights differently and that they may reconstruct their views of such rights over time, and not in predictable sequences or with characteristic end-states. Even certain rights around which a global consensus has emerged can be interpreted variably, depending on the social context. For sociologically explicable reasons, people differently located within social structures and under different historical local, national, and international circumstances may embrace different values, including values that directly relate to rights and rights-violations, which are contingent on their own, distinctive, lived experiences and on the "cultural repertoires" that guide their actions in situations both familiar and unprecedented. Given such sheer variability, one group's sense of its unchallengeable social and economic rights may be viewed by others as unfair or unprincipled; this is especially true of people in dominant versus subordinate positions within social structures. Even in the test case of basic human subsistence needs—where there is an irreducible biological component—we will argue that human definitions of and responses to subsistence crises are socially constructed and hence only intelligible in social terms.

In gathering together the authors whose work appears herein we deliberately assembled contributors from different scholarly disciplines and we intentionally included a focus on different types and conceptions of rights among diverse groups in the region. We focus specifically on Latin America because we believe the understanding of rights is enhanced by the examination of groups in a historical and cultural context that has some common ground. These chapters are revised versions of papers presented at the Congress of the Latin American Studies Association (LASA) over which we (Susan Eckstein and Timothy Wickham-Crowley) respectively served as president and program chair. LASA is an association premised on the principle that the most enlightened understanding of peoples comes from cross-disciplinary analyses placed in their historical, structural, and cultural context. The multiple and complementary viewpoints of sociology, anthropology, history, economics, political science, and literary criticism all find voice in this volume. The scholars of different disciplines, as well as of different analytical perspectives, provide a broad tapestry of pertinent and often poignant information about social rights, violations of those rights, and people's responses in the face of rights-based grievances.

As a collection this book offers a humble effort to broaden the global understanding of conceptions of social rights, conditions that do and do not allow perceived rights to be enjoyed, and how more people can enjoy the rights to which they feel entitled. In chapter 1, the editors provide a broad treatment and synthesis of many of the issues interwoven and (re-)appearing in the chapters of our able contributors. We focus on four types of social rights: (1) on rights to material subsistence, broadly defined and historically mutable, in both the countryside and the city; (2) on rights to work-linked benefits in all forms; (3) on rights and just treatment across genders and sexual orientations; and (4) on rights-claims and justice-claims made by Latin Americans of varied race and ethnicity. In our collective efforts we address how, when, and where the social construction of those rights and access to those rights have varied, and why. We argue that changing conditions at the most macrolevels of human experience affect those matters, to be sure—hence the real import of the oft-aired references to "globalization"—yet powerful as well are far more microinfluences such as local social relations and cultural traditions. Both sets of forces have influenced visions of rights and claims to rights, including side effects not intended by the principal contenders.

Therefore we stress here a theme that recurs throughout this book: People's experiences of and struggles over social rights are *globally lived, but locally felt.* Again and again our authors forcefully draw our attention to the international and transnational economic, political, cultural, and social forces that, along with local conditions, shape rights as they are locally felt, including the all-too-frequent restrictions, repression, and retraction of those rights.

In the assemblage of these chapters we also try to give voice to the many Latin Americans whose voices have gone unheeded in the rush toward neoliberal market reforms and the complacent satisfaction with recurrent elections as "enough" democracy for one and all. "Giving voice" should be considered one of the basic goals of good social science. As our chapters collectively demonstrate, many Latin Americans under different circumstances *have* given voice: They have pressed for the restoration of rights that they felt came to be denied, sought retribution for past wrongs, and asserted rights they previously did not enjoy but to which they have come to feel entitled.

For assistance at the LASA Congress we organized, we are indebted to the staff of the LASA Secretariat with whom we then worked: Reid Reading, Sandy Klinzing, Stacy Maloney, and Mirna Kolbowski. We are also indebted to the Rockefeller Center at Harvard and to Georgetown University for hosting the LASA Presidency and the LASA Program Office, respectively. At Harvard we are especially indebted to John

Coatsworth and Steve Reifenberg, who helped make the LASA presidency affiliation possible, smooth running, and enjoyable. And at Georgetown we thank Graduate Dean Bruce Douglass and Arturo Valenzuela of the Center for Latin American Studies for willing financial support. We would also like to acknowledge the generosity of the Ford Foundation and the William and Flora Hewlett Foundation for LASA support that helped in this project. We also thank Ilene Kalish, Kimberly Guinta, and Arlene Belzer of Routledge for guidance and efficient efforts in bringing this volume speedily to press. Last but far from least, for valuable commentary on the entire manuscript, we are indebted to June Nash.

*March, 2002*

*Susan Eva Eckstein*    *Timothy B. Wickham-Crowley*
*Boston University*    *Georgetown University*

# Struggles for Social Rights in Latin America: Claims in the Arenas of Subsistence, Labor, Gender, and Ethnicity

*Susan Eva Eckstein and Timothy P. Wickham-Crowley*

The new millennium began with the triumph of democracy over dictatorship and market economies now minimally encumbered by interventionist states. The Soviet Cold War alternative fell with the Berlin Wall. So too did the new millennium begin with a growing global consensus concerning basic human rights, including those for social minorities, and new transnational alliances and groups to address such rights worldwide. The changes were partially rooted in increased globalization, and with it the permeation of Western values and Western institutions to the most remote corners of the globe. But do people worldwide enjoy more rights, and a broader range of rights, as a consequence? And how can we account for lingering differences in rights?

In that ideas of rights hinge on people's values, we cannot look mainly to philosophical reasoning, such as to preeminent scholars such as John Rawls (1971) and Nobel Laureate Amartya Sen (2000), for an adequate understanding of the variability in conceptions of rights in different times and places or of the social conditions that generate such perceptions. A full understanding of rights begs for empirically grounded analyses, not philosophical "what ifs."

The term *social rights* best conveys the book's underlying thesis. That term helps convey to the reader that both popular viewpoints and the actual attainment of rights are sociologically contingent, the products of social construction, negotiation, contestation, and possible reconstruction. Both conceptions and the actual enjoyment of rights also hinge on historical circumstances, along with people's positions in social hierarchies and group identities. Once secured, rights may also be denied, especially by the more powerful. In contrast, the term *human rights* is too closely associated with the axiomatic view that such rights are, in principle, universal and applicable across the globe, a view suggested in resolutions adopted by the United Nations, such as its "Universal Declaration of Human Rights."

## The Social Construction of Social Rights

While situationally defined, the patterning of social rights is explicable theoretically, to wit, in terms of people's values, group involvements, and institutionally grounded experiences. Recognizing the variability of people's values and experiences, this book focuses on a single region, Latin America, and on the social (re-)constructions of social rights that have occurred there.

Latin American countries have shared a common colonial heritage, and they share contemporary exposure to similar global economic, political, social, and cultural processes. Due to historically specific experiences, for example, Latin America today has the worst distribution of wealth and income of any world region (see IDB 1997; 1998a: 13, 25), and the neoliberal restructuring that took the region by storm since the mid-1980s (and especially since the 1990s) has reinforced and deepened such longstanding inequities. The electoral democracies that restored political and civil rights (denied by military governments in the region in the 1960s and 1970s) have done little to reduce inequalities between the poor and laboring classes, women, and sexual, racial, and ethnic minorities on the one hand, and dominant classes and privileged groups on the other hand. Yet in the less politically repressive milieus, those disprivileged groups have begun to *contest* social-rights issues as never before.

This book focuses on four historical and more recent arenas of claimed social rights in the region: rights to subsistence protection and social consumption, rights to work-linked benefits, rights based on gender, and rights based on race/ethnicity. These are not the only socially grounded rights-claims, but we hold them to be the most important. Both viewpoints about and the materiality of subsistence and labor rights have been the focus of broad-based struggles for a long period of time. Unlike the industrial countries where there has been a gradual expansion of political to economic to social rights (see Marshall 1950), in Latin America access to such rights has ebbed and flowed with changing national political and economic conditions (Oxhorn 2003). Moreover, conceptions of these rights were redefined in the course of the twentieth century; they have come to include rights to social consumption, that is, to state-provided or state-subsidized goods and services. Concomitantly, racial/ethnic and gender claims were added to the repertoire of social rights in the latter twentieth century, but the additions did not occur because such rights-violations first occurred then. Indeed, rights-violations in these arenas were longstanding, and they had occasionally evoked localized resistance in times past (especially over ethnic rights). The new concern rather reflects an emergent global consensus about such rights, changes in views of these rights, and new mobilizations to secure these rights.

Because we believe that a full understanding of the patterning of social rights rests not only on comparisons of multiple and contested domains, but also on patterns in time and in different settings, we include in this volume both comparative and historical case studies. The latter provide a window through which to view better continuities and ruptures between current and past contestations of social rights. Since social rights are embedded in group life, even similar historical heritages and subjugation to similar global economic, political, social, and cultural forces will still elicit different responses within and among the nations of Latin America. And because contestations take on cultural dimensions—with culture both fueling and reinforcing grievances rooted in social hierarchies—we include literary, textual, and popular-cultural analyses here alongside more structural ones. While typically omitted from many societal analyses, literary criticism helps highlight how fictional characters can draw attention to hidden subtleties of class, gender, and race/ethnicity often concealed in real life and accordingly ignored by social scientists.

## Institutional Foundations of Social Rights, Rights-Claims, and Rights-Violations

We feel that the four arenas of contested rights on which the book focuses are best examined from an institutional vantage point. The institutional factors likely to influence socially perceived rights, violations thereof, and responses thereto include, minimally, conditions rooted in actual (and perceived) social relations as well as broader community, national, and international structures in which people's lives are also embedded.

Relations of domination and subordination are fundamental features of institutional life and sources of contradictory interests. Top positions incline occupants toward preserving and exploiting the status quo to their own collective and personal advantage, while persons in bottom positions are less likely to view demands placed on them as ideal or reasonable, whether or not they feel they can change conditions they consider unjust. Both those "above" and "below" in social-class hierarchies often justify their claims as "rights," however different the content of their claims. Yet independently of, and in combination with, class-linked rights-claims, status group differences based on gender and on race/ethnicity also influence conceptions about, and capacities for, attaining social rights.

Beyond positions in hierarchies of (dis-)advantage, the patterning of social rights is shaped by broader societal dynamics. When a range of institutional settings brings people together in similarly structured situations, individuals are most likely to perceive their private grievances as collectively shared and perhaps collectively soluble. Collective views of violated rights are especially likely to crystallize when persons similarly situated in multiple institutional hierarchies share common values, customs, and beliefs, including so-called cultures of resistance. They are yet more likely to do so when macropolitical conditions are also conducive to collective efforts to assert and defend rights and when the disadvantaged have some support from politically, religiously, socially, or economically advantaged individuals or groups. Since members of advantaged groups often have greater organizational skills, networks, and other resources; enjoy greater social stature and thereby greater influence; and benefit from a broader understanding of the social setting, they are well situated to know how to exploit "the system" to the advantage of the disadvantaged.

State institutional arrangements may be a further contextual factor influencing conceptions of rights and how people respond to felt rights-violations; the state is therefore not just an agent or abetter of violated rights. The democratic versus exclusionary nature of regimes on the one hand, and the state's material, symbolic, and organizational resources on the other, influence which rights are enjoyed and whether and how rights-violations are addressed. Sidney Tarrow (1998) refers to these factors as the political opportunity structure (see also Goodwin and Skocpol 1989; Goodwin 2001). State institutional arrangements in essence can influence whether people turn to collective or individual, and formal or informal strategies to secure or protect social rights and to redress violations thereof.[1]

Furthermore, in the increasingly globalized world in which people and information easily and quickly move across borders, certain ideas, groups, and alliances originating abroad may influence people's very conceptions of rights and their local responses to perceived rights-violations. We will see that such global features are not merely an important contextual factor, but also a set of forces contributing to new definitions of social rights at the local level.

People's general perceptions, and not merely their objective options, may also shape their specific views of rights and especially their responses to rights-violations. The greater the diversity of options and the more attractive alternatives seem, the less likely people are to attempt to directly address local violations. In Albert Hirschman's (1970) words, they are likely instead to opt out, to "exit" instead of objecting via "voice." Such options, of course, vary with historical circumstance and might include a shift to a new source of employment or a physical escape through internal migration or international emigration. In such "exits," solutions to perceived deprivations are, although individualized, socially patterned by family networks and community relations. Indeed, the options people *consider* themselves to have, not necessarily the full range of objectively available choices, shape the pattern of their responses. When turning to collective efforts at redress, people may even *create* options, including newly formed organizations and social movements.

### Analytic Frames and the Study of Social Rights

Even well-contextualized studies are influenced by the analytic frames through which scholars view society. What social scientists see, highlight, and prioritize depends on their a priori assumptions and analytic frames. For this reason we deliberately include contributors who represent a variety of perspectives and scholarly disciplines, as well as analyses of different groups, countries, and historical periods.

Neoliberal economists, for example, who see the world through modernization-theoretical and transnational-homogenizing lenses, presume that the world is increasingly following a Western developmental course and also that such a path is normatively preferred. The reforms that such economists have advocated and convinced multilateral institutions and governments around the world to pursue since the mid-1980s center on the privileging of market forces. They thus prompt states to rescind trade, consumer, and other protections; to privatize state-owned enterprises; and to remove barriers to foreign investment. Whether or not such economists focus specifically on issues of social rights, their conceptual frame presumes that people will be best off with a bourgeois–democratic capitalist order premised on individual civic, political, and property rights.

Historical and more recent social inequities generated by unfettered capitalism have, attracted the criticisms not only of Marxists and neo-Marxists of course, but also of some non-Marxists (e.g., Moore 1972; Heilbroner 1974). The Marxists have seen rights and efforts to redress perceived rights-violations as driven first and foremost by class interests and class tensions, in turn traced to relations of production or to global market forces. Their conceptual frame accordingly leads them to focus on the unequal benefits that accrue to different social classes under global neoliberal restructuring (such as the proponents of modernization have privileged), inequities often concealed in aggregated macroeconomic data on national growth rates, export-sector performance, and so forth.

State-centered analysts, in turn, regularly highlight how the state, both institutionally and ideologically, may mediate between globalizing tendencies and forces on the one hand, and civil society on the other (Evans 1979; 1995; Evans, Rueschemeyer, and Skocpol 1985). Some studies of social and economic rights that begin from a "statist" vantage point focus on certain material or political rights guaranteed (or not) by states, often in the context of globalizing processes. Correspondingly from a grassroots perspective, popular concerns with rights-violations typically focus on the denial or retraction of such state protections.

Also in contrast to neoliberal economists, postmodernists see no unilinear path of development or universal value consensus concerning social rights that transcends time and place (see Alvarez, Dagnino, and Escobar 1998). Postmodernists do not see people in the Third World uniformly welcoming modernizing practices and ideas emanating from "above" and abroad. Focusing on what they call "decentered" particularities, postmodernists highlight local variability, in line with people's individual "bundles" of beliefs, norms, and wants, independent both of state institutional arrangements and practices and of society-wide class dynamics. Conceptions of social rights and of conditions perceived as violations thereof, in this view can *only* be understood situationally, not through the master (more commonly "meta-") narratives found in either modernization or Marxist theories.

One postmodern variant, known as *postcolonialism*—a name selected to connote the potential break with the Western institutions and thought processes imposed on Third World regions by colonial powers—centrally concerns itself with the politics and putative empirics of subaltern populations. While the term originated among scholars who study South Asia, an increasing number of Latin Americanists have found virtue in these ideas, notwithstanding the fact that most of Latin America's "postcolonial" period began almost two centuries ago. The best-known postcolonial theorist, Gayatri Spivak (1988), for example, has asked the question, "Can the Subaltern Speak?" and has generally answered it negatively, especially when subalterns' "voices" have been filtered by social analysts or judicial proceedings. The postcolonial and subalternist viewpoint now deeply influences many Latin Americanists' concerns with social rights and (especially) with indigenous experiences in the region (e.g., Beverly 1999). Like Spivak, such scholars often recoil from any assertion of "fact" about human behavior or culture among so-called subalterns, endorsing instead what anthropologist Sherry Ortner (1995) has critically labeled a tactic of "ethnographic refusal." Yet postcolonial theory may have its own blind spots. Like other postmodernisms, it fails to take class and globalizing economic forces seriously, and its theorists tend to essentialize, totalize, and homogenize into nonhybrid types "the" experiences of "the" subaltern group, even in the act of refusing to characterize them (contrast García Canclini 1995). Following from that conceptualization, they fail to give full recognition to cultural complexities and hybridities, even when they seem to discuss them. Their anti-anthropological assertion that one can never really understand "the other" continues to be challenged deeply and implicitly by the research of many of the contributors here and explicitly elsewhere by critical anthropologists (Gellner 1992; Ortner 1995; Spiro 1996).

"Moral economists" in turn argue that people's understandings of rights and rights-violations are grounded in institutional arrangements but filtered through distinctive (sub-)cultural views of the world, including class, group, and community-specific frames, a frame of analysis that challenges postcolonialists' empirical skepticism. Ordinary people are especially likely, from a moral economy perspective, to envision any economic situation threatening their subsistence as unacceptable (see Thompson 1971; Scott 1976). Popular views and "readings" of rights-violations are not, they acknowledge, necessarily transparent. People in subordinate positions may feel the risks are too great to publicly challenge conditions they consider unjust. Instead, they may turn to "everyday forms of resistance" and "hidden transcripts," to borrow James Scott's by-now-famed terms, namely to foot-dragging, passive noncompliance, deceit, pilfering, slander, sabotage, and arson (see Scott 1985; 1990). They may also generate ballads, folktales, popular theater, religious rites, and other cultural forms that express their sense of their rights and rights-violations. Such covert activity and cultures of resistance reflect underlying views of what is and what is not morally acceptable. Over time covert resistance may do more to bring about change than overt challenges to authority, since publicly concealed noncompliance may undermine productivity and legitimacy to the point that elites feel the need to institute significant reforms.

Since the closing decades of the twentieth century, feminist analyses have cut across many paradigmatic frames. While feminist thinking has evolved and taken different turns, feminists share the view that non-feminist studies typically fail to (1) account adequately for gendered experiences and (2) deploy conceptual frames that are truly gender neutral. Accordingly, feminists have highlighted how women's experiences, independent of class, race/ethnicity, and other socially grounded experiences, are engendered and engendering. Although early feminist thinking focused on universalistic, transhistorical, and cross-cultural patriarchal dynamics whereby women were at times portrayed as passive and powerless, research and analytic attention since the 1980s have focused on differences among women. This focus looks at gender not merely as an individual, if structurally grounded, attribute, but also as a processual attribute socially constructed—especially through power relations—with symbolic, ideological, organizational, and identity components (Scott 1988). While in this context we highlight how and explain why gender is neither an omnipotent explicator of all social life nor the sole basis of perceived and constructed social rights, we cannot fully understand the patterning of social rights, rights-violations, and rights-claims without taking gender relations into account.

In essence, different analytic perspectives focus on distinctive features of a world that, in the concrete, is complex. Each frame conceptualizes social rights differently and highlights certain tendencies, while leaving others unnoticed, undocumented, and unanalyzed. Although a specific frame of analysis may reveal more about the origins and outcomes of perceived rights and rights-violations, precisely because different frames privilege different information, each is more illuminating in certain contexts than others. Collectively, they can deepen our understanding of perceived rights-abuses and how they might be corrected.

While the chapters that follow deliberately draw on the combined strength of multiple analytic frames, they all highlight the institutional patterning of social rights, cultural repertoires that shape conceptions of rights, and responses to perceived rights-violations. So too do the chapters provide a window through which to unravel the relationship between structure and agency. As we shall see here, historically rooted social conditions and cultural practices do not in themselves predetermine conceptions of social rights or responses to rights-violations. Within structural and cultural parameters human agency mediates, in ways that may modify institutions, laws, and cultural codes governing life at the local, if not at the broader societal, level. Marx remains correct in his argument that men (and women) make history, but, as he stressed, not under conditions of their choosing.

The remainder of this chapter focuses on the four arenas of social and economic rights to which the chapters speak. While analytically distinct, the arenas are not necessarily experienced independently. In different settings and circumstances, though, one of the concerns typically takes center stage.[2]

## Subsistence and Social-Consumption Rights: Changing Conceptions, Claims, and Struggles

Although Latin America has the most unequal distribution of wealth and income of any world region, conceptions of socioeconomic rights in Latin

America have tended not to center on issues of equality. The wealthy and powerful, who would lose out with redistribution and on whom governments have depended for support, have overseen a cultural order that provides no underpinnings to legitimate economic equality as such. Only in Cuba under Fidel Castro has a Latin American government advocated equality in both discourse and practice. Instead, regional conceptions of socioeconomic rights have centered more on rights to subsistence and what we refer to as *social consumption*: housing, schooling, health and environmental welfare, and rights to electricity, potable water, and transportation and to collective goods such as free or affordable roads and public safety. Also included are labor-linked rights for the more privileged urban labor force. But even conceptions of subsistence rights have differed historically and among socioeconomic groups, varying with both local and macroinstitutional conditions; and the claims to and enjoyment of such rights have not evolved in a unilinear manner, nor mimicked the experience of industrial countries.

Subsistence at its most fundamental level is biologically driven by the body's need for a minimum caloric and nutritional intake. Yet access to and allocation of food is socially, culturally, economically, and politically contingent; it is not merely a matter of production. In this vein, Sen (1999) highlights how significant macropolitics may be for subsistence. Famines, he argues, occur only under repressive nondemocratic regimes because electoral competition sensitizes politicians to people's needs and induces responsiveness to those needs. For this reason, says he, although equally poor over the last half century, Communist China has experienced mass starvation—during its Great Leap Forward (1959–1962)—while India has not. While Latin America has been spared widespread famine, the urban and rural poor in the region have suffered serious problems of malnourishment, even under democratic rule. Moreover, regional conceptions of subsistence rights have changed in the course of the twentieth century, with the denial of claimed rights becoming highly contentious.

*The "Squeezing" of the Peasantry and the Expansion of Urban Subsistence Claims: From Colonialism to Import-Substitution Industrialization (ISI)*

Historically, the peasantry has been the least privileged socioeconomic group in Latin America, the region with the world's most unequal distribution of land, and most governments have done little over the years to alter the extreme inequalities in the distribution of rural resources. The antipeasant bias has roots in colonialism. Beginning in colonial times and continuing after independence, rural oligarchs ensured exploitation of rural laborers through their domination of the state. Exacerbating conditions for the peasantry, in the mid-1800s many states enacted what were known as *liberal reforms*—with key provisos insisting on privatized, individual ownership of all lands—which had the effect of prying yet more lands away from peasant communities and into the hands of large estates. Forced into servile relations with landowners, peasants' subsistence claims were highly circumscribed, centering either on rights to small land parcels to which they had historical claims, or to some modest (if historically variable) share of the surplus they produced.

When promoting import-substitution industrialization after World War II, Latin American governments yet again joined rural oligarchs in "squeezing" the peasantry and rural labor more generally. The governments came to favor the urban-industrial sector through food policies and other policies that are discussed below. Most fundamental, they regulated basic food prices, which kept the cost of living for the growing urban population low. It thereby became transparent whose "moral economy" governments would privilege: that of peasants or urban consumers. They thus kept a lid on smallholders' ability to profit from their own labors and also tacitly supported the exceedingly low wages that large landowners paid their estate workers (to compensate for the low prices farmowners received for their domestic sales) and, in so doing, drove poor agrarian laborers to the brink of malnourishment, if not starvation. Pressures on the subsistence of the rural poor were made worse by high population growth rates and by landlords' (or foreign firms') large-scale land grabs in certain regions, such as the northern highlands of Guatemala and the Brazilian Amazon region (Wickham-Crowley 1992: 239–41; page 1995: chap. 12).

Despite such rural pauperization, peasant revolutions have been rare. The three peasant-fought twentieth-century revolutions in Latin America—in Mexico in the early 1900s and in Bolivia and then Cuba in the 1950s—were contingent on broader, cross-class support and did not stem merely from violations of peasants' perceived subsistence rights. Agrarian laborers resentful of perceived landowner transgressions have more commonly, quietly, and covertly sought redress for abuses through pilfering, foot-dragging, and the like (Colburn 1989). While such covert economic insubordination is difficult to document, it can be inferred from the notoriously low productivity of wage laborers on large estates in the region. Indicative that low productivity reflects labor recalcitrance, the work-breaks that hacienda workers in 1950s Peru demanded in order to rest and chew coca leaves seemed rather less necessary when they were working on their families' own usufruct tenant plots (Paige 1975: 170; see also Colburn 1989).

Yet even the more restricted types of agrarian uprisings rarely ensued.

Unlike Southeast Asia, where peasants protested against violations of claimed subsistence rights (cf. Scott 1976; Scott and Kerkvliet 1973/1977), in Latin America import substitution opened up the possibility for exit: Peasants could migrate to cities where opportunities were greater. Indeed, the most dynamic economies in the region during this period came to have urban population percentages comparable to those of industrial countries and far greater than those in Asia and other Third World regions.

But urban growth soon far exceeded the capacity of the urban-industrial sector to absorb labor. Consequently, migration contributed to an urbanization of poverty. Nonetheless, migrants until the 1980s typically viewed their economic situation in the cities as an improvement over life in the countryside and were optimistic about future prospects, especially for their children, who could benefit from the greater educational opportunities cities offered (see Eckstein 1990 and references therein). Such perceptions at the time helped to defuse urban mobilizations for subsistence-rights claims.

*State and Market Erosion of Subsistence-Rights Claims in the Neoliberal Era*

Debt crises in the region in the 1980s—rooted in heavy foreign bank borrowing to finance development and in subsequent loan repayment difficulties owing to weak export sectors—provided the coup de grace to the nationalist industrial-development model. Import substitution was discredited, and the debt crises created the conditions under which the United States and the International Monetary Fund (IMF) pressed for economic restructuring. Under foreign pressure to reduce fiscal expenditures and increase revenue, Latin American governments cut back the subsidization of subsistence to which the urban populace had come to feel entitled. The state became leaner and, from the vantage point of many in the lower and working classes and even portions of the middle class, meaner.

The assault on moral-economy claims to subsistence rights in the cities did not focus on sheer survival needs as such, a telling illustration of the point that even rights so deeply rooted in biological essentials are socially constructed. Experiencing the sudden and collective retraction of food and other subsidies that had come to be considered subsistence rights, at the same time that neoliberal-linked monetary policies caused their earnings to fall, city dwellers took to the streets in anger. While mainly directing their rage at authorities, some urbanites also looted supermarkets, where they directly experienced the strains of heightened prices. Urban consumer revolts occurred in at least half of all Latin American countries in the 1980s (cf. Walton 1989/2001), and countries such as Ecuador, Bolivia, and Argentina experienced them well into the early years of the new century. The material bases of these uprisings make them rather clearly the contemporary equivalent of the *sans culottes'* and workers' bread riots of eighteenth- and nineteenth-century France and England (see Rudé 1981; Thompson 1971).

Yet price hikes alone neither stirred unrest nor determined the form resistance took. The Latin American protests displayed various combinations of demonstrations, *paros cívicos* (civic or general strikes), riots, laborers' strikes, looting, and attacks on government buildings in different countries, in line with different national repertoires of resistance (Tilly 1978: 151–58, 224–25), different macropolitical-economic conditions, different state-society relations, different group alliances, and different organizational involvements. Subsidy cutbacks, for example, stirred riots in Jamaica, Argentina, and Venezuela, street demonstrations in Chile, and strikes and roadblocks in Andean nations. One monster riot, dubbed the *caracazo*, rocked Venezuela's capital and other cities in early 1989 in response to such cutbacks and was only put down after the loss of hundreds of lives (Coronil and Skurski 1991: 291). Dubbed *IMF protests*, these seemingly spontaneous eruptions typically involved some degree of coordination. They occurred especially where unions and Liberation Theologyinspired clergy backed them,[3] where political divisiveness and power struggles prepared the ground, and where governments were weak and unpopular (see Walton 1998; 1998/2001). The groundwork prepared by unions illustrates how social class, in its organized form, soon came to shape economic claims outside the workplace. Where such union, religious, and state conditions did not prevail, as in Mexico, no such protests occurred despite widespread cutbacks in consumer subsidies.

The impact of the cost-of-subsistence protests also varied. When unrest was broad-based, insurgents typically succeeded in getting governments, anxious to reestablish order and their own claims to rule, to retract or reduce the price hikes. Even when storing consumer subsidies, governments on occasion collapsed under the weight of the claims to subsistence rights. This occurred, for example, in Ecuador, where protesting trade unionists, teachers, and indigenous groups paralyzed the country and put government officials between a rock and a hard place. In attempting to appease the populace by rolling back price increases, fiscally bankrupt governments defaulted on foreign loans and, in desperation, turned to hyperinflationary policies that made them yet more unpopular. Continued resistance to price hikes, in the context of the devalued worth of the national currency, contributed to the deposing of two elected presidents there, in 1997 and 2000. Argentina roughly echoed Ecuadoran events in late 2001 and early 2002, when massive consumer protests forced President Fernando de la Rúa and short-lived successors from office as Argentina's "dollarized" economy faltered, the peso-dollar linkage was scrapped, the government defaulted on international loans, and a major peso devaluation followed (*Boston Globe* 2002: A6).

While consumer revolts and the forms they took hinged on locally variable conditions, data on price increases for basic goods and services give a sense of why so many Latin American countries experienced such revolts with neoliberal restructuring. Although the first dramatic cutbacks in state subsidies occurred in the 1980s, during the 1990s only two countries, Costa Rica and Panama, experienced less than a doubling of food prices, and Brazil, Ecuador, Peru, Uruguay, and Venezuela experienced more than five-fold increases. Adding fuel to the fire, in the general region the minimum wage as of the latter 1990s still had not rebounded to the level of 1980 (i.e., before the explosion of debt crises) and industrial wages, on average, only surpassed the 1980 level in 1996 (Eckstein 2002).

Latin America was not alone in restructuring so as to drive subsistence costs up, yet no other world region experienced as many protests centering on food and other consumer-claimed rights. Within Latin America, the most urbanized Third World region, more of its people depended on the market for food. Moreover, in Latin America such protests were more gendered, that is, more female-based, as well as more secular in orientation, especially in comparison to North Africa and the Middle East (Walton 1998). Women's greater involvement in Latin America reflected their greater absorption into the paid labor force, their greater involvement in the public sphere, and their greater dependence on the market for subsistence (compared to other Third World regions). Moreover, in some Latin American countries, such as Peru, Guatemala, and Chile, women's involvement in consumer protests was stirred by their involvement in neighborhood soup kitchens and food-purchasing cooperatives, which they had formed to address assaults on subsistence needs when their respective governments introduced austerity policies. Parish priests, often inspired by Liberation Theology and its emphasis on a "preferential option for the poor," as well as new nongovernmental organizations (NGOs) with access to international funds and organizational skills, also helped women seek collective solutions to their plight.

While state removal of consumer food subsidies in theory reversed the longstanding "squeezing of the peasantry," in allowing agriculturalists to price their products at market-driven rather than government-driven prices, neoliberal-linked trade liberalization simultaneously subjected farmers to competition from cheaper foreign imports. And in Mexico the market bias of the Carlos Salinas de Gortari administration

(1988–1994) ushered in new legislation that led in many locales to the dismantling of the village-based *ejido* system of communally held lands, a system that the constitution had guaranteed since the consolidation of the early twentieth-century revolution. This new restructuring squeezed the peasantry all the more, and it became yet more vulnerable to market vicissitudes, including the vagaries of global markets. Evidence from the Inter-American Development Bank's mid-1990s household survey of eleven nations in the region shows that rural wage levels remained sharply below urban earnings: 13 percent to 44 percent lower, depending on the country, even *after* controlling for differences in workers' gender, work experience, and education. Mexico and Brazil, the two largest Latin American economies, showed the most extreme rural/urban earnings differentials (IDB 1998b: 5). Economists Jaime Ros and Nora Lustig discuss the situation in Mexico in detail in chapter 5.

Concomitantly with the new squeezing of the peasantry on the one hand, and city struggles over subsistence rights on the other hand, the "urban alternative" for all intents and purposes closed down. Rates of urbanization reached over 70 percent in the more economically advanced countries in the region, at the same time that employment and income opportunities contracted and urban living costs rose. Even under the new circumstances, though, agrarian uprisings framed around subsistence rights remained rare. Rural unrest was defused when the rural populace increasingly turned to emigration abroad, seasonally or more permanently, rather than to internal migration as an attempt to address its plight. And those not emigrating turned to emigrant family members for remittances, that is, money sent home from abroad to help them.[4] Such families soon came to view the resolution to their subsistence needs as a transnational kinship matter.

In chapter 2, anthropologist Donna L. Chollett illustrates in rich detail how one group of rural laborers has experienced globalization and neoliberal restructuring. The reduction of international barriers to trade with the implementation of the North American Free Trade Agreement (NAFTA) subjected Mexican-based sugar producers and processors to massive competition from U.S. high fructose corn syrup exports, while also confronting export barriers that the U.S. producers successfully lobbied Washington to impose. Meanwhile, the state-overseen, neoliberal-friendly privatization of state-owned sugar-processing units followed. The new private owners then tried to consolidate those holdings by closing mills like the one in Puruarán, Michoacán, the focus of Chollett's study. The sugar mill shutdown adversely affected thousands of townspeople, whose well-being was either directly or indirectly linked to the local sugar economy.

Chollett's study of Puruarán provides a window through which to observe how neoliberal changes in the sugar sector, historically one of the main sources of rural income, hurt peasant livelihoods. She highlights the combination of ways—individually and collectively, overtly and covertly—by which villagers responded to a new subsistence crisis that they came to experience through no fault of their own, a crisis concealed at the macroeconomic level. Viewing the mill closing as unjust, since without the facility their sugarcane was worthless, they illegally took it over. But the owner thwarted their ability to sell what they were processing in the "closed" mill, and had the state governor send police and dismantle the mill. Disillusioned with their collective efforts at resistance, community members turned to more individual coping mechanisms. With alternative local survival opportunities close to nonexistent, some villagers joined the ever-larger number of Mexicans who legally and illegally went to the United States for work. Others remained in their village but became dependent on remittances from family members who left. But villager responses to their newfound plight were also dysfunctional, at both the individual and community level, as evidenced by rising rates of alcoholism, robberies, narcotrafficking, and interpersonal violence. To add another wrinkle to this tale, in September 2001 the new Vicente Fox administration moved to take over nearly half of Mexico's sugar mills in response to their economic hardships and cane-farmer protests (Weiner and Gori 2001).

Amid the neoliberal era's eroding subsistence claims, Cuba proves an interesting test case of how a country not subjected to direct U.S. and IMF pressure can resist global macroeconomic tendencies. As a self-defined (and often defiant) socialist state, Castro's government subsidized consumption even more than had the market-based regimes of Latin America in the heyday of import substitution, and it increased food subsidies precisely when other governments were reducing such supports. Although the island government in the 1970s and 1980s had gradually reduced the role of costly and cumbersome rationing, in the early 1990s it officially put almost all goods back on the state-administered system. As the economy contracted some 40 percent with the cut-off of Soviet and Soviet bloc aid and trade, the new scarcities otherwise would have driven prices beyond most islanders' means. Rationing thus formally equalized consumption for all, at affordable prices. The government clearly understood how politically explosive price increases could be, especially with the populace having benefitted from widespread, low-cost, state food provisioning for decades.

While rationing in principle "equalized sacrifice," islanders resorted to "weapons of the weak," to borrow Scott's (1985) phrase, at every step from the point of rural production to final consumption in the cities, and covertly took advantage of the "real" market value of scarce goods. They diverted supplies to a mushrooming black market, so much so that rationing effectively covered only about half of a family's monthly needs. While Cubans with limited economic resources experienced malnutrition and sometimes starvation, political repression and continued official state commitment to food subsidization managed to contain subsistence protests. Especially vulnerable to such plights were those Cubans without access to dollars. Cubans, like other Latin American émigrés, now remit hard currency from abroad, and the dollar soon became the de facto (if initially illegal) black-market survival currency .

Only once, in August 1994 when the food supply reached rock bottom, did an estimated 1,000 to 2,000 islanders actually risk the consequences of rebellion and protest in downtown Havana. The revolt was the largest ever in Castro's Cuba, as rioters looted stores and carried placards calling for Fidel's downfall. Intolerant of protests, Castro craftily defused the defiance by opening up the option to exit, allowing islanders to board boats and rafts and leave for the United States. And soon thereafter he initiated market reforms: He broke up state farms and opened private farmers' markets to help increase the food supply quickly. Accordingly, the Cuban experience suggests how even when a Latin American state seeks to subsidize subsistence, in the global neoliberal era formal and illegal market dynamics make it difficult. And with Washington refusing to allow bilateral economic relations, despite its free trade bias, residual Cold War politics also contributed to the subsistence crisis in Cuba.

## Struggles over Social Consumption Rights

*Environmental Claims.* At multiple touch points subsistence rights and claims intertwine with environmental conditions and with the ability of environments to sustain people. The claimed right to a healthy environment is relatively new to the Latin American social-rights repertoire. It is a response to air, water, and soil pollution and to accumulated mountains of garbage, derelict or absent sewage disposal systems, the (associated) spread of parasites and diseases like cholera, and rampant deforestation in rural areas—by-products of economic development as conventionally conceived. Such conditions threaten Latin Americans' economic and social livelihoods, rights previously taken for granted.

Newly asserted environmental claims also reflect global processes. They are partly a response of domestic groups to growing environmental movements in industrial nations. While Western-influenced, they do not result from the permeation of foreign values per se, as modernization theorists might suggest. Rather, they are a by-product of Latin American groups deliberately and strategically responding to new international discourses and to new international NGOs' commitment to environmental issues. Latin Americans were, after all, participants in the Kyoto and Rio de Janeiro meetings seeking solutions to global environmental problems.

Agrarian groups, including indigenous peoples, like their urban counterparts, have become preoccupied with a "good" and "safe" environment. However, rural and urban conceptions of environmental justice typically differ. The agrarian perspective is raised vividly, and with an anthropologist's attention to ethnographic detail, here in chapter 3 by Nora Haenn. She explores deep tensions between the Mexican state and certain peasant communities concerning environmental rights, but she also delves into class-based tensions between farm-colony communities seeking lands for crop cultivation and the Calakmul Biosphere Reserve, the country's largest protected area for tropical ecosystems, in which 25,000 *campesinos* seek subsistence.

Haenn's topic of interest suggests two well-understood but competing tropes, premised on different political viewpoints. In the first trope are people close to nature who are trying to live out ecologically sensitive, traditional agrarian ways apart from the interference of government officials, know-it-all international aid workers, and capitalist incursions. The second trope, in contrast, pits ignorant, selfish (if admittedly land-needy), slash-and-burn, and precious-tropical-resource-destroying farmers—who to boot do not understand the principles of sustainable agriculture under tropical soil conditions—against the knowledgeable experts trying to preserve habitat and species in the face of yet one more population-driven incursion by ecology-destroying humanity.

Haenn, like the Calakmul project, manages not to get trapped by the tropes. She grounds the ecological concerns in the dense, rival-ridden thicket of Mexican local politics, in class conflicts and *ejidal* politicking, and in changing local events and national politics. She notes that the Calakmul *ejidatarios* (villagers with inalienable community-based land claims) even turned the second trope against the "champions of environmental protection," in taking the ecologists to task for their conservation money being siphoned off to "rock concerts, exotic meals, and travel." As Haenn argues, the *campesinos'* understanding of social rights in this setting is one animated by an ethic of care, of creating "a community of justice between themselves and government agents," with strong patron-client (or *cacique*) overtones. Yet this envisioned community excludes not only the nongovernmental environmentalists, but also the physical environment itself as "actors" worthy of systematic consideration by the *campesino* community.

One common trope in the literature of environmental concern portrays peasants, deprived of alternative food and other resources, as prime agents of deforestation and other ecological damage. That is, under such circumstances they unwittingly undermine their own longstanding — and environmentally linked—claims to material rights. Yet, such an option is only *one* potential response to a shortage or collapse of the economic basis of subsistence. Peasants and other lower-class groups might also "raid the cash economy," as James Scott puts it (1976: chap. 7). In essence, they may compensate for land or harvest shortages by establishing short- or long-term connections to the (typically urban) cash economy, especially in the "informal sector" of that economy (which is discussed below in conjunction with labor rights). The important point about such economic "make-do" patterns is that they do not necessarily entail deeper ecological damage but may instead be agents of more frugal use of already available resources.

A rather extreme version of informality and of raiding the cash economy, one with *positive* environmental ramifications, involves scavenging. One form of scavenging entails the commodification of garbage dumps themselves, that is, the marketing, often under highly conflictual circumstances, of materials retrieved from trash heaps controlled by garbage *caciques* (strongmen). The related type of scavenging that Martin Medina explores in chapter 4 focuses on Mexicans from Nuevo Laredo who collect and recycle for sale used cardboard gleaned from Texas. Scavenging here takes on an international dimension, made easier with the increased integration of the U.S. and Mexican economies in NAFTA. Some Mexicans can thus find ways to make a living from wastage the U.S. economy and society reject. In keeping with the observation that the "informal economy" fills in the interstices of material life with activities and products that the formal economy does not provide (most notably argued by de Soto 1989), Medina shows how cardboard scavengers (as well as recyclers of aluminum cans) have quite important economic linkages, both backward and forward, to the formal economy and that they thereby provide an important service. Implicit in this whole scavenging subsystem are claims made by these industrious poor that they have the right to make use of the scraps that fall from the rich man's table, even if in this instance that New Testament metaphor has moved from the interpersonal to the international level.

In Medina's view, however, this system is not a case of "charity." As he argues, there is a positive contribution here from the ecological viewpoints of energy efficiency and pollution reduction, in that such cross-border recycling offers a far more energy efficient way to produce new paper than by using wood pulp (the normal mode of paper production, a notoriously polluting process). But the environmental gains are an unintended consequence of humble Mexican efforts to invent right-to-work opportunities that have been bypassed by the labor force north of the Rio Grande with better income-earning options.

*Housing, Community Services, and Safety.* Under import substitution the definition of subsistence rights for city dwellers was broadened to include more than food, the typical concern of moral-economy theorists (cf. Scott 1976 and Walton 1989/2001). In cities throughout the region, conceptions of rights to livelihood came to include inexpensive housing plus affordable (collective?) goods and services, like public transportation, piped water, and electricity. Populist regimes governing during the import-substitution era extended such rights to encourage rural-to-urban migration, so as to consolidate an urban political base while ensuring a cheap labor force for industry. Against this backdrop, the neoliberal government hikes in prices of fuel, transportation, and water, and not just food, triggered subsistence protests. Four of the ten countries with available information—Ecuador, Honduras, Uruguay, and Venezuela—experienced at least a doubling of fuel prices between 1990 and 1997 (see Eckstein 2002). It was official gasoline price hikes, designed to raise money for bankrupt state coffers, and not merely cutbacks in food subsidies, that proved the undoing of the two democratically elected presidents deposed in Ecuador. Gasoline price hikes were also implicated in Venezuela's 1989 *caracazo*. Meanwhile in Bolivia, only through the imposition of a state of siege did the government put a stop to coordinated multicity protests in 2000 against water price hikes.

Movements for housing rights took a somewhat different turn. The period saw the decline of squatter invasions, which had previously mushroomed in cities across the region with tacit state support under the populist governments of the import-substitution era. Urban land invasions tapered off for several reasons. First, the less populist, neoliberal governments felt less pressed to respond to neighborhood demands for the urban and social services that squatter settlements required. Second, under import substitution policies governments had merely tolerated squatters on public lands, and by century's end most such property had already been claimed. Third, the neoliberal governments were biased toward market processes, not political ones. Consistent with their bias, they favored informal commercial dealings over land invasions to address pent-up demand for affordable housing, a more costly solution for people of humble means.

In the changed milieu two interesting new movements for housing rights arose in Latin America, both involving the same inner-city poor whom urbanists had dismissed as apathetic, incapable of organizing, and entrenched in a culture of despair, in contrast to "activist" squatters on the periphery of cities (see Eckstein 1990). In Mexico City inner-city residents successfully pressured the government after the 1985 earthquake to rebuild their neighborhood for them, despite initial government efforts to take advantage of the disaster damage and clear the area for commercial development. And in Brazil in the 1990s very poor people who lived in slums or on the streets organized seizures of unoccupied urban buildings (Duarte and Kostman 2000). By the turn of the century the Roofless People's Movement was one of the strongest movements in urban Brazil, especially in (but not limited to) the largest cities, and it was energized by support from the left-leaning Workers' Party and the progressive wing of the Catholic Church. Aside from obtaining housing, the Roofless People's Movement succeeded in getting legislation passed on matters of land tenure and housing (Sandoval 2001).

We should also note, at least in passing, that struggles for property rights did not occur only in cities. In Brazil the most dynamic and influential social movement of the 1990s and the early years of the new century, for rights to social welfare as well as land, was rural-based. The Landless Workers' Movement (*Movimento dos Sem Terra*, MST) organized family-based rural land invasions. In the resulting settlements, called *encampments*, the MST emphasized community building, and successfully pressed for state healthcare, education, and agricultural extension service (Sandoval 2001).

Yet other claims appeared in urban areas. City dwellers of all classes, along with the poor, by the 1990s became preoccupied not merely with rights to certain material conditions, but also to public safety. In the context of the plunge in living standards that came with state-initiated austerity policies, crime rates soared, including rates of violent crime. Theft, pilfering, looting, illicit dealings, kidnappings, and homicides rose to unprecedented levels. The region became the most violent in the world, and Colombia became the kidnapping capital of the world (for the region's crime rates in international context see Newman 1999: 285–88). By 2001 a kidnapping occurred in Colombia every three hours. Crime generated more crime as a culture of illegality became entrenched, and violations increasingly went unpunished. Poverty and unemployment, the spread of drugs—with Latin America becoming not merely a producer for industrial-country markets but increasingly a consumer of drugs as well—and police corruption were at the root of the problem. Indeed, in many countries law enforcement agents became part of the problem, not its solution, as they joined the ranks of the criminals and operated with impunity.

Against this backdrop arose civic movements centering on the right to public safety. In Rio de Janeiro in 1995, for example, a civic group, *Viva Rio*, oversaw a massive demonstration for a cleanup of the police department, as well as improved urban services. Hundreds of thousands of rich and poor and old and young, cloaked in white, joined the demonstration, "React Rio." Similarly, in Mexico City two years later, tens of thousands of frustrated and frightened residents of all social classes, but especially the middle class, paraded with white ribbons and blue flags in outrage over a mounting wave of violent crime there. Like the Brazilians, they demanded an end to police corruption and violence as well as common crime.

*Educational Rights.* In the latter twentieth century a yet broader notion of social and material entitlement appeared. Increasingly groups clamored for the right to a free education. Led by youth of the middle and organized working classes, they focused upon access to university education from which they could benefit, not on the persistent and, in some nations, massive lacunae in primary and secondary school opportunities that severely limited life's chances for the rural and urban poor (IDB 1998a: 27 for data). When neoliberal governments in the region sought to charge for previously gratis university studies, the students collectively protested. Thus Venezuelan students rioted in 1997 against cuts in school and transportation subsidies, and in Nicaragua students protested cutbacks in university funding (together with shantytown dwellers who took to the streets in rage over consumer price increases). Students were enraged more by what they considered an infringement of their rights than by the new tuition costs per se.

Mexican students have been more persistent than their peers elsewhere in the region in protesting state-initiated tuition charges. In 1988 hundreds of thousands of students in the capital marched in protest against government efforts to impose fees (along with entrance exams), just when a major peso devaluation, along with austerity measures, had dramatically driven up living costs. The government did not dare to fire on students as it had in 1968, for it had never fully recuperated legitimacy after the student massacre. Capturing the imagination of Mexico City, the students won: The government retracted the newly imposed charges (Castañeda 1993: 204).

History somewhat repeated itself a decade later when students again closed down the main public university campus in the capital (the National Autonomous University of Mexico) (*Universidad Nacional Autónoma de México, UNAM*) after the government announced that enrollment charges would rise from a few cents to $140 per year. This time, though, strike organizers refused to back down when the government offered to make the tuition payments voluntary. Instead, they broadened their demands, also calling for university democratization, the resignation of the rector, and increased student involvement in university decision making. However, as the paralysis of university education dragged on, the protest movement fragmented, and after ten months the government finally broke it up. Learning from history, President Ernesto Zedillo ordered the police to enter the UNAM campus unarmed, and he made sure that the operation was conducted under the watch of official human rights observers.

In sum, in both the city and the countryside, among consumers and producers, among peasants, workers, and others, sentiments first about subsistence and more recently about social-consumption rights loom large. Yet only in exceptional cases are contemporary subsistence claims grounded in bottom-line survival needs. And conceptions of those rights have both broadened and changed over time, in part with changing state policies and the permeation of global forces.

### Labor Rights

When wage labor meets capital-controlling management in the context of the workplace, the authority relations by themselves create a structural setting of potential tension, conflict, and open struggle, as both Ralf Dahrendorf and Randall Collins argued in their foundational contributions to conflict theory, and as Milovan Djilas argued for Soviet-style economies (Wallace and Wolf 1999: chap. 3). Although owners and/or managers control both capital and the raw materials necessary for production, hired hands have not necessarily viewed their employers as "naturally" entitled to total control over conditions at work and the division of work-generated revenue streams.

Over the years, a number of conflicts and struggles created by conditions at the workplace have been extended from shop floors into the realm of politics. First, the workers' rights to organize into unions and to withdraw their labor collectively by striking have been hard-won gains. Through legal recognition, labor's right to organize and strike became part of the institutional structures of more-developed societies. Second, wage levels and fringe benefits have been contentious, and have been routinely displaced into the political realm, notably in the form of minimum wage laws, mandatory insurance and benefits, and so on. Third and fourth, the number of hours in the workday has also been a source of struggle, along with workplace conditions, including the pace of work (speedup, slowdown, and "work-to-rule" issues) and workplace safety. These issues furthermore have not remained housed within the firm, becoming repeated targets of national contention and legislation. Fifth, questions of hiring, firing, job security, and promotion, which also became subjects of contention between labor and management, have given rise to protective legislation and massive nationwide labor-management agreements brokered with state officials, especially in Europe, but extending to Latin America, such as in the National System for Support of Social Mobilization (*Sistema Nacional para Apoyo de Mobilizaciòn Social*, SINAMOS) program of worker-managed firms established under Juan Velasco Alvarado's (1968–1975) left-leaning military government in Peru.

*Import-Substitution Industrialization and the Expansion of Labor Rights*

With regard to collective claims to work-linked rights, Marx gave us reason to believe that industrial workers would be more militant than peasants, not because their work conditions were worse but because large numbers of them experienced perceived injustices in collective, interdependent ways. With Latin American governments promoting industrialization (initially under ISI), Marx's logic would lead us to expect a related increase in labor strife for labor rights to be directed at the polity.

We might expect industrialization in Latin America to stir unrest for other reasons. Factory workers in the region earn little compared to their equivalents in the highly industrial countries, even if the region's workers, especially skilled workers, view their situation within the context of their own countries. Workers in the so-called formal sector, covered by labor laws and typically protected by unions, have ranked among the minority in the work force earning at least the official minimum wage and qualifying for unemployment, health, pension, and other social security benefits. Industrial workers won such concessions in part because they were few in number, and also because their work was considered central to their countries' economic advancement, and because political and economic elites valued their political support. With the onset of industrialization, manufacturers sought labor support in their struggle against entrenched oligarchies for control of the state, and the populist governments they backed, between the 1930s and 1960s, viewed labor as an important political base. For this combination of reasons, and consistent with the region's previously mentioned state-centralist tradition, ISI-oriented governments in the region privileged labor in the industrial and expanding public sectors after World War II. It was during this period that organized workers were most adept at effectively broadening their social and economic claims, notably through exercising their right to strike.

Their success, however, came to a precipitous end as countries in the region fell under military rule like dominoes in the 1960s and early 1970s, even where import substitution remained the official policy of choice. Labor's rights to unionize independently of the state and to strike for improved wage and work conditions collapsed in most countries. And as governments rescinded workers' rights, labor's real earnings and its share of national income declined. Here we see how labor rights did not expand over time, as they historically did in the countries that industrialized first, and as modernization theory would lead us to expect. In Latin America macropolitical conditions and then macroeconomic conditions (see below) catalyzed reversals in rights-claims, even for the privileged segment of the labor force. Those reversals even included labor's loss of the right to contest openly for its rights.

*The Contraction of de Facto vs. de Jure Labor Rights under Neoliberalism*

While workers formally regained their de jure (legal) rights to organize and strike with redemocratization in the 1980s, they never fully recuperated their de facto (factual) rights. Strikes in Latin America picked up with democratization but soon tapered off, even in the wake of cutbacks in earning power and increases in living costs with neoliberal restructuring. Strike activity tapered off especially in the private sector, where it had historically been concentrated. By the 1990s, indeed, more countries experienced decreases than increases in the standard indicators of workplace disruptions: number of strikes, number of workers involved, and lost workdays. Strike activity declined even though (1) industrial wages in the region, on average, declined in the course of the decade and did not surpass the mid-1980s level until 1996, and (2) the minimum wage, which had dropped in the 1980s, had not yet rebounded by the later 1990s (Eckstein 2002). One careful analysis of Brazil's recent cyclical strike experience from the later 1970s to the turn of the new century showed an initial explosion of strike activity—its volume without parallel either there or elsewhere in the world—peaking in the late 1980s, then followed by sharp downturns through the 1990s. Eduardo Noronha and his colleagues demonstrated that that cycle is mostly explicable in terms of the changing political opportunities within the democratization process in Brazil, even as strike activity also waxed and waned (if less markedly) according to economic conditions, including those induced by Brazil's increasingly globalized economic milieu. Moreover, neither political nor economic forces affected strikes in "obvious" ways. Yet, as the 1990s proceeded both types of forces—consolidation of democracy at home and globalizing economic pressures from abroad–worked in concert to produce much lower levels of Brazilian strikes (Noronha, Gebrim, and Elias 1998).

The tempering of strike activity in Latin America takes on added significance when compared to labor mobilizations in the United States. There, too, the bargaining power of workers declined in the last decades of the century; in the 1990s the number of strikers increased, but there were no increases in the other measures of intensity of labor unrest. The comparative data highlight how globalization has weakened workers' power in both the north and the south. Global neoliberal restructuring had this effect despite falling real earnings and growing inequality in the distribution of wealth. With increased global competition-cum-neoliberalism, and with the rise of labor-unfriendly government initiatives in Latin America, the "invisible hand" replaced military repression as the source of weakened labor power. With capital ready to move around the globe wherever labor was cheapest (especially in the low-skilled sectors), workers risked losing their jobs if they made defensive claims, much less pressed for expanded rights. Classic Marxist analyses that focus narrowly on relations of production, rather than on global market dynamics, cannot account for the diminution of strikes in the context both of falling wages and increased political tolerance of the right to strike.

While globalization weakened workers' ability to contest rights both in the north and south, the Latin American setting was distinctive. In Latin America it occurred at a time of dramatic increases in living costs. The same was not true in the United States. While all but two Latin American countries between 1990 and 1997 experienced at least a doubling (and typically more) of food costs, as noted above, in the United States prices rose merely 19 percent (Eckstein 2002). Workers thus were hit much harder by neoliberal-linked global restructuring in Latin America than in the United States. The "squeezing" of employment options in the formal sector, and the de facto difficulty of staging work strikes under the circumstances, help further explain, in the context of dramatic increases in living costs, the previously noted mushrooming of consumer protests south of the Rio Grande since the mid-1980s. National and international dynamics displaced contestations over labor rights from the workplace to the neighborhoods where people lived, from the realm of production to consumption, a shift explicable within a global market frame of analysis (even if not determined by global market forces alone).

By the turn of the century remaining strike activity centered, as in Brazil (Noronha, Gebrim, and Elias 1998), primarily in the public sector, in response to job cutbacks there linked both to the privatization of state-owned enterprises that had proliferated under import substitution and to neoliberal fiscal belt-tightening in the public sector that remained. With the shift from import substitution to the new economic model, the region experienced some of the most far-reaching privatization programs in the world. In this changed economic context state-based unionized employment, which had offered since the import-substitution era a range of social and economic guarantees, underwent dramatic cuts. In the process, large numbers of middle- and working-class employees lost formerly secure rights, not merely to a minimum wage, and to health and other benefits, but to work itself. In extreme cases, such as Argentina, workers even lost the right to payment for labor rendered; there, provincial government workers went months without receiving cashable paychecks. Meanwhile, neoliberal governments throughout the region reformed their official labor codes to weaken workers' legal rights.

Labor's responses to the deprivations caused by public-sector downsizing and private-sector restructuring must be understood as well in the context of opportunities to exit to other jobs. With the contraction of formal-sector job options (which had had wage and social guarantees), as well as falling formal-sector earnings, the workforce increasingly turned to self-employment and other easy-entry jobs (in terms of skills or financing) on a full- or part-time basis. This refuge, in turn, helps account for the defusion of collective, work-based protests, just as rural-to-urban migration has had such an effect. Reactions to perceived work-based injustices were shaped by the total labor-market context in which formal-sector downsizing and earnings cutbacks were embedded, not merely by direct employer-employee relations.

Given that logic, the significance of *informalization* stands out in high relief when Latin America is viewed both comparatively and historically. While informalization picked up in the region with the shift to neoliberalism, in the United States during the same period the portion of the labor force employed in the informal sector tapered off (Eckstein 2002; Castells and Portes 1989: 19). Informal-sector employment typically is associated with lower earnings, no social benefits, and less income security than formal-sector work. Yet it still helped address people's needs for work in the narrowest sense, as Medina's previously noted analysis of cardboard scavenging attests. Meanwhile, the individuation that most informalization entails, involving jobs in small businesses if not self-employment, further contributes to a social milieu not conducive to collective work-based activity for improved earnings and social benefits, and that despite the insecurity inherent in the work.

Closely related to the direct and asymmetrical relations between labor and capital are the unequal macroeconomic consequences now clearly visible in overall national contexts. Jaime Ros and Nora Lustig show here in chapter 5 how contemporary macroeconomic policies exacerbate rather than mitigate longstanding regional, sectoral, and class inequalities. Focusing on Mexico, they show how the privileging of market forces and, with it, the removal of import-substitution barriers to trade and foreign investment, increased employment vulnerability, increased the wage gap between those with and without skills, increased income inequality nationwide and poverty rates regionally (especially in the country's south), and lowered agriculturalists' earnings (e.g., among coffee producers). The authors show that subsistence as well as job and income equality can be deeply buffeted by macroforces far beyond the control of localized policies and institutions, and that such conditions can be exacerbated yet further by a decline in institutional supports. They note, for example, how the decline in institutional supports for farmers with small and medium holdings, in the forms of access to credit, water, and technical assistance, along with state deregulation, contributed to increased inequality in Mexico's distribution of income.

Aside from the interesting, if deeply sobering, findings that trade liberalization and neoliberal monetary policy have far-reaching, unequal distributional impacts on the country's poor, the Ros-Lustig chapter sheds light on the analytic strengths and weaknesses of macroeconomic analyses that build on neoclassical economic assumptions. On the one hand, their work provides superb insight into the macrostructural dynamics shaping the locally lived experiences that Chollett, Haenn, and Medina dissect; on the other hand, it cannot account for the interplay between the economic and the social, cultural, and political forces for which the case studies allow. And, to their credit, they address distributive effects of macroeconomic policies and trends that many neoliberal-modernization analyses ignore. Meanwhile, their comparison of the experiences of the skilled versus the unskilled, and of different regions, reveals that less skilled workers, above all in the region where indigenous peoples are concentrated, benefit least from neoliberalism in general and business-cycle fluctuations in particular.

*The International and Transnational Faces of Work and Labor-Rights Issues*
Another low-end, income-earning option picked up toward the turn of the century, especially for women (and girls) at the Mexican border but elsewhere in the region as well, notably in Central America and the Caribbean. So-called *maquila* (subcontracting) firms are directly tied to the global restructuring of production that occurred once neoliberal reforms reduced cross-border trade barriers and relaxed import-substitution foreign investment restrictions. *Maquilas* produce and assemble manu-

factured goods, especially apparel and electronics, for the U.S. (and European) consumer markets.

Latin American governments courted the so-called offshore industries not only because they created much-needed jobs for an underemployed workforce, but also because production in the firms, explicitly designed for export, generated hard currency that the debt-ridden countries needed. Foreign capital, for its part, was attracted by the lower wages (and lower tax rates) in the south, so as to increase their profit margins. The expansion of offshore production thus is the harsher flip side to U.S. deindustrialization: Global competition for job-creating and hard currency–earning firms plus employers' own antiunionization efforts depress *maquila* wages. Given fierce global competition for *maquila* contracts, laborers in this most rapidly expanding manufacturing sector faced an uphill battle in attempting to secure the types of labor rights, benefits, and protections that earlier industrial workers in the region had secured.

Mark Anner's chapter 6, on Central American labor, focuses on transnational social-movement efforts to improve conditions for *maquila* workers. He points to the importance of cross-border political alliances for the advancement of such labor rights. Along with cross-border organizing coalitions came a new labor rights strategy, one that focused on the points of consumption abroad, and not merely, as in labor organizing in years past both in the United States and in Latin America, on conditions at the point of production (paralleling the shift within Latin American economic collective actions from labor strikes to consumer protests). In increasingly globalized economies labor rights thus must be understood and organized beyond the workplace, in contrast to the earlier national import-substitution contexts. Anner's analysis, in turn, highlights how labor trends can be shaped by politics and how they are gendered and not shaped simply by the invisible market forces that neoliberal economists favor.

Anner shows a "collision" between two very different global forces: the growing scope, size, and export power of the *maquila* garment industries generated by foreign investment on the one hand, and on the other hand the labor-organizing and labor-protective efforts of NGOs working in Latin America, as well as labor-solidarity efforts like the antisweatshop movement in the United States and Europe. His work strongly suggests that the greater power of the foreign investors in this situation derives from their single-minded, top-down actions. Whereas the diverse cross-border labor alliances tend to be difficult to control and at times conflictive, foreign contractors are more able to speak and act univocally, even at the industrywide level. The divisive weakness of the more "bottom-up" grass-roots groups became especially visible when domestic labor unions became wary of the new independent NGOs' labor-standards watchdogs, including those concerned with child labor. Unions also clashed with domestic women's groups, some of which felt that the male-dominated unions refused to address the gender discrimination that women experienced and the failure of the male-dominated labor movement to accommodate women's new industrial roles; in turn, some unionists felt that those groups knew little about labor organizing and that women were undermining the unions' role in representing labor at the workplace.[5] In terms of our analytical frames, both viewpoints suggest the limits of "only class" or "only gender" approaches to labor issues.

The multinational firms, nonetheless, were not without their own vulnerabilities, including public exposure in the United States of their sweatshop conditions—as in the Kathie Lee Gifford/Honduras uproar. Threats of consumer boycotts in the United States, pressure from the multicampus United Students Against Sweatshops movement, and embarrassment from bad media exposure, exerted some pressures on companies to temper their exploitation of Latin American labor.

With the closing of domestic income-earning opportunities, especially outside of the low-paid and largely female *maquila* sector, Latin Americans by the closing decades of the twentieth century increasingly looked abroad for work. Their emigration reflects the uneven distribution of work opportunities, among rich and poor countries in the region, but especially between Latin America and the United States, the main magnet for cross-border labor migration.[6] So determined are Latin Americans to come to the United States that growing numbers of them enter illegally if they cannot enter legally, owing to Washington-imposed immigration restrictions. Thus as capital moves south to take advantage of cheap labor, Latin American labor heads north to take advantage of better work prospects there, and Latin Americans have become the main source of U.S. immigrants, legal and illegal.

Yet the experiences of Latin American immigrants must be understood in the new macroeconomic context of the United States. By the late twentieth century the manufacturing jobs that provided secure employment for earlier European immigrants no longer were to be found. Those jobs, as we have seen, have been moving offshore, to Latin America and elsewhere in the Third World. Consequently, Latin Americans were pressed to fill mainly low-paid service jobs in the United States. Although the nonimmigrant populace usually avoids these minimum wage jobs offering no career prospects and few if any social benefits, the lower-, working-, and even lower-middle-class migrants see these "bad jobs" as offering better earnings than their home countries afford.

In chapter 7, Alejandro Portes and Patricia Fernández-Kelly—sociologist and anthropologist, respectively—point to the increasingly globalized context in which such (often displaced) Latin American lives are led. They very interestingly note how laborers do not merely respond to better opportunities abroad. Sometimes they *construct* new opportunities, including opportunities embedded in cross-border networks previously unimaginable. In the process they also improve the livelihoods of family left behind, through remittances, and infuse their communities, and countries of origin more generally, with new skills and monetary resources. However unevenly and unequally, cross-border socioeconomic, political, and cultural flows move from "south" to "north" as well as the reverse, and the former flow is neither noticed nor theorized about within a modernization-analytic frame that focuses merely on the Third World's mimicking of industrial countries.

In pointing to the increasingly mobile, transnational nature of people's lives, Portes and Fernández-Kelly make hash of the aphorism that labor is merely local, whereas capital has a global reach. The range of cross-border minientrepreneurial practices that Portes and Fernández-Kelly portray also subverts and undermines such neat categories as citizen, national identity, and domestic—"versus"—foreign in almost every realm, for example, labor, capital, income, social ties, and community. In light of their argument, the classic assertion that governments effectively "control" a wide range of activities within their national borders becomes increasingly suspect across the Americas.

### Gender, Sexuality, and Social Rights

*Struggles over Gender and Women's Rights*

Women in Latin America historically have not enjoyed the same prerogatives as men, and such inequities are legitimated culturally and made especially transparent via machismo, its most explicit and vulgar variant. However, even when aware of gender injustices, women often have acquiesced publicly if unhappily. Why? Within society as well as within their households they have felt weak and meek, but class and racial/ethnic boundaries have also divided women, undermining gender solidarity and consciousness wherever those other identities are perceived as more central, as they often have been.

Gender disparities have persisted into the modern era in different institutional domains, even though women throughout Latin America have come to enjoy the legal right to formal equality with men. Yet, as in so many human societies, custom is not dictated by law: Legal equality has failed to erase historically rooted and lingering gender injustices in custom and practice. Such countervailing forces notwithstanding, women's rights did improve in the last decades of the twentieth century. With occasional setbacks, their rights expanded from the political realm to encompass economic and social rights, which came to comprise not only rights to gender-equal treatment, but also rights framed specifically for women.

In that groundbreaking political realm, women in most Latin American countries gained voting privileges in the middle third of the twentieth century (Ochoa 1987: 904; Loveman 1999: 208). But they, like men, also had the right rescinded by the repressive military governments ruling in the region between the 1960s and 1980s. Yet, paradoxically, the military governments that clamped down on mass politics created the very conditions that brought women across the class divide together into the public arena in novel ways, based on shared grief. In Argentina, Chile, El Salvador, and Guatemala, military governments unwittingly politicized the personal while depoliticizing institutional politics. As hundreds of thousands of civilians lost their lives at military gunpoint, women took to the streets to protest the loss of their loved ones, despite the risks of publicly defying the regimes. The movements were defensive, to *reestablish* women's claims to the most fundamental of rights, that of motherhood; they were not mobilizations to transform or transcend women's place in the home. The *Madres* movement in Argentina became especially renowned and a source of inspiration for the other women's movements in the region (see Navarro 1989/2001; Stephen 1997), as women in crisis learned from each other across national borders. And, in publicly exposing military atrocities, the defiant women helped bring down repressive authoritarian regimes and reestablish political rights for both women and men.

Redemocratization eliminated most of the human rights abuses that had first brought women into the public arena (with Guatemala a notable exception). Under the changed circumstances, women's activism became less broad-based, more focused on class- and gender-specific concerns, and less visible in the streets. It also became less defensive and confrontational and more proactive. But most noteworthy, women's concerns now came to be incorporated into the new institutional milieu. Women's mobilizations under the military regimes helped transform societal expectations and practices, often generating unintended outcomes. They influenced political discourse, political strategies, and official policies under the new regimes, and in so doing they opened up opportunities for women. The new democracies now incorporated women's rights into their new constitutions and established women's agencies, so unprecedented was official preoccupation with gender equity in the region. The women's movements did not alone induce these changes, but they were central to the remaking of gender relations and gender expectations.

With redemocratization women also gained for the first time new rights to formal representation within political parties and elected offices. A number of countries even introduced gender quota rules for political parties, so that parties now included gender-balanced candidate lists for national elections, thereby guaranteeing women formal political representation. Accordingly, the proportion of women in the Argentine house of representatives rose from 4 percent in 1991 to 28 percent four years later, while in Brazil the number of women legislators in 1997, when quotas began, increased nearly 40 percent over the preceding election. In Mexico, in turn, the *Partido Revolucionario Institucional* (Party of the Institutionalized Revolution, PRI) and its leftist opposition, the *Partido Revolucionario Democrática* (Party of the Democratic Revolution, PRD), also adopted quotas, although they were not codified into law. Meanwhile, in the changed regional context, other countries debated gender quota systems as well (Jaquette 1997).

Despite the upsurge in the quota-linked proportion of women in national legislatures, and in women's political presence more broadly, women continued to hold but a small fraction of positions of high power in the region as a whole (and very high percentages have been achieved to date virtually only in Scandinavian nations; Jaquette 1997; Constance 1998; Craske 1999: 64, 66). Where they became elected heads of state in the new democracies, as in Bolivia, Nicaragua, and Panama, they often owed their electoral positions more to family preeminence and connections than to gender rights, gender political equality, or feminist claims.

Yet, correcting gender injustices rooted in the past entails more than expanding women's formal political representation and rights. For one thing, women in high positions do not necessarily identify more with gender than with class concerns and, even when gender-conscious, do not necessarily consider it politically expedient to place a high priority on gender justice. Thus office-holding women to date have not commonly used such formal power to usher in substantial legislation advancing gender rights. Second, even when gender-friendly laws are enacted, there is no guarantee of their implementation, especially in the face of sharply unequal gender customs and practices (Craske 1999). Indeed, even though democratization was accompanied by anti-sex-discrimination laws and constitutional provisions specifying women's rights, such laws have yet to end sharply etched economic inequalities between the sexes. Carefully conducted studies on the experiences of Cuban women similarly show how customary gender biases continue to constrict women's rights. The Cuban government, though not democratic, codified gender rights and, for a period, pressed for equality between men and women in the home as well as in the workplace and broader society, but without striking success (Smith and Padula 1996).

The new regional concern with gender justice is a response not only to a changed domestic milieu, but also to a growing international concern with women's rights that captured the imagination of Latin American women, especially those of the middle class who traveled abroad and who were politically and media informed. Indeed, by the early 1980s Robin Morgan (1984) declared that sisterhood had become global and included Latin American feminists in her volume. New international groups and NGOs further fostered the new regional concern with gender rights. NGOs provided women with new material resources, new organizational skills, new international networks, and new expectations, all of which served to induce women to take advantage of new political openings, especially with formal redemocratization in the region in the 1980s.

Gender-oriented NGOs initially made their way to Latin America during the dark days of military rule. But their continued presence contributed to the deepening of the democratization process in gender-consequential ways beyond the emergent party system. Often provided with new NGO assistance, women's groups began to address for the first time gendered social rights that focused on such issues as (1) domestic violence; (2) health, psychological, and legal services for women; and (3) reproductive rights. In such instances, women pressed not for equality but for rights rooted in women's distinctive experiences, consonant with the growing international shift in gender concern to *difference feminism*. That last phrase denotes a trend among scholars and activists who focused less on pure equity with men and more on women's peculiar attitudes, experiences, and needs (see Gilligan 1982 for a text central to this shift).

In chapter 8 Susan A. Berger highlights women's unequal experiences within both custom and law, in the face of the power of a male-dominated state in Guatemala, including problems with formal democratization. She shows how difficult it can be for women, even when organized and given formal political representation, to make clear breakthroughs. She notes particular paradoxes and contradictions for women attendant on the country's political opening, in a setting where there were no democratic traditions on which to build.

Against the backdrop of some 200,000 Guatemalans having lost their lives in the nation's civil war, women organized as mothers, wives, and daughters to defend the right to life, as elsewhere in the region. The regionwide economic crisis of the 1980s also brought women, especially poor ones, together for the first time to seek collective solutions to their plight, both in Guatemala and in other nations. These claims, like the mobilizations in defense of disappeared kin, were rooted in traditional, family-related conceptions of gender roles.

But in response to conditions more specific to Guatemala, newly politicized women insisted on participation in the country's peace negotiations, which sought to restore civilian rule. They sought to use the opportunity to press for an expanded set of rights, which ranged from gender equity (e.g., access to education) to gender-specific concerns (e.g., protection of women from violence against them). In the process, their public involvements (again with regionwide parallels) became more conciliatory and less confrontational, but also had less solidarity than during the dark years of the 1980s civil war. Women of different socioeconomic and ethnic backgrounds came to push for distinctive claims, often with the assistance of diverse NGOs. These claims might encompass women in general, only indigenous women, and/or poor women.

For reasons different from those of international NGOs, policies of multilateral lenders have had a mixed effect on the expansion of women's rights in the region, even as such funders began to address a variety of women's issues in response to new international concerns with gender justice. Cynthia Wood, in chapter 9, provides a gender-oriented dissection of World Bank policies in Latin America. Along with the IMF, the World Bank dispenses large sums of funds for development throughout the Third World. While certain Bank policies became more gender sensitive, Wood shows that the effects of others worked to the disadvantage of many women. Her feminist perspective uncovers how apparently universalistic economic processes and neoclassical/neoliberal economic analyses leave invisible gender (and class) inequities. As the Bank's policies became oriented in the 1980s toward fostering unfettered market activity, so as to deepen neoliberal restructuring, it privileged paid labor while ignoring the unpaid, domestic labor tasks of food preparation, clothing repair, care of the sick, and childcare, all done overwhelmingly by women. The Bank's frame—more efficient and productive market activity—kept it from taking gender both seriously and separately as central to achieving higher levels of human welfare. Wood carefully skirts the temptation to attribute these gender-discriminatory effects to malintentioned Bank bureaucrats. Instead, she traces the effects to policies not designed with gender in mind. Such "unanticipated consequences of purposive social action" are at the very heart of interesting social science, a point made by Robert Merton (1936) long ago. Yet, for Wood, as well as for other gender-oriented scholars, such inattention to policy effects, whatever the intent, is precisely why gender sensitivity should be a routine consideration in global financial planning.

Independent of the effects of such biases in multilateral lending policies, women's labor force experiences have not been uniform. Despite
the incorporation of gender-equality provisions in the new democratic
constitutions of the region, more privileged women have experienced
labor force gains, while other women have been left behind. Economic
opportunities have especially opened up for educated women of the
middle class, who have entered the labor force across the region in record
numbers, especially in the public sector, for example, healthcare,
teaching, and public administration. Yet, unlike the industrial countries,
the middle class remains small, and public-sector job options have
declined with neoliberal fiscal belt-tightening. Meanwhile, industrialization, first under import substitution and second under neoliberalism,
generally opened up only semi-skilled, low-paying, dead-end jobs for
women, such as in the previously described *maquilas*. Employers have
also favored younger women, who are cheaper to hire and less likely to
organize for improved worker's rights since they have a tendency to quit
when they have children. Most poor women, as a consequence, must rely
on the informal sector for work, with no job protection and poor earnings prospects. They have turned to this option especially since more of
them have become heads of households (due to rising divorce rates), and
since male earning power has diminished. Wood argues that this sector
has especially suffered from the benign neglect of the multilateral aid
agencies.

As if to instruct us in the difficulties (even literary) of breaking free
from the constraints of gendered systems of inequality, Judith
Morganroth Schneider, in chapter 10, reveals how even in the realm of
fiction, women's experiences bear the weight of history, a history that
has not only denied women the same rights as men but has also denied
the same rights to women of different socioeconomic classes (and eth-
nicities/races). Schneider provides us with a graceful, almost seamless
blending of social science and literary analysis on the issue of mistresses,
their maids, and their relations with men. The multiple and intersecting
social divisions of class, gender, and race are shown to pose persistent
social structural constraints on solidarity among women.

Schneider shows us repeatedly how mere "right thinking" cannot
alter the stubbornly complex and hierarchical elements inherent to the
mistress-maid relationship. To paraphrase Marx, women who employ
maids may "make" decisions about how to treat their employees, but not
under conditions of their own choosing. One subtext that arises from
Schneider's multiple analyses concerns the limited but possible "agency"
of mistresses to move toward solidarity with their maids. By contrast,
maids, given their low status, are far more limited in their room to

maneuver and to alter relations with their mistresses. That partition of agency nicely captures the very power inherent in the relation itself: While the more powerful member in a social relationship may make moves toward a more egalitarian and more emotionally involved stance vis-à-vis the less powerful, the mistress also has the power to rescind such moves, to put the maid "back in her place," or remove her completely from the setting. Schneider argues that novels suggesting rosier scenarios ("sisterhood is powerful") inherently contain unpersuasive, utopian elements.

Power in social relationships also depends in part on the options parties have outside the dyadic pair itself. Again, Schneider nicely alerts us to recurring contexts in which alternatives are few or absent for maids: A maid often has cut herself off from her family of origin in moving to a large city and, if a nanny, is typically so immersed in that role that her options to marry and raise her own children are cut off. Schneider accordingly shows us how literature reflects the gender (together with class and ethnic) injustices of the societies in which the stories are embedded, as well as constraints on efforts made to modify social relations between women of different statuses and between men and women.

### Struggles for Gay and Lesbian Rights

If gender inequities raise issues of social rights, so too does the differential treatment of Latin Americans depending on their sexual orientation. As with workers, rights of homosexuals have neither progressed in a unilinear manner nor reproduced the experience of the countries that industrialized first. Gays and lesbians have experienced setbacks and reversals in their rights-claims over the years, partly owing to macropolitical conditions beyond their control.

Socially constructed views and treatment of homosexuality have changed over the years in response to broadened global respect for the right to be different. Yet, unlike subsistence and labor concerns, they were unaffected by economic globalization. By the later twentieth century, in response to increased domestic tolerance as well as changed international conceptions of gay rights, a number of countries in Latin America experienced an upsurge in activism and homosexual scholarship. On the scholarly side there emerged varied and subtle attempts at cultural understandings of how gay men and women "fit" within the universe of Latin American sexualities and interaction, both hetero- and homosexual (see Murray et al. 1995; Kutsche 1995; Green 1999; Streicker 1993; Babb 2001; Thayer 1997). Studies also point to cross-national variation in the lifestyles and perceptions of gay men (Kutsche 1995). As for activism, gay-rights mobilizations joined the Latin American social movement repertoire, most notably in Argentina, but in other nations as well (e.g., see Babb 2001 on Nicaragua; Thayer 1997, comparing Costa Rica and Nicaragua), partly in response to divergent local political dynamics, or, in Tarrow's (1998) words, political opportunity structures.

In Argentina, as Mario Pecheny reports in chapter 11, there have been periods, such as the nineteenth century, when all private sexual acts between consenting adults, including homosexual ones, were treated equally within the law and, later, even within the 1853 constitution. Still, equity in treatment varied over the years, and was partly shaped by national politics. Even in the later twentieth century, gay rights waxed and waned with political repression and liberalization. Persecution rose with the return to power of Juan D. Perón in the mid-1970s, with the subsequent rule of his widow Isabel, and with the military juntas that followed. With democratization in the 1980s, in contrast, the defense of human rights agendas in part encompassed gay and lesbian issues. In that context, the gay and lesbian communities' discourse argued that homosexuality should be viewed as a private matter between consenting adults with equal protection under the law, reminiscent of the nineteenth-century conception. In the face of this discourse, public officials backed away from treating homosexuality as criminal, and spoke instead of the incompatibility of homosexuality with the "common good" and "family formation." Although these competing conceptions remain, the view that homosexuality entails the free actions of consenting adults has (re-)gained ground. And Pecheny suggests that the shift reflects the political impact of what could be the region's largest and most active gay community.

The growing tolerance and visibility of gay and lesbian communities coincided by chance with the spread of the AIDS epidemic, which had the effect of intensifying stigmatization of gays, who, in turn, were redefined in terms of vulnerability to getting AIDS. While initially the disease was concentrated in Argentina among urban, educated, middle-aged gay men (as was initially typical in the industrial world), the "gay" imagery of AIDS did not change when the numbers of intravenous drug needle sharers surpassed gay men among new cases.

Changes in macropolitical conditions and the views held by officialdom, as well as the growing incidence of AIDS, in turn, led not only to shifts in the framing of the gay rights movements, but also to their fragmentation. Gay rights efforts were still sufficiently effective to get official laws and practices changed. In sum, state structures both influenced and were influenced by the homosexual community. In the early 1990s, for example, the federal government forcefully took over the national campaign against AIDS by parliamentary law and imposed its more liberal and educative stance, superseding (often) more repressive provincial laws and policies. And, later in the decade, the new city constitution of Buenos Aires abrogated certain police edicts that had tolerated discriminatory practices toward homosexuals. Instead, it recognized the "right to be different" and accordingly condemned all manner of discrimination based on sexual orientation. While the legal and institutional changes in themselves provide no guarantee of equal rights irrespective of sexual orientation, the interplay between changing macropolitical structures and mobilization within civil society "liberalized" the broader culture in which Argentinian homosexuality is embedded.

From Pecheny's perspective there is thus much to learn. He shows how a social minority can press for the inclusion of new rights, how the AIDS tragedy has ironically precipitated greater tolerance and acceptance in attitudes about homosexuality, how a social movement can further the human rights of a socially marginal group, and how new social relations and social "spaces" can be turned into political action and social movements. In so doing, he also shows how conceptions of social rights and actual rights-claims result from an interplay of structure and agency, and respond to global as well as domestic forces.

## Racial and Ethnic Rights

In Latin America, race and ethnicity tend to be defined in social and cultural, rather than biological, terms. Since the colonial conquest, privilege has been linked to those of European stock and, less so, to some persons of mixed-race ancestry: to those mestizos (Indian-cum-white) and mulattos (African-cum-white) who assimilated and acculturated to the mores of the dominant class. While mobility between social classes was historically limited, the dominant ethos spoke to the possibility thereof: An individual could move upward in the class- and status-systems if willing to shed social and cultural distinctiveness. Modernization theory adopted this conception of the world in presuming that the importance of race and ethnicity would wane, and that Indians and blacks would experience upward mobility as they learned Spanish (or Portuguese, in the case of Brazil), dressed in Western-style clothes, and moved to cities: that is, if they adopted the dominant culture, partook in the institutional life of the nation-state, and suppressed their ethnicity. Insofar as elites and their intellectual allies still adhere to such views, such discourses veil the palpable continued presence of racial and ethnic discrimination.

Indeed, discourses and modernization theory aside, interethnic and interracial relations in the region have remained characterized by both racial and ethnic prejudice and discrimination, that is, by biased attitudes and unjust social practices. Racial and ethnic inequities have been so embedded in social life that they have been presumed over the centuries, especially by elites, to be aspects of "human nature." Visible "markers" of ethnic differences were seen as so "natural" as to account per se for maltreatment by the privileged of the dark-skinned and the ethnically different. With racial and ethnic differences closely correlated with socio-economic and class differences, this naturalistic view of social stratification gained added credibility. Yet careful sociological study has shown that prejudice and discrimination are social constructions and, hence, can also be subject to social de-construction.[7]

As deeply embedded and "natural" as racial and ethnic inequalities have been in Latin America, changing international as well as national conditions (including conditions not pointed to in studies of the industrial world) have stirred claims for racial, ethnic, and other social rights during the later decades of the twentieth century. And, as in other institutional domains, notably that of gender, the repertoire of racial and ethnic claims came to focus not only on rights to equality, but also on the right to be different. Moreover, that repertoire came to include not just individual claims but collective ones as well, notably, collective claims for ethno-specific territorial and constitutional rights.

The now-familiar changes in domestic and international macropolitical, economic, social, and cultural conditions of the 1980s and 1990s stirred the new assertion of rights. First, democratization reduced the risks to racial and ethnic minorities of pressing for rights to which they felt entitled. Second, the very constitutions of the new regimes often specified racial, ethnic, and other minority rights, which reflected the new international concern with human rights and also official efforts to be more inclusive and protective of rights that had been denied under the repressive regimes they displaced. Third, political parties were anxious to pick up votes as democracies were established, and accordingly became somewhat responsive to racial and ethnic claims.

But other institutional changes also induced the new focus on racial and ethnic rights. In particular, neoliberalism unwittingly stirred claims to such rights when generating new and intensified forms of market-based and property-based economic competition, inequalities, and insecurities, phenomena that many of this book's contributors discuss, in both their ethnic and nonethnic dimensions. Given those neoliberal changes, and in light of the preceding theoretical discussion (see note 7), we would *not* expect to see easy rapprochement between the different ethnic groups now competing in situations of yet greater scarcity.

Furthermore, certain state-driven actions would be expected only to exacerbate intergroup tensions. These include the state's interventions in, definitions of, and access to property itself, as in Mexico's privatization of collective *ejido* land claims, and state (in-)actions, as in the Brazilian Amazon, where the government tolerated massive land grabs by large-property holders. However, as social-movement theorizing has stressed for more than half a century, grievances alone, even exacerbated ones, do not by themselves mobilize people collectively for change. Other phenomena must come into play as well.

Improved means of communication, for example, brought new ideas and new modes of coordinating social claims to the most remote of regions. The Internet, in particular, became a catalyst for indigenous mobilization to claim new rights, in that it was a source of information sharing, consciousness raising, and solidarity building across nations and national borders. The *Zapatista* movement in Chiapas, Mexico, became known for popularizing indigenous use of the World Wide Web. At the same time, a growing international consensus crystallized about the rights of racial and ethnic minorities, and new NGOs that provided human and social capital and other material resources to help pursue these rights.

This international dimension reveals that values that stress the *universality* of human rights paradoxically contributed to the growth of movements premised on the right to be *distinctive,* the very differences to which postmodern and subaltern studies often alert us.[8] But while postmodernists offer a frame that does allow for the privileging of racial, ethnic, and other local variegation, they have also regularly asserted insuperable barriers to intergroup communications—the "heteromorphous nature of language games" (Lyotard 1984/2000: 428)—a formulation that ipso facto essentializes racial and ethnic identities. They also offer no analytic frame to account for the manner in which broader forces influence and interact with these local, racial, and ethnic dynamics.

Subaltern-studies analysts provide a more structural frame (implicitly, if not explicitly) to understand the patterns of racial and ethnic relations and the ways victims of prejudice and discrimination may covertly resist, if not overtly challenge, perpetrators of injustice and the institutions in which racial and ethnic injustices are embedded (on Latin America, see Beverly 1999). They accordingly can explain why manifest claims to racial and ethnic rights may increase—not decrease, as modernization proponents posit—over time, even (or especially) among those with *increased* intergroup contacts and exposure to Western ways.[9] These processes may bring to the fore grievances that, until then, were privately experienced or collectively shared, but kept contained among the politically weak.

Catherine Héau, whose contribution to this volume (chapter 14) is detailed below, nicely shows that fuel for the covert challenges to intergroup race/ethnic relations may reside in the shared beliefs, traditions, and folk histories among the subalterns, including cultures of resistance expressed in folktales, ballads, popular theater, resistance rituals, and status-inversion festivals (see also Nash 1989/2001; Stone 2001). Yet, when she demonstrates that we can gain at least approximate knowledge of subalterns' lives and worldviews, Héau parts sharply, if only tacitly, with a key claim that Spivakian postcolonialists have made.

*Struggles for Race-Based Rights*
Most but not all concentrations of Afro–Latin Americans are associated with the history of slave labor, which continued in the region well into the 1800s.[10] Despite a prevailing discourse asserting that race-based social and cultural mobility was individually possible with cultural assimilation, in countries such as Colombia and Brazil skin color still became a focus of racialized claims toward the later years of the twentieth century. These race-based movements built simultaneously on traditions brought from Africa and on contemporary global black culture, but their nature and the rights they demanded varied with local conditions, including class-based experiences. And so, too, did they vary with local social constructions of race.

Castro's Cuba demonstrates that the new international milieu congenial to human rights cannot alone account for stepped-up mobilizations for race-based rights in the region. The Cuban Revolution officially eliminated racial discrimination traceable to the slave era, and improved opportunities for the country's blacks, although the improvements lasted only up until the 1990s, when the economy went into deep recession following the cut-off of Soviet aid and trade. While Communist Party politics did not permit public focus on racial claims, Afro-Cuban identity fueled broad-based syncretic religious movements that gained popularity and public expression with the crisis of the 1990s. The homegrown syncretic religions, which represented cultures of resistance in that they fused African with colonial-imposed Catholic beliefs, provided solace when subsistence became problematic. When the formerly self-professed atheist state showed more tolerance, it catalyzed a growing public expression of such racialized religious activity. Indeed, authorities became more tolerant of all religions as Communism lost its appeal following the delegitimation of its Soviet-style variant, which no longer satisfied islanders' most basic subsistence needs. The new tolerance suggests that authorities understood Karl Marx, who perceived religion as the "opiate of the masses," and decided that, in a time of crisis, such an opiate might not be a bad policy. Yet they also understood the subversive effect homegrown religion could have when it brought Cubans together in the streets. Although *santeros* (the priests of the popular, syncretic, Afro-Cuban religion *Santería*) typically provided diffuse support for the government, ordinary islanders' religious engagements did not preclude oblique critiques of officialdom (Montoya 2001). Indeed, government's fear of the subversive effects of homegrown religion may have led authorities in 1990 to suspend a pilgrimage to the shrine of the Virgin of Cobre, the much-revered patron saint of Cuba, whose appeal derives from Afro-Cuban beliefs merged with Catholicism (see Eckstein 1994: 122). Officials particularly feared that the procession might turn into an antigovernment demonstration. Thus, history could yet repeat itself, for *Santería* was central to the political struggle both for independence in the later nineteenth century and to Castro's own movement to oust Fulgencio Batista in the 1950s.[11]

Meanwhile, in Colombia, the 1991 constitution formalized collective rights for black communities as well as the goal of a pluriethnic and multicultural society (Gureso, Rosero, and Escobar 1998). The new national vision consecrated in the document served as the basis of incipient black community mobilization for cultural, ethnic, and territorial rights in the Pacific portion of the country. The leadership framed the movement partly in terms of the government's redefinition of citizenship. The movement, however, had difficulty getting support across the racial class divide, as Marxist analyses might have led us to expect. Uninterested in being singled out as a social minority, Colombia's black elite rarely supported efforts to make racialized claims, and the concern with race-based rights accordingly became class-specific.

In a different manner, a highly complex racial structure in Brazil also accentuated differences along the crucial racial divide. Brazil has the second largest black population in the world (after Nigeria): Apart from whites (*brancos*), about 40 percent of its 170 million people are identified as *pardo* (mixed African and European ancestry, sometimes with indigenous blood, too), and 5 percent as *prêto*, or black (Jordan 2001). Censuses and data-gathering surveys in Brazil for many years have employed solely these three categories, even though every Brazilian and every scholar of these matters knows of and uses a far more varied list of terms. Scores of such terms differentiate subtleties of skin tones and facial features within broad racial groups, and that variety, in turn, is associated in people's minds with differences in socioeconomic status. Yet the very multitude of race/color distinctions works against *both* class solidarities *and* broad-based racial identity.[12] Further working against race-based claims was the state, which, through much of the previous

century, routinely perpetuated the mystique of Brazil as a "racial democracy" by denying race-based inequities, injustices, and rights (Jordan
2001). In so doing, politicians built on and deepened themes most influ-
entially propagated in the writings of Gilberto Freyre (Page 1995: 71–78),
despite ample long-term evidence of the very phenomena that the myth
denies (Marger 1994: chap. 13).

For such reasons Brazil's raced-based movements have had difficulty
transcending class divisions. Movement-building was thus contingent
on the leadership's inventing "flattened," simplified, and polarized racial
identities and appealing to shared cultural motifs (Gomes da Cunha
1998). But middle-class mulattos and lower-class, racially mixed (and
black) populations over the years tended to have different concerns and
different identities. Race-based movements in the country's Northeast,
where there is the greatest concentration of poor blacks—their ancestors
were brought there in mammoth numbers as slaves for the local sugar
economy—focused on issues of poverty and demands for government
services, and thus reflected a class-specific appeal. Homegrown Afro-
Catholic religions provided a bedrock on which such movements built.
As in Cuba, then, race was not the salient feature around which most
blacks mobilized, even though the social base of movements was race-
specific, and the underlying source of grievances was rooted in racial
inequities.

Although race was not the public focus of rights-claims among Brazil's
racial minorities, Brazil's somewhat low interracial marriage rates, the
best single indicator of interracial mutual acceptance, reveal the continued significance of race there (Telles 1993). Nor is that the only challenge to the official and dominant discourse of "racial democracy," for
educational and income data also speak to race-based inequities. Only 2
percent of all university graduates are nonwhite. Whites have, on
average, 2.4 more years of schooling than either *pardos* or *prêtos*. Because
of publicly concealed hiring biases as well as educational disparities, few
blacks are in high positions. Whites' monthly income, on average, is now
twice that of *either* nonwhite group in Brazil (Jordan 2001), confirming
earlier research reporting a similar income gap between whites and all
nonwhites. In that study, which directly compared Brazil and the United
States, the income gap between whites and all nonwhites (*pardos* and
*prêtos*) was *greater*, and earnings were *less varied* across African skin tones
in Brazil than in the United States (Telles 1999: 86). Both sets of data
strongly suggest that Brazil's multiracial gradations have social, not economic, significance, and that the United States, despite its bifurcated
black/white social divide, actually conceals a more graduated, color-
linked economic opportunity structure than Brazil can boast.

Against this backdrop, Brazilian president Fernando Henrique Cardoso broke with history in 2001. He publicly acknowledged raced-based inequities, and initiated raced-based quotas in state hiring to correct the situation. Two ministries took the lead by requiring 20 percent of all outsourced workers to be black. (Nearly half of all employees in the country's massive federal bureaucracy are outsourced.) Consistent with the new federal emphasis, lawmakers in the state of Rio de Janeiro voted that 40 percent of all slots in state universities be reserved for minority students. The quota system was to apply only to those who identified themselves as black, even though many blacks do not consider themselves in such terms. Racial inequities alone did not lead authorities to change their stance. While the new concern reflects a commitment of the country's top leader to make racial justice a legacy of his administration, initiatives were also a response to pressure from Brazilian black activists at a time of heightened international concern with race-based rights following the 2001 United Nations' antiracism conference (Jordan 2001). Not only did the state's changed stance demystify the dominant ethos of multiethnic harmony, it also pried open the very meaning of race and racial identity.

### Claims for Indigenous and Ethnic Rights

Changes in the macroinstitutional and cultural milieus (both domestic and global), when combined with changes in locally lived experiences and conceptions of rights, brought previously latent identities and new ethnic-based claims to the forefront of political life in those countries with substantial indigenous populations. The selfsame indigenous peoples whom elites and modernization theorists led us to assume would assimilate and acculturate, instead pressed during the 1990s for certain rights premised on social difference.

Best known abroad of these new indigenous (or partly indigenous) mobilizations is the *Zapatista* movement of Chiapas. Chiapas is one of Mexico's southern states, and Ros and Lustig (chapter 5) show that economic marginalization there deepened with the neoliberal transition; Chiapas is also at the very core of the most indigenous of all Mexican regions.[13] Yet, Ecuador and Guatemala also experienced important new ethnic-based movements. In all three countries the movements were premised on attempts to redefine citizenship by focusing on indigenous rights to cultural distinctiveness, including some elements of political-juridical autonomy. In so doing, the movements strengthened indigenous identities and indigenous cultural life. In a novel and intriguing fashion, they channeled localized ethnic solidarities into newly constructed pan-ethnic social formations through which new, broader Indian identities

were socially constructed. Especially in Mexico and Ecuador the movements' grievances were also fueled by neoliberal reforms that threatened
subsistence claims: in Mexico by the state's removal of legal guarantees
to land rights and its retraction of crop (along with consumer) subsidies;
in Ecuador by state-initiated cost-of-living increases.

In Guatemala frustration with continued de facto exclusion from full
participation in the country's institutional life following formal democratization contributed to an evolving pan-ethnic movement there as well.
Participation of indigenous organizations in the Guatemalan peace negotiations (along with the women's groups described by Berger in chapter
8) served indirectly to strengthen the Mayan movement, because it legitimated indigenous groups and indigenous rights and created a political
opening for the movement. Fueling the movement was an emergent
group of Mayan intellectuals who produced new school texts criticizing
the racism of official national histories, who promoted Mayan language
retention, and who disseminated information on indigenous rights. They
also criticized the Western development model, which favored assimilation over ethnic retention and indigenous claims. In essence, leadership
contributed to a redefinition of indigenous rights along with a new
indigenous identity, and it also helped remake a culture imposed on
them by elites for centuries.

The intersections between economic and political changes and the
assertion of ethnic identity concern Amalia Pallares in chapter 12. She
highlights how newly awakened concerns among indigenous peoples
may be focused on specifically localized matters, even in the context of a
growing, national, pan-village indigenous movement. In her study of
Cacha, Ecuador, she takes a close look at the transformation of class-
linked ethnic relations there. She offers an almost textbook example of a
change from a highly institutionalized, consent-cum-coercion system of
social patronage to newly liberated options. The Cacha moved from a
situation of what Pierre Bourdieu (1984: 471) terms *doxa*—in which
extant, socially oppressive relations were taken for granted and seen as
both natural and unchangeable—to the recognition and seizure of new
social possibilities, both individually and collectively.[14] The indigenous
Cacha were able to resist subversion of their culture and to transform
their relations with the nation-state, undermining the doxa that sustained their subordination to the higher-status, white-mestizo Yaruquíes.

Pallares intriguingly points to the importance of controlling *space*:
defined not only in terms of physical territory, but also in terms of the
social, economic, cultural, and political meanings embedded therein.
Central to the preexisting exploitation of the highland Cacha by the
neighboring lowland Yaruquíes was the latter's control of crucial spaces

Cacha needed to cross in order to reach markets vital to their economy and subsistence. The control of that space had conferred power on the Yaruquíes and contributed to that doxa quality of everyday life for the Cacha. The ethnic-geographic overlay that intensified barriers between the two groups was further strengthened by *caciquismo* (political bossism) and patron-client relations involving both coercion and consent. The fiesta and *compadrazgo* (fictive kin relations) systems, which the Yaruquíes deliberately cultivated across the community divide, also served to reinforce doxa.

Such a closed system is vulnerable to externally induced disruption, especially by new political and economic intrusions. In the Cacha region the Pandora's box was unwittingly opened when a variety of state interventions, including but not restricted to agrarian reform laws, freed the Cacha from heretofore servile labor relationships and (later) from direct political control by the Yaruquíes. Laborers' consequent use of the option to exit—embodied in the massive migration to the Ecuadorian coast, where earning possibilities were greater—accentuated the growing independence of the Cacha. In essence, as the Yaruquíes' town was bypassed by growth in the lowland Guayaquil region, the site for the old forms of subordination no longer served. The old order began to crack once the mestizo elite had their liquor profits undercut. With these changes, the Cacha transformed local power relations and replaced mestizo authority. As such changes unfolded, and as the Yaruquíes mobilized defensively against their loss of control over their neighbors and tried to reclaim the status quo ante, their efforts were met with the blossoming of the Cacha community organizing in opposition, culminating in the formation of their own parish and their political autonomy from the Yaruquíes. Liberation Theology–inspired clergy—here as elsewhere in the region— helped prepare the groundwork for the change.

James Scott or scholars of the subaltern might raise the issue of whether the "reading" of the initial set of conditions as *doxa* was accurate, or whether "hidden transcripts" of the sort that James Scott points to had already laid the cultural basis for the exuberant resistance movement that clearly appeared once the structural monopolies of Yaruquíes oppression had been cracked open. A juxtaposition of the contributions of Pallares' and Héau to this volume (we discuss Héau's chapter below), for example, suggests that hidden transcripts may have lurked beneath the overt signs of doxa that the Cacha exhibited. No matter: Pallares alerts us to the highly localized ways in which subalterns may respond to conditions they find oppressive, as postmodernists would lead us to expect. The Cacha response is particularly interesting in that it occurred at a time when a pan-ethnic indigenous movement swept the country, as we noted above. The response shows that claims for indigenous rights, as for other rights, are shaped but not predetermined by broader structures, beliefs, and processes.

That hidden transcripts may have been long in the making gains credence from elsewhere in the Andean region: in the eighteenth-century Peru explored by Alcira Dueñas in chapter 13. Her analysis can be thought of as a textual counterpart to the long history of peasant-originated lawsuits, wherein the indigenous tried to turn laws against the very elites who had fashioned the legal system. In parallel form, Dueñas considers how Christian religious scriptures and symbolism imposed by the conquistadores had the effect, although not the intent, of serving as bases for criticizing those very elites. She illustrates these matters through an analysis of the text "Representación verdadera" (shortened title), written in 1748 by Peruvian Fray Calixto, a mestizo Franciscan. The text, written and printed clandestinely, documents colonial injustices and calls for a reformulation of colonial Christianity in a manner that both legitimated and evoked Andean resistance. Within the "Representación" are found denunciations of abuses against Indians by *corregidores* (colonial officials in charge of indigenous communities), priests, and judges; allegations of illegal behavior by the rulers of Peru; unflattering comparisons of the Spanish empire to the Moorish rule of Spain; calls for equal status of Indians and Spaniards under the king's rule; and moral remonstration because Indians and colonists were denied equal access to Church life and secular benefits, owing partly to the purportedly sinful, non-Christian ways of the pre-Columbians. The document goes on to call for a certain equality of rights for Indians and colonists, for example, to carry out trade and not be subjugated to sales taxes (borne by indigenous peoples but not by European settlers), as well as the rights to greater indigenous autonomy and self-government and to indigenous juridical power-sharing (claims that would resurface in the indigenous movements of the late twentieth century). Thus the "Representación" acutely illustrates how elite discourses can be turned against their creators as well as later elite carriers of those viewpoints: an example of hidden transcripts at work. In particular, Fray Calixto and his indigenous followers found potent criticism of their Christian oppressors in the oppressors' own sacred texts, notably Jeremiah's Lamentations.[15]

Although a key defender of indigenous rights, Fray Calixto himself yet personified a mixture of social roles and beliefs, thus negating any easy attribution to him or to his comrades of "the" subaltern label. As a mestizo and a friar, he mediated between the white conquerors and the native peoples and between traditional Andean religion and Iberian Christianity. Also negating any easy attribution of the subaltern label, the "Representación" itself was, in the words of Dueñas, an Indian-mestizo collective project of writing and social activism, based on input from Indian-mestizo "scholars, teachers, and sympathetic priests, who provided skills, experience, and knowledge for the advancement of" the indigenous peoples. Fray Calixto even discussed the document with various *caciques* (leaders) of indigenous communities before presenting it in its (culturally indicative) Spanish-language form for the eyes of the king. Indigenous *caciques*, presumably co-opted by the Spaniards, in due course became critics of the colonizers they served, even by drawing on European liberal thought for their critiques. Subaltern theoretical approaches might well mask the hybridities and mixtures at work here, given their focus on "the" voice(s) of "the" subalterns (*mestizo* derives from the Spanish verb *to mix*). The mestizo friar, along with the other intellectually creative members of the mestizo intelligentsia that Dueñas discusses, were structurally well positioned to create novel and synthetic discourses that could be turned against the legal and religious foundations of colonialism.[16]

While steeped in colonial history, Dueñas provides insight that helps us better understand and contextualize today's indigenous movements, including their religious inspiration and (in part) religiously derived meaning. For example, the Catholic clergy's shaping of *cacique* ideology in eighteenth-century Peru, particularly the references to Jeremiah and the enslavement of the Israelites, has parallels in the *Zapatista* movement today in Chiapas. There in the Lacandon area, the favorite passages of the Christian Base Communities (the core organizations of Liberation Theology) have come from Exodus, and the peasants who went to the jungle area to seek salvation from plantation exploitation have identified with the Israelites of old (see Nash 2001).

Similarly focusing on cultural texts that build on an indigenous sense of violated rights, Catherine Héau analyzes Mexican popular music in chapter 14. Through ethnomusicology, she unravels changing notions of popular culture and how they correspond to the dominant culture without replicating the latter's original intent. In particular, Héau focuses on a classic form of veiled protest expressed through *corrido* lyrics sung by villagers in southern Mexico during the *Porfiriato* (1876–1910), the period of backdrop and prologue to the country's revolution. The *corrido* as a popular form of music typically involved a narrative tale, and into its basic musical structure many politically potent lyrics were poured. In the very region where Emiliano Zapata's movement (the core of the country's revolution-fostering peasant rebellion) would flare up in the 1910s, *corrido* creators had earlier turned their symbolic guns on the dictator Porfirio Díaz and on Porfirian social conditions.

In noting the longstanding vintage of popular, indigenous, and sub-terranean expressions of cultural resentments against elites, Héau implicitly rejects Bourdieu's idea of doxa and, for that matter, any casual Gramscian reading. The Gramscian view might argue that an already intact and upper-class–based "hegemony" was being undermined (here and in the later context of the country's revolution) by a newly evolved "counterhegemony" among the masses, the latter worldview thus both providing and fostering revolutionary perspectives.[17] Héau instead indicates that, through the lyrics of the *corridos*, certain "hidden transcripts" that had long existed simply *emerged* into (partial) public view. Not unlike Dueñas, Héau also highlights how *corrido* lyricists in their discursive efforts took hold of the language and viewpoints of the nineteenth-century elite—reflected in Mexican liberalism (*la Reforma*)—revised them, and created a *negation* of the official *reformista* ideology. And they did so in a manner that laid down clear ideological-political precedents for Zapata's later revolt.

The *corridos* symbolically reflected the growing, real-life, indigenous indignation toward violations of longstanding community-based rights, especially claims for communal landholding, regularized access to water, and village political autonomy. They counterposed their view of a native "Indian Republic" with the view of a new nation dominated by the "Spanish Invaders." *Corridos* evinced especially deep anger with the large-estate land grabs that the *Reforma* made possible—via the privatization of property rights previously held collectively by villages and the Church—and their lyrics painted Díaz as a traitor to those concerns. Lyricists and singers of the ballads even sanctioned protection of social bandits, who stole from the rich, and depicted such bandits as agents of resistance against an illegitimate elite.[18] We see here an early expression of collective indigenous claims that would frame and inspire the *Zapatista* movement of Chiapas a century later. Héau's analysis implies that victims of the unleashing of economic globalization today might also nurture cultures of resistance that could form a bedrock on which antiglobalization political movements might build, just as victims of Porfirian liberalization policies did earlier.

Both Dueñas and Héau implicitly address Spivak's previously discussed questioning of whether scholars can speak for and accurately understand the subaltern. Unlike Spivak, who argues that far too much information/communication is lost when a nonsubaltern (fails in) attempts to present the subaltern view, these two contributors show in a refreshingly straightforward manner—and very much in the historiographical and anthropological tradition—that we can indeed get closer approximations of how the meek (or not so meek) view their rights and the violations thereof. The two authors also show how subaltern cultures, in a veiled manner, may offer critiques of those rights-violations, appropriate the discursive and symbolic tools of their oppressors, and turn those discourses against elites to demand redress (cf. Scott 1990). More specifically, Dueñas implicitly debunks any postcolonial theorizing that conceptually portrays "the" subaltern as an essentialized, homogenized, totalized, and culturally nonhybrid human type whose life is, furthermore, phenomenologically unavailable to outsiders. Through her consideration both of the "Representación" itself and of its authors, Dueñas demonstrates such social pigeonholing to be both theoretically and empirically unsustainable. Quite apart from the difficulty of unambiguously plugging real persons into such preformed conceptual pigeonholes, nonsubalterns may well serve as important allies and articulators of subaltern lives and perspectives, as Dueñas reveals. Héau, in turn, nicely furthers the unveiling of indigenous conceptions of justice in suggesting that, even when subalterns cannot speak (or write), they sure can sing!

There could hardly be a better place to end our introductory chapter than with Héau's contribution. Her work well encapsulates many of the thematics we have developed throughout this introduction: concerns over assaults on laborers' subsistence claims; official ideologies and discourses; the contrary views of the subaltern stratum that may draw upon and transform dominant discourses; and the sheer range of ways—culturally as well as socially, from music and lyrics all the way to openly rebellious actions, and proactive as well as reactive views and collective actions—through which victims of historical "progress" attempt to cope with and redress their situations. Readers may see what the fine contributors have to say about these and other matters concerning the social construction of rights, claims to such rights, and efforts to correct perceived rights-violations, after we discuss the sequence we have followed.

### The Ordering of the Essays

The essays are grouped according to the main type of social rights they address and upon which they shed light. We begin with the chapters by Chollet, Haenn, and Medina, which focus on different aspects of subsistence rights and their connections to socioeconomic inequities. Then follow three chapters on historical shifts in labor rights and claims to and struggles for such rights within the domestic and increasingly globalized world order, by Ros and Lustig, Anner, and Portes and Fernández-Kelly. The next group of chapters addresses gender- and sexuality-based rights, and includes contributions by Berger, Wood, and Schneider on gender, and Pecheny on gay experiences. The final group of chapters addresses claims to racial and ethnic rights, including rights based on new pan-ethnic social formations, identities, and cross-border networks, and contemporary as well as historical efforts to challenge socially and culturally elite-imposed race/ethnic views and structures. This section includes contributions by Pallares, Dueñas, and Héau.

The four types of social rights on which we focus are presented in the approximate order in which public concern about them came to span the region: subsistence and labor rights, and then gender and racial/ethnic rights. However, as this introduction elucidates and as we find in the chapters that follow, Latin Americans have also experienced reversals in their enjoyment of rights, and thus, over time, they have revisited, redefined, and renegotiated (or attempted to renegotiate) previously enjoyed rights and claims. For this reason, when addressing each of the four types of social rights, we have ordered the chapters thematically and not in terms of the historical period on which the authors focus. In essence, the sequencing of the chapters is analytically, not historically, grounded.

And because our categorization is analytical, the concrete themes considered in these chapters are not so neatly separable. As many of the contributors make clear, struggles for each category of social rights are often tied to struggles for others. Ordinary people, and Latin Americans are no exception, respond to their lived experiences and their understandings of those experiences, not to the intellectual frames the scholarly community imposes to make sense of those experiences. We need to understand Latin Americans on their own terms, though ultimately we hope that, if we can make sense of their lived experiences, it will help them determine the rights they aspire to and how to secure them.

### Notes

1. On political rights and political injustices, see Eckstein and Wickham-Crowley (2003) and the references therein.
2. The preceding section and arguments substantially replicate arguments we make elsewhere (Eckstein and Wickham-Crowley 2003: chap. 1). Such replication stems from our development of an analytical frame of reference that helps us to gain insight into *both* the struggles for social rights treated here *and* the issues of politically grounded injustice treated in *What Justice, Whose Justice?*.
3. Latin American theologians in the 1960s formulated a biblically inspired social doctrine that called for a "preferential option for the poor." Subsistence struggles accordingly became one of their foci of concerns.
4. Just as one folksy example: offers to send money orders to El Salvador and other Latin destinations are common signs in the doorways of Latina/o-run *mercados* (grocery stores) in the Washington, D.C., metropolitan area, home to many migrants from El Salvador.
5. For similar issues of male laborers' economic and social concerns over women employed in *maquilas*, and so on, see also Safa (2001).
6. While most immigrants come for economic reasons, the civil wars in Central America in the 1980s stirred refugee flows as well.
7. The experience of industrial countries suggests that where contact between groups occurs in the context of *relative equality of status*, where competition is

muted, and where economic and social cooperation and informal contacts become part of everyday life, ethnic and racial prejudice and discrimination tend to dissipate and social acceptance and mobility become more routine. Allport (1958) developed the classic argument; for later developments see Bonacich (1972), Lieberson (1980), and Stark (1998: chap. 11).

8. There is a parallel here to gender trends previously noted. Women's movements and groups first focused mainly on equal rights, then on rights to differences from the (male/white) mainstream.

9. The theorists cited in note 7 argue that more intergroup contact will *not* reduce prejudice and increase assimilation if the groups are in intense competition for resources in unequal settings; that is quite an accurate portrait of many indigenous communities in Latin America under threat by developers, landlords, and/or internal migrants threatening their traditional lands. They have responded by seeking various (and sometimes novel) protections in law and in fact, including especially their recognition as semisovereign communities with special rights over the use and disposition of their lands.

10. The exceptional instances usually cited are along the Caribbean coasts of the Central American nations, to which persons of African descent were brought or attracted after the era of slavery, most famously for work on the Panama Canal, but also for banana-plantation labor and similar economic activities. Coming from the English-speaking islands of the Caribbean, their language and religion as well as skin color accentuated their differences from the already established racial/ethnic groups where they (re-)settled. Even in such exceptional cases, however, the black populations originally came to the Western hemisphere in conjunction with the slave trade.

11. Castro enjoyed the support of *santeros,* and many of the rebels carried with them *santería* bead collars as well as rosaries. *Santeros* placed "protections" in Castro's path, and Castro came to be known as *El Caballo* (The Horse). The horse had mysterious qualities to believers, the *Santería* priest being known as the "horse" of the saints (Geyer 1991).

12. It also makes it most difficult to create Jim Crow–style segregation policies in Brazil, given what comparative U.S.-Brazilian historian Carl Degler (1971: chap. 5) dubbed Brazil's "mulatto escape hatch."

13. The *Zapatista* movement in Chiapas is described in greater detail in essays by Nash and Peeler in our companion book on the politics of injustice in Latin America (Eckstein and Wickham-Crowley 2003). In focusing on women in Chiapas, Nash nicely illustrates how claims for gender as well as ethnic rights may reinforce and even strengthen one another.

14. Such a shift in subordinate group perceptions of the "politically possible" has many Southeast Asian parallels, among others. See Schmidt et al. (1977) and Scott and Kerkvliet (1973). For greater elaboration on the Latin American context, see Wickham-Crowley (1991: chap. 2).

15. In a remarkably similar manner, enslaved Africans in the United States found powerful, antislavery readings and comfort in the book of Exodus and in the Bible-inspired lyrics of spirituals, which can easily be read for their messages of longing for freedom and even specific mechanisms of liberation (Roberts 1990: 250–53).

16. In contrast, sociological analyses of the intersections of group identities provide us here with insight. One of the most influential early sociologists, Georg Simmel (1971: 143–49), pointed out that persons socially located "in between" two collectivities are *especially* well situated to give clear insights into the lives of both. This perception helps us understand the social conditions that contributed to Fray Calixto's special role.

17. See Gramsci (1971), and Boggs (1976: chap. 2) for the Gramscian position, which virtually begins by *assuming* the existence of such ideological hegemony over the masses, and pays attention mainly to slight variations on that theme. For withering critiques that deny that upper-class hegemony exercises decisive influence over the lower classes, see Scott (1977), on peasants, and Abercrombie, Hill, and Turner (1980), on the working class. For further critical comments on that concept and its companion, false consciousness, see Wickham-Crowley (1991: chap. 4).

18. Their view of social banditry has parallels elsewhere. See Hobsbawm (1959; 1981) and Wickham-Crowley (1991: chap. 2).

# References

Abercrombie, Nicholas, Stephen Hill, and Bryan S. Turner. 1980. *The Dominant Ideology Thesis*. London: Allen and Unwin.

Allport, Gordon. 1958. *The Nature of Prejudice*. New York: Doubleday.

Alvarez, Sonia, Evelina Dagnino, and Arturo Escobar, eds. 1998. *Cultures of Politics/Politics of Cultures*. Boulder, Colo.: Westview Press.

Babb, Florence. 2001. "Out in Nicaragua: Queer Desires, Local and Transnational." Paper delivered at the 23d International Congress of the Latin American Studies Association, Washington, D.C., September 6–8.

Beverly, John. 1999. *Subalternity and Representation: Arguments in Cultural Theory*. Durham, N.C., and London: Duke University Press.

Boggs, Carl. 1976. *Gramsci's Marxism*. London: Pluto Press.

Bonacich, Edna. 1972. "A Theory of Ethnic Antagonism: The Split Labor Market." *American Sociological Review* 37: 547–59.

Bourdieu, Pierre. 1984. *Distinction: A Social Critique of the Judgement of Taste*. Translated by Richard Nice. Cambridge, Mass.: Harvard University Press.

Castañeda, Jorge. 1993. *Utopia Unarmed: The Latin American Left after the Cold War*. New York: Alfred A. Knopf.

Castells, Manuel, and Alejandro Portes. 1989. "World Underneath: The Origins, Dynamics, and Effects of the Informal Economy." Pp. 11–37 in *The Informal Economy: Studies in Advanced and Less Developd Countries*, edited by Alejandro Portes, Manuel Castells, and Lauren A. Benton. Baltimore: Johns Hopkins University Press.

Colburn, Forrest D., ed. 1989. *Everyday Forms of Peasant Resistance*. Armonk, N.Y.: M. E. Sharpe.

Constance, Paul. 1998. "Sudden Surge in Women's Representation." *IDBAmerica* (September-October): 23.

Coronil, Fernando, and Julie Skurski. 1991. "Dismembering and Remembering the Nation: The Semantics of Political Violence in Venezuela." *Comparative Studies in Society and History* 33, no. 2 (April): 288–337.

Craske, Nikki. 1999. *Women and Politics in Latin America*. New Brunswick, N.J.: Rutgers University Press.

Degler, Carl N. 1971. *Neither Black nor White: Slavery and Race Relations in Brazil and the United States*. New York: Macmillan.

de Soto, Hernando, with the Instituto de Libertad y Democracia. 1989. *The Other Path: The Invisible Revolution in the Third World*. Translated by June Abbott. New York: Harper and Row.

Duarte, Alessandro, and Ariel Kostman. 2000. "Os invasores urbanos: Histórias surpreendentes de famílias que ocupam prédios abandonados e improvisam lares que chegam a ter videocassete e computador." *Veja* (April 26): 16–20.

Eckstein, Susan. 1990. "Urbanization Revisited: Inner-City Slum of Hope and Squatter Settlement of Despair." *World Development* 18, no. 2 (February): 165–81.

———. 1994. *Back from the Future: Cuba under Castro*. Princeton, N.J.: Princeton University Press.

———. 2002. "Globalization and Mobilization: Coping with Neoliberalism in Latin America." *Economic Sociology at the Millennium*, edited by Mauro Guillen, et al. New York: Russell Sage.

———, and Timothy P. Wickham-Crowley, eds. 2003. *What Justice? Whose Justice? Fighting for Fairness in Latin America*. Berkeley: University of California Press.

Evans, Peter B. 1979. *Dependent Development: The Alliance of Multinational, State, and Local Capital in Brazil*. Princeton, N.J.: Princeton University Press.

———. 1995. *Embedded Autonomy: States and Industrial Transformation*. Princeton, N.J.: Princeton University Press.

———, Dietrich Rueschemeyer, and Theda Skocpol, eds. 1985. *Bringing the State Back In*. Cambridge and New York: Cambridge University Press.

García Canclini, Néstor. 1995. *Hybrid Cultures: Strategies for Entering and Leaving Modernity*. Translated by Christopher L. Chiappari and Silvia L. López. Minneapolis: University of Minnesota Press.

Gellner, Ernest. 1992. *Postmodernism, Reason, and Religion*. London: Routledge.

Geyer, Georgie Anne. 1991. *Guerrilla Prince: The Untold Story of Fidel Castro*. Boston: Little, Brown.

Gilligan, Carol. 1982. *In a Different Voice*. Cambridge, Mass.: Harvard University Press.

Gomes da Cunha, Olivia Maria. 1998. "Black Movements and the 'Politics of Identity' in Brazil." Pp. 220–51 in *Cultures of Politics/Politics of Cultures*, edited by Sonia Álvarez, Evelina Dagnino, and Arturo Escobar. Boulder, Colo.: Westview Press.

Goodwin, Jeff. 2001. *No Other Way Out: States and Revolutionary Movements, 1945–1991*. New York and Cambridge: Cambridge University Press.

———, and Theda Skocpol. 1989. "Explaining Revolutions in the Contemporary Third World." *Politics and Society* 17, no. 4 (December): 489–510.

Gramsci, Antonio. 1971. *Selections from the Prison Notebooks*. Edited and translated by Quentin Hoare and Geoffrey Nowell Smith. New York: International Publishers.

Green, James N. 1999. *Beyond Carnival: Male Homosexuality in Twentieth-Century Brazil*. Chicago: University of Chicago Press.

Gureso, Libia, Carlos Rosero, and Arturo Escobar. 1998. "The Process of Black Community Organizing in the Southern Pacific Coast Region of Colombia." Pp. 196–219 in *Cultures of Politics/Politics of Cultures*, edited by Sonia Alvarez, Evelina Dagnino, and Arturo Escobar. Boulder, Colo.: Westview Press.

Heilbroner, Robert. 1974. *An Inquiry into the Human Prospect*. New York: W. W. Norton.

Hirschman, Albert. 1970. *Exit, Voice, and Loyalty*. Cambridge, Mass.: Harvard University Press.

Hobsbawm, E. J. 1959. *Primitive Rebels: Studies in Archaic Forms of Social Movement in the 19th and 20th Centuries*. New York: W. W. Norton.

———. 1981. *Bandits*. Revised edition. New York: Pantheon Books.

Inter-American Development Bank (IDB). 1997. "Money Isn't Everything." *The IDB* (July): 9.

———. 1998a. *Facing up to Inequality in Latin America*. Washington, D.C.: Johns Hopkins University Press.

———. 1998b. "Unequal from Any Angle: A Closer Look at the Income Gap." *IDBAmerica* (November-December): 4–5.

Jaquette, Jane. 1997. "Women and Power: From Tokenism to Critical Mass." *Foreign Policy* 108 (Fall): 23–37.

Jordan, Miriam. 2001. "Quotas for Blacks in Brazil Cause Hubbub." *Wall Street Journal*, December 27: A6.

Kutsche, Paul. 1995. "Two Truths about Costa Rica." Pp. 111–37 in *Latin American Male Homosexualities*. Stephen O. Murray et al., contribs. Albuquerque: University of New Mexico Press.

Lieberson, Stanley. 1980. *A Piece of the Pie: Blacks and White Immigrants since 1880*. Berkeley: University of California Press.

Loveman, Brian. 1999. *For La Patria: Politics and the Armed Forces in Latin America*. Wilmington, Del.: Scholarly Resources.

Lyotard, Jean-François. 1984/2000. "The Post-Modern Condition: A Report on Knowledge." Pp. 418–32 in *Readings in Social Theory: The Classic Tradition to Post-Modernism*, 3d ed., edited by James Farganis. New York: McGraw-Hill.

Marger, Martin. 1994. *Race and Ethnic Relations: American and Global Perspectives*. 3d ed. Belmont, Calif.: Wadsworth.

Marshall, T. H. 1950. *Citizenship and Social Class and Other Essays*. Cambridge, England: Cambridge University Press.

Merton, Robert K. 1936. "The Unanticipated Consequences of Purposive Social Action." *American Sociological Review* 1: 894–904.

Montoya, T. Mark. 2001. "Redefining the Cuban Revolution: The Cultural Politics of Santería." Paper delivered at the 23d International Congress of the Latin American Studies Association, Washington, D.C., September 6–8.

Moore, Barrington, Jr. 1972. *Reflections on the Causes of Human Misery, and Upon Certain Proposals to Eliminate Them*. Boston: Beacon Books.

Morgan, Robin, ed. 1984. *Sisterhood is Global*. Garden City, N.Y.: Anchor Books.

Murray, Stephen O., et al. 1995. *Latin American Male Homosexualities*. Albuquerque: University of New Mexico Press.

Nash, June. 1989/2001. "Cultural Resistance and Class Consciousness in Bolivian Tin-Mining Communities." Pp. 182–202 in *Power and Popular Protest: Latin American Social Movements*, edited by Susan Eva Eckstein. Berkeley: University of California Press.

———. 2001. *Mayan Visions*. New York: Routledge.

Navarro, Marysa. 1989/2001. "The Personal is Political: Las Madres de Plaza de Mayo." Pp. 241–58 in *Power and Popular Protest: Latin American Social Movements*, edited by Susan Eva Eckstein. Berkeley: University of California Press.

Newman, Graeme, ed. 1999. *Global Report on Crime and Justice*. The United Nations Office of Drug Control and Crime Prevention. New York and Oxford: Oxford University Press.

Noronha, Eduardo Garuti, Vera Gebrim, and Jorge Elias Jr. 1998. "Explicações para um ciclo excepcional de greves: o caso brasileiro." Paper delivered at the 21st International Congress of the Latin American Studies Association, Chicago, September 26–28.

Ochoa, Enrique C. 1987. "The Rapid Expansion of Voter Participation in Latin America: Presidential Elections, 1845–1986." Pp. 861–904 in *Statistical Abstract of Latin America*. Vol. 25, edited by James W. Wilkie and David Lorey. Los Angeles: UCLA Latin American Center Publications, University of California.

Ortner, Sherry B. 1995. "Resistance and the Problem of Ethnographic Refusal." *Comparative Studies in Society and History* 37, no.1 (January): 173–93.

Oxhorn, Philip. 2003. "Social Inequality, Civil Society, and the Limits of Citizenship in Latin America." Chap. 2 in *What Justice? Whose Justice? Fighting for Fairness in Latin America*, edited by Susan Eckstein and Timothy P. Wickham-Crowley. Berkeley: University of California Press.

Page, Joseph A. 1995. *The Brazilians*. Reading, Mass.: Addison-Wesley.

Paige, Jeffery M. 1975. *Agrarian Revolution: Social Movements and Export Agriculture in the Underdeveloped World*. New York: The Free Press.

Rawls, John. 1971. *A Theory of Justice*. Cambridge, Mass.: Belknap Press of Harvard University Press.

Roberts, Keith. 1990. *Religion in Sociological Perspective*. 2d ed. Belmont, Calif.: Wadsworth.

Rudé, George. 1981. *The Crowd in History, 1730–1848*. Revised ed. London: Lawrence and Wishart.

Safa, Helen I. 2001. "Women and Globalization: Lessons from the Dominican Republic." Paper delivered at the 23d International Congress of the Latin American Studies Association, Washington, D.C., September 6–8.

Sandoval, Salvador A. M. 2001. "The Demobilization of the Brazilian Labor Movement and the Emergence of Alternative Forms of Working-Class Contention in the 1990s." Paper presented at the 23d International Congress of the Latin American Studies Association, Washington, D.C., September 6–8.

Schmidt, Steffen W., Laura Guasti, Carl H. Landé, and James C. Scott, eds. 1977. *Friends, Followers, and Factions: A Reader in Political Clientelism*. Berkeley: University of California Press.

Scott, James C. 1976. *The Moral Economy of the Peasant: Rebellion and Subsistence in Southeast Asia*. New Haven: Yale University Press.

———. 1977. "Hegemony and the Peasantry." *Politics and Society* 7, no. 3: 267–96

———. 1985. *Weapons of the Weak: Everyday Forms of Peasant Resistance*. New Haven: Yale University Press.

———. 1990. *Domination and the Arts of Resistance: Hidden Transcripts*. New Haven: Yale University Press.

———, and Benedict Kerkvliet. 1973/1977. "How Traditional Rural Patrons Lose Legitimacy (in Southeast Asia)." *Cultures et Developpement* 5: 501–40. Reprinted as Pp. 439–57 in *Friends, Followers, and Factions: A Reader in Political Clientelism,* edited by Steffen W. Schmidt, Laura Guasti, Carl H. Landé, and James C. Scott. Berkeley: University of California Press.

Scott, Joan. 1988. *Gender and the Politics of History*. New York: Columbia University Press.

Sen, Amartya. 1999. *Development as Freedom*. New York: Alfred A. Knopf.

Simmel, Georg. 1971. *Georg Simmel on Individuality and Social Forms*, edited by Donald N. Levine. Chicago: University of Chicago Press.

Smith, Lois C., and Alfred Padula. 1996. *Sex and Revolution: Women in Socialist Cuba*. New York: Oxford University Press.

Spiro, Melford. 1996. "Postmodernist Anthropology, Subjectivity, and Science: A Modernist Critique." *Comparative Studies in Society and History* 38, no. 4 (October): 759–80.

Spivak, Gayatri. 1988. "Can the Subaltern Speak?" Pp. 271–316 in *Marxism and the Interpretation of Cultures*, edited by Cary Nelson and Lawrence Grossberg. Urbana: University of Illinois Press.

Stark, Rodney. 1998. *Sociology*. 7th ed. Belmont, Calif.: Wadsworth.

Stephen, Lynn. 1997. *Women and Social Movements in Latin America: Power from Below*. Austin: University of Texas Press.

Stone, Samuel Z. 2001. *Telltale Stories from Central America: Cultural Heritage, Political Systems, and Resistance in Developing Countries*. Albuquerque: University of New Mexico Press.

Streicker, Joel. 1993. "Sexuality, Power, and Social Order in Cartagena, Colombia." *Ethnology* 32, no. 4 (Fall): 359–74.

Tarrow, Sidney. 1998. *Power in Movement: Social Movements, Collective Action and Politics*. 2d ed. Cambridge, England and New York: Cambridge University Press.

Telles, Edward. 1993. "Racial Distance and Region in Brazil: Intermarriage in Brazilian Urban Areas." *Latin American Research Review* 28, no. 2: 141–62.

———. 1999. "Ethnic Boundaries and Political Mobilization among African Brazilians: Comparisons with the U.S. Case." Pp. 82–97 in *Racial Politics in Contemporary Brazil*, edited by Michael Hanchard. Durham, N.C.: Duke University Press.

Thayer, Millie. 1997. "Identity, Revolution, and Democracy: Lesbian Movements in Central America." *Social Problems* 44, no. 3 (August): 386–407.

Thompson, E. P. 1971. "The Moral Economy of the English Crowd in the Eighteenth Century." *Past and Present* 50 (February): 76–136.

Tilly, Charles. 1978. *From Mobilization to Revolution*. Reading, Mass.: Addison-Wesley.

Wallace, Ruth A., and Alison Wolf. 1999. *Contemporary Sociological Theory: Expanding the Classical Tradition*. 5th ed. Upper Saddle River, N.J.: Prentice-Hall.

Walton, John. 1989/2001. "Debt, Protest, and the State in Latin America." Pp. 299–328 in *Power and Popular Protest: Latin American Social Movements*, edited by Susan Eva Eckstein. Berkeley: University of California Press.

———. 1998. "Urban Conflict and Social Movements in Poor Countries: Theory and Evidence of Collective Action." *International Journal of Urban and Regional Research* 22, no. 3: 460–81.

Weiner, Tim, and Graham Gori. 2001. "In Mexico, Bitterness is Sugar's Legacy." *New York Times*, December 30, Business section: 5.

Wickham-Crowley, Timothy P. 1991. *Exploring Revolution: Essays on Latin American Insurgency and Revolutionary Theory*. Armonk, N.Y.: M. E. Sharpe.

———. 1992. *Guerrillas and Revolution in Latin America*. Princeton, N.J.: Princeton University Press.

# part I.

## *Subsistence Rights*

# 2

# In Defense of Social Justice:
# From Global Transformation to Local Resistance

*Donna L. Chollett*

## Introduction

The global transformations that enveloped Latin America over the past decade resulted in uneven consequences for diverse social groups. Scholars witness an increasing tension between a macroeconomic agenda concerned with profitability and local community access to employment and sustenance. As neoliberal reforms intensify Latin America's integration into the world economy, they may adversely impact local communities. Should local people lose their ability to obtain basic rights, will they be able to effectively challenge the neoliberal model? In the absence of more adequate attention to social justice, it is probable that occurrences of local resistance in defense of these rights will escalate.

From the perspective of policy makers, neoliberalism promised important advantages. Debt-ridden Latin American countries adopted International Monetary Fund (IMF)–mandated policies as a condition for debt restructuring. In turn, they received access to new loans. Neoliberal policies also promised to stimulate economic growth. According to this logic, the privatization of inefficient parastatal industries would contribute to modernization and greater profitability. As a result, an increase in export production would generate revenues for the benefit of the national economy.

From the perspective of those who live with the consequences of neoliberal policies, the benefits remain elusive. Privatizations replaced state paternalism inherent in parastatal industries with a more profit-oriented managerial system. Frequently, this change involved large worker layoffs and a reduction of credit to small-scale producers. Simultaneously, global market integration placed local producers in competition with more economically competitive international actors. As a result, many small-scale producers and workers suffered a decline in income.

Below I analyze the impact of neoliberalism on the Mexican sugar sector. Privatization of Mexican sugar mills from 1988–1992 and the inclusion of sugar trade into the 1994 North American Free Trade Agreement (NAFTA) pact dramatically transformed sugar production and marketing. In the 1990s, food and beverage processors in Mexico began to replace cane sugar with lower-costing high fructose corn syrup (HFCS) in their products. Competition with alternative sweeteners imported from the United States hindered the ability of Mexican refineries to market their sugar, leaving them with severe cash-flow problems that imperiled the industry. Sugar industry officials predicted that HFCS would force twenty sugar mills to close. In addition, pressure by political interest groups to modify NAFTA in regard to trade in sugar and HFCS circumvented the "free hand of the market," placing sugar mills at greater risk.

Next, I present an in-depth community study of Puruarán, Michoacán, to examine the local consequences of these transformations. In this case, the mill owner closed down the community's sugar mill, leaving residents unemployed. While mill owners tend to view cane growers and workers as unproductive, local growers and workers at the Puruarán mill mobilized in defiance of police repression to defend their right to employment.

The research is based on fieldwork from 1997 to 2001 that addressed several research questions: Did privatization of sugar mills contribute to productive efficiency and increased earnings? By 1997, some growers who earlier experienced debts succeeded in earning small profits. Was this experience universal? While some mills showed economic recovery, corporate consolidation (the concentration of production into fewer mills), and market opening under NAFTA contributed to the closure of the Puruarán mill.

Six of Mexico's sixty sugar mills closed their doors between 1986 and 1997. Thus, *Ingenio* (sugar mill) Puruarán, with its community of 11,373 inhabitants, is not representative. The importance of this case lies in the absence of research that examines the impact of agroindustrial shutdowns on rural communities. Puruarán is unique because it is the only community where a social movement emerged to contest the mill closing. What makes this community significant is the potential closure of twenty more Mexican sugar mills as HFCS imports under NAFTA displace cane sugar. Events that jeopardized social justice in Puruarán stand to be replicated.

My research involved formal and informal interviews with a non-random sample of cane growers, ex-mill workers, and community leaders, to ascertain the impact of the mill closure on the community.

These data reveal changes in economic strategies, household income, attitudes about the mill closure, and involvement in efforts to reopen the mill. Sugar industry offices in Mexico City provided additional data to situate Puruarán within the national context.

## Global Transformations

Mexico's 1980s debt crisis served as a catalyst for neoliberal reforms aimed at economic restructuring. The IMF's solution for debt restructuring and economic recovery called for the privatization of industries and the dismantling of barriers to international trade. Privatization became the antidote for government mismanagement of Mexico's parastatals. While privatization freed up government resources, market integration contributed to foreign exchange earnings. The privatization of state-owned sugar mills from 1988 to 1992 and the enactment of NAFTA in 1994 brought profound consequences for Mexican sugarcane growers and mill workers.

Privatization resulted in the consolidation of fifty sugar mills into eleven consortiums. These consortiums maintained linkages to a variety of enterprises[1] and established easy access to sugar for their sugar-based products. Twenty-five mills, for example, held soft drink franchises with Coca-Cola, Pepsi-Cola, and Mexican soft drinks.

Initially, a severe crisis besieged the sugar sector: New owners failed to invest in modernizing their mills, market opening flooded the country with imported sugar,[2] mechanical failures left unprocessed cane rotting in the fields, and cane growers experienced large debts to mill owners (Chollett 1995). Buyouts of one consortium by another and the splitting of certain consortiums reflected the volatility of the sugar sector. By 1994, however, the sugar sector showed signs of recovery. As new investments rejuvenated the industry, Mexico regained its sugar-export capacity, and cane growing became somewhat profitable. In 1997, acreage, yields, and factory efficiency all showed significant increases.[3]

Despite record production, by 2000 industrialists accumulated debts of $2 billion. Inability to pay off loans provoked the failure of FINASA, the Financiera Nacional Azucarera, S.A. (National Sugar Financial Corporation), the government financial institution for the sugar sector. The cane harvest of 2000–2001 ended in May, yet industrialists were unable to pay growers for their cane. During July and August 2001, cane growers marched on Mexico City and seized government buildings, including the Secretariat of Agriculture, in demand of back payments in the amount of $500 million. *Grupo Santos*, owner of the Puruarán sugar mill, owed a debt of $200 million. President Vicente Fox, in response, expropriated twenty-seven of Mexico's fifty-nine sugar mills in September with the intention of consolidating and reselling them. Many of these mills may face the same fate as *Ingenio* Puruarán. Among the expropriated mills are those belonging to *Grupo Santos* (Mutual Support Group), Grupo Azucarero México (GAM) (Mexico Sugar Group), Consorcio Azucarero Escorpión (CAZE) (Scorpion Sugar Consortium), and Machado.

The impressive national-level achievements cited above were not uniform. Private mill owners increased profitability of their mills by favoring more efficient cane growers. They denied credit to less efficient growers, often forcing them out of cane production. In some cases, mill managers assumed direct control of the land until the *cañeros'* (cane growers) debts were paid off. In other cases, they denied entry of low-yielding cane for processing. These policies marginalized producers with fewer resources, and created substantial hardships for family survival.

Similarly, mill owners concentrated their interests in fewer mills by favoring their more productive refineries and excluding their less efficient mills. Six sugar refineries closed following privatization: *Ingenio* Oacalco, Morelos (1988); *Ingenio* Estipac, Jalisco (1988); *Ingenio* José López Mateos Juchitán, Oaxaca (1992); *Ingenio* Purísima, Jalisco (1992); *Ingenio* Puruarán, (1992); and *Ingenio* Rosales, Sinaloa (1997).

*Grupo Azucarero México*, affiliated with Pepsico, exemplifies this process. Its owners bought out *Grupo Sucrum*, formerly owned by Alberto Santos de Hoyos. Santos purchased four mills in 1991, forming *Grupos Santos*. This entrepreneur sealed the fate of the Puruarán mill in 1992 when he claimed that the mill was unprofitable, closed it, and consolidated his interests in the three remaining Santos refineries (*Alianza Popular*, San Luis Potosí; *Bellavista*, Jalisco; and *Pedernales*, Michoacán). While this strategy promotes productive efficiency, it disregards the social and economic impact on sugar-producing communities.

## NAFTA

NAFTA integrates Mexico into the North American market in consequential ways. Pre-NAFTA studies offered varying predictions concerning NAFTA's impact on employment, yet many projected substantial job increases. The creation of hundreds of thousands of new jobs benefitted the automotive, electronics, and *maquiladora* industries. Since enactment of NAFTA, however, the economic crisis and competition with foreign firms and goods caused 28,000 businesses and two million Mexican jobs to disappear (Hansen-Kuhn 1997). Imported commodities that flooded the Mexican market in the 1990s undermined many rural producers. With respect to the sugar sector, Mexico's integration into

NAFTA threatens the livelihoods of unprecedented numbers of *cañeros* and workers.

Important considerations distinguish sugar production in the United States and Mexico. Subsidies to U.S. sugar growers and a restrictive tariff-rate quota on sugar imports maintain an artificially high price for U.S. sugar. The beneficiaries of U.S. sugar policy accrue to 1 percent of American farmers as a form of corporate welfare. In contrast to the United States, where 851,000 hectares of land were in cane and sugar beet production, Mexico had 582,746 hectares of cane under cultivation in 1997. The United States concentrates its sugar industry in twelve sugar refineries, while the Mexican industry extends across sixty production zones. U.S. cane and sugarbeet growers hold, on average, 100 to 150 hectares in Louisiana and Texas, and 11,000 hectares in Hawaii and Florida. Mexican cane growers average 3.5 hectares on *ejido* (agrarian reform) lands, and 12 hectares on private landholdings (Buzzanell and Lord 1993). In Mexico, 145,145 *cañeros* and 264,411 workers directly depend on the sugar industry; the sector indirectly supports 2,424,969 individuals (CNIAA 1995). Thus, market integration affects fewer, wealthy industrialists in the United States, while thousands of Mexicans representing a range of social classes depend on the sugar industry for their survival.

Competition between the two countries sharpened with enactment of NAFTA. NAFTA prescribes a fifteen-year phaseout of tariffs. During the first six years, NAFTA allowed Mexico to export 25,000 tons of sugar to the United States (.0055 percent of its national production); in year seven, it could export up to 250,000 tons. If, after six years, Mexico acquired surplus producer status for two consecutive years, it could then export all of its surplus, duty-free, to the United States. NAFTA defines *exportable sugar* as the surplus that exceeds domestic sugar consumption. The potential to export sugar to the United States represented a major benefit for Mexico under NAFTA. Nonetheless, the United States allowed Mexico to export only 25,000 tons until 2000–2001, increasing allowable exports to 116,000 tons in 2000–2001 and 137,788 tons for 2001–2002.

A closer look at trade between the two countries reveals an uneven playing field. In addition to disparities in the two economies, political interests circumvented the free trade principles stipulated by the original NAFTA document.

U.S. cane and sugar beet growers formed a powerful lobby to oppose NAFTA. They feared that Mexico would switch to HFCS in its soft drink industry, and thus generate a larger sugar surplus for export. An increase in Mexican exports threatened to depress U.S. sugar prices. Under this pressure, last-minute modifications to NAFTA provided U.S. sugar producers a decided advantage. NAFTA redefined Mexico's exportable sugar as the excess above domestic consumption of cane sugar *and* HFCS (Butler and Otero 1995). High fructose corn syrup generated a war of sweeteners within the context of NAFTA. As the U.S. fructose industry expanded at the expense of sugar in the 1970s and 1980s, the government protected U.S. growers by imposing quotas on sugar imports (Buzzanell and Lord 1993). Sugar imports retracted from five million to one or two million tons.

Mexico, however, regained its sugar export capacity, and in 1997 production reached a historical benchmark of 5,174,028 tons. Just when Mexico placed more of its surplus sugar on the world market, world overproduction brought international sugar prices down. Therefore, SECOFI, the Secretaría de Comercio y Fomento Industrial (Mexico's Secretariat of Commerce and Industrial Promotion), requested an increase in Mexico's quota to the United States since U.S. sugar prices exceeded those on the world market. Officials in Mexico's sugar industry complained that the persistence of U.S. quotas prevented Mexico from taking advantage of market integration under NAFTA.

U.S. companies that promoted HFCS as a sugar substitute in Mexico also undercut demand for cane sugar on Mexico's domestic market. In 1992, the United States exported 20,000 tons of HFCS to Mexico (Kessel, Buzzanell, and Lord 1993); this amount increased to 350,000 tons in 1997 (Muñoz 1997). The United States exported 1.3 million tons of HFCS to Mexico from 1994—when NAFTA came into effect—until the year 2000 (Ortiz 2000). In 2000–2001, the United States exported 400,000 tons of HFCS to Mexico, in addition to U.S.-based plants that produced 300,000 tons of HFCS within Mexico, leaving warehouses stocked with surplus sugar. The lower price of HFCS relative to cane sugar and a NAFTA phaseout of tariffs on HFCS will further increase the flow of HFCS to Mexico. The USDA projects that by the year 2008, HFCS is expected to capture 90 percent of the soft drink market and 37 percent of the total sweetener market (Cruz 1997; Kessel, Buzzanell, and Lord 1993; Rudiño 1998).

The connection between soft drink production and HFCS in Mexico is significant in this context. Industrial sugar consumption, a mere 762,386 tons in 1970, reached 2,534,929 tons by 1995. In 1991, soft drinks alone accounted for 55 percent of industrial sugar consumption in Mexico (Buzzanell and Lord 1993; García Chávez 1997). However, domestic sugar consumption contracted in response to its displacement by HFCS, especially in its use for Mexican soft drinks.

In 1997 a bitter conflict emerged when Mexico initiated an antidumping investigation and raised tariffs on HFCS imports. Sugar industrialists and soft drink companies reached an accord to limit use of HFCS to 380,000 tons over a three-year period. This agreement committed the bottling industry to meet any increase in demand with sugar, rather than HFCS (Flores 1997; Rudiño 1997). The U.S. Senate Agricultural Committee accused the Mexican government of illegal actions for limiting the purchase of HFCS. The United States brought the matter before the World Trade Organization (WTO) for violation of NAFTA principles. The committee denounced this action, stating, "The establishment of limits sanctioned by the government would promote protectionism that NAFTA has sought to eliminate" (González 1997: 27). A WTO decision in February 2000 determined that Mexico must repay, with interest, provisional tariffs charged to U.S. corporations for HFCS imports (U.S. Trade Representative 2001). Since NAFTA gives Mexico the right to export all of its surplus sugar once it achieves surplus-producer status for two consecutive years, Mexicans argue that they have the right to export 600,000 tons of sugar to the United States. The Kantor-Serra Puche parallel letters of 1993 are at the heart of the current trade controversy. U.S. trade representative Robert Zoellick argues that this side-agreement limits imports of Mexican sugar to 250,000 tons until the year 2007. Mexico's secretary of commerce Ernesto Derbez disclaims the parallel letters with the argument that they were never ratified by the Mexican congress and asserts his unwillingness to comply with resolutions of the WTO dispute-settlement body. President Fox stated his resolve to defend the industry's right to export all of its sugar surplus and retain tariffs on HFCS imports. President George W. Bush insists that the United States retain full rights to duty-free HFCS exports and maintain its own protective barriers for the U.S. HFCS and sugar industries.

My interview with a representative of the national cane growers' union captured this critique of the unequal trade relationship:

> The U.S. imports 4,200,000 tons of sugar, but purchases only 25,000 tons from Mexico. According to the agreement we made with the industrialists, no more than 380,000 tons of HFCS can be sold in Mexico. Whereas sugar is the survival of the cane grower, fructose is death for us. We intend to confront NAFTA. We are not going to allow one sugar mill to close. We cannot let the people die; it is necessary to defend them. This is the only industry that employs so many people in the rural sector. We are trying to protect the work of 2,000,000 cane growers. If we leave so many people without employment, where are they going to work? When a sugar mill closes everything ends. When a sugar mill goes under, the community goes under. This is the oldest industry, with a history of 400 years. Never in the history of this country has it been as threatened as now.

It is within this context that small-scale producers and workers must confront neoliberalism and its impact on their communities.

### Local Transformations

Studies that document the impact of neoliberalism indicate a growing consensus that these transformations place local societies at increasing risk and often foster social injustices (Carton de Grammont 1995; Gates 1993; Phillips 1998). While neoliberalism may resolve problems of international capital accumulation, as an *economic* model it often fails to address increasing poverty, social disparities, and political unrest that may accompany such transformations (Carton de Grammont 1995).

Policies that marginalize small-scale producers pose an important challenge for social science analysis. Marilyn Gates (1993) documents cases of economic triage, a practice that denies credit to less efficient producers and downsizes the work force in the name of efficiency. As Phillips (1998: 196) points out, "Critical social science requires an engagement that ... actively listens to representations of the world that vary from those being offered by ... neoliberalism." Below, I introduce these alternative representations.

David Barkin and his co-authors advise researchers to consider two significant forces in dynamic interaction—neoliberalism and resistance to it (Barkin, Ortiz, and Rosen 1997). Hernández and Nigh (1995) assert that ideologies associated with globalization tend to underestimate the powers of local cultures. Therefore, analysis proceeds by situating the community of Puruarán within the interaction of global and local forces. This analysis privileges both the impact of neoliberalism on the community and the multiple ways that local people contested its repercussions. In analyzing both local discourse and acts of confrontation, I illustrate how the closure of the Puruarán mill fostered the reassertion of community identity and a social movement in defense of social justice.

### *Puruarán and the Community Sugar Mill*

Puruarán's historical dependence on sugar production commenced with the founding of its hacienda in 1772. Agrarian reform in 1938 severed the unity of factory and field formerly maintained by the hacienda. The mill eventually came into the hands of an American, Thomas D. Boyd. When the mill went bankrupt in 1966, the National *Ejidal* Credit Bank took it over.

A plaque on the mill wall, dated January 31, 1966, documents the historic event of President Gustavo Díaz Ordaz (1964–1970) refinancing the refinery through the *Ejido* Bank and improving it "in benefit of the *ejidatarios* [agrarian reform recipients] and inhabitants of the region." Based on this event, residents claim that the mill rightfully belongs to the community. This understanding shapes local cultural identity and reinforces the importance of the community's 300-year tradition of sugar production.

During the 1970s, the government assumed ownership of decapitalized sugar mills to preserve economic stability of the sector. It took over the Puruarán mill in 1971. But by the 1980s, neoliberal policies called for privatization. Santos de Hoyos purchased *Ingenio* Puruarán in 1991. Local residents, however, believed the mill to be the property of the community and contested the legitimacy of its sale to Santos de Hoyos.

The Puruarán and Pedernales mills were the least productive of the four refineries in the sale package. Santos, claiming it was unprofitable, closed the Puruarán mill on May 25, 1992. The rationale for closing "inefficient" sugar mills can be measured against data that reveal the place of *Ingenio* Puruarán among other mills in the country. In 1991, Puruarán had 2,062 hectares of cane in cultivation, industrialized 158,498 tons of cane, and produced 15,400 tons of sugar. Puruarán represented the fifth smallest refinery in the country in volume of production. Nonetheless, in 1992, the year the mill closed, the field yield (tons of cane per hectare) at Puruarán averaged 91.63, in contrast to the national average of 74.34. Only fourteen of Mexico's sixty-two mills surpassed Puruarán's yields, and forty-eight had lower averages. While the factory yield (tons of sugar produced per ton of cane) at Puruarán reached 9.7, the national average registered 9.28. Eighteen mills surpassed Puruarán, and forty-four achieved lower factory yields. Also in 1992, extraction of sucrose during the processing of cane at Puruarán reached 13.01 percent, while the national average registered 12.36 percent. Puruarán ranked twelfth in the nation (CNIAA 1995). Santos' other mills surpassed Puruarán in volume, yet Puruarán ranked relatively high in measures of efficiency.

Overemployment contributed to inefficiency of sugar mills and taxed their profitability. Representatives from the national mill workers' union warned workers at Puruarán in 1991 that, without a major worker layoff, the mill would be closed. An ex-worker recalled, "We did not want to leave—we said 'all' or 'none.' Well, we were ignorant, right? Because we did not know what agreements they had made. We said, 'If you are going to hang some, hang everyone.'" Workers at Santos' Pedernales mill, 11 kilometers away, agreed to accept some worker layoffs, which most likely played an important role in the rationale for keeping it open. Puruarán, on the other hand, is a substantially larger community with an infrastructure that supports a larger number of people. In terms of employment, the decision to close the Puruarán factory held greater impact.

The realization that HFCS reduced demand for cane sugar constituted another factor that influenced the owner's decision to close the Puruarán mill. Low world market prices for sugar exports and emerging competition with HFCS within Mexico made the decision to concentrate investments in fewer mills a logical strategy.

Whereas neoliberal incentives played a major role in the decision to close the Puruarán mill, Santos' strategy overlooked the impact borne by local residents. This refinery served as the economic hub for Puruarán and surrounding communities. *Ingenio* Puruarán supported 2,260 cane growers, 800 cane cutters, 244 truck and tractor drivers, and 530 mill workers. The economic activity directly and indirectly benefitted 36,050 inhabitants of the region. Its demise stifled economic activity throughout the region.

### The Social Impact of Mill Closure on Puruarán

The impact of neoliberal policy often goes unnoted. The abrupt termination of economic activity in 1992, however, imposed a severe crisis regarding peoples' ability to sustain family and community forms of survival. Unemployment, increased poverty, emigration, and violence born of social stress played havoc in a community formerly knit by cultural traditions extending back to the colonial period.

Economically, loss of income affected access to housing, food, clothing, education, and medical care. Socially, Puruarán's residents experienced profound distress, mixed with rage over their exclusion from the benefits of modernization. Many turned to robbing, alcoholism, narcotrafficking, and violence when no other solution materialized. Below, I draw on local discourse to give voice to their outrage.

Concerns with preservation of their families, their community, and the right to work punctuate conversations that fill the everyday lives of people in Puruarán. The parish priest, perceptively attuned to the needs of the community, confided:

> I arrived when it was very critical, after they closed the mill. You can still see the great poverty because many jobs were lost. The pay from the mill that was received in all the region, all this brought people for commerce— the commerce was lively. [But now] the stores are barely surviving. Many [of them] closed and many ex-workers had to leave Puruarán—they had to migrate. This was a consequence of the closing.
>
> The first six months after I arrived, pickups with high-powered weapons passed, firing at all hours. The people, at six in the afternoon, no longer left their houses. I believe that for lack of employment and with the crisis here, it provoked peoples' nerves. Many young boys have been killed by police while robbing in the streets. How many have been killed? Well,

we lost count. Here we say that when 15 days pass without an assassination, it is a long time. And the violence continues.

This reality contrasts sharply with the historical legacy of cane and sugar production that gave form to community life. An 82-year-old cane grower elaborated on this cultural tradition. His father had worked at the Puruarán mill and labored in the cane fields to provide for the family. His father taught him to cultivate cane when he was a boy. In 1938, when President Lázaro Cárdenas (1934–1940) distributed land to *campesinos* (rural workers), he received his *ejido* parcel of two hectares. All of his own seven children became cane growers. Like most families in Puruarán, the tradition of working in the cane or the mill spanned many generations.

This *cañero* assessed the mill closure: "We don't have any other industry. . . . As long as I remember this has been the only industry here. Now we have no money—from where?" He received his highest profits, $2,567 (U.S.) at *Ingenio* Puruarán. After the mill closed in 1992, he delivered his cane to *Ingenio* Pedernales. From 1993 to 1994, he received no profits, and in 1995 earned only $135 (U.S.). In his words, "The cane growers are sweating so that others can benefit. The mill owners are enjoying their life, and the poor cane grower is suffering."

Many sugarcane growers opted to deliver their cane to the Pedernales mill after the Puruarán mill closure. Of the 1,140 *cañeros* who delivered cane to the Puruarán mill in 1991, 74 percent of these delivered cane to Santos' Pedernales mill in 1998. The Pedernales mill could not process all the cane in the two zones; *cañeros* paid higher transportation costs, and contracting with *Ingenio* Pedernales often resulted in debts. Thus, many of these growers decided to quit sugarcane production.

One of the *cañeros*, who received a profit of $1,605 (U.S.) at the Puruarán mill before it closed, lost his earnings once he contracted with Pedernales in 1994. In 1995, mill supervisors left his cane in the field, unharvested. Nonetheless, he still owed $1,500 (U.S.) for production costs. The manager of the Pedernales mill denied him credit the following year, and he quit cane production. No longer a contracted cane grower, he lost access to health insurance and retirement benefits. Subsequently, mill supervisors attempted to rent his land. Rather than rent to the mill, he rented out his land for pasture, providing him an income of $135 (U.S.) per year.

Unlike *cañeros*, all mill workers faced unemployment. One of the mill workers, with twenty-four years' experience in the mill, received $4,000 (U.S.) in severance pay. He related how the loss of employment affected him:

The money ran out after two months. Now I work in the *campo* like an animal and barely earn $3 (U.S.) a day. This is how our government has us. Here is the part I don't understand. We are cut off, working like monkeys cutting cane, and the clothing and everything is running out.

Another ex-mill worker lamented the hardships he endured once the mill closed:

My father worked in the mill. Here his life ended, here in Puruarán. There were four children; we were all boys. Two of my brothers worked in the mill. Well, my father earned very little, but he earned enough to pay the bills and to have money to spend.

I earned a little [in the mill], to buy something for my wife, or to buy shoes—I had a family too. I was earning $42–45 (U.S.) a week when they closed the mill. And no, they did not pay us [a severance pay] according to the law—they only gave me $1,700 (U.S.). It was gone after three months. Everything has killed me and all this money is spent. With all the obligations I have, what am I to do? And then with no work in the *campo*?

Rural workers who were neither *cañeros* nor mill workers also experienced the effects of the mill closure. One of these workers related:

I have been a *campesino* all my life. I cut cane and whatever work there was to do. My sons also depended on this source of work. Now, I have no work. I have looked, but there isn't any. The people here in Puruarán need this source of work so they can survive. If our government doesn't reopen our source of work, how are we going to live? We have to rob or we have to plant other things, like marijuana. That is what our government is pushing us to do. We are not to blame, if suddenly we have to rob because we are hungry. They closed this mill only for the caprice of a single person. Imagine, for the caprice of a single person, how many people are suffering here!

Even those with no direct relationship to the mill suffered consequences. Cane growers and mill workers patronized local businesses and contributed to cash flow in the community. Owners of small businesses, teachers, doctors, and others confirmed that many residents lost, on average, 30 percent of their incomes, and some faced bankruptcy.

A restaurant owner earned approximately $40 (U.S.) per day before the mill closed; subsequently, his earnings dropped to $13 to $17 (U.S.). He reflected:

The sugar mill has always been the source of work here. Before, on Fridays—payday—the restaurant was filled, and now it is empty. In that time, on Sundays, the people formed a line all the way down the stairway, waiting for a table. Now there is no way to maintain myself. Well, it is very hard to keep going.

The owner of a clothing store, the only source of income for her family of seven, complained, "Yes, you can see that [the mill closing] affected us because the sales are not the same. Before, in one day I would sell twelve dresses, and now, one dress." She related that previously most people bought merchandise with cash, but since the mill closed, they rely on credit: "they buy on pure credit. Also, I am risking because many don't pay me back." Before the mill closed, she sold about $670 (U.S.) in clothing per week (before discounting her costs). In 1997, she averaged $400 (U.S.)—a drop of 40 percent in her business.

These two businesses are representative of the numerous commercial enterprises in Puruarán. All revealed a common pattern of economic decline. The mill closing also affected education in Puruarán. Unable to pay for school uniforms, lunches, and supplies, many parents withdrew their children from school. Enrollment at the primary and secondary level dropped by 30 percent from 1992 to 1997. Professionals, whose parents often paid for their educations with income derived from the sugar mill, also felt the impact. A dentist in Puruarán obtained his professional education with the earnings of his father, a sugarcane grower. The dentist served 15 to 20 patients per day before the mill closed; that number fell to 5 to 7 per day after 1992. Both dental and medical care have suffered, as only cane growers who contract with the Pedernales mill are covered by health insurance. Health insurance and pension funds for all mill workers terminated when the mill closed.

The mill closing not only imposed obvious economic repercussions on the community, but also brought psychological stress that translated into alcoholism and violence. These destructive forces tore some families apart.

The extraordinary number of homes with the words *se vende* (for sale) on their exteriors also provides testimony of the hardships. Immigration to the United States is not new, yet the mill closure forced many more to leave Puruarán. Those who left send remittances to family members in Puruarán. Here, remittances are used for survival purposes, rather than for home improvements or acquisition of consumer goods. Census data verify the scope of out-migration. The population declined 16.6 percent, from 13,638 to 11,373, between 1987 and 1996.

These consequences generated diverse responses. Alternative strategies to cope with marginalization and ensure livelihoods ranged from efforts to find alternative sources of employment, to thievery and drug trafficking, to out-migration. Most of the community's residents, however, joined in a social movement to reopen the Puruarán sugar mill.

*Emergence of the Social Movement*

The social movement that emerged following the mill closure drew on the community's tradition of *cultura cañera* (cane culture). The movement fortified community solidarity by calling on shared cultural understandings of Puruarán's historical dependence on cane and sugar production. The forging of the social movement reinforced notions of local community identity and bound people together in common purpose. On December 7, 1992, community residents mobilized across class and occupational lines and illegally seized the abandoned sugar refinery. Under the leadership of Gregorio Alvarez Vargas, cane growers, mill workers, and townspeople surrounded the mill and removed six guards placed there by the owner.

After the seizure, 180 workers volunteered their labor to repair the factory and put it back in operation. The illegal harvest, known locally as the *miniharvest*, lasted from March through May 1993. Workers operated the sugar mill without the aid of engineers, chemists, or other technicians. They processed 36,000 tons of cane (almost one-fourth of the cane in the zone) into 3,300 tons of sugar, valued at $93,333 (U.S.) and made partial payments to some 500 to 700 cane growers. Nonetheless, the mill owner prohibited them from selling the sugar that remained in the warehouse.

A boiler mechanic explained his involvement in the illegal mill seizure. His discourse illustrates how strong community ties, local work ethics, and ideas about social justice shaped local understandings that led him to join the social movement:

> I did not think just in [sic] myself. I was thinking about my community, that the government was going to leave it a pure ghost town, without employment, without this source of work. Because if you had seen how in the mill all the people were active, the extensive activity, and it made a lot of money flow. Then it ended and look how we are. Never was it like this when we had the mill. Our goal is to open the Puruarán mill. We are struggling only so we can work, that is all. We are working people and we demonstrated that with the miniharvest that we made, without even one engineer, with no one else but the workers. And we produced sugar and we are not afraid to present it before any sugar mill that has all its engineers, all its technicians.

This action, however, brought Puruarán residents into direct conflict with the mill owner and the government. Santos called on the state governor, who ordered police to arrest the leaders of the social movement. Police removed seven people from their homes at gunpoint and incarcerated them. Released on bail after twenty days, they were put on parole for four years. One of the parolees, suffering from diabetes and heart disease, died before his release from parole obligations. He had migrated with his family to Veracruz after the mill closed, but returned to Puruarán to engage in the struggle to reopen the sugar mill. Another of the detainees related, "We did not rob, we did not kill, we did not take anyone's property away from them. The crime was to work. That was the crime. The crime was to work, that is why they jailed us."

The day of the arrests, July 3, 1993, armed police besieged the town. One hundred and fifty to 200 police entered Puruarán at 5:00 A.M. and began to dismantle the sugar mill. As the church bells tolled, townspeople united in a demonstration that prohibited the police from removing additional mill equipment. Subsequently, sixty preventative police arrived to guard the mill, from 1993 to 1996. While under their "protection," police guards dismantled and destroyed machinery, cut cables, broke windows, and fired numerous rifle shots through the roof. They intended to destroy the mill to prevent the community from operating the factory.

The leader of the social movement, Gregorio Alvarez, escaped after absconding with much of the profit from the illegal miniharvest. His deceit contributed to a series of divisions within the social movement and left residents disillusioned and mistrustful. As community tensions increased, a struggle for control of the social movement began. Violence in the community escalated. In 1995, the *comisariado ejidal* (president of the *ejido*) became the victim of murder. The 1996 murder of Gregorio Alvarez followed. In this context of escalating violence, conflicts over the sugar mill resulted in the murder of fifteen individuals within a three-year period. The community lost its former unity as new groups emerged to take control of the social movement to reopen the sugar mill.

Puruarán's priest assumed leadership of the social movement in 1995, at the insistence of 500 to 600 people attending a community meeting. The Committee for the Struggle to Reopen *Ingenio* Puruarán (henceforth, the Committee) formed under his leadership. The Committee began a three-year legal campaign to oblige the government to intervene on behalf of the community. Members of the Committee presented petitions for expropriation of the mill to Michoacán's governor, state officials, national officials, and President Ernesto Zedillo. The Committee based its demand for expropriation on alleged violations of the sale contract, which obligates purchasers to maintain the factories as sources of employment and to improve their productive capacities. Furthermore, it requires them to "foment modernization, rehabilitation, diversification, integration, and agricultural development." The Committee argued that the owner's noncompliance with the sale contract justified expropriation.

In 1995 the Committee met with Santos and proposed three alternatives: (1) that he sell or rent the mill to the community; (2) that he remain owner and let the community operate the mill; or (3) that he reopen the mill and operate it himself. Santos' response illustrates the exclusionary character of the current development trend and its inability to address social injustices: "The social aspect, the development [of the region], to remove so many people of the region from poverty, this is not my responsibility. As a businessman, it has to be a business that gives me earnings." Santos planned to salvage equipment from the Puruarán mill to use in his Pedernales refinery. Ultimately, he demanded that the community vacate and return the mill to him and threatened to close the nearby Pedernales mill, as well, if it were not returned. After failing to achieve a favorable response, in 1996 townspeople again seized the Puruarán mill and forced Santos' police guards to leave.

In the meantime, the Committee began to work with the Michoacán government to establish small factories as alternative sources of employment. None materialized. Nonetheless, these projects turned many people against the official Committee. The movement fractured with accusations that the priest's Committee "sold out" to the government and was no longer interested in reopening the sugar mill. Charges flourished that its leaders became involved in the movement only for political purposes. When the president of the Committee ran for *Presidente Municipal* on the *Partido Revolucionario Institucional* (PRI) ticket in 1998, many claimed that he had supported the mill opening in order to win votes.

A new faction emerged under the leadership of Pedro Tapia (pseudonym), a former mill accountant. On December 11, 1998, Tapia formed the *Sociedad Cooperativa Trabajadores del Ingenio Puruarán* (henceforth, *Sociedad Cooperativa*), comprised of loyal members of the *Partido Revolucionario Democrática* (PRD*istas*). Some of them, as well, aspired to local offices in the 1998 elections. Political opening in Mexico and politicization of the struggle along party lines further disunited the social movement. Tapia's faction forced the Committee's guards out of the mill on April 20, 1998, and initiated a second illegal operation of the mill, with poor results. Because of mechanical failures, they processed only twenty tons of sugar from five thousand tons of cane delivered by loyal *cañeros*.

Curiously, the mill owner and state authorities did not intervene in the 1998 operation. Indirectly, however, the manager of the Pedernales mill denied further credit to *cañeros* who delivered cane to Puruarán. The government, in turn, dismissed workers involved in repair and operation of the mill from employment in the construction of irrigation canals. The irrigation project offered the most important, if temporary, source of employment since the mill closure.

*Cañeros* who delivered cane to Santos' Pedernales mill in 1998 suffered different consequences. In August, with 60 percent of its sugar still in the warehouse, competition with HFCS left *Ingenio* Pedernales without the cash flow to make payments to cane growers. Lists posted on the door of the *casa ejidal* (*ejido* building) advised *cañeros* when they would receive payment for their cane. People lined up daily to check the lists and desperation mounted, since over two and one half months had passed since the end of the harvest.

Tapia's faction quickly lost most of its support after the leader sold the sugar and syrup, stored since the 1993 miniharvest, and then claimed that he had no money to pay *cañeros* or mill workers. This created greater discontent among those who labored for months growing cane, repairing the mill, and processing the cane without pay. Accusations spread through the community that Tapia pocketed money from the sale of sugar, that the priest's group confiscated cash donations made to the social movement, and that the Committee had been bought off by the government. Even so, the desire to reopen the mill rivaled the force of increasing factionalism. One resident's commentary illustrated this greater common aim:

> Well, there were certain things about the priest's Committee that we did not like, but we are in the same boat. Thus, if they get it opened, well fine. And if Tapia achieves it, good, or another group, good. Here, if the virgin opens it, if the Señor San José [the village patron saint] opens it, but [what matters is] that it gets opened.

Political will to reopen the mill transcended the sharp divisions in 1998 as events unfolded that promised to reenergize the local economy. In August Tapia's faction visited officials of Pascual, a manufacturer of the natural fruit drinks marketed under the Boing label. Pascual works with cooperatives, financing their operations, and purchasing their sugar for its products. On January 28, 1999, the Puruarán mill once again opened its doors, this time under contract with Pascual. During the 1999 harvest, between 200 and 300 cane growers, including those associated with the official Committee, delivered their cane to Puruarán. Mill workers, who processed three thousand tons of sugar, again received their bimonthly paychecks. By 2000, from 60,470 tons of cane, the

Puruarán mill produced 5,134 tons of sugar, valued at $2,247,000 (U.S.). Production directly benefitted 1,250 *cañeros* and 237 mill workers. This solution provides people with work and income, and guarantees a market for their sugar. People in this community, acutely aware of global trends that threaten their livelihoods, sought an alternative solution. As one mill worker asserted, "Pascual does not use one drop of fructose."

## Conclusions

In the Mexican sugar sector, privatization initially showed poor perfor-mance as a result of deficient investments, excessive sugar imports, and rising debts among *cañeros*. A strategy of triage—the exclusion of ineffi-cient cane growers and unproductive sugar mills—accompanied eco-nomic recovery of the industry in the mid-1990s. Gains made in the sector were not equitably distributed. While some *cañeros* benefitted, others found themselves marginalized.

Recovery of Mexico's sugar-export capacity coincided with imple-mentation of NAFTA. Even though neoliberalism promotes laissez-faire principles, political pressure to protect the U.S. sugar market circum-vented dictums for "free trade." Whereas quotas limited Mexico's access to the U.S. market, HFCS presented fierce competition in its domestic market. The import of HFCS from the United States threatened to close twenty of Mexico's sixty remaining sugar mills. From the perspective of the government, overproduction on the world market and displacement of cane sugar with alternative sweeteners makes consolidation into fewer mills a logical choice. The recent expropriation of mills, while contradic-tory to neoliberalism, may represent an initial move in this direction. A number of expropriated mills will likely meet the same fate as *Ingenio* Puruarán.

In the context of global transformation, this chapter examined one community's response to the closure of its sugar mill. This closure may be viewed as an outcome of the macrolevel forces cited above. Residents of Puruarán, Michoacán, united to reject the neoliberal model that threat-ened community integrity and their means of family survival. Puruarán may not be representative of other communities that struggle with neoliberalism, yet this community demonstrates how, through local resistance, its residents managed to restore social justice.

A large volume of theoretical literature addresses macrolevel per-spectives of neoliberalism (Gustafson 1994). Transformations taking place in rural communities may be less visible, but equally dramatic. This chapter takes into account "the impact of neoliberal policies on the people we do not usually hear from" (Phillips 1998: xi) without neglecting the dynamic interaction of global and local perspectives and processes. It accounts for global transformations in neoliberal ideology and practice, yet gives voice to those who mobilized to confront its consequences.

Literature on alternatives to the neoliberal model suggests much room for theoretical debate on the ability of neoliberalism to hold sway against local will. Yet, despite the probability that Latin American governments will continue to extend neoliberal policies, there is evidence for growing popular resistance among those subjected to marginalization (Petras 1999; Phillips 1998; Stephen 1997). As Jonathan Fox (1994) clarifies, when the state withdraws social guarantees, militant opposition increases, along with the capacity of *campesino* movements to seek alternative means of survival. The social movement that emerged in Puruarán exemplifies growing discontent and willingness to find alternative solutions. The cooperative continues to operate the mill, but is plagued by ongoing internal struggles and bossism, and production costs that exceed income.

Resistance to neoliberalism expresses itself in diverse ways, from accommodation to more high-risk, independent collective action (Chollett 1997; Petras 1999; Phillips 1998). The factors that condition alternative strategies remain obscure, but preliminary analysis of Puruarán's social movement suggests several factors that led to political mobilization: historically deep cultural traditions, abrupt closure of the community's main source of employment, lack of economic alternatives, inability of most residents to sustain their families, and a capacity to forge unified action based on identification with the community.

Several research questions remain for future analysis: Will *campesinos* benefit from neoliberalism in the long run? Will they compensate for the retrenchment of market-driven forces by abandoning small-scale production for wage labor? Can emigration resolve unemployment caused by corporate consolidation? As traditional crops lose their competitive value, will more lucrative illegal crops become the strategy of preference? Or, alternatively, will future macrolevel economic policies be flexible enough to incorporate concern with cultural integrity, community social institutions, economic self-sufficiency, and demands for autonomous political action that emanate from local communities?

## Notes

1. For example, *Empresas Gamesa*, whose owner purchased the Puruarán mill, is a consortium comprised of numerous enterprises: *Promotora Agropecuaria Gamesa, Productos* Gerber, *Ingenios Gamesa*, and *Grupo Gamesa. Grupo Gamesa* includes Nabisco *Famosa, Harinera Santos, Dulces* Lady Baltimore, *Mareas Alimenticias Internacionales, Galletera Palma, Gamesa Comercial, Desarrollo*

*Industrial Gamesa, Almacenadora Gamesa, Desarrollo Inmobiliario Gamesa, Pastas Tepeyac, Inmobiliario Jalisciense, Corporativo Gamesa,* and *Acrosantos* (Ortega 1990).

2. Mexico imported sugar from Colombia, Guatemala, Honduras, Venezuela, Argentina, Brazil, Cuba, the Dominican Republic, Haiti, Jamaica, Korea, and the Philippines (*Diario de Colima* 1991; Zúñiga 1992).

3. These increases included: hectares of cane, 14 percent; tons of cane, 21 percent; field yield (tons of cane per hectare), 6 percent; tons of sugar, 43 percent; kg. of sugar per hectare, 25 percent; sucrose content of cane, 16 percent; and factory yield 18 percent (CNIAA 1995).

## References

Barkin, David, Irene Ortiz, and Fred Rosen. 1997. "Globalization and Resistance: The Remaking of Mexico." *NACLA Report on the Americas* 30, no. 4: 14–27.

Butler Flora, Cornelia, and Gerardo Otero. 1995. "Sweet Neighbors? The State and the Sugar Industries in the United States and Mexico under NAFTA." Pp. 63–74 in *Mexican Sugarcane Growers: Economic Restructuring and Political Options*, edited by Peter Singelmann. San Diego: Center for U.S.-Mexican Studies, University of California.

Buzzanell, Peter, and Ron Lord. 1993. "Sugar and Corn Sweetener: Changing Demand and Trade in Mexico, Canada, and the United States." *Agriculture Information Bulletin*, no. 655. Washington, D.C.: Economic Research Service, U.S. Department of Agriculture.

Cámara Nacional de las Industrias Azucarera y Alcoholera (CNIAA). 1995. *Desarrollo Agrícola Cañero, Zafra 1989/90–1994/95*. Mexico City.: CNIAA.

Carton de Grammont, Hubert, ed. 1995. *Globalización, Deterioro Ambiental y Reorganización Social en el Campo*. Mexico City: Universidad Autónoma de México (UNAM).

Chollett, Donna L. 1995. "Restructuring the Mexican Sugar Industry: Campesinos, the State, and Private Capital." Pp. 55–62 in *Mexican Sugarcane Growers: Economic Restructuring and Political Options*, edited by Peter Singelmann. San Diego: Center for U.S.-Mexican Studies, University of California.

———. 1997. "Culture, Ideology, and Community: The Dynamics of Accommodation and Resistance to Transformations in the Mexican Sugar Sector." *Culture and Agriculture* 18, no.3: 98–109.

Cruz Romero, José. 1997. "El TLC-Azúcar y los sinsabores de la fructosa." *La Jornada* 10, no. 1: 3.

*Diario de Colima*. 1991. "Importaciones de Azúcar por $3 Millones: CNPP." June 21: 1.

Flores, D. 1997. "Mexican Agreement Limiting the Use of HFCS" [Internet], AGR Number MX7092, Washington, D.C.: USDA [U.S. Department of Agriculture]. Available from: <http://www.fas.usda.gov> [Accessed October 2, 1997].

Fox, Jonathan. 1994. "Political Change in Mexico's New Peasant Economy." Pp. 243–76 in *The Politics of Economic Restructuring: State-Society Relations and Regime Change in Mexico*, edited by Maria Elena Cook, Kevin J. Middlebrook, and Juan Molinar Horcasitas. San Diego: Center for U.S.-Mexican Studies, University of California.

García Chávez, Luis Ramiro. 1997. *El Mercado Azucarero Mexicano y el Tratado de Libre Comercio*. Chapingo, Mexico: Universidad Autónoma Chapingo.

Gates, Marilyn. 1993. *In Default: Peasants, the Debt Crisis and the Agricultural Challenge in Mexico*. Boulder, Colo.: Westview Press.

González Pérez, Lourdes. 1997. "Recrimina EU las restricciones a la fructosa." *El Financiero* 9, no. 9: 27.

Gustafson, Stephen. 1994. *Economic Development under Democratic Regimes: Neoliberalism in Latin America*. Westport, Conn.: Praeger.

Hansen-Kuhn, Karen. 1997. "Clinton, NAFTA and the Politics of U.S. Trade." *NACLA: Report on the Americas* 31, no. 2: 22–26.

Hernández Castillo, Rosalva Aída, and Ronald Nigh. 1995. "Global Processes and Local Identity: Indians of the Sierra Madre of Chiapas and the International

Organic Market." Paper delivered at the annual meeting of the American Anthropological Association, Washington, D.C., November 18.

Kessel, Fred, Peter Buzzanell, and Ron Lord. 1993. "Mexico's Sugar Industry—Current and Future Situation." Washington, D.C.: U.S. Department of Agriculture.

Muñoz, Cuauhtémoc. 1997. "Amenazan azucareros con bloqueo nacional a empresas embotelladoras." *Cuestión* 9, no. 9: 2.

Ortega Pizarro, Fernando. 1990. "El porvenir de la industria mexicana, ser devorada por trasnacionales, dice Alberto Santos." *Proceso* 728: 10–15.

Ortiz Moreno, Humberto. 2000. "El TLC, inequitativo: Seoane." *La Jornada*, August 19.

Petras, James. 1999. *The Left Strikes Back: Class Conflict in Latin America in the Age of Neoliberalism*. Boulder, Colo.: Westview Press.

Phillips, Lynne. 1998. "Conclusion: Anthropology in the Age of Neoliberalism." Pp. 193–198 in *The Third Wave of Modernization in Latin America: Cultural Perspectives on Neoliberalism*, edited by Lynne Phillips. Wilmington, Del.: Scholarly Resources Inc.

Rudiño, Lourdes Edith. 1997. "Fructosa, Amarga Competencia para la Industria Azucarera." *El Financiero* 8, no. 18: 28–30.

———. 1998. "Persiste el Riesgo de Quiebra de Ingenios Nacionales." *El Financiero* 2, no. 3: 13.

Stephen, Lynn. 1997. *Women and Social Movements in Latin America: Power from Below*. Austin: University of Texas Press.

U.S. Trade Representative. 2001. "Dispute Settlement Update" [Internet]. Available from: <http://www.ustr.gov-enforcement-update.pdf> [Accessed March 15, 2001].

Zúñiga, María Elena. 1992. "En Crisis la Industria Azucarera Nacional por Voluminosas Importaciones a Precio *Dumping*." *El Financiero*, 6, no. 15: 6A.

# 3

# Risking Environmental Justice:
# Culture, Conservation, and Governance
# at Calakmul, Mexico

*Nora Haenn*

In rural Latin America, environmental programs must balance conservation with demands for economic development. In the past two decades, policy makers have addressed these conditions through a combination of sustainable development programs and biosphere reserves—a protected area status that allows some human activity (Brandon, Redford, and Sanderson 1998; Wells and Brandon 1992). In this chapter, I use the case of Mexico's largest protected area for tropical ecosystems, the Calakmul Biosphere Reserve, to show how these well-intentioned aims generate ambiguous social consequences.[1] At Calakmul,[2] national conservation policies were reconfigured at the local level to re-create both populist and authoritarian styles of governance. This contradiction further heightened local debates regarding what kinds of government activity were appropriate in Calakmul, debates that emphasized the government's role in providing access to farmland. In response to these tensions, Calakmul's people used their class position as *campesinos* (subsistence farmers, see below) and their role as determiners of the region's ecology to navigate contradictions within conservation and these same government-farmer relations. As I show below, the end results of these processes were equally problematic. Calakmul's people now live with more government intervention, both desired (in the form of greater local representation) and undesired (in the form of an expanding military presence). Conservation policies that once acknowledged local people's role in Calakmul's environmental future now focus on the presence of nonlocal ecotourists.

Research in environmental justice addresses situations like Calakmul's by highlighting how distinct social groups share unevenly in the burden of environmental degradation and protection (Miller, Hallstein, and Quass 1996). For example, international conservationists travelled by plane and rental car to Calakmul, where they hoped to change the swidden agriculture practiced in the region. This stereotype, however, may obscure more complex questions of environmental and social justice. Calakmul's people resisted some aspects of conservation, but not others. They operated simultaneously within multiple political frameworks and contrary norms for relating. I explore this variability by describing conservation programs and policies at Calakmul, as well as local responses to these programs and policies. In my conclusions, I use this material to suggest localized definitions of environmental justice at Calakmul. Because of the government's central role in land distribution, I concentrate on how local ideas emphasized a community of justice between government agents and *campesinos* and the regulation of that relationship through patron-client ties.

I base my evidence on fourteen months of participant observation conducted at Calakmul during 1994 and 1995 with brief subsequent trips in 1996, 1999, and 2001. I spent most of that time living in two *ejidos* (communally managed farm communities) located within the Reserve buffer zone. There I documented the effects of aid projects on village political structures and household economies. I also made weekly trips to the town of Zoh Laguna, headquarters of the Calakmul Biosphere Reserve and of the Xpujil Regional Council. The Council is a *campesino* organization, and, during my research, the group allied itself to the Reserve while spearheading a pervasive program of small-scale, sustainable development. While I learned about the Reserve and Council's operations by attending meetings and conducting interviews, I also followed the connections between these organizations and regional *ejidos*. Reserve and Council staffers regularly visited *ejidos* as they oversaw conservation development programs. The Council also held monthly assemblies attended by hundreds of delegates from its forty-three–member *ejidos*. As I explain below, Reserve and Council officers sought to transform national environmental policies into locally acceptable programs that empowered Calakmul's *campesino* community. The officers' intentions, however, never appeared straightforward. Corruption accusations swirled around both administrations. This association between corruption and conservation indicates the importance people ascribed to the goods at risk in Calakmul's political game, as well as the contradictory quality of conservation's message. In these paragraphs, I describe how these discrepancies accompanied conservation's arrival to Calakmul and were never entirely clarified.

## Declaration of the Calakmul Biosphere Reserve

Calakmul sits in the southeast corner of Campeche state, where Mexico borders Belize and Guatemala. In this section, I describe the political scene preceding the Reserve's declaration, which contributed to conservation's local formulation. In the early 1990s, government authorities asociated with the Institutional Revolutionary Party (PRI) imposed conservation development at Calakmul using a rhetoric of neopopulist politics. Development programs were aimed at appeasing Calakmul's people, then known for their support of Mexico's opposition, the Party of the Democratic Revolution (PRD). In creating a base of PRI support, government agents never set aside conservation objectives. Instead, they characterized Calakmul as an impoverished agricultural frontier, rich in natural resources, in order to rationalize both conservation and development initiatives (see also Li 1999).

Centered on the Mayan archaeological site of the same name, Calakmul, the Reserve was formed by presidential decree in 1989. Mexican and international archaeologists and environmentalists had lobbied for the Reserve throughout the 1980s (Folan n.d.). Some conservationists, however, admit privately that the declaration finally came about only after Mexico's sullied 1988 presidential elections. Entering office under accusations of election fraud, Carlos Salinas de Gortari turned to environmental protection as a way to gain support for his administration.[3] This decision alienated Calakmul's people, who suddenly found themselves living near a reserve.

Calakmul's people say they only learned of the Reserve's existence a year after its declaration, when scientists arrived to inventory the region's resources. It was at this time that they also learned that *ejidos* with lands inside the Reserve might be relocated. These threats proved an especially sore point in *campesino*-government relations at the time. *Campesinos* complained that the Reserve was an added insult in an area long neglected by government authorities. The area's history of colonization helps explain their discontent.

Calakmul is home to 24,000 migrant farmers who colonized the area's extensive forests over the past thirty years. As with similar frontiers in the state of Chiapas (Arizpe, Paz, and Velazquez 1996; Harvey 1998b), some families arrived through government-sponsored relocation programs that aimed to relieve pressure on agrarian lands in northern Mexico. Others learned of land availability through word of mouth and squatted on national lands until their situation was legalized in the form of *ejidal* grants.

*Campesinos* who arrived at Calakmul before the 1990s complained that local conditions did little to improve their quality of life. Calakmul houses a seasonal tropical forest that undergoes marked dry periods. Droughts occur one out of every four years and often cause food shortages. Until the early 1990s, difficult living conditions forced many people out of Calakmul, and population turnover in the region's *ejidos* was high (Boege and Murguía 1989). People asserted that government agents were unresponsive to these hardships. State and municipal authorities, located at least four hours away by bus, seldom visited the region. Calakmul received agricultural programs but had few schools or health clinics. Slighted by governing authorities, the people allied themselves with the opposition PRD. The ruling PRI, in the words of one farm leader, "had no influence here."

In order to counter anti-PRI sentiment, organizers with the government's National Solidarity Program, *Programa Nacional de Solidaridad* (PRONASOL) worked in the early 1990s to build a *campesino* organization (the Xpujil Regional Council) capable of administering PRONASOL development funds. Through astute political maneuvers, PRONASOL organizers utilized anti-PRI and anti-conservation sentiment to intensify government-farmer relations at Calakmul. Campeche's 1991 gubernatorial election served as a platform for this renegotiation. In return for supporting the PRI candidate, the residents of Calakmul —through the PRONASOL-funded Regional Council— would receive increased development funds. They would also find relief from relocation threats. One of the Regional Council's first board members described this votes-for-development deal:

> We wanted to form a group that could sell its product with the aid of technical advice. But then came the problem of the Reserve and that, in 1990, we learned some people were inside it. When the first investigators came, birders and all those people who go into the forest, we realized there were *campesinos* inside the Reserve. SEDUE (Secretaría de Desarrollo Urbano y Ecología, Secretariat of Urban Development and Ecology [federal environment and development authority) said they had to leave, and they began to hold meetings with villages. In that time ... ecologist[s] ... went to the village of Colón for a meeting, and there the people told them that if they weren't smart, they were going to be lynched. The [Regional] Council talked with the government. [We said] it wasn't right, that if the *ejidal* decrees were from before the Reserve's, you cannot place one decree on top of another. The governor said, "I promise to bring the President here, but you all are going to work out this problem with him, that you don't want to move and that you want to care for the Reserve."

Calakmul's people did vote for the PRI candidate, after which Salinas made a personal visit to the region. In a speech to hundreds of *campesinos*, he promised development programs that would contribute toward a "productive ecology." He furthermore charged area residents with "caring for the Reserve." In practice, this caring entailed considerable financial support for the Regional Council. In the mid-1990s, the budget of this (technically) nongovernmental organization rivaled that of any government office in southeastern Campeche.

## A Regional Environmental Agenda

If it ended here, this story would be a familiar one of pork-barrel politicking (Molinar Horcasitas and Weldon 1994). The implementation of the 1991 deal, however, strengthened *campesinos'* position within environmental policy-making and, more generally, within government-farmer relations. The PRONASOL organizer who became the Reserve's first director, Deocundo Acopa, steered this empowerment. Acopa asserted that Campeche's farmers "owned" the Reserve and should benefit from its presence. Under his direction, Reserve and Council administrations became virtually indistinguishable. Without denying the electoral implications of his work, Calakmul's director saw himself as using conservation development to train *campesino* leaders, while empowering Calakmul's *campesino* sector. Here I examine PRONASOL's expansiveness to show how notions of equity and redistributive justice played out in the context of governing institutions characterized by a blending of populism and authoritarianism.

PRONASOL was its most developed when Calakmul's Reserve director, the Regional Council, and nongovernmental groups working in southeast Campeche met with state environmental officers to review the region's conservation initiatives in February 1995. Acopa began by explaining the importance of having the Regional Council coordinate nongovernmental activities. He argued that independently operating nongovernmental organizations (NGOs) could become embroiled in rivalries in which groups duplicate programs, become territorial, and generally operate within a "feudal" atmosphere. After this introduction, technical staff employed by the Reserve, Council, and NGOs presented their programs, stressing a common focus on projects that met developmental needs as expressed by Calakmul's people.

The variety of programs highlights how Calakmul's local conservation practitioners viewed development as serving conservation aims and vice versa. Technical staff described water management programs that included damming seasonal streams and constructing ponds. A global information systems (GIS) project aimed to delineate *ejidal* boundaries. An environmental educator had built an educational center, complete with botanical garden and zoo, in which she hosted local schoolteachers and children. Organic agriculture programs aimed to enrich soil which would end the need for field rotation. The agroforestry program addressed forest management from numerous perspectives. The Regional Council operated four nurseries that supplied saplings to Council members. *Campesinos* planted hardwoods and fruit trees in their house gardens and farm parcels. Technical staff gave advice for caring for the trees and combating arboreal diseases. While the Council board explored markets for less valuable woods, foresters evaluated rates of secondary growth to assess the economic potential of pioneer species.

In the Council's flagship program, *campesinos* voluntarily established protected areas on *ejidal* lands. These reserves aimed at some use particular to an *ejido's* resources. *Ejidos* with archaeological ruins and wildlife populations hoped to capture part of the tourism market. While Council staff emphasized the reserves' practical value, policy makers saw the *ejidal* reserves as a proselytizing tool. They hoped the reserves would provide a foundation for relating to the Calakmul Biosphere Reserve, as Calakmul's people continued to oppose protected areas, despite widespread support for sustainable development projects (see below and Haenn 1999a).

As technical staff reported one after another, director Acopa interjected the philosophy behind each program. The water programs, he explained, aimed at stressing that "if people want water, they have to care for it." People did not have to participate in Council projects, but if they did, the projects would allow them "to see for themselves that the forest is being destroyed." Acopa believed people would protect only those species they found economically valuable. Acopa thus described the sum total of the projects as supporting biodiversity by demonstrating the value of a variety of forest products (Acopa and Boege 1998). Acopa was a consummate cultural broker. In his conservation philosophy, he easily combined the neopopulist and neoliberal rhetoric of the Salinas administration with growing support in conservation circles for community-based management (Dresser 1991; Haenn 2000; Western and Wright 1994).

At the meeting's close, a state representative described Calakmul as a national example. Calakmul's conservation community was creating "new and rational ways to take advantage of the environment." Most important, he noted, these programs were "based on the people, with the people, and for the people." Although presenters listed among their funders the MacArthur Foundation, the World Bank, Canada's Eastern Ontario Model Forest, and various federal agencies, the programs' grassroots tint was noticeable. In its management role, the democratic Regional Council provided the appearance of a local environmental movement.

## New Environmental Populism

Originally formed to administer PRONASOL funds, the Regional Council grew far beyond this mandate. By 1995 the Council was a quasi-governmental group with whose power everyone in Calakmul had to reckon. The source of this power was the group's alliance with the Reserve, an alliance that underpinned receipt of conservation development funds. In Mexico organizations like the Council form part of a complicated drama in which nongovernmental groups variously (sometimes simultaneously) strive for political independence and governmental support for small-scale producers (Harvey 1998a; Otero 1999; Stanford 1994). At Calakmul, the Council became a site for the creative blending of hegemonic and nonhegemonic discourses (cf. Stephen 1997), as Council members attempted to reconfigure government policies. Elsewhere I describe this blending in respect to conservation ideologies (Haenn 1999a). Here, I consider how the Council served as a place where people replicated and attempted to work through tensions between ideals of social hierarchy and equality. As people worked through these tensions in the context of authoritarian and populist governing styles, they also had to deal with contrasting ideals of development, including differences among locally desired development and the aims of various funding agencies.

By 1995 more than half of the villages located in Calakmul's buffer zone belonged to the Regional Council. To join, an *ejido* simply requested acceptance at one of the Council's monthly assemblies. *Ejidos* then accessed projects by petitioning the assembly. Acopa encouraged individual *ejidos* to conduct annual assessments of their development needs. Ideally, petitions would reflect these assessments. Given the top-down nature of the Council's funding; however, these assessments never influenced development expenditures. Instead, the assessments provided Acopa and the Council's board with material to pressure funders for changed development priorities. In the meantime, *ejidal* petitions reflected available funding with its overwhelming emphasis on environmental issues.

Council assembly meetings were day-long affairs in which hundreds of elected representatives promoted their personal interests, those of their *ejidos*, and their visions of a social order in which *campesinos* would dominate. These representatives oversaw the work of a board, voted from within the assembly's ranks. While men voted for their own delegates, women also voted for representatives from organized women's groups. As such, women comprised one third of Council delegates, and the Council provided the only place in Calakmul where women held formal power. Because a single *ejido* could have as many as four representatives (in addition to hangers-on), assembly attendance ranged from one to three hundred people. This size made Council assemblies the most representative *campesino* forum in Calakmul.

Acopa and the Council's board built on this representativeness to further enhance the group's power. Populism and *caciquismo* (local bossism), rather than standing as polar opposites, shaded into each other as the government agent mandated popular oversight of regional conservation and development. In addition to the Council's coordinating role, Acopa required that all nongovernmental groups (including university researchers) receive public, that is, Council assembly, approval for their programs. This approval was never denied, and *campesino* input had little effect on program design. Still, the process reminded powerful outsiders of the similarly influential position held by Calakmul's inhabitants.

Meanwhile, government agents repeatedly acknowledged the Council's authority. They used the assembly to disseminate information on topics ranging from fire control techniques to future development planning. In one assembly, the state governor and Canadian ambassador to Mexico signed a binational pact that delivered aid to Calakmul. The fanfare surrounding the event reiterated a government-*campesino* alliance forged previously in the votes-for-development deal. Speaking to the assembly, one federal agent asserted that: "We chose to work here because of the Reserve director and the support of the state government. But, none of that matters without your support. If [conservation] doesn't work here, it won't work anywhere." By asserting that successful conservation required both a commanding government presence and popular support, federal agents contributed to the Council's role in repainting tensions between hierarchy and populism reflective of the region's relationship to federal authorities. Not coincidentally, these tensions were similarly characteristic of political life in Calakmul's *ejidos*. An important difference at the *ejidal* level was the tenor with which people acknowledged that these tensions invariably play out in contests surrounding control of land.

## Old *Ejidal* Politics

Within Calakmul's *ejidos*, this conservation agenda had a mixed reception. People struggled to put off unwanted government interference while they also took advantage of conservation's development aspects. In exploring this mixed reception, I noted how conservation had become caught up in *ejidal* politics at all levels of governance. At a regional level, Salinas' call to "care for the Reserve" echoed the usufruct rights associated with *ejidal* donations. At the *ejidal* level, conservation programs touched on people's worries about defending their access to land. Before exploring how Council programs reinforced these fears, I first turn to the broader basis for *campesino* resistance to conservation.

In opposing conservation, Calakmul's people called on a social contract with federal agents, one in which government authorities should facilitate access to farmland and agricultural inputs. This position, with its roots in Mexico's revolution of 1910, will sound familiar to researchers of Mexico's agrarian reform. The enduring relevance of this contract finds its most potent expression in the *Zapatista* uprising in Chiapas, a movement instigated partly to resist conservation programs in that state (Collier 1994; Harvey 1998a, 1998b; Nigh 2001). At Calakmul, people opposed environmentalism, arguing that such policies countered this social contract. Protected areas take land out of the agricultural base. Restrictions on hunting and felling and burning forests threaten subsistence. Part of the *Zapatista* platform protests changes made in Article 27 of Mexico's constitution, changes that officially ended distribution of farmland and that encourage privatization of existing *ejidal* lands. At Calakmul, concerns about land insecurity have focused on the Calakmul Biosphere Reserve. Privatization has been a slow and uneven process at Calakmul (Klepeis and Vance 2000), where government agents have countered national policies by creating two new communities composed of families relocated from the Reserve. With public support and government actions leaning toward land redistribution, people who participated in sustainable development programs did so while resisting conservation in the form of protected areas.

Jerónimo provides an example of how this selective approach to conservation found roots in ideals of land distribution. Jerónimo joined every Council project offered in his *ejido*. He spoke with me about his *ejido's* reserve and the need to protect forests to counter global environmental change. However, responding to government mandates that farmers build firebreaks during the burning season, Jerónimo became angry, protesting that:

> What we are going to care for is the [Calakmul Biosphere] Reserve, and we are not going to care for the forest, because the government gave it to us. If the government prohibits something on the land it gives, why give it in the first place?

Although willing to appear conservationist in order to appeal to outside interests (cf. Tsing 1999), Jerónimo was unwilling to alter his farming practices. His stance suggests that, in addition to threats to land and livelihood, *campesino* resistance also countered the unpredictability of ambivalent government policies.

More than social contracts, ideals of land distribution contributed to social identities at Calakmul. Thus far, I have used the word *campesino* as a gloss for *farmer*. Local descriptions of *campesino* pointed to the word's use as a class marker that describes an identity built partly on farm work and partly on people's unique relationship to government authority. A *campesino*, one man said, "lives by his hands, eats because of his pure strength. When there is no money, a *campesino* looks for work to buy food, soap. This is how the years pass." One of the most important markers of a *campesino* was that he or she did not receive a regular salary. Dependent on agriculture and occasional wage labor, they were also dependent on government authorities who provide access to land and welfare aid. This relationship, however, was never easy. While governing authorities could facilitate subsistence, they were also described as extortionists who were predatory toward *campesino* interests. Government structures acted as an antagonistic source of *campesino* identity. Thus, a man drunk on the proceeds of a government subsidy check harangued a soldier conducting a routine search on a local bus. He lectured that "Article 27 says a *campesino* has the right to decide his life for himself. Nobody can manipulate him." Being a *campesino*, this situation suggests, entailed negotiating ideals of dignity in autonomy and the reality of an interdependence built on *campesinos'* humiliation and exploitation. In this way, conservation's double-edged sword was familiar to *campesinos* accustomed to equivocal government actions.

In pressing for more consistent government policies, *campesinos* invoked the social contract outlined in the original Article 27, and attempted to force government agents to live up to promises of patronage (see below). Along these lines, Juan echoed Jerónimo, although the two men did not know each other, and Juan lived two hours driving distance from Jerónimo's *ejido*. Juan did not participate in any Council activities, but he still saw the need for such programs:

> Well, the government should come and explain exactly why it doesn't want [us to fell forest]. If the government gave us land, it gave us land to work. Then after giving us the land to work, it doesn't want us to fell. Then what it should do is give us other lands, give us the support to be able to live from one or two hectares, with mechanized agriculture or something else.

While Juan and Jerónimo drew on national-level *ejidal* politics to formulate anticonservation positions, their positions in Calakmul's conservation arena reflected localized *ejidal* politics. In Juan's *ejido*, Council projects were controlled by a village faction of which Juan was not a member. Council projects were part of a deeper division in which the *ejido's* two blocs divided between themselves the various programs that were then entering the community. Because of this division, Juan saw little need to feign support for conservation. Contrastingly, Jerónimo rarely uttered a word against conservation. Instead, he actively cultivated Council projects. Jerónimo, along with a handful of other men, controlled Council projects in his *ejido*. In addition to agricultural inputs, they benefitted from the day wages, foodstuffs, and household supplies that programs offered only the most active participants. By dominating projects, individuals also might develop opportunities for more illicit gain. Project accounting at the *ejidal* level was not transparent. Council staff disregarded people who complained about a neighbor's handling of project materials; it regarded these issues as a matter of internal *ejidal* politics and, thus, beyond Council jurisdiction. The Council's goals of grass-roots empowerment met serious obstacles in the factional politics and unaccountable leadership often typical of Mexico's *ejidos* (DeWalt and Rees 1994; Galletti 1998).

At the same time, Council programs actually reinforced *ejidal* inequalities by organizing project implementation in a way that mirrored the *ejido's* governing structure. For each project, farmers voted a management group consisting of a *presidente* (president), *tesorero* (treasurer), *secretaria* (secretary), and a *consejo de vigilancia* (oversight council). The *ejidal* governing structure was similarly comprised of two committees, each containing a president, secretary, and treasurer (roughly, one committee is charged with managing internal *ejidal* affairs and another with managing the *ejido's* external affairs). In addition to these, a third committee, similarly designated the *consejo de vigilancia,* acted as a check on the others to see that officeholders fulfill their obligations. Although outsiders saw this organization as evidence for an environmentalism rooted in the local culture, they overlooked the extent to which Calakmul's people themselves saw this structure as problematic.

"In *ejidos* there are always problems," people told me. In saying so, they indicated their personal experience of Mexico's variable and complex *ejidal* sector (Cornelius and Myhre 1998; Snyder and Torres 1998). Many of Calakmul's migrants fled impossible economic and political situations (Haenn 1999b) only to find that Calakmul's *ejidos* similarly presented "population pressures, boundary disputes, competition for ejidal rights, . . . entrenchment of certain leaders in ejidal office, factional power struggles, intrigues with outside political and economic interests, corruption and favoritism, agitation and demagoguery, violence and assassination" (Ronfeldt 1973: 216). Cognizant of their vulnerable position, *campesinos* jockeyed to use the new sustainable economy to reconfigure *ejidal* relationships to their benefit. At the same time, they struggled with the environmental ideas that brought about this particular political game. In the following sections I explore *campesino* thoughts about conservationists' hidden agendas along with *campesinos'* attempts to move political relations at Calakmul beyond their base in environmentalism.

### ¿Qué Hace Esta Persona En Mi Casa?

By the end of 1995, the Calakmul Biosphere Reserve was six years old, and the Regional Council was at its zenith. Conservation goals had been broadcast in Council and *ejidal* assemblies. Yet, at a conference with Mexican and international environmental groups, a former Council board member asked of the environmentalists, "*¿Qué hace esta persona en mi casa?*": "What are these people doing in my house?" People were suspicious that the programs were not what they seemed. The notion of setting aside land that nobody would touch remained alien to Calakmul's people, who viewed the landscape as a place of work (see Haenn 1999c; Murphy 1998; Schwartz 1999). Faced with such incomprehensible actions, *campesinos* began to surmise that environmentalists harbored malevolent motives (cf. Brydon 1996).

In brief, Calakmul's people concluded that there must be something of wealth in the forest that environmentalists wanted to keep for themselves. People viewed some outsiders as stealing recognizable forms of wealth. For example, Canadian interests in conservation were seen as a land grab, as one man avowed that "Canada owns [the] Calakmul [Biosphere Reserve]." Outsiders might as likely translate forest goods into items whose market value is unknown in Mexico. One group of biologists was thought to be stealing bats, even though people could not imagine what commercial use the animals would have. The biologists' tendency to work clandestinely in the forests at night provided some clues. A rumor circulated that they were drug traffickers; when the biologists announced their intentions by painting a batman sign on their car, however, the rumor ceased.

Along these lines, people saw urban-based, nongovernmental groups not as champions of environmental protection, but as self-interested actors. Another former board member of the Regional Council complained: "That's why the money ecologists have for conservation doesn't arrive here. It all goes to rock concerts, exotic meals, and travel." Critiques of conservation thus doubled as critiques of Mexican and international class structures. *Campesinos* often said that people who receive regular salaries are wary of losing that income. Because of this, salaried workers would do what they must to maintain financial security, even if it meant making hypocrites of themselves or enforcing regulations detrimental to farm activities. On this basis, people were indignant, though unsurprised, at reports that environmentalists illegally hunted wildlife. As conservation became caught up in class conflict, tools for resisting conservation similarly employed class statements. In addition to issues of land reform, Calakmul's people drew on class-based discourses and strategies made available by PRD activists and the *Zapatista* movement. These strategies effectively gained additional government aid for Calakmul. They did not, however, counter conservation's role in Calakmul's political organization or the more oppressive aspects of conservation policy.

### Reconfiguring Conservation

As the Regional Council grew, its critics objected that not everyone benefitted from the new sustainable economy. Council board members aroused suspicions of corruption as they began to live lifestyles beyond the means of their salaries. Impatient with a hegemonic Regional Council, hundreds of farmers blocked a federal highway during the busy Easter weekend of 1995. They exacted tolls from passing drivers, charging foreigners more than Mexicans. Tractor trailer drivers refused to pay and found themselves unable to traverse one of only two roads connecting the Yucatán peninsula to the rest of Mexico. Strikers requested the governor's personal presence to address their complaints. By challenging the Regional Council, the strike and its aftermath would reshape government structures at Calakmul.

Protestors' grievances centered on government subsidies that, for the most part, were unrelated to the conservation-development schema. Strikers criticized the government's program for children's scholarships, which, at that time, was in arrears on its payments. Representatives of individual *ejidos* presented petitions for issues particular to their communities. These problems included long-standing requests for either a school, electrification, or legalization of land tenure.

Rumors circulated that the strike had been aided by PRD and *Zapatista* organizers. This *Zapatista* connection merits brief attention. Following the 1994 uprising, Calakmul received an influx of migrants fleeing violence in Chiapas. These refugees provided a personal connection to the rebellion's issues and discourses. Farmers and government agents alike drew parallels between Chiapas and Calakmul, and the Easter protest raised awareness of the possibility of armed resistance to conservation in Calakmul. Following the protest, for example, one of its participants complained about regulations that ban cutting older growth forest:

I don't understand them [conservationists], because if a fellow does not have land already felled, how is he going to feed his family? That's why the farmer becomes rebellious, like in Chiapas, where they don't allow even a small part of the forest to be felled.

I asked this man if he were a PRD supporter, and he responded with an ironic tone: "No, I've always voted PRI, although they steal from me." Public disassociation from the PRD may be advisable in Calakmul, where PRD organizers have been jailed for their activities. This particular man went on to work with PRI government agents to address his community's development needs. Still, the PRD and *Zapatistas* offered Calakmul's people alternative avenues for understanding conservation and for framing responses to it.

A *Zapatista* presence and threats of violence in Calakmul assured the governor's interest. On his arrival, protestors engaged the governor in theatrical displays of poverty. They fed him a plate of unsalted beans and requested he drink a glass of the filthy water typical of regional water sources during that drought season. The governor conceded to few demands, but he assigned a team of bureaucrats to meet with community leaders. Numerous problems cited by demonstrators began to receive attention. Calakmul's Reserve director reflected that the PRI's pork-barrel tactics had returned to haunt the party as Calakmul's people demanded increasingly higher prices for their allegiance.

Conservation issues were on the sidelines of these events, and, as such, the political reorganization that followed the protest might have detached conservation from Calakmul's political arena. After the Easter protest, no fewer than three new farm organizations arose to challenge the Regional Council. Unallied with the Reserve, these groups made little pretense of harboring conservationist sentiments in order to access government funds. Government reaction to the protest, however, reinforced the environmental connection.

Before the protest, the Council and Reserve director had considered pressuring state authorities for the creation of a *municipio*, akin to a U.S. county, to encompass the Reserve and its buffer zone. After the Easter protest, people saw the *municipio* as a way to quell potential rebellion. Declared in 1996, lawmakers heralded Calakmul as the country's first "ecological" *municipio*, a place where environmental regulations and conservation development programming weighed significantly. The creation of the *municipio* increased the local administrative budget from 441,527 pesos in 1996 to 9 million pesos in 1997 (*Diario de Yucatán*, January 2, 1997). A Reserve director (distinct from the person mentioned above) became the *municipio's* first president.

Since 1995, Calakmul has seen an increasing state presence, though the region's reputation for political rebellion and grass-roots activism has lessened. Following the Easter protest, the Regional Council began to decline, and today has only a handful of members. Regional development now focuses on ecotourism (see *Diario de Yucatán*, September 10, 1999), an industry that benefits mainly local and urban elites who finance its infrastructure. Rumors of guerilla activity in Calakmul persist. As in other parts of southern Mexico, the military has a growing presence in Calakmul. Military authorities include in their mandate protection of natural resources, alongside "the fight against drug trafficking and illegal arms shipments" (*Diario de Yucatán*, January 13, 2000). Overall, Calakmul serves as a powerful example of how conservation can be used to extend state power and incorporate undercapitalized regions into larger economic structures (Escobar 1996).

Nonetheless, Calakmul's people feel pride in their *municipio*. Government agents are more locally available, and the presence of local people in *municipio* offices allows for personalized interactions with officeholders. At the same time, an increased government presence raises the specter of greater interference in farm practices and *ejidal* life. Today, Calakmul's people continue to negotiate a series of contradictions characteristic of their relationship to government authority: autonomy and dependence, the need for government aid and fear of predatory government actions, and the desire for a dignified place in the Mexican nation-state and the ambivalent quality of government policies that appeal to divergent interests.

### Discussion

Within this contradictory setting, sustainable development briefly worked as a *metafix* (see Lélé in Dobson 1998), a set of ideas and programs capable of appealing to conflicting interest groups. What relationship, then, did this sustainable development agenda have to notions of justice? Members of the international environmental community, who view poverty and environmental degradation as mutually causative, often see sustainable development as a more solid form of justice (Dobson 1998). Contrastingly, *campesino* opposition to conservation and continued pressuring for certain kinds of government activities suggest that they viewed sustainable development not as a definitive form of justice, but as a single event within a larger process. This difference raises broader questions about the existence of localized ideas of environmental justice at Calakmul. Here, I make some suggestions for these ideas, while assessing the challenge that Calakmul poses for such delineation.

The above list of contradictions points to my own notion of how just environmental and social structures at Calakmul might appear. An autonomous, empowered *campesino* sector would influence transparent government policies that benefit the farm sector. Many of Calakmul's people pressure for this kind of setting. Teasing out variable local ideas of justice, however, can be quite difficult. The political maneuvering of the mid-1990s entailed games within games, and individual motivations were never transparent. Often, it is only in retrospect that such dense political scenes can be assessed, when results of the games materialize. With this hindsight, commentators on the events I describe suggest that these games were simply about extending PRI control. Descriptions of events as they happened show how such statements can overdetermine government actions while denying *campesino* agency (cf. Moore 1999). In addition to resisting conservation, *campesinos* took advantage of contradictory government actions. Because of this, Calakmul shows how, in addition to expressions of abstract norms, researchers must examine actions and processes as sources of ideas about justice.

A primary question within these local ideas is *justice for whom?* Given that social justice entails the distribution of particular goods to a particular group of people, whom do Calakmul's people see as belonging to a local community of justice? *Campesinos'* active role in the votes-for-development deal of 1991 and Easter strike of 1995 suggests that Calakmul's people worked to create a community of justice between themselves and government agents. Government-farmer relations at Calakmul supported Adolfo Gilly's (1998) assertion that governance in Mexico entails ongoing negotiations of authority, often built on instances of revolt. Furthermore, the personalized quality of these negotiations suggest that Calakmul's people viewed an ideal community as operating within what has been called "an ethic of care," or the notion that obligations arise out of relationships (Gilligan 1982). Thus, absent from this community were nongovernmental environmentalists. Both national and international environmental agents remained suspect because they had not established sustained relationships of give-and-take with Calakmul's people. Also absent from this community was the physical environment, an entity that many environmentalists view as deserving or requiring a place within discussions of justice. The reasons for this omission are too lengthy to explore here, but rest on local ideas of the environment as a separate social world, linked to human society through people's labor.

As *campesinos* worked to enforce the boundaries of this community of justice, they also strove toward regulating that community and, in particular, the actions of government agents. In this regulation, Calakmul's people resisted the letter of the law while invoking the spirit of Mexico's constitution. People resisted environmental laws but were not willing to entirely dismiss a legal framework. Instead, they used the social ideals that underpin such frameworks to make moral statements about government-farmer relations. They invoked Article 27 as both an identity marker and a guide for appropriate government behavior. They emphatically insisted on continued land distribution and government aid. At the same time, they suggested that government authorities should better protect *campesinos* from the vagaries of the marketplace, as well as from the malevolent intentions of national and international upper-class representatives.

In order to goad the government into action, *campesinos* drew on the law's symbolism to imbue its mandate with emotive content. Symbols and emotions then provided material for mapping ideas of a personalized, procedural justice (in which the outcome is determined by process, rather than regulation, see Collier 1973) onto Mexico's political system. When the Easter protestors fed the governor a meal of dirty water and unsalted beans, they demanded that he recognize poverty as experienced in the particular lives of Calakmul's people. The governor responded in kind by forming a group that could negotiate responses to highly localized needs. Given the final outcome of the strike, however, negotiation through protest provided only a limited way to advance *campesino* interests.

With few tools of accountability and the social demands posed by close-knit life in small communities, the *ejido* also lent itself to personalized, procedural forms of justice. Procedural justice at the *ejidal* level, however, presented particular difficulties. Past experiences of agrarian strife left many of Calakmul's people deeply suspicious of their new neighbors (Haenn 2000). Calakmul's newness as a social arena meant that institutions for handling disputes were relatively weak. In this setting, many of Calakmul's *ejidos* housed powerful men who used their strength of character to enforce a (sometimes controversial) social order.

This contradiction at the *ejidal* level resonated regionally in the person of Acopa, whose early success suggested that some of Calakmul's people remained comfortable with features of *cacique* rule. Rather than emphasizing more egalitarian political relations, Calakmul's people seemed to assert a different set of criteria for assessing justice within power relations. Various kinds of power relations could be just, as long as they benefitted the *campesino* sector and were accountable, that is, carried out on transparent terms. Ongoing grievances against the Calakmul Biosphere Reserve, thus, noted how conservation entailed secret deals in which environmentalists enriched themselves at *campesinos'* expense. Acopa's authoritarianism came under fire when *campesinos* decided that it was providing a cover for corrupt Council board members, some of whom grew imperious toward their constituents.

Changing attitudes toward authoritarianism provide one more example of how Calakmul in the 1990s was a dynamic frontier setting, characterized by shifting political frameworks and relationships whose transparency was often suspect. Conservation did little to provide coherence to this political scene. Instead, conservation added to the series of contradictions by placing *campesinos* within an ill-defined development trajectory in which farm activities were often viewed a priori as destructive. Conservation development programs underscored the extent to which regional power plays required *campesinos* to gamble their own subsistence on an unknown future. In 1995, policy makers admitted that the programs outlined above remained experimental. Even if the programs were implemented to their fullest, project designers did not know if the projects would generate farm income or protect the environment. *Campesinos* who adopted the programs whole-heartedly risked the lives of their families. Luckily, skepticism about agricultural programs remained the norm, and few people took such chances.

In light of these conclusions, localized environmental justice at Calakmul might go beyond fulfilling promises of land distribution and rectifying government-farmer relations. Environmental justice also requires that *campesinos* no longer risk their subsistence in order to receive aid. Such a reformulation entails movement toward a broader notion of social justice, one characterized by responsive governing authorities and transnational funding agencies. Given the operation of both procedural and regulatory frameworks in Calakmul, defining what constitutes *responsive action* may be difficult. This complication, however, may be overcome by greater attempts at transparency in government practices and the international structures that support biodiversity protection. For example, policy agents might use public forums to solicit public opinion at the earliest stages of policy formulation. In the past, public forums at Calakmul have operated to soften the impact of non-local decision-making. Unfortunately, present governance at Calakmul is ambivalent about *campesino* influence on policy. The *municipio* allows for the election of more locally accountable officials, but these officials reportedly avoid staging large-scale assemblies where *campesinos* might develop a strong, collective voice. Reserve managers largely focus their attention inside Reserve limits. Calakmul's small but growing tourism sector offers menial employment in the service of nonlocal tourists. Among the many interest groups associated with the Calakmul Biosphere Reserve, the protected area now rationalizes a military presence, just as it once served as a tool for *campesino* empowerment.

## Notes

1. This chapter was aided by the insightful comments of Madelaine Adelman and Jennifer Culbert. In the Calakmul area, special thanks go to Mauro Sanvicente, Deocundo Acopa, Eckart Boege, Esteban Martínez, area technical staff, and the residents of southeast Campeche, whose time and patience in contributing to this research are greatly appreciated. Fieldwork for this chapter was carried out with support from the Wenner-Gren Foundation for Anthropological Research, the Fulbright program's U.S.-Mexico Commission for Educational and Cultural Exchange, the Mellon Foundation's Program in Anthropological Demography, and the National Science Foundation.
2. The name applies to both the Calakmul Biosphere Reserve and the *municipio*, or county, which currently houses the Reserve and its buffer zone. I use *Calakmul* to speak generally about the *municipio*, while employing *Reserve* to speak about the Biosphere Reserve.
3. See also O'Neill (1996)and Umlas (1998) for the influence of international environmental groups on Mexican policy makers.

## References

Acopa, Deocundo, and Eckart Boege. 1998. "The Maya Forest in Campeche, Mexico: Experiences in Forest Management at Calakmul." Pp. 81–97 in *Timber, Tourists, and Temples: Conservation and Development in the Maya Forest of Belize, Guatemala, and Mexico*, edited by Richard Primack, David Bray, Hugo Galletti, and Ismael Ponciano. Washington, D.C.: Island Press.

Arizpe, Lourdes, Fernanda Paz, and Margarita Velazquez. 1996. *Culture and Global Change: Social Perceptions of Deforestation in the Lacandona Rain Forest in Mexico*. Ann Arbor: University of Michigan Press.

Boege, Eckart, and Raúl Murguía. 1989. "Diagnóstico de las Actividades Humanas que se Realizan en la Reserva de la Biosfera de Calakmul, Estado de Campeche." Mérida, Yucatán: PRONATURA–Península de Yucatán.

Brandon, Katrina, Kent H. Redford, and Steven E. Sanderson, eds. 1998. *Parks in Peril: People, Politics, and Protected Areas*. Washington, D.C.: Island Press.

Brydon, Anne. 1996. "Whale-Siting: Spatiality in Icelandic Nationalism." In *Images of Contemporary Iceland*, edited by G. Palsson and E. P. Durrenberger. Iowa City: University of Iowa Press.

Collier, George. 1994. *Basta! Land and the Zapatista Rebellion in Chiapas*. Oakland, Calif.: Food First.

Collier, Jane Fishburne. 1973. *Law and Social Change in Zinacantan*. Stanford: Stanford University Press.

Cornelius, Wayne A., and David Myhre, eds. 1998. *The Transformation of Rural Mexico: Reforming the Ejido Sector*. San Diego: Center for U.S.-Mexican Studies, University of California.

DeWalt, Billie, and Martha Rees. 1994. *Past Lessons, Future Prospects: The End of Agrarian Reform in Mexico*. San Diego: Center for U.S.-Mexican Studies, University of California.

*Diario de Yucatán*. January 2, 1997. "Desde ayer Campeche tiene 10 Municipios: el Congreso Aprobó Crear el de Calakmul." Internet edition.

———. September 10, 1999. "El Turismo Cultural Sería una Opción para el Desarrollo en el próximo milenio." Internet edition.

———. January 13, 2000. "Ofrecen Respeto del Ejército para los Indígenas de Xpujil." Internet edition.

Dobson, Andrew. 1998. *Justice and the Environment: Conceptions of Environmental Sustainability and Theories of Distributive Justice*. Oxford: Oxford University Press.

Dresser, Denise. 1991. *Neopopulist Solutions to Neoliberal Problems: Mexico's National Solidarity Program*. San Diego: Center for U.S.-Mexican Studies, University of California.

Escobar, Arturo. 1996. "Construction Nature: Elements for a Post-Structuralist Political Ecology." *Futures* 28: 325–44.

Folan, William, and José García Ortega. N.d. "Reserva de la Biosfera de Calakmul: Los Primeros Esfuerzos." Author manuscript.

Galletti, Hugo A. 1998. "The Maya Forest of Quintana Roo: Thirteen years of Conservation and Community Development." Pp. 33–46 in *Timber, Tourists, and Temples: Conservation and Development in the Maya Forest of Belize, Guatemala, and Mexico*, edited by Richard Primack, David Bray, Hugo Galletti, and Ismael Ponciano. Washington, D.C.: Island Press.

Gilligan, Carol. 1982. *In a Different Voice*. Cambridge, Mass.: Harvard University Press.

Gilly, Adolfo. 1998. "Chiapas and the Rebellion of the Enchanted World." Pp. 261–334 in *Rural Revolt in Mexico: U.S. Intervention and the Domain of Subaltern Politics*, edited by Daniel Nugent. Durham, N.C.: Duke University Press.

Haenn, Nora. 1999a. "The Power of Environmental Knowledge: Ethnoecology and Environmental Conflicts in Mexican Conservation." *Human Ecology* 27, no.3: 477–90 .

———. 1999b. "Community Formation in Frontier Mexico: Accepting and Rejecting Migrants." *Human Organization* 58, no. 1: 36–43.

———. 1999c. "Working Forests: Conservation and Conflict in Tropical Mexico." *Delaware Review of Latin American Studies*. Available from: <http://www.udel.edu/LASP/vol1Haenn.html>

———. 2000. "Biodiversity is Diversity in Use: Community-Based Conservation in the Calakmul Biosphere Reserve." Working Paper no. 11, América Verde Series. Arlington, Va.: The Nature Conservancy.

Harvey, Neil. 1998a. *The Chiapas Rebellion: The Struggle for Land and Democracy*. Durham, N.C.: Duke University Press.

———. 1998b. "Illegality and Economic Viability on the Post-Modern Frontier: Marqués de Comillas, Chiapas." In *The Future Role of the Ejido in Rural Mexico*, edited by Richard Snyder and Gabriel Torres. San Diego: Center for U.S.-Mexican Studies, University of California.

Klepeis, Peter, and Colin Vance. 2000. "Government Policy and Tropical Deforestation in Southeastern Mexico: Land Reform, PROCAMPO, and Land-Use/Land-Cover Change." Paper delivered at the 22d International Congress of the Latin American Studies Association. Miami, FL. March.

Li, Tania Murray. 1999. "Marginality, Power and Production: Analysing Upland Transformations." Pp. 1–44 in *Transforming the Indonesian Uplands: Marginality, Power, and Production*, edited by Tania Murray Li. Amsterdam: Harwood Academic Publishers.

Miller, Vernice, Moya Hallstein, and Susan Quass. 1996. "Feminist Politics and Environmental Justice: Women's Community Activism in West Harlem, New York." In *Feminist Political Ecology: Global Issues and Local Experiences*, edited by Dianne Rocheleau, Barbara Thomas-Slayter, and Esther Wangari. New York: Routledge Press.

Molinar Horcasitas, Juan, and Jeffrey Weldon. 1994. "Mexico's National Solidarity Program: An Overview." Pp. 123–41 in *Transforming State-Society Relations in Mexico: The National Solidarity Strategy*, edited by Wayne A. Cornelius, Ann Craig, and Jonathan Fox. San Diego: Center for U.S.-Mexican Studies, University of California.

Moore, Donald S. 1999. "The Crucible of Cultural Politics: Reworking 'Development' in Zimbabwe's Eastern Highlands." *American Ethnologist* 26: 654–89.

Murphy, Julia. 1998. "Ways of Working in the Forest: Mediating Sustainable Development in Calakmul." Paper delivered at the 97th Annual Meeting of the American Anthropological Association. Philadelphia, PA. November.

Nigh, Ronald. 2001. "Maya Pasts, Maya Futures: The Reflexive Consumption of Nature and Culture in Laguna Miramar Chiapas Mexico." Paper delivered at the 61st Annual Meeting of the Society for Applied Anthropology. Mérida, Yucatán, Mexico.

O'Neill, Karen. 1996. "The International Politics of National Parks." *Human Ecology* 24: 521–39.

Otero, Gerardo. 1999. *Farewell to the Peasantry? Political Class Formation in Rural Mexico.* Boulder, Colo.: Westview Press.

Ronfeldt, David. 1973. *Atencingo: The Politics of Agrarian Struggle in a Mexican Ejido.* Stanford: Stanford University Press.

Schwartz, Norman B. 1999. "An Anthropological View of Guatemala's Peten." In *Thirteen Ways of Looking at a Tropical Forest,* edited by James D. Nations. Washington, D.C.: Conservation International.

Snyder, Richard, and Gabriel Torres, eds. 1998. *The Future Role of the Ejido in Rural Mexico.* San Diego: Center for U.S.-Mexican Studies, University of California.

Stanford, Lois. 1994. "Ejidal Organizations and the Mexican State: Confrontation and Crisis in Michoacan." *Urban Anthropology* 23: 171–207.

Stephen, Lynn. 1997. "Pro-Zapatista and Pro-PRI: Resolving the Contradictions of Zapatismo in Rural Oaxaca." *Latin American Research Review* 32: 41–70.

Tsing, Anna Lowenhaupt. 1999. "Becoming a Tribal Elder, and Other Green Development Fantasies." Pp. 159–202 in *Transforming the Indonesian Uplands: Marginality, Power, and Production,* edited by Tania Murray Li. Amsterdam: Harwood Academic Publishers.

Umlas, Elizabeth. 1998. "Environmental Networking in Mexico: The Comité Nacional para la Defensa de los Chimalapas." *Latin American Research Review* 33: 161–89.

Wells, Michael, and Katrina Brandon. 1992. *People and Parks: Linking Protected Management with Local Communities.* Washington, D.C.: The World Bank.

Western, David, and Michael Wright, eds. 1994. *Natural Connections: Perspectives in Community-Based Conservation.* Washington, D.C.: Island Press.

# 4

# The Cardboard Collectors of Nuevo Laredo: How Scavengers Protect the Environment and Benefit the Economy

*Martin Medina*

In most developing countries, the informal recovery of materials from waste constitutes a common activity for disadvantaged populations. But both scavenging, as an occupation, and scavengers, as people, are poorly understood. They are perceived as poor and as living and working on the margins of the economy and society, and, in many areas, they are subject to exploitation and discrimination by middlemen and by local and federal government policies. Yet, when scavenging is supported—ending that exploitation and discrimination—it represents a perfect illustration of sustainable development that can be achieved in the Third World: jobs are created, poverty is alleviated, raw material costs for industry are lowered (while improving competitiveness), resources are conserved, pollution is reduced, and the environment is protected.

This chapter undertakes an analysis of the scavenging population involved in the informal recovery of cardboard in one of the "twin cities" located along the U.S.-Mexico border (Laredo, Texas, and Nuevo Laredo, Mexico). The case provides a clear demonstration of the economic and environmental benefits that scavenging renders. On this basis, I argue that public policy should support—or at least tolerate—scavenging activities. Most Third World cities perceive scavengers as a problem, and enact policies and ordinances that attempt to eliminate their activities. Rather than being a problem, scavengers can be part of the solution to the insufficient collection and inappropriate disposal of solid wastes in developing countries. Two conflicting theoretical views on scavenging exist: those of Chris Birkbeck (1978; 1979) and Daniel Sicular (1992: 3–25). This chapter attempts to resolve the debate on scavenging in a different empirical setting, namely, the U.S.-Mexico border. In order to better understand the scavenging population, I first estimate the size and importance of the informal recycling sector, and examine the role that scavenging plays in the recycling system. This activity is placed in broader context through an overview of scavenging in the developing world and an examination of the main changes that cardboard collecting has undergone over the past fifty years. This is followed by an analysis of the linkages with the formal sector and a discussion of the effect that globalization and free trade have on scavenging. Finally, I examine the questions of whether scavengers in the area are poor and marginal. I demonstrate that scavenging is not an occupation operating on the margins of society. Rather, scavenging has strong and direct forward and backward linkages with the formal economy, and with the international economy as well. I also propose that cardboard collecting in Laredo and Nuevo Laredo exemplifies the ongoing process of economic integration between Mexico and the United States.

The analysis is based on a joint qualitative/quantitative study carried out in 1994–1995. The qualitative methods used included observation of recycling activities; participant observation of cardboard collecting, processing, and shipping; and in-depth interviews with scavengers, middlemen, local government officials, and Mexican paper industry executives. In order to obtain statistically significant data, I conducted a survey among scavengers in the area. The survey comprised one hundred questionnaires, but the sample included only thirty cardboard collectors. The other seventy scavengers in the sample recovered other materials, such as aluminum cans, glass, and ferrous scrap metal. The results discussed here refer only to cardboard recycling.

## Scavenging in the Developing World

The consumption of manufactured products by the population translates into industrial demand for inexpensive raw materials. Scavenging provides an occupation for some unemployed individuals while supplying low-cost materials—paper, glass, metals, plastics, and so forth—to industry. Manufacturing companies reuse or recycle these materials, incorporating them into new products. The primary causes of scavenging are fundamentally economic, and these activities exist because they make economic sense for all parties involved. In contrast, environmental considerations form the basis of recycling activities in the developed world (Medina 1997b: 191–233).

A large and dynamic informal recycling sector exists today in most developing countries. The World Bank estimates that up to 2 percent of the population in the developing world—as many as 30,000 to 40,000 individuals in cities like Jakarta, Bangkok, Mexico City, or São Paulo—engage in scavenging as a primary occupation and as a means of survival (Bartone 1988: 3–5).

Scavenging takes place in a wide variety of settings: At the source of generation, collection crews sort recyclables prior to their disposal; scavengers salvage materials from communal storage sites, from illegal dumping sites, littered on the streets, at composting plants, and at municipal open dumps and landfills. In many areas itinerant buyers purchase materials separated by households or small businesses. And in cities where canals and rivers cross the urban area, such as in Bangkok and Manila, scavengers recover items floating on the water (Medina 1997b: 128).

Scavengers face multiple problems. Due to their daily contact with garbage and often ragged appearance, scavengers are usually associated with dirt, disease, and squalor and are perceived as a nuisance, a symbol of backwardness, or even as criminals. They survive in a hostile physical and social environment. In many cases, public policy toward scavengers reflects this view, and, as a result, their activities are persecuted and banned in many cities. Sometimes scavengers face extreme animosity and violence. In some Colombian cities, for example, organized groups established, in the 1980s, a campaign of "social cleansing" (*limpieza socia*). Those groups either kill or kidnap and transport to the countryside individuals they consider "disposables" (*desechables*), such as beggars, prostitutes, and scavengers. As a result of the social cleansing campaign, over 2,000 "disposable" individuals had been killed in Colombia by mid-1997 (Medina 1997a: 12–13).

In order to earn cash, scavengers must sell the materials they gather. When purchasing recyclables, industry requires a minimum quantity of materials (usually a truckload) and that they be sorted, clean, and baled. Industry encourages the existence of middlemen/waste dealers, who purchase the recyclables recovered by scavengers and then process and sell them. Consequently, industry will not buy materials from individual scavengers, and opportunities arise for the exploitation and/or political control of scavengers, particularly at open dumps/landfills. These waste disposal facilities are often located at remote locations, making it impossible for scavengers to transport the materials to town, where they may be able to obtain a higher price. Scavengers at dump sites form identifiable groups with limited mobility (in contrast, street scavengers walk up to several miles a day searching for materials). This situation facilitates control of scavengers. Sometimes large scavenging communities form around the dumps/landfills, such as the settlements that surround the Dhapa dump in Calcutta, with an estimated population of twenty thousand, and the Smokey Mountain dump in Manila, where approximately seven thousand scavengers lived. Under these conditions, some unscrupulous individuals become middlemen and exploit scavengers. Indeed, the low incomes that many scavengers earn are largely attributed to the low prices middlemen pay them. In some Indian, Colombian, and Mexican cities, middlemen pay scavengers as low as 2 percent of the price they get from industry for recyclable materials, and thus obtain high profits (Holmes 1984: 181).

Middlemen/waste dealers often operate in monopsonistic markets (markets where there is only one buyer, as opposed to a monopoly, where there is only one seller) and pay lower prices than in a competitive market. Sometimes authorities sanction these monopsonistic markets by awarding concessions. In other cases, authorities and scavenger leaders develop clientelistic relationships that allow for mutual gain from scavenger exploitation. Relationships of political clientelism are common in Mexican cities. Scavenger leaders, popularly known as *caciques*, develop close ties with government officials and the *Partido Revolucionario Institucional* (PRI), Mexico's former ruling party. In Mexico City, for example, Rafael Gutierrez, the only scavenger leader at the dumps until 1987, became a middleman, exploiting and controlling over ten thousand scavengers. As a reward for his loyalty, the PRI nominated him as an alternate Mexican Congress representative in the early 1980s. The authorities legitimized scavenging operations and guaranteed *caciques* unimpeded access to waste at the disposal sites, while ignoring the exploitation of scavengers. In return, officials received payoffs from the *caciques*, political support for the ruling party, and scavenger votes for the PRI (Castillo 1990: 75–99). The patron-client relationship between scavenger leaders and Mexico City authorities continued after Gutierrez's death in 1987, and today five *caciques* control dumpsite scavengers in the city. In conclusion, many scavengers in Third World cities are indeed poor, largely due to the low prices they are paid by the middlemen, relationships of political clientelism, and repressive government policies that hinder their access to materials.

## Twin City Economic Integration

Long before the North American Free Trade Agreement (NAFTA) went into effect on January 1, 1994, the U.S. and Mexican economies were undergoing a process of economic integration (Weintraub 1990: 11–26). Through trade, investment, and financial transactions, economic ties between the two countries deepened. NAFTA merely codified and accelerated the process of integration (Lang and Ohr 1995: 245–57).

The process of economic integration is apparent along the common border of Mexico and the United States. In the so-called *Los Dos Laredos*, for instance, economic integration began soon after the present borderline went into effect. In 1848, when the town split into two as a result of the Guadalupe-Hidalgo Treaty, ferries began transporting people and goods across the Rio Grande between *Los Dos Laredos* (Hinojosa 1983: 73–83). The state of Tamaulipas declared Nuevo Laredo a free trade zone in 1861, and immediately merchants in Laredo, Texas, opened stores to take advantage of the benefits derived from investing there (Sanchez 1981: 87–100).

During the 1860s, the U.S. Civil War encouraged exports of food, alcohol, clothing, and cotton through *Los Dos Laredos*, which benefitted the area. Also during the Civil War, unionists recruited Mexicans and Mexican-Americans on both sides of the border; these recruits became known as *enganchados* (Thompson 1991: 28–29). By the end of the nineteenth century, the Laredo electric and water utilities provided service to Nuevo Laredo (Sanchez 1981: 87–100). This expansion across the border suggests that the Laredo utilities considered Nuevo Laredo a segment of their market.

The labor market in the area was also integrated. During the 1880s, destitute Mexican immigrants constituted most of the miners at the Santo Tomas coal mine in Laredo, and approximately two hundred Nuevo Laredo men, then known as *barrileros*, hauled water from the Rio Grande in donkey carts for the daily needs of Laredo residents. During elections in the 1880s, Laredo political parties "imported votes" by paying a fee to Nuevo Laredans, and bringing them to the United States to cast their ballots illegally (Thompson 1991: 34). Thus, Mexicans from the interior have been migrating to *Los Dos Laredos* for over a century, attracted by the possibility of a better life on the border. Mexicans have provided inexpensive labor for agriculture, industry, and services, while Americans have provided capital as well as demand for various goods and services. The recovery of cardboard in *Los Dos Laredos* illustrates the ongoing international economic integration between Mexico and the United States.

## Cardboard Collecting in Historical Perspective

The informal recovery of waste materials in *Los Dos Laredos* is hardly new. Studies note the use of scavenger carts in Laredo at the end of the nineteenth century (Thompson 1991: 103). Before cities instituted municipal waste collection, scavengers performed this activity in many U.S. cities, and recovered recyclables prior to the disposal of the wastes (Melosi 1981: 51). Thus, it is possible that those scavengers in Laredo at the turn of the century were Mexicans.

Mexican scavengers have been crossing the border to collect cardboard in Laredo for at least sixty years. The cardboard collectors, locally known as *cartoneros*, live on the Mexican side, recover cardboard in Texas, and transport it across the border to be recycled in Mexico. The oldest active *cartonero* started collecting cardboard for a living in the 1940s. He reported that at that time a large number of scavengers collected cardboard on the Laredo streets and other items at the open dump then existing in Laredo. In those years, scavengers used pushcarts to transport the cardboard across the border. Scavengers commonly used horse carts in Nuevo Laredo in the 1940s, but U.S. authorities would not allow the entry of horses from Mexico for sanitary reasons. The so-called *carretoneros* (informal refuse-collectors operating in low-income areas not served by the city sanitation crews) still use horse carts today in Nuevo Laredo. These informal collectors pick up garbage for a fee in areas that lack municipal collection, and salvage any recyclables prior to the disposal of the wastes at the Nuevo Laredo dump (Medina 1997a: 20–4).

In 1956, Enrique Tomás Lozano, a Nuevo Laredo Catholic priest, played a crucial role in the formalization of the transborder recovery of cardboard in the area. He brought together a group of *cartoneros* and contacted Laredo authorities, ultimately reaching an agreement. This agreement sanctioned the *cartoneros'* activities, providing them with a steady income, while helping keep Laredo clean. His efforts would later result in the creation of a *cartoneros* cooperative, the *Sociedad Cooperativa de Recuperadores de Materiales de Nuevo Laredo*, one of the few scavenger co-ops that currently exists in Mexico (Medina 1997b: 195).

Cardboard collecting in *Los Dos Laredos* has undergone dramatic changes over the last five decades. Due to the higher volume of retail sales in Laredo, which results in more cardboard boxes discarded by stores, a greater amount of cardboard is available today than fifty years ago. Laredo is an important commercial center that caters to Mexican shoppers from as far away as Mexico City. Purchases by Mexicans account for nearly 60 percent of the retail sales in Laredo. In fact, due to the influx of Mexican shoppers, Laredo had in 1993 the highest per capita retail sales rate in the United States. While its income per capita was $7,300, its retail sales rate amounted to $12,300 per person per year (Althaus 1993). Such an active retailing sector generates large amounts of cardboard boxes, since the merchandise sold at the stores is shipped in cardboard boxes.

Furthermore, the assembly plants, known as *maquiladoras*, that today constitute an important source of cardboard, did not exist in the 1940s. The *maquiladoras* receive shipments of the parts and components to be assembled in cardboard boxes, which then must be disposed of. Until 1989, U.S. and Mexican laws required *maquiladoras* to dispose of all of their wastes in the Unites States. That year, new Mexican regulations came into effect

allowing *maquiladoras* to dispose of or recycle their nontoxic wastes in Mexico ("Summary of the New Maquiladora Program Decree" 1990). Not being a hazardous material, all cardboard discarded by *maquiladoras* can be recycled in Mexico. This change in the law gave rise to an innovative recycling activity in Nuevo Laredo. The local *maquiladoras* began donating the cardboard to charities. The charities, in turn, sell the cardboard to dealers or to the *cartoneros* cooperative and use the revenue for their programs. Since the donations of cardboard are tax deductible the *maquiladoras* lessen their tax burden (Medina 1997b: 197).

In the United States large reserves of softwood keep demand for wastepaper low. Sometimes the demand for discarded cardboard is so low that its price is negative. That is, recycling programs must pay wastepaper dealers to have their cardboard hauled away and recycled. If the *maquiladoras* shipped their cardboard back to the United States, soft demand and low prices could translate into disposal costs. Alternatively, by donating the cardboard to charities, the *maquiladoras* avoid such disposal costs. Moreover, the fact that proceeds from the sale of cardboard benefit local charities is good public relations (Medina 1997b: 197–98).

With scavenging an informal occupation,[1] no official statistics exist on the number of people involved in it. Therefore, it is possible neither to estimate the volume of cardboard recovered that has been recycled in the past nor to estimate the number of *cartoneros*, the fluctuations in quantities, or the number of individuals engaged in this activity throughout the years. Nevertheless, *cartoneros* and middlemen reported a cyclical pattern in the availability of cardboard: periods of economic growth in Mexico translate into more shoppers in Laredo and more cardboard generated. Economic crises and an unfavorable peso-dollar exchange rate bring about the opposite result. Accordingly, the amount of cardboard available dropped in the aftermath of the Mexican peso devaluations of 1982 and 1994. When the peso-dollar exchange rate is favorable and Mexicans have disposable income, they can afford more purchases in Laredo, which translates into more cardboard discarded by stores.

Even though no federal laws regulate the *cartoneros'* activities, they must comply with all the regulations that impinge on their operations. Middlemen and *cartoneros* reported that the Mexican government has sometimes hindered their recovery activities. In the 1960s, for instance, the government banned the importation of discarded cardboard into the country. Despite the ban, the *cartoneros* smuggled the cardboard by throwing it into the river from the American side and having other individuals retrieve it downstream on the Mexican side.

Then, in the mid-1980s, the Mexican government established a quota system, which required a permit to transport the cardboard from Nuevo Laredo to the paper mills in Monterrey. The liberalization of economic policy carried out by the Carlos Salinas de Gortari administration eliminated the quota system in 1992. In the late 1980s Mexican sanitary authorities required that discarded cardboard be sprayed with pesticides prior to its entry into the country, but this requirement was dropped soon afterward. At present, no limits exist on the amount of discarded cardboard that can be imported into Mexico, but an import tariff of 10 percent must be paid, and the process must be conducted by a Mexican customs broker (Medina 1997a: 203).

*Cartoneros* reported receiving a friendlier reception and more tolerant attitude to their activities from U. S. authorities than from Mexican authorities. In addition to the legal barriers to their occupation, *cartoneros* sometimes face hostile Mexican customs officials, who contend that the *cartoneros* smuggle various goods into Mexico. Not one *cartonero* interviewed reported having problems with U.S. officials, while 70 percent indicated that they have had some kind of problem with Mexican officials. Laredo government officials are aware of the *cartoneros'* activities, and indicated the absence of problems with them. Over the last eleven years no *cartonero* has been brought to court for violating local ordinances. The Laredo officials I interviewed expressed their support for the continuing operation of the *cartoneros*, since, in their opinion, they provide a useful service to the city.

### Cardboard Recovery and the Formal Sector

Several factors have created and influenced the recovery of cardboard in *Los Dos Laredos*. The market conditions for discarded cardboard in Mexico and the United States differ markedly. While the United States possesses vast forestry resources and plays a dominant role in the world's paper industry, Mexico produces less than 40 percent of its domestic demand for wood pulp (Espinosa 1994). Further, the U.S. forestry industry uses advanced technology, benefits from large economies of scale, receives governmental subsidies, and has integrated vertically with the paper industry. The more than six thousand local recycling programs throughout the United States have steadily increased the volume of cardboard available to the paper industry for recycling, while the number of paper mills that can process it has not expanded significantly (Jaffe 1995).

Industrial demand and prices of cardboard in the United States show wide fluctuations. For example, in 1994 New York City had to pay dealers $25 per ton in order to have its source-separated cardboard picked up, while in 1995 the city was being paid $60 per ton, due to the changing market conditions ("Paper Chasing" 1995). In sharp contrast, the Mexican paper industry shows a steady demand for discarded cardboard and wastepaper.

The Mexican paper industry has suffered a chronic shortage of raw materials since the first paper mill was established in 1590 near Mexico City. Throughout the seventeenth, eighteenth, and nineteenth centuries, the Mexican paper industry made paper from old rags. Rags were scarce in colonial Mexico due to the fact that inhabitants used their clothes as long as possible and discarded them infrequently and in small quantities. For three centuries, Mexican rag collectors, then known as *traperos,* constituted the main source of rags for papermaking (Medina 1997b: 118–19). The *traperos'* activities had such economic importance that they commanded royal attention. Felipe II of Spain, for instance, authorized the *Reglamento de Libre Comercio de Indias* (free trade law between the Spanish Crown and its territories in the Americas) in 1778, which exempted from the payment of taxes the rags collected in the Spanish possessions in the Americas. This law attempted to encourage Mexican *traperos* to increase their gathering of rags, which would be exported to Spain and transformed into paper, which would be sent back, in part, to New Spain (Lenz 1990: 16–48).

In the early twentieth century, the Mexican paper industry began making paper from wood pulp, but this did not alleviate the shortage of raw materials. Mexican Indians own most of the forested areas in the country, but many lack deeds, or their ancestral rights to the land have not been recognized. The lack of definition of property rights has led to the plundering of forestry resources by outsiders as well as reluctance to invest in commercial timber plantations (Cortez 1993). Moreover, the remaining woodlands in the country are located in remote and inaccessible areas, requiring the construction of expensive access roads, which account for about 50 percent of a logging project's total costs (Lenz 1990: 16–48). The Mexican government does not subsidize the construction of access roads (as the U.S. government does). Finally, the small scale of logging operations and the use of outdated technology drive up the cost of the timber obtained to such a degree that the prices of domestic forest products often exceed international prices ("Días de guardar" 1993: 551). The previous factors translate into an insufficient domestic supply of wood pulp.

Due to the impracticality of achieving backward vertical integration with the forestry sector, the Mexican paper industry has undertaken vigorous efforts to increase the use of recycled fiber. In 1984 the Mexican paper industry used 58.3 percent of wastepaper as a fiber source, and in

1993 it had increased to 73.8 percent. Correspondingly, primary fiber utilization decreased from 41.7 percent in 1984 to 26.2 percent in 1993 (Espinosa 1994). The paper mills' consumption of the cardboard collected by the *cartoneros* in *Los Dos Laredos* illustrates these recycling efforts.

*Cartoneros'* activities represent important cost savings for the Mexican paper industry: they paid scavengers 300 Mexican pesos a ton in June 1994, while a ton of U.S. market pulp cost 2,250 pesos, plus transportation costs (Medina 1997b: 274; Jaffe 1995). Faced with such a large difference in costs, the Mexican paper industry integrated vertically with scavengers via middlemen. In order to obtain the high-quality U.S. cardboard collected by the *cartoneros*, the paper industry helped set up two of the middlemen by providing loans to start their operations. Paper industry executives periodically visit Nuevo Laredo to devise ways that could increase cardboard collection. As a result of such efforts, in 1994 *cartoneros* collected approximately 620 tons of cardboard per month, worth $53,125 (U.S.) (Medina 1997b: 271–74).

NAFTA will phase out market barriers to trade in most paper products. It will first eliminate tariffs on corrugated boxes, then tariffs on most converted paper products (Jaffe 1995). Since Canadian and American paper product companies are larger and more efficient than their Mexican counterparts, Mexico may face fierce competition when NAFTA takes full effect. The United States and Canada produce two-thirds of the world's supply of wood pulp and more than 40 percent of its supply of paper and cardboard. The Mexican paper industry is trying to survive by upgrading its processes and by lowering its costs: The latter centers on maximizing the use of wastepaper and cardboard collected by scavengers. Thus, Mexican paper mills expect to survive NAFTA competition by further strengthening their ties with scavengers (Medina 1997b: 226–30).

Other global structures and processes besides NAFTA affect *cartoneros*. For one, more and more products made in East Asia arrive in Laredo shipped in cardboard boxes. Typically, the higher the percentage of Asian boxes there, the lower the *cartoneros'* income tends to be. Recycling of paper is more intensive in East Asia than in the United States. Paper can be recycled only a few times because every time it is recycled the fibers get shorter, until they finally can no longer be used. Because of the longer fibers in U.S. cardboard, Mexican paper mills prefer U.S. to Asian cardboard and pay nearly twice as much for the former. Second, the greater the number of *maquiladoras* and the higher their production levels, the more cardboard boxes are available for recycling. Third, factors that determine the global supply and demand of paper affect the *cartoneros*.

For instance, a strike of mill workers in British Columbia in 1992 caused the price of pulp to increase. The Mexican mills raised the price of cardboard paid to the *cartoneros* in order to increase the amount of cardboard collected and avoid the payment of the still higher prices of North American market pulp.

In conclusion, scavengers *(traperos* during the seventeenth, eighteenth, and nineteenth centuries, and *cartoneros* in the twentieth century) have played a critical role in supplying raw materials to the Mexican paper industry. For its entire existence, the Mexican paper industry has had backward vertical integration with *traperos* and *cartoneros*. Rag and cardboard collectors, therefore, have never operated on the margins of the Mexican economy, despite the low earnings many of them obtained.

### Socioeconomic Characteristics of the *Cartoneros* and Recovery Patterns

A survey was conducted among *cartoneros* during 1994. Since *cartoneros* must sell the collected cardboard to middlemen, and since they collect cardboard in various areas and at different times, I decided to approach them just outside the middlemen's warehouses. There, a systematic random sampling was used; every other *cartonero* arriving to sell cardboard was interviewed. Thirty cardboard collectors were included in the sample, which represented about 60 percent of the *cartonero* population at the time.

The cardboard boxes discarded in Laredo are large and bulky so that a vehicle is needed to transport them to Nuevo Laredo. The cheapest vehicle to transport cardboard, and the most commonly used, is a three-wheeled cart called a *tricicleta*. Maneuvering a fully loaded *tricicleta*, which may contain up to 880 pounds of cardboard, requires physical strength. As a consequence, cardboard collecting is a predominantly male occupation. The only female collector in the area received help from her teenage children.

*Cartoneros* received 0.12 to 0.15 Mexican pesos per kilogram for U.S. cardboard and 0.06 to 0.08 pesos for Asian cardboard. Mexican cardboard commands the same price as the Asian. Because of the low price Asian cardboard commands, sometimes *cartoneros* leave it behind to be picked up by the Laredo sanitation crews. For economic reasons, they concentrate on collecting U.S. cardboard.

The survey suggests that the typical *cartonero* is forty years old, is a migrant, has four years of formal education, is married, knows how to read and write (Spanish), and collects cardboard in Laredo. The average *cartonero* has been collecting cardboard in the area for thirteen years, and works eight to nine hours a day, six days a week (Monday through Saturday). Eighty percent of the *cartoneros* transport cardboard in *tricicletas*, while 20 percent use pickup trucks. Ninety percent of the *cartoneros* interviewed reported that they collect cardboard on a full-time basis year-round, while the rest engage in it only seasonally.

The most common areas where cardboard recovery takes place are the Laredo downtown commercial district and shopping centers. Most *cartoneros* had previous work experience. Several factors attracted them to scavenging: flexibility of work hours, ability to work independently, and the possibility of earning a higher income. In mid-1994 *cartoneros* earned a median weekly income of 270 pesos (approximately $77 U.S.), three times the local minimum wage at the time and more than was earned by 95 percent of all Nuevo Laredo income earners (Medina 1997a: 259). The average *cartonero* had collected cardboard for thirteen years, which suggests that it is a stable occupation.

Scavenging offers opportunities for income supplementation, as well. Forty-six percent of the interviewed scavengers reported collecting aluminum cans for additional income. Some are paid cash to help Mexican smugglers pack various goods, especially electronics, which are then taken across the border into Mexico. Some perform odd jobs for Laredo store-owners, such as cleaning up sections of stores and running errands for a tip; they also salvage discarded furniture, appliances, building materials, and food with expired consumer purchasing dates. They retrieve the food for their own consumption.

Table 4.1 presents a comparison between *cartoneros* and the general population of Nuevo Laredo. *Cartoneros* differ from the population at large in several respects. Migrants constitute a greater percentage of the *cartonero* population; *cartoneros'* literacy rate and years of formal education are lower and fewer of them are affiliated with the system of socialized medicine. Yet, *cartoneros* enjoy greater access to public utilities and a higher median weekly income. Nearly three-fourths of the *cartoneros* are homeowners, and nearly 60 percent of them consider their standard of living to be "fair" or "good." In essence, given Nuevo Laredo market options, scavenging offers economic, if not social, benefits.

Nearly two-thirds of the interviewed *cartoneros* considered, before becoming cardboard collectors, migrating illegally to the United States. One-quarter reported having worked in the United States in the past, and some of them were deported back to Mexico. Middlemen's warehouse employees earn lower incomes than the *cartoneros,* and they tend to consider their occupation as a temporary form of employment. But *cartoneros* tend to stay in this occupation.

Table 4.1. Comparison of Socioeconomic Characteristics of *Cartoneros* and the General Population of Nuevo Laredo

| Characteristic | *Cartoneros* | General Population |
| --- | --- | --- |
| Migrants | 69.6% | 41.0% |
| Illiterate | 16.6% | 7.4% |
| Completed at least Elementary School | 39.1% | 73.5% |
| Homes Connected to Sewer System | 96.6% | 81.8% |
| Homes with Tap Water | 100% | 92.5% |
| Homes with Electricity | 96.6% | 95.1% |
| Workers Not Affiliated with Socialized Medicine | 92.9% | 27.9%* |
| Hours Worked per Week | 48 | 40.8* |
| Household Size | 4.1 | 4.6 |

*These figures refer to Nuevo Laredo's labor force and not to the general population.
Sources: My own survey research; INEGI 1993; Alegria 1990; Gonzalez 1990.

## Environmental Impact of *Cartoneros'* Activities

The recovery of cardboard by *cartoneros* renders several environmental benefits. Cardboard recycling reduces energy and water use (23–74 percent and 58 percent, respectively) and lessens water and air pollution (35 percent and 74 percent, respectively), compared to the production of cardboard from wood pulp (Cowles 1986). Moreover, the diversion of cardboard saves landfill space, extending the life of the local landfills. Assuming that each ton of cardboard recycled saves 106 cubic feet,[2] then the space savings from the recycling of cardboard amounts to 65,720 cubic feet per month.

Cardboard collecting diminishes the amount of waste that needs to be collected and transported. This translates into fewer trips made by garbage trucks, less gasoline burned, and less air pollution in the area. The *cartoneros* also pick up aluminum cans and other items they find in waste bins, littered on the streets, and in illegal garbage dumps. By engaging in these activities, they help clean up the two Laredos (Medina 1997b: 284).

## Economic Impact of Cardboard Collecting

Economic benefits include employment opportunities and industrial cost savings. While employment generation is limited (mainly because Mexicans need a visa to cross the border into the United States, and this is hard to get for low-income individuals), in a tight labor market it is welcomed. At least sixty individuals collect cardboard in the area, nearly all of them on a full-time basis. In addition, ten persons work at middlemen's warehouses and at the scavenger co-op.

Scavengers recovered approximately 900 tons of cardboard and aluminum in *Los Dos Laredos* each month, valued at $440,000 (U.S.). This amount contributes to the local economies by way of scavengers' income, middlemen's profits, warehouse employees' wages, import tariffs, truck drivers' fees (who transport the cardboard to the paper mills), international bridge tolls, and Mexican customs brokers' fees. Therefore, recycling activities have an economic impact of over $5 million (U.S.) a year.

The cardboard supplied by *cartoneros,* moreover, lowers costs. For one, salvaged cardboard costs at least 20 percent less than imported cardboard and only one-seventh as much as imported pulp. Second, it saves the country hard currency: the cost of importing supplies. Third, scavenging reduces the volume of waste that needs to be collected, transported, and disposed of, and this saves the two towns nearly $9,000 (U.S.) per month (Medina 1997a: 272).

### The Future of Cardboard Collecting?

Politics and market forces both influence cardboard collecting in the area. As previously discussed, cardboard collecting is affected by and dependent on Laredo/Nuevo Laredo local ordinances and U.S. and Mexican regulations, as well as the interplay of factors determining the global supply and demand for paper products.

The tolerance of the Laredo authorities for the *cartoneros* could change in the near future. Texas Senate Bill 1340, enacted in 1993, mandates all municipalities in the state to reduce the amount of solid waste sent to landfills by 40 percent (Cardenas 1993). In response to the legislation, Laredo launched a recycling program using the "blue-bag" concept (residents put their recyclables in a blue bag provided by the city. Once the bag is filled, the municipal collection crews pick it up at the curbside). The city plans to attain the 40 percent goal by recycling only.

The new law notwithstanding, scavengers may subvert this initiative. In pursuit of their own economic interests, some scavengers open the blue bags to steal aluminum cans. Authorities may, in turn, respond by banning scavenging altogether, to maximize revenue from the recycling program. The California experience may be telling. There, 220 cities and 33 counties promulgated antiscavenging ordinances to enhance recycling income (Lacey 1994).

Cardboard collecting is likely to continue on the Mexican side of the border, though illegally. Cityregulations prohibit scavenging on the streets and impose fines as high as the minimum weekly wage. Although the ordinance is rarely enforced, it allows the police to demand bribes from the scavengers to avoid prosecution. Scavengers report extortions. Such corruption and illegal activity will persist unless the law changes.

Dump site scavenging, long a tradition at the Nuevo Laredo dump, is under attack. In March 1994, the city awarded a concession to Setasa, a private company, for the collection and disposal of municipal refuse. Setasa, fearing that scavenging would obstruct the new landfill operations, announced a ban on the informal activity. Private interests are more likely than officials to enforce policies. Job and income opportunities for scavengers will suffer as a consequence (Medina 1997b: 201).

### Theoretical Implications: Are Scavengers Poor and Marginal?

Despite the fact that scavenging occurs throughout the developing world, it has received scant attention from scholars. Scavengers are often portrayed in the media as poor and on the margins of society. That view is shared by scholars, such as Larissa Lomnitz (1987: 23–45) and Paulo Souza (1980: 22–25), who consider Mexican and Brazilian scavengers, respectively, to be marginal groups, and argue that scavenging shows weak or nonexistent linkages with the formal sector.

Birkbeck (1978; 1979), by contrast, argues that scavengers are poor and exploited, but not marginal. Daniel Sicular (1992), criticizes Birkbeck and contends that scavenging is a precapitalist form of production and considers scavengers both poor and marginal.

My field research demonstrates that scavengers may engage in non-market activities, but in ways integrated into capitalist, not precapitalist, economies on both sides of the U.S.-Mexican border. Rather, my research supports Birkbeck's thesis. Scavenging in *Los Dos Laredos* has strong backward and forward linkages to the formal sector, both domestically and transnationally. Scavengers help lower industrial raw-material costs. However, in contrast to Birkbeck's contention, the *cartoneros* of Nuevo Laredo were not, by labor market standards, poor. In conclusion, *cartoneros* are neither poor nor marginal. Rather, *cartoneros* should be considered informal entrepreneurs: They invested, by saving or obtaining loans, to purchase *tricicletas* or pickup trucks, and their income depends on their efforts (number of cardboard collection trips) and business acumen in salvaging other recyclable or repairable items that can later be sold in Mexico.

### Policy Implications: Should Scavenging be Supported?

Cardboard collecting has both individual and societal benefits. It is a source of income for individuals, saves costs to businesses, and is environmentally friendly. Such benefits have been documented not only in the border zone, but also elsewhere. First, studies of the Philippines, Egypt, Argentina, and China demonstrate the income-generating gains of scavenging. In Manila, the Linis Ganda program grants scavengers access to middle- and upper-income neighborhoods, which earns scavengers up to $20 (U.S.) a day. In Cairo and Buenos Aires, informal refuse collectors and scavengers earn up to three times the minimum wage in their respective cities, and, in Beijing, three times the monthly salary of college professors (Medina 1993; Medina 1997a: 14–5; Medina 1998; Furedy 1990: 80–4). Second, evidence from Colombia, Brazil, and Indonesia indicates that scavenger cooperatives promote grass-roots development as well as provide environmental and economic benefits to cities there (Medina 2000: 35–51; Medina 1998).

Benefits aside, the privatization of trash collection and the promotion of private solid-waste services, in conjunction with neoliberal reforms, undermines scavenging and thus reduces the earning power of scavengers. The adverse effects have been documented in Colombia, for example (see Cadena, Gonzalez, and Suremain 1993: 45–67). Local governments rarely respond to scavengers' cooperative bids for the provisioning of solid waste services. Instead, they favor large companies. When Porto Alegre, Brazil, formed a private-public partnership with scavengers to incorporate them into a recycling program, waste-management costs diminished. Similarly, a contract signed with a scavenger co-op in Guarne, Colombia, saved the city $5,000 (U.S.) a year (Medina 1998). Labor-intensive solutions that recognize and support informal refuse collectors and scavengers can promote poverty alleviation, help clean up the urban environment, supply inexpensive raw materials to industry, and provide low-cost collection of mixed wastes and/or recyclables in areas where municipal collection does not currently exist.

Scavenging may involve social costs, such as the health risks dump site scavengers face and the possibility of disease outbreaks. Scavengers searching for recyclables in curbside containers may spread the wastes into the streets. Scavengers may also interfere with the normal operation of recycling programs and transfer and disposal facilities. When authorities accept or support scavenging, however, these problems can be greatly diminished or eliminated completely.

## Conclusions

Despite appearances and arguments to the contrary, the *cartoneros* of *Los Dos Laredos* are an important component in the operation of the recycling system. Scavenging also plays an important role in improving the competitiveness of the Mexican paper industry because of the cost savings realized. Consequently, cardboard collecting in *Los Dos Laredos* can hardly be considered a marginal occupation, since it shows direct, strong backward and forward linkages with the formal sectors of both Mexico and the United States. Scavenging has direct linkages with, and is affected by, the international economy. Cardboard collecting is influenced by the interplay of factors that affect the global supply and demand for paper products. Cardboard collecting provides the *cartoneros* a relatively stable occupation, has enabled them to raise a family, and provides them with a modest income, an activity they like, and living conditions they rate as "fair."

Cardboard collecting in *Los Dos Laredos* constitutes one example of the increasing economic integration between Mexico and the United States. It represents a mutually beneficial activity: It provides a steady income to Mexicans while reducing the amount of wastes that Laredo needs to collect and dispose of as well as the tax burden on the *maquiladoras*. Recycling of cardboard also renders environmental benefits compared to the use of virgin resources.

Scavenging constitutes an adaptive response to scarcity, particularly for migrant individuals. My research supports theorists who argue that the informal sector is a structural component of the type of development experienced by developing societies, and therefore is closely linked to the formal sector.[3] Tolerance and support for scavengers in their efforts to organize cooperatives, to create microenterprises, or to form public-private partnerships that include scavengers should form the basis of a sensible solid-waste policy in developing countries.

## Notes

1. Informal economic activities have been defined as characterized by ease of entry, reliance of indigenous resources, family ownership, small scale of operation, labor-intensive methods of production and adapted technology, skills acquired outside the formal school system, and unregulated and competitive markets (Thomas 1992: 53).
2. Figure used in a previous study (CEPAL 1992).
3. Authors such as Portes, Castells, and Benton (1989); Arizpe (1989); Beneria and Roldan (1987); Soto (1990); Fernández-Kelly (1989); and Sassen-Koob (1989) maintain that view.

## References

Alegria, T. 1990. "Ciudad y Transmigración en la Frontera con Estados Unidos." *Frontera Norte* 4, no. 2: 51.

Althaus, D. 1993. "NAFTA May Lead to Decline of Border Towns." *The News* (Mexico City), November 3: 33.

Arizpe, L. 1989. *La Mujer en el Desarrollo de México y de América Latina*. Mexico City: Universidad Nacional Autónoma de México (UNAM).

Bartone, C. 1988. "The Value in Wastes." *Decade Watch*, September: 3-4.

Beneria, L., and M. Roldan. 1987. *The Crossroad of Class and Gender: Industrial Homework, Subcontracting and Household Dynamics in Mexico City*. Chicago: University of Chicago Press.

Birkbeck, C. 1978. "Self-Employed Proletarians in an Informal Factory: The Case of Cali's Garbage Dump." *World Development* 6, nos. 9-10: 1173–85.

———.1979. "Garbage, Industry and the 'Vultures' of Cali, Colombia." Pp. 161–83 in *Casual Work and Poverty in Third World Cities*, edited by Ray Bromley and Chris Gerry. New York: John Wiley.

Cadena, M.; J. González, and M. Suremain. 1993. *Estudio Sobre Los Circuitos de Reciclaje de Desechos Sólidos en la Ciudad de Bogotá*. Bogotá: ENDA America Latina.

Cardenas, A. 1993. "City to Launch Recycling Program." *Laredo Morning Times*, December 22: AI.

Castillo, H. 1990. *La Sociedad de la Basura: Caciquismo Urbano en la Ciudad de México*. Mexico City: Universidad Nacional Autónoma de México (UNAM).

Comisión Económica para América Latina (CEPAL) 1992. *Reciclaje de Papel en América Latina: Tendencias y Desafíos*. Santiago, Chile: CEPAL: 11.

Cortez, C. 1993. "El Sector Forestal: Entre la Economía y la Ecología?" *Comercio Exterior*: 370–77.

Cowles, R. 1986. "Source Separation and Citizen Recycling." *The Solid Waste Handbook*, edited by W. Robinson. New York: John Wiley & Sons: 151.

de Soto, H. 1990. *The Other Path: The Invisible Revolution in the Third World*. New York: Harper & Row.

Diario de Yucatán. 1997. "Desde ayer Campeche tiene 10 Municipios: el Congreso Aprobó Crear el de Calakmul." Internet edition. January 2.

———. September 10, 1999. "El Turismo Cultural Sería una Opción para el Desarrollo en el Próximo Milenio." Internet edition.

———. January 13, 2000. "Ofrecen Respeto del Ejército para los Indígenas de Xpujil." Internet edition.

"Días de guardar en la industria editorial." 1993. *Comercio Exterior* (May): 546–51.

Espinosa, M. J. 1994. "Recesión e Importaciones Deprimen la Industria de Celulosa y Papel." *Excelsior*, September 21: 1F, 3F.

Fernández-Kelly, P. 1989. "Informalization at the Core: Hispanic Women, Homework, and the Advanced Capitalist State." Pp. 247–64 in *The Informal Economy: Studies in Advanced and Less Developed Countries*, edited by A. Portes, M. Castells, and L. Benton. Baltimore: Johns Hopkins University Press.

Furedy, Ch. 1990. "Waste Recovery in China." *BioCycle*, June: 80-84.

González, R. 1990. "Evaluación de la Encuesta socioeconómica de la Frontera." *Frontera Norte* (Tijuana, Mexico) 4, no. 2: 99–110.

Hinojosa, G. 1983. *A Borderlands Town in Transition: Laredo 1755–1870*. College Station: Texas A&M University.

Holmes, J. 1984. "Solid Waste Management Decisions in Developing Countries." Pp. 5-25 in *Managing Solid Wastes in Developing Countries*, edited by J. Holmes. New York: John Wiley & Sons.

Instituto Nacional de Estadística, Geografia e Informática (INEGI). 1993. *La Frontera Norte: Un Panorama de la Población y las Viviendas. Resultados Definitivos. XI censo General de Población y Vivienda*. Aguascalientes, Mexico: INEGI.

Jaffe, M. 1995. "Paper Industry's Amazing Resurgence." *Standard & Poor's Industry Surveys: Building and Forest Products* 163, Sec. 1 (August 10): B76.

Lacey, M. 1994. "Crackdown on Scavenger Squads Proposed." *Los Angeles Times,* September 10: B1:2.

Lang, F. P., and R. Ohr, (eds.). 1995. *International Economic Integration.* Heidelberg, Germany: Springer Verlag.

Lenz, H. 1990. *Historia del Papel en México y Cosas Relacionadas 1525–1950.* Mexico City: Porrúa.

Lomnitz, L. 1987. *Cómo sobreviven los marginados.* Mexico City: Siglo XXI.

Medina, M. 1993. "Collecting Recyclables in Metro Manila." *BioCycle* (June): 51–3.

———. 1997a. "Informal Collection and Recycling of Solid Wastes in Developing Countries: Issues and Opportunities." Working Paper no. 24. Tokyo: United Nations University/Institute of Advanced Studies.

———. 1997b. "Scavenging on the Border: A Study of the Informal Recycling Sector in Laredo, Texas and Nuevo Laredo, Mexico." Ph.D. dissertation, Yale University.

———. 1998. "Scavenger Cooperatives in Developing Countries." *BioCycle* (June): 70–2.

———. 2000. "Scavenger Cooperatives in Asia and Latin America." *Resources, Conservation and Recycling* 31: 51–69.

Melosi, M. 1981. *Garbage in the Cities.* Austin: Texas A&M University Press.

"Paper Chasing." 1995. *The New Yorker.* February 6: 5.

Portes, A., M. Castells, and L. Benton. 1989. "Introduction." Pp. 1–7 in *The Informal Economy: Studies in Advanced and Less Developed Countries,* edited by Portes, Castells, and Benton. Baltimore: Johns Hopkins University Press.

Sánchez, R. 1981. *Frontier Odyssey. Early Life in a Texas Spanish Town.* Austin, Tex.: San Felipe Press.

Sassen-Koob, S. 1989. "New York City's Informal Economy." Pp. 60–77 in *The Informal Economy: Studies in Advanced and Less Developed Countries,* edited by A. Portes, M. Castells, and L. Benton. Baltimore: Johns Hopkins University Press.

Sicular, D. 1992. *Scavengers, Recyclers, and Solutions for Solid Waste Management in Indonesia.* Berkeley: University of California Center for Southeast Asian Studies.

Souza, Paulo. 1980. *Emprego, Salario e Pobreza.* São Paulo, Brazil: HUCI-TEC Fundação de Desenvolvimento da Universidade Estadual de Campinas. (FUNCAMP/UNI-CAMP).

"Summary of the New Maquiladora Program Decree Established in 1989." 1990. *Codein* (August): 3–4.

Thomas, J. 1992. *Informal Economic Activity.* Ann Arbor: University of Michigan Press.

Thompson, J. 1991. *Warm Weather & Bad Whiskey: The 1886 Laredo Election Riot.* El Paso: Texas Western Press.

Weintraub, S. 1990. *Marriage of Convenience: Relations Between Mexico and the United States.* New York: Oxford University Press.

# part II.

## *Labor Rights*

# 5

# Economic Liberalization and Income Distribution in Mexico: Losers and Winners in a Time of Global Restructuring

*Jaime Ros and Nora Claudia Lustig*

In Mexico, as in many other Latin American countries, the 1980s were a decade of economic decline, increasing poverty, and worsening income distribution, the joint outcome of the 1982 debt crisis and the additional difficulties created by the collapse of oil prices in early 1986. Following a successful heterodox stabilization program that began in late 1987, and a large reduction in domestic and external public debt, which was financed with revenues from the privatization of state enterprises and facilitated by the first Brady agreement in mid-1989, the end of the decade witnessed a reawakening. Mexico returned to the international capital markets, and its economy finally appeared to be on its way to recovering economic growth and price stability. Many observers at the time believed that Mexico, a model reformer and successful emerging market, was going to turn into a Latin American economic miracle. When the North American Free Trade Agreement (NAFTA) was approved in 1993, optimistic expectations became even more rampant. The optimistic view was also reinforced by the fact that, besides wide-ranging economic reforms, the Mexican government had engaged in an antipoverty program geared to reduce the gap in health and education infrastructure. To many, thus, Mexico appeared to be on a firm path toward economic and social modernization.

Events turned out to be quite different. The legacy of increased poverty and inequality of the 1980s was reflected in 1994 in an explosion of social violence and political turmoil. Political shocks followed in succession: the armed uprising by the *Zapatistas* in January (on the day NAFTA came into effect), the assassinations of the presidential candidate in March and of the Secretary General of the ruling party in September, and the resignation in November of the assistant attorney general who had been in charge of investigating the assassination of his brother (the PRI's secretary general). At the end of 1994, scarcely a year after

NAFTA's approval, the Mexican economy was in a financial crisis and entering its worst recession since the Great Depression of the 1930s. Whatever progress had been made in the early 1990s in reducing poverty was reversed by the sharp decline in real wages and the increase in unemployment and underemployment that followed from the 1994 devaluation of the peso and the deep recession in 1995.

What explains that the country, which was supposed to enter a period of sustained economic and social modernization, found itself in the mid-1990s immersed in the worst economic crisis in the last seventy years? How are these developments related to the economic liberalization measures undertaken during the late 1980s? These are the questions addressed in this chapter. In section 1, the chapter briefly reviews the balance-of-payments liberalization measures that preceded the episode of massive capital inflows of the early 1990s, and discusses its macroeconomic consequences. Section 2 examines how these macroeconomic developments were reflected in the labor market, in the evolution of productivity, in employment, and in the distribution of labor incomes. Section 3 looks at how labor market developments affected overall income, inequality, and poverty. A concluding section draws lessons from the Mexican experience and discusses the prospects of the economy after the crisis.

## 1. Economic Liberalization, the Capital Surge, and the Financial Crash

The main balance-of-payments liberalization measures were adopted in the second half of the 1980s and early 1990s (for a detailed discussion of policy reforms, see Lustig and Ros 1999, and Lustig 1998). These changes culminated with NAFTA, which came into effect in January 1994. Since then NAFTA has constituted Mexico's basic institutional framework for trade and capital movements, including a regime of free trade and capital mobility with the United States, its main trading partner and source of foreign investment.

The opening of the domestic bonds and stock markets to foreign investors in 1989 and 1990 was followed by a veritable surge in capital inflows, which rose from insignificant numbers in 1988 and 1989 to represent 12.6 percentage points of Mexico's gross domestic product (GDP) at their peak in 1993 (see table 5.1). From 1990 to 1993, Mexico accounted for nearly half of all capital flows into Latin America. Fueled by favorable external circumstances—a continuous reduction (up to early 1994) of foreign interest rates, a U.S. recession in the early 1990s, and regulatory changes introduced by the U.S. Securities and Exchange Commission, which facilitated portfolio investments abroad[1]—the composition of these inflows was strongly biased toward highly liquid assets.

For a while, these large capital inflows and the stabilization and reform processes mutually reinforced each other. The renewed access to international capital markets was an indicator of the positive response of local and foreign investors to the reform process since the mid-1980s. On the other hand, the capital inflows themselves, by reversing the sign of the massive transfer of resources abroad that Mexico had been making during the previous decade, put an end to the financial difficulties that followed the 1982 debt crisis and contributed, in particular, to the success of the stabilization program of late 1987.

At the same time, however, the liberalization process and the capital surge were followed by a number of macroeconomic developments that were to play major roles in the unfortunate conclusion of the episode of massive capital inflows at the end of 1994. A first and persistent trend was the real appreciation of the peso, and, thus, a decline in the external competitiveness of the economy. Against the background of an exchange rate–based stabilization program that had been successful in bringing inflation down, the large amounts of capital inflows applied pressure for a real appreciation of the domestic currency (see table 5.1). Even when the exchange-rate regime passed through several modifications—from a fixed peg to a crawling peg and, subsequently, to an adjustable band (which, in time, had its boundaries widened)[2]—the appreciation continued as actual inflation remained systematically above the target. Thus, from 1988 to 1993, the peso appreciated by over 40 percent in real terms (the real exchange rate fell by 30 percent). By 1993, the real value of the peso was only around 10 percent below that of 1981, before the massive devaluations of early and mid-1982, albeit because the economy in the meantime had undergone a radical trade liberalization and had much less oil-export revenues than in the early 1980s. This explains the highly unbalanced expansion of foreign trade: of the 14-percentage-point increase in the trade-to-GDP ratio, nearly 11 points are accounted for by a boom in imports, while the export ratio rises by only a little more than 3 percentage points (see table 5.1).

Combined with trade liberalization, the real appreciation of the peso meant a shift in relative prices against tradable goods, which led to a profit squeeze in the tradable-goods sectors (i.e., those exposed to international competition). This profit squeeze is shown in table 5.1: The property income share falls continuously from 1988 to 1994, with a cumulative decline of 7 percentage points. The impact of the profit squeeze is very different among sectors, with a large redistribution taking place from the tradable- toward the nontradable-goods sectors,

**Table 5.1. Mexico: Macroeconomic Performance Indicators since 1988 (percentages)**

| | 1988 | 1989 | 1990 | 1991 | 1992 | 1993 | 1994 | 1995 | 1996 | 1997 | 1998 |
|---|---|---|---|---|---|---|---|---|---|---|---|
| GDP Growth | 1.2 | 4.2 | 5.1 | 4.2 | 3.6 | 2.0 | 4.4 | -6.2 | 5.2 | 6.7 | 4.8 |
| Inflation | 51.7 | 19.7 | 29.9 | 18.8 | 11.9 | 8.0 | 7.1 | 52.0 | 27.7 | 15.7 | 18.6 |
| Real Exchange Rate (index) | 100 | 94.6 | 89.9 | 82.0 | 75.0 | 70.8 | 73.6 | 106.6 | 96.7 | 85.5 | 86.4 |
| Real Interest Rate [1] | 7.3 | 13.8 | 1.0 | -1.3 | 3.4 | 14.0 | 13.3 | 6.6 | 9.2 | 8.8 | 10.1 |
| Private Savings Rate [2] | 17.5 | 14.8 | 13.2 | 10.6 | 10.5 | 11.6 | 11.4 | 15.8 | 16.7 | | |
| Domestic Savings Rate [2] | 21.4 | 19.5 | 20.3 | 19.0 | 18.1 | 18.2 | 18.0 | 18.5 | 22.5[3] | 24.1[3] | 20.5[3] |
| Fixed Private Investment [2] | 11.7 | 11.8 | 12.8 | 14.1 | 15.6 | 14.8 | 14.3 | 11.0 | 13.2 | 15.3 | 16.8 |
| Fixed Public Investment [2] | 3.9 | 4.0 | 4.2 | 4.1 | 3.8 | 3.8 | 4.9 | 3.6 | 2.9 | 3.0 | 2.5 |
| Urban Unemployment | 3.6 | 3.0 | 2.8 | 2.6 | 2.8 | 3.4 | 3.7 | 6.2 | 5.5 | 3.8 | 3.2 |
| Average Real Wage (index) | 100 | 105.9 | 107.4 | 114.2 | 122.8 | 130.6 | 136.9 | 118.8 | 109.1 | 112.5 | 115.7 |
| *Trade[2]* | | | | | | | | | | | |
| Exports | 13.9 | 14.0 | 14.1 | 14.2 | 14.4 | 15.2 | 17.2 | 23.9 | 26.8 | 27.9 | 29.2 |
| Imports | 11.7 | 13.2 | 15.0 | 16.6 | 19.2 | 19.2 | 22.3 | 20.2 | 23.6 | 27.1 | 29.5 |
| *Capital Account[2]* | | | | | | | | | | | |
| Direct Investment | 1.6 | 1.5 | 1.1 | 1.8 | 1.6 | 1.5 | 3.5 | 3.1 | 2.9 | 3.7 | 2.9 |
| Portfolio Inflows | 0.5 | 0.2 | 1.4 | 4.9 | 6.6 | 10.1 | 2.6 | -3.2 | 4.2 | 1.5 | 0.4 |
| Loans | -1.8 | 0.4 | 4.7 | 3.1 | -0.6 | 1.0 | 0.4 | 7.5 | -3.8 | -2.6 | 1.1 |
| *Debt[2]* | | | | | | | | | | | |
| Gross External | 43.7 | 36.6 | 32.1 | 30.1 | 28.4 | 27.5 | 27.1 | 31.0 | 30.8 | 26.9 | 24.9 |
| Gross Internal | 22.4 | 23.4 | 20.9 | 16.8 | 11.8 | 10.2 | 10.8 | 9.5 | 6.8 | 7.4 | 8.9 |
| *Income Shares* | | | | | | | | | | | |
| Profits and Interest [4] | 56.5 | 56.0 | 54.5 | 52.9 | 51.8 | 50.4 | 49.8 | 54.6 | 55.9 | | |
| Tradable-goods sectors | 25.1 | 21.3 | 19.1 | 17.5 | 16.0 | 14.2 | 13.8 | 17.0 | 19.2 | | |
| Nontradable-goods sectors | 31.4 | 34.7 | 35.4 | 35.4 | 35.8 | 36.2 | 36.0 | 37.6 | 36.7 | | |
| Skilled Labor [5] | 9.8 | 11.7 | 12.3 | 14.0 | 15.6 | 17.2 | 18.2 | 16.6 | 15.5 | | |
| Other [6] | 33.8 | 32.3 | 33.2 | 33.0 | 32.6 | 32.4 | 31.9 | 28.7 | 28.6 | | |

*Notes*

[1] Discontinuous series: 1988–1992 Economic Commission on Latin America and the Caribbean (ECLAC) data; 1993–1998 calculated based on International Monetary Fund (IMF) statistics.

[2] Displayed as a percentage of GDP.

[3] Value not comparable with earlier series.

[4] Operating surplus (excluding oil, agriculture, commerce, and other services) minus property income paid abroad, plus government interest payments to the private sector.

[5] Estimated using the average wage in construction as an upper limit to the wage of unskilled labor.

[6] Unskilled labor and self-employed earnings. Estimated as a residual.

*Sources*: Instituto Nacional de Estadística, Geografía e Informática (INEGI) National Accounts: Indicators of Competitiveness; Banco de México: Economic Information; Organization for Economic Cooperation and Development (OECD): Economic surveys, various years; Secretaría de Hacienda y Crédito Público: historical data; IMF: International Financial Statistics; ECLAC, *Economic Survey of Latin America and the Caribbean 1996–97*.

that is, from those exposed to international trade to those sheltered from foreign competition.

The profit squeeze in the tradable goods sectors contributed in turn to a fall in business savings, and also had adverse effects on *aggregate* investment, to the extent that the increased profitability in nontradable goods was less than the reduced profitability of the tradable goods sectors.[3] Together with the distributive effects of the profit squeeze against incomes with relatively high savings rates, these adverse effects on investment explain why the rapid expansion of bank credit that accompanied the capital surge ended up fueling a consumption boom. Indeed, the large increase in the gap between private investment and savings was associated with a collapse in private savings (6 to 7 percentage points of the GDP), rather than with a significant increase in the investment rates (see table 5.1).

The implication of the path followed by the economy—real currency appreciation, falling competitiveness, and a consumption boom—was a continuous accumulation of external liabilities. Between 1989 and 1993, the current account deficit (excluding debt service) averaged 31.7 percent of exports. Given an export growth rate of 8.7 percent per year (the average for 1989–1993), Dadush and his colleagues estimate that the foreign-liabilities-to-export ratio would converge to a steady-state value of 3.6.[4] This figure is so high that well before reaching the steady state, the Mexican economy would likely face a slowdown of capital inflows and thus severe balance-of-payments problems.

The slowdown of capital inflows came in 1994 and, given the political shocks of that year, partly took the form of a series of speculative attacks associated with these shocks. In an effort to reverse the slowdown, and in the midst of electoral campaigns, the government made a number of policy decisions—the dollarization of domestic debt, the shortening of its average maturity, and the sterilization of reserve outflows—that set the stage for the financial crisis at the end of the year.[5] The outcome of the slowdown in capital inflows and these policy decisions was a loss of $20 billion (U.S.) of reserves by the end of the year and the buildup of nearly $30 billion (U.S.) of additional short-term debt indexed to the dollar (the Treasury Bonds, or TESOBONOS). In this way, the conditions were created for a financial panic following the devaluation of December 20, 1994. A $50-billion package was necessary to calm down the markets after the financial panic, but the need for adjustment was such that it could not prevent a deep recession in 1995.[6] The severe hit to the living standards of Mexicans—with real manufacturing wages falling over 20 percent in 1995—will take several years to reverse.

## 2. The Labor Market: Employment, Productivity, and Wage Inequality

The loss of external competitiveness and the profit squeeze in the tradable-goods sectors resulted in a slow expansion of these sectors (agriculture, mining, and manufacturing). This slow expansion of output and investment implied sluggish job creation, especially in manufacturing, where a poor output performance combined with an acceleration of labor productivity increases.

### *Productivity and Employment in Manufacturing*

The high rate of growth of labor productivity in manufacturing (6 percent per year, see table 5.2) in the face of a relatively slow rate of output growth (4.2 percent per year)—with a resulting negative contribution of manufacturing to employment growth—appears to be closely related to the profit squeeze and import penetration. The reaction to the profit squeeze varied across manufacturing industries, however, depending on the extent of import penetration, the fall in profit margins, and the sector's potential for intraindustry trade (see Ros and Bouillon 2001). In one group of industries, import penetration is inversely correlated with output and employment growth. Firms in these sectors reacted to the fall in profit margins with defensive increases in productivity. Where the decline in profit markups was very large, many firms did not manage to cover variable costs and they disappeared. This generated a contraction of employment as imports crowded out domestic production. This is the case of a number of segments of the textile, wood, and nonmetallic mineral industries.[7] Where the decline in markups was more moderate, or nonexistent in the case of food-processing, papermaking, and printing, the slowdown in output and employment growth was also less pronounced. In all these cases, initial import ratios were relatively low, indicating an initially high degree of protection of the domestic market, and export ratios were also relatively low, suggesting lack of experience with exporting activities by frims in these sectors.

In a second group of industries, with the initially highest import and export ratios and a large potential for intraindustry trade, import penetration is positively correlated with export growth. This is the case of the chemical, basic metals, machinery and equipment (including, in particular, the automobile industry), and other manufacturing industries. By modifying the output mix (reducing diversity), reducing value added (complementing with imports), investing in labor-saving technologies, increasing their specialization in intraindustry trade, and adopting organizational changes to reduce direct labor costs (downsizing and out-

Table 5.2. Output, Employment, and Productivity Growth
(average percentage growth rates per year)

| Sector | Employment Growth | | Output Growth | | Productivity Growth | |
|---|---|---|---|---|---|---|
| | 1988–93 | 1993–97 | 1988–93 | 1993–97 | 1988–93 | 1993–97 |
| Total | 3.1 | 3.2 | 3.7 | 2.4 | 0.6 | −0.8 |
| Mining[1] | −7.4 | 8.8 | 2.0 | 4.1 | 9.4 | 4.7 |
| Manufacturing | −1.8 | 4.9 | 4.2 | 4.7 | 6.0 | −0.2 |
| Agriculture | 5.8 | 0.5 | 1.9 | 1.7 | −3.9 | 1.2 |
| Nontradables | 3.6[3] | 3.9[3] | 3.1 | 1.8 | −0.5 | −2.1 |
| Construction | 4.1 | −1.7 | 4.9 | 0.1 | 0.8 | 1.8 |
| Transport and Communication | 5.0 | 2.7 | 4.1 | 5.0 | −0.9 | 2.3 |
| Commerce[2] | 5.1 | 3.4 | 4.3 | 1.0 | −0.8 | −2.4 |
| Services | 3.0 | 5.5[4] | 3.9 | 1.6[4] | 0.9 | −3.9[4] |
| Government | 0.8 | | 0.9 | | 0.1 | |

*Notes*
[1]Includes electricity
[2]Includes restaurants and hotels
[3]Includes unspecified activities
[4]Includes government

*Source*: INEGI, National Accounts and National Survey of Employment 1997.

sourcing), firms in these sectors managed to survive and prosper. Here import penetration leads, through specialization in intraindustry trade, to high rates of export growth and, in almost all cases, to the highest rates of output and productivity growth. In fact, these four industries are those with the highest rates of both import penetration and export growth.

*The Slowdown of Productivity Growth in the Whole Economy*

The acceleration of productivity growth in manufacturing did not lead, however, to a trend of increased productivity growth in the economy as a whole (see Ros and Lustig 2001). In fact, this acceleration in manufacturing from 1988 to 1993 was, paradoxically, accompanied by a very low overall rate of productivity growth (0.6 percent per year), well below that of the second half of the 1970s (when it had been 1.6 percent per year). The reasons for this behavior are related to the effects on productivity growth of the reallocation of the labor force during the period and to the slow growth of productivity in the nontradable-goods sectors and agriculture (see table 5.2). Before the crisis of the 1980s, the reallocation of labor from low- to high-productivity sectors used to make a large contribution to overall productivity growth (in fact, in the second half of the 1970s, this contribution was equivalent to slightly more than the overall growth of productivity). While the reallocation effects on productivity remained positive in the 1988 to 1993 period—indicating that, on average, high-productivity sectors grew faster than low-productivity sectors—they were much smaller than in the 1970s. In fact, the slowdown in overall productivity growth was equivalent to the reduction in the size of these reallocation effects between the two periods (Ros and Lustig 2001). Since, at the same time, the contribution to productivity growth by manufacturing increased considerably, this means that this higher contribution was counteracted by a reduction in the contribution of productivity growth in other sectors.

Another factor behind the slow rate of overall productivity growth is the evolution of productivity growth in the nontradable-goods sectors and agriculture. The productivity slowdown here can be related to the sluggish, and later negative, rate of employment creation in manufacturing—first as a result of the recession of the 1980s and later due to the acceleration of productivity growth—as well as to the slow rate of output growth in agriculture. The result of these trends was higher rates of underemployment in services, commerce, and agriculture that hindered the growth of productivity in these sectors. It is in this way that the low-productivity growth in these sectors is itself related to the decline in the size of reallocation effects.

### Trade Liberalization and Wage Inequality

All the available evidence points to a substantial increase in wage inequality since the mid-1980s. According to income and expenditure household surveys, the Gini coefficient of wage inequality increases from 0.44 in 1984 to 0.46 in 1989, then to 0.49 in 1992 and 0.53 in 1994 (Lustig and Székely 1998). Table 5.1 illustrates the redistribution between skilled and unskilled labor earnings that took place from 1988 to 1994. Figure 5.1 illustrates the rising trend up to 1996 of white-collar-worker earnings relative to blue-collar worker earnings in all manufacturing industries. Other evidence reported in a number of studies similarly documents the decline since 1988 in the relative labor earnings of the low-wage sectors of agriculture, construction, commerce, and services (see Ros and Bouillon 2001) and the increase in wage dispersion, showing that it largely revolves around the increase in skilled- relative to unskilled-labor incomes (see Hanson and Harrison 1995; Cragg and Epelbaum 1996; Alarcón and McKinley 1997).

The rapid increase in the wage premium for skilled labor raises an initial question: Is it the result of a demand shift in favor of skilled labor, or is it largely a supply-side phenomenon resulting from either a relatively fast growth of the unskilled labor force or a higher labor-supply

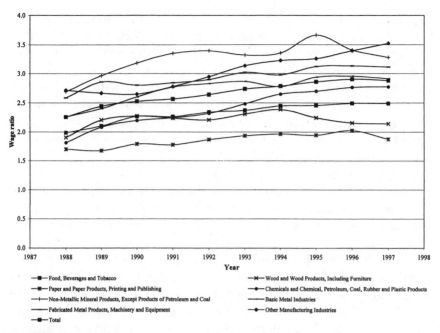

Source: INEGI Cuentas Nacionales.

**Figure 5.1. Ratio of White-Collar to Blue-Collar Workers' Earnings in Manufacturing**

elasticity for unskilled labor? The available studies on the subject have focused on explaining the shift in the composition of labor demand. The evidence confirms the importance of demand factors within manufacturing: The change in the employment ratio of skilled to unskilled labor (measured very imperfectly by the ratio of white-collar to blue-collar employment) tends to be positively correlated across industries with the change in the relative wages of skilled labor, that is, those industries where unskilled labor falls more rapidly, relative to skilled labor, are those where the skill premium increases faster (see Ros and Bouillon 2001). If supply factors were responsible for the substitution of skilled for unskilled labor, we should observe the contrary: a negative relationship between relative earnings and employment ratios, with an increase in the skill premium leading to a fall, rather than an increase, in the employment ratio of skilled to unskilled labor.

The evidence also suggests that the shift in labor demand in favor of skilled workers and the increasing skill premium can be explained only to a small extent by intersectoral employment shifts from unskilled-labor-intensive industries[8] Hanson and Harrison (1995) found, for example, that the shifts in the composition of employment account for 7 percent and 20 percent of the change in the white-collar wage share, depending on the data source (respectively: the Industrial Census, or a sample of medium and large plants from the Secretariat of Commerce and Industrial Promotion [SECOFI]).[9] These findings imply that a complete explanation of the increasing wage inequality must take into account other effects of a "within industry" nature, that is, a full explanation must rely more on the fact that the increase in the skill premium and the relative demand for skilled labor took place within specific industries, even at the firm or plant level, and less on intersectoral changes in employment and wages.

Our hypothesis is that the intensified competition from imports, resulting from trade liberalization and the real overvaluation of the peso, accelerated the rate of technology adoption and reduced the demand for low-skilled workers in manufacturing.[10] This hypothesis can be elaborated in the framework of a two-sector model (tradables and nontradables), in which tradable goods are produced under imperfect competition with unskilled labor as the variable factor, while skilled labor, being complementary to physical capital, is largely fixed in the short run. Trade liberalization implied greater competition in the domestic market, and increased the share of imports in domestic demand. As a result of this increased competition and of the real currency appreciation associated with capital inflows, increased demand for nontradables, and exchange rate policies, there was a fall in profit markups over costs in the import-competing sectors. Thus we saw the profit squeeze in the traded-goods sector documented in section 1. The lower profit markup means an increase in the product wages (i.e., the wage measured in terms of the sector's output) of skilled and unskilled workers. The negative effect on employment falls on unskilled workers, as their employment is the variable factor that firms can adjust to in the short run. Thus, we can observe the tendency to substitute skilled for unskilled labor that is observable in the industrial employment data.

In this view, the effects of trade liberalization on the labor market operated as follows: The relative price of imported goods fell and thus reduced the demand for locally produced importable goods. With sluggish nominal wages, the adjustment involves a reduction of employment and of output in the import-competing sectors as well as an expansion of employment in the nontradable-goods sector. The higher employment there reduced productivity and wages. This opened a gap between the wages of unskilled labor employed in the two sectors (observable in Mexico in the increasing wage inequality among sectors). Eventually, the downward pressure on real wages in the import-competing sectors tended to reduce the *product* wage of unskilled labor there, in turn generating an intrasectoral increase in the wage premium of skilled labor.

The cost reductions tended to reestablish the initial relative prices. However, even if the initial relative prices were reestablished in the long run, the displacement of local production by imports may have hysteretic effects that lead to a permanent increase of the ratio of imports to domestic production of importable goods. In this case, trade liberalization has long-lasting effects on employment and real wages in the import-competing and nontradable-goods sectors.

Finally, the intensified competition in the local market leads to an increase in the price elasticity of demand facing producers of importable goods. The higher price elasticity reduces the firms' profit margins in the sector. This has two consequences. First, it implies a fall in the relative price of importable goods relative to nontradable and imported goods, which increases demand for importables. The second effect is the fall in profitability, which tends to reduce investments in the import-competing sectors, and has negative long-term effects on employment. As is argued below, this second effect—together with the short-run and long-run effects of import penetration discussed above—appears to have clearly dominated in the Mexican experience.

The empirical evidence appears to clearly support this explanation, based on import competition and declining profit margins. First, this hypothesis implies that the shift in the composition of labor demand should be limited to the tradables sector and not observable in the nontradables sectors, where there was no such intensified competition from imports. This is precisely what happend: The substitution of skilled labor for unskilled labor was much faster in the tradables sector, specifically in manufacturing, and was largely limited to this sector (see Cragg and Epelbaum 1996). If the cause of the demand shift had been, for example, a fall in capital goods prices, the substitution of skilled for unskilled labor should have been equally present in the nontradable sectors.[11]

Second, if trade liberalization affected the skill premium through the fall in profit margins, we should expect that the industries in which the skilled-unskilled employment ratio increased faster are those that reduced most their overall employment (since, in this hypothesis, the shift in the composition of labor demand reflects the changes in the variable factor, unskilled labor). This negative correlation is observable in the data (see Ros and Lustig 2001).[12] Moreover, the fact that the ratio of white- to blue-collar employment in manufacturing increases as a result of a *decline* in the employment of blue-collar workers, rather than an increase in the employment of white-collar workers, raises serious doubts about any explanation of the increased skill premium that relies on a rising demand for skilled labor (rather than a falling demand for unskilled labor, as our hypothesis suggests).

Finally, it is worth noting that, within manufacturing, the rate of employment decline is positively correlated, with two exceptions, to the percentage decline in profit margins. This suggests that, indeed, the employment reductions were a reaction to the fall in markups. And, since the shift in the composition of labor demand is closely related to the change in employment, these two observations link the shift in the composition of labor demand to the fall in profit margins. The two exceptions (metallurgy and other manufacturing) are the two industries with the fastest and the lowest rates of productivity growth during the period. Due to these characteristics, the behavior of their profit margins is consistent with our hypothesis. Indeed, in our explanation the employment reductions on the part of firms are, strictly speaking, a reaction to the ex ante fall in profit margins, that is, to the fall in margins before taking into account the effects that the more or less successful increases in productivity (resulting from the employment falls) had on the ex post evolution of margins. If our hypothesis is correct, the industry with the fastest rate of productivity growth (metallurgy) can be expected to become an outlier because it managed to offset the effects of a large ex ante decline in margins with those very large productivity gains: thus its relatively small ex post reduction of profit margins in the context of a sharp decline in employment. The sector least successful in increasing productivity (other manufacturing) is also an outlier because its relatively small employment contraction determined a relatively large ex post reduction in profit margins.

So far we have focused on explaining the change in the composition of labor demand. Yet, supply factors also appear to have had some role in the increase in skill premium. First, the labor demand shift in manufacturing implies a shift in the composition of labor supply growth from the perspective of other sectors in the economy. In their 1996 paper, Cragg and Epelbaum illustrate the fact that low-skill occupations (such as salespersons, service workers, and transport workers) experienced rapid employment growth and relatively small wage increases between 1987 and 1993.

Second, even if a shift in the composition of labor demand was absent, the composition of labor supply for the economy as a whole may have favored an increase in the skill premium. Alarcón and McKinley (1997) refer to evidence, based on household surveys, suggesting a relatively fast growth of the unskilled labor force: according to this evidence, between 1984 and 1992 the fraction of urban employees with tertiary education fell from 18.5 percent to 15.5 percent, and the fraction of those with secondary education fell from 53.7 percent to 46.3 percent.[13]

Finally we should add the fact, already alluded to, that trade liberalization did not benefit unskilled-labor-intensive agriculture. The resulting slow growth of the *demand* for unskilled labor in this large economic sector—which is not inconsistent with the rapid increase in the agricultural labor force, resulting from the difficulties unskilled workers have in finding employment in other sectors—drove down rural earnings. This reduced the supply price of unskilled labor to the urban sectors and, as seen in the next section, contributed to the increase in poverty in the rural areas (particularly in southern Mexico).

### 3. Income Distribution and Poverty

The crisis and adjustment of the 1980s led to sharp declines in income and, in particular, wages.[14] Given the characteristics of Mexico's labor market (with real wages being very flexible), the adjustment primarily involved a reduction in real wages, while the increase in open unemployment was short-lived. As might be expected, the fall in wages was accompanied by an increase in the incidence of extreme and moderate poverty. Lustig and Székely (1998) estimate that extreme poverty rose from 13.9 percent to 17.1 percent, and moderate poverty increased from 28.5 percent to 32.6 percent, between 1984 and 1989. The depth and severity of poverty also increased considerably. Moreover, the burden of adjustment was not equitably distributed.[15] While the share of income in the upper 10 percent of the population rose, it fell in the remaining 90 percent. Income concentration, as measured by the Gini coefficient, increased quite sharply (and unambiguously) between 1984 and 1989. As the Lorenz curves present no crossings, the results are unambiguous.

*Trends in Poverty and Inequality*

During the incipient and frustrated recovery of the early 1990s, moderate poverty and income inequality remained virtually unchanged, while extreme poverty declined slightly and wage inequality rose.[16] To test for the sensitivity of the results on poverty due to the selection of poverty line, the income frequency curve was estimated from zero income up to the highest available poverty line. Visual examination shows that, for the lower poverty lines, the function corresponding to 1989 is stochastically dominant with respect to the function for 1994, meaning that, for the lower poverty lines, the incidence of poverty was always lower in 1994 than in 1989. However, for higher poverty lines no clear conclusion could be drawn as to the direction of the change. The results presented are obtained by "adjusting" the household survey data for underreporting.

We performed several robustness tests to check for the sensitivity of our results to different methods of correction, and found that in terms of trends our results are robust.

Since in this period the structure of relative wages changed significantly and wage inequality rose considerably, as we have seen in section 2, it is unlikely that these trends in poverty were fairly uniform for all population groups. If we classify households by occupation, economic activity, and geographic location, we observe a differentiated pattern. Unlike what happened with the national head count between 1989 and 1994, poverty rates increased among rural workers in the primary sector (agriculture, in particular) and in the southern (Tabasco and Veracruz) and southeastern (Chiapas, Guerrero, and Oaxaca) regions of Mexico.[17] The proportion of poor increased in occupational categories, regions, and production sectors associated with the rural areas, and in which the poverty incidence was highest in 1989. Those are also the groups or sectors where a high proportion of the total population lives in extreme poverty.

Given that the total poverty practically remained unchanged, these trends mean that the decline in poverty in other population groups and/or migration to richer regions (or activities) were sufficiently large: enough to offset the negative trends in the groups that did not do well. Using the disaggregation formula applicable to additive poverty measures, we determined the contribution of each of the above categories to the total change in poverty, distinguishing the portion that should be attributed to demographic changes among categories and to changes in poverty within individual categories (Morley 1995; Ravallion and Huppi 1991). The total contribution of the three subcategories—rural workers, household units operating in the primary sector, and households in southeastern Mexico—to changes in total poverty turns out to be negative. This finding can be attributed to the fact that, despite the increase in poverty within the subgroups, demographic changes also occurred, offsetting the changes in poverty. In other words, there were household units that "moved out" of these subcategories. The only subgroup in which both effects were positive is the southern region.

*Causes of Increasing Inequality*

In section 2 we saw that the wage gap between skilled and unskilled workers went up considerably, and that this increase is primarily the result of trade liberalization and skill-biased shift in the demand for labor. How much of the trends in overall inequality can be explained by the rising gap in returns to skill? How much is accounted for by other factors, such as regional disparities?

Applying a simulation methodology, Bouillon, Legovini and Lustig

(1998) looked at the sources of the observed increase in overall income inequality applying a decomposition methodology first developed by Almeida dos Reis and Paes de Barros (1991). The methodology is similar to that applied by Juhn, Murphy, and Pierce (1993) in the context of earnings inequality in the United States, but was generalized to the household level in a model first proposed by Bourguignon, Fournier and Gurgand (1998). In essence, the methodology allows the identification of the contribution of the changes in income distribution by source: endowments (education, experience, etc.) and the returns to those endowments.

The results of this exercise revealed that the widening gap in the "returns" to education explain close to 50 percent of the observed increase in household income inequality, while the "returns" to regional location explain over 15 percent and to geographic location (urban/rural) explain another 9 percent. Hence, most of the rising inequality in Mexico should be ascribed to increasing disparities in returns. Population effects—that is, the distribution of skills, and so on—account for about one-fourth of the increase in inequality. In Mexico, therefore, the widening gap in the returns to skill was not compensated by a more equal distribution of skills.

The exercise also showed that the returns for households in the rural sectors deteriorated between 1984 and 1994, particularly in the south and center regions. The fixed effect of the south region alone can explain 9 percent of the increase in income inequality. It is also the only region where both the urban and rural fixed effects are negative and worsening over time. This points to a divergence of the conditions in the south from those prevailing in the rest of the country. Hence, dynamics in the south may be able to explain about one-fifth of the rising income inequality in Mexico attributable to changes in returns. The greatest contribution may come from the southeast region, which includes Chiapas, Guerrero, and Oaxaca, where poverty rates increased from 17 percent to 37 percent in the 1984 to 1994 period (see Lustig and Székely 1998).

*Causes of the Worsening Conditions in Rural Areas and the South*

As indicated above, between 1989 and 1994, both extreme and moderate poverty increased among rural workers, in the primary sector, and in southern and southeastern Mexico, while it declined or remained unchanged in the rest of the country's sectors and regions.

When income is broken down by sector, we can observe the deficient performance of agriculture during the period. As a result, households whose principal source of income was agriculture were necessarily affected. Indeed, in the case of agriculture, the shift in relative prices against tradable goods and the resulting profit squeeze meant a decline in real incomes for small and medium farmers. Moreover, the trends in relative wages against unskilled labor adversely affected rural workers.

We must also consider other factors in determining why poverty increased in agriculture. According to a study on the agricultural sector focused on the common land, or *ejido* sector, the income collected by the common land farmers, or *ejidatarios*, was adversely affected not only by the appreciation of the peso, but also by the collapse in the real guaranteed price for the major basic crops, by the high interest rates, and by the loss of subsidies in the sector (de Janvry, Gordillo, and Sadoulet 1997). Privatization, reduction, or liquidation of many government institutions supporting the sector also occurred in connection with the modernization process. In general, this reduction in the institutionalized support for agriculture drove up the cost of access to credit, insurance, markets, modern inputs, seed, water, and technical assistance. In this context of more flexible public controls, an unfavorable macroeconomic cycle, and institutional gaps, a process of social differentiation occurred, a process in which a small group of farms became successful businesses while others were left behind, with some farmers even abandoning their properties. Those who created successful businesses were relatively wealthy; that is, they possessed larger land areas or had greater access to credit and irrigation services. At the other end of the spectrum were the small farmers and members of indigenous communities, for whom it was difficult to modernize and diversify their activities as a result of limited access to financial resources and institutional services.

The increases in extreme poverty observed in southern and southeastern Mexico may also be attributed to the trends in prices of the major crops produced by the farmers in these regions. Between 1984 and 1992 the prices of coffee and cocoa declined by more than 70 percent in the international market. It is estimated that the subsistence income for small farmers in the southern states of the Pacific coast declined an average of 15 percent (World Bank 1996a). The states of Chiapas, Veracruz, and Oaxaca are Mexico's three leading coffee producers. In the early 1990s, primarily as the result of the dismantling of the International Coffee Agreement,[18] the price of coffee on the international market plummeted from an average of $1.32 (U.S.) per pound in 1986 through 1988 to $0.53 (U.S.) per pound in 1992 (FAO 1992; 1994). Although direct calculations are not available, it seems reasonable to attribute some (if not all) of the observed increase in poverty in Mexico's southeastern and southern states to coffee price trends. In fact, indigenous producers comprised one of the groups most severely affected by the decline in the price of coffee, as 65 percent of all coffee producers are indigenous and produce one-third of Mexico's coffee output (World Bank 1996a, 1996b).

## 4. Concluding Comments: The Medium-Term Prospects for the Economy

The liberalization of the balance of payments in Mexico took place in the midst of a loss of external competitiveness and a persistent volatility of capital flows. The inconsistency between trade and exchange-rate policies, and the vulnerability generated by massive portfolio capital inflows, had an unfortunate denouement in late 1994. After a deep recession in 1995, and unlike what had happened after the 1982 debt crisis, the economy recovered a growth rate of the order of 5 percent to 6 percent per year, and open unemployment has fallen to rates of the order of 3 percent. How viable is a scenario of sustained growth at rates higher than those observed since the early 1980s, on which a substantial reduction of poverty and an improvement in income distribution depend?

A number of factors lend some credibility to such a scenario. First, the international environment is more favorable in the late 1990s than in the aftermath of the 1982 debt crisis, despite the increased volatility and probability of contagion effects, such as those experienced in the aftermath of the East Asian and Russian financial crises. As compared with the early 1980s, foreign interest rates remain low, and, unlike what happened then, the international rescue package successfully prevented a financial panic from degenerating into a decade-long credit run in the international credit markets. In this setting, fiscal and exchange-rate policies that ensure that the economy is operating at high levels of activity and with a high real exchange rate have greater chances of success than in the 1980s.

Second, despite the fact that the adverse consequences of the 1994 to 1995 crisis on living standards and income distribution will take years to reverse, the crisis itself may have substantially altered the long-term macroeconomic outlook in a positive direction. The huge real devaluation of the peso abruptly eliminated the inconsistency between trade and exchange-rate policies that, as argued earlier, played a major role in the process leading to the crisis. The macroeconomic impact of the export expansion is enhanced in the context of a more open economy and greater integration with the U.S. economy under NAFTA.[19] Net exports have had an expansionary effect since 1995, contrary to what happened in the period of 1988 through 1994.

Given its large size, the real devaluation of the peso has also contributed to a reversal of the factors underlying the profit squeeze in the tradable-goods sector and the fall of the private savings rate (see table 5.1). Private savings increased substantially in 1995, following the real devaluation, and domestic savings continued to increase until 1997. The increase was probably due not only to the real devaluation, but also to the domestic banking crisis and the associated credit crunch. As credit constraints become less acute, the upward trend of private savings may be reversed. In fact, a negative recent development was the significant decline in the domestic savings rate in 1998, much of which must have come from private savings. Through its positive effects on the profitability of the tradable-goods sector, the higher real exchange rate must also have contributed to the increase in foreign direct investments. These investments now represent nearly 20 percent of total private investment and, between 1996 and 1998, around 60 percent of total foreign investment (including portfolio inflows). This means that the current account deficit is now being financed much less by short-term capital than in the first half of the 1990s, thus making the economy less vulnerable to new domestic or external shocks.

Without a sustained recovery, little progress can be made in the reduction of poverty and inequality. Yet the scenario outlined above may be insufficient by itself to improve income distribution. This is not because growth would not "trickle down"—in fact, fast growth per se can do a lot to reduce inequality through its positive effects on employment creation and wages. The reason is, rather, that the distributional consequences of the new trade regime have been highly disappointing. The initial expectation that unskilled labor would benefit from trade liberalization turned out to be simply wrong. This increases the burden that social, health, and educational policies will have to carry in improving the material conditions of the poor and counteracting the tendencies to the concentration of income and wealth.

## Notes

A previous version of this chapter was presented at the CEPAL's conference on Globalization and Social Policy, New York, January 1999. The authors acknowledge the support of the United Nations Development Programme. The authors are grateful to Maiju Perala for research assistance and to Susan Eckstein, Bill Gibson, Jorge Katz, Lance Taylor, and an anonymous reviewer for comments on an earlier version of the chapter. The usual caveat applies.

1. See on the subject French-Davis and Reisen (1998), Comisión Económica para América Latina (CEPAL) 1998.
2. The policy based on a fixed exchange rate, designed to fight inflationary pressures, was implemented at the end of February 1988. Beginning in 1989, the fixed exchange regime was replaced by a crawling peg. In November 1991, the crawling peg was replaced by a band within which the exchange rate was allowed to fluctuate. On December 20, 1994, the ceiling of the band was increased by 15 percent, while its subsequent daily increase of 0.0004 new pesos was maintained. This policy proved to be unsustainable and was abandoned two days later when the Mexican authorities were forced to adopt a floating exchange-rate regime because they had run out of international reserves.
3. This also makes the reasonable assumption that the capital intensity at the margin in the tradeable-goods sectors is higher than in nontradable goods.
4. Jaime Ros (1994) reaches similar conclusions (See also McLeod and Welch 1992;

Oks 1992; Oks and van Wijnbergen 1992.) This ratio is well above the 220 percent of exports or 80 percent of the GDP that the World Bank uses in its debit tables to classify a country as "severely indebted." It is thus unlikely that foreign investors would have been willing to finance the required factor service payments.

5. The sequence of events and policy dilemmas in 1994 leading to the December crisis in that year has been examined in Norma Claudia Lustig and Jaime Ros (1999) (for more details, see Lustig 1998: chap. 7).

6. The final package included $20 billion of loan guarantees from the U.S. government, $17.8 billion of credit from the IMF, $10 billion in short-term loans from central banks via the Bank for International Settlements, and several billion dollars in loans from other governments in North and South America. The IMF loan amounted to over seven times Mexico's IMF quota in and was unprecedented in the history of the IMF. The Mexican government declared its intention to reduce government spending by 1.3 percent of the GDP and to cut the amount of credit granted by state development banks. A national accord among workers, business, and government was set up to contain the inflationary pressures arising from the devaluation. The Mexican government also emphasized its commitment to market-oriented reforms, and pledged to propose constitutional amendments to open previously restricted areas of the economy to private investment and to increase foreign participation in the domestic banking system. As a source of collateral, the Mexican government agreed to have importers of Mexican oil products make payments through an account at the Federal Reserve Bank of New York.

7. We emphasize segments of these industries. Other segments, as would be revealed by a more disaggregated analysis, follow different patterns that fit better with the second group of industries discussed below. One example is the restructuring of the garment industry, where a number of activities are successful cases of export growth. Still, even here, success became clear only after the currency devaluation of late 1994.

8. Hanson and Harrison (1995) for the period 1984–1990 and Cragg and Epelbaum (1996) for the period 1987–1993.

9. It is worth noting that the quantitative strength of interindustry effects operating in possibly different directions is hard to assess through these accounting exercises. The fact that the net balance of these effects is small is not inconsistent with important interindustry effects that tend to neutralize each other. Findings by Revenga (1995), cited by Hanson and Harrison, indicate that Mexico's net exports are negatively correlated with skill intensity, suggesting that Mexico has a comparative advantage in many goods produced with a relatively high intensity of unskilled labor.

10. This hypothesis is suggested by Cragg and Epelbaum (1996), who, however, do not explore it further. Instead, they focus on the effects of trade liberalization on the prices of imported capital goods under the assumption of complementarity between skilled labor and physical capital. To the extent that trade liberalization drove down the relative price of imported capital goods, it stimulated the adoption of more capital-intensive techniques, and thus a skill-biased shift in the demand for labor given the complementarity between skilled labor and physical capital. This increased demand for skilled labor caused, then, the increase in the skill premium.

11. In fact, one can argue that it should have been faster in these sectors. To the extent that the composition of investment shifted in favor of these sectors, in the face of a decline in the profitability of the tradable-goods sector, the complementarity between physical capital and skilled labor should have induced a faster rate of unskilled-skilled labor substitution in the nontradable-goods sector.

12. This correlation is inconsistent with the alternative hypothesis: If the stimulus to labor substitution came from the fall in the relative prices for capital goods, the industries that benefitted most from the lower prices of capital goods should be those where the capital stock and employment increased most, and also those that increased their skilled-unskilled employment ratios faster. The expected correlation in this case should thus be positive rather than negative.

13. Other data sources do not, however, confirm the same trends. The data from INEGI's urban employment surveys used by Cragg and Epelbaum (1996) suggests an increasing percentage of skilled workers in the urban labor force.

14. This section draws from Lustig (1998) and Lustig and Székely (1998).
15. These estimates are calculated from household income and expenditure surveys for 1984, 1989, 1992, and 1994. Although the survey for 1996 has been completed, the results had not been released by the time of completion of the Lustig and Székely (1998) study.
16. To measure the incidence of poverty, we used the extreme and moderate poverty lines for urban and rural areas developed by the Mexican National Institute of Statistics, Geography, and Informatics.
17. A more detailed discussion of poverty profiles is available from the authors upon request.
18. The International Coffee Agreement, the member countries of which undertook to reduce wide swings in coffee prices, was eliminated in 1989 and reinstated in March 1994.
19. A comparison of the performance of Mexico's exports during the 1995 crisis with the 1983 recession may be illustrative of the positive side of the legacy of a more open economy. In 1995, the exchange rate increased by 86 percent (end of period). In that year, non-oil and non-*maquiladora* exports expanded by 37 percent, while *maquiladora* exports increased by 30 percent. Instead, in 1983, following a 466 percent increase in the exchange rate in 1982, *maquiladora* exports increased by 29 percent, while non-*maquiladora*/non-oil exports fell by nearly 6 percent.

## References

Alarcón, D., and T. McKinley. 1997. "The Paradox of Narrowing Wage Differentials and Widening Wage Inequality in Mexico." *Development and Change* 28, no. 3: 505–30.

Almeida dos Reis, J., and R. Paes de Barros. 1991. "Wage Inequality and the Distribution of Education: A Study of the Evolution of Regional Differences in Inequality in Metropolitan Brazil." *Journal of Development Economics* 36: 117–43.

Banco de México. 1995. *The Mexican Economy 1995: Economic and Financial Developments in 1994,Policies for 1995.* Mexico City: Banco de México.

Bouillon, C., A. Legovini, and N. C. Lustig. 1998. "Rising Inequality in Mexico: Returns to Households Characteristics and the Chiapas effect." Preliminary draft. Washington, D.C.: Poverty and Inequality Advisory Unit, Inter-American Development Bank (IDB).

Bourguignon, F., F. Ferreira, and N. C. Lustig. 1998. "The Microeconomics of Income Distribution Dynamics in East Asia and Latin America." Research Proposal. Washington, D.C.: Inter-American Development Bank–World Bank.

———. M. Fournier, and M. Gurgand. 1998. "Labor Incomes and Labor Supply in the Course of Taiwan's Development, 1979–1994." Mimeo.

Comisión Económica para América Latina (CEPAL). 1998. *Políticas Para Mejorar la Inserción en la Economía Mundial.* Santiago, Chile: Fondo de Cultura Económica.

Cragg, M., and M. Epelbaum. 1996. "Why Has Wage Dispersion Grown in Mexico? Is it the Incidence of Reforms or the Growing Demand for Skills?" *Journal of Development Economics* 51, no. 1.

De Janvry, G. Gordillo, and E. Sadoulet. 1997. *Mexico's Second Agrarian Reform.* San Diego: Center for U.S.-Mexican Studies, University of California.

FAO (Organización de las Naciones Unidas para la Alimentación y la Agricultura/Food and Agricultural Organization). 1992. *Commodity Review and Outlook 1991–1992.* Rome: FAO.

———. 1994. *Commodity Review and Outlook 1993–1994.* Rome: FAO.

French-Davis, R., and H. Reisen. 1998. *Capital Flows and Investment Performance.* Paris: Organization for Economic Cooperation and Development (OECD) Development Centre.

Hanson, G., and A. Harrison. 1995. *Trade, Technology and Wage Inequality in Mexico. Working Paper no. 5110, May.* Washington, D.C.: National Bureau of Economic Research (NBER).

Juhn, C., K. Murphy, and B. Pierce. 1993. "Wage Inequality and the Rise in Returns to Skill." *Journal of Political Economy* 3: 410–48.

Londoño, J., and M. Székely. 1997. "Persistent Poverty and Excess Inequality: Latin

America During 1970–1995." Working Paper no. 358, OCE Series, September. Washington, D.C.: Organization for Economic Cooperation/World Bank.

Lustig, N. C. 1998. *Mexico: The Remaking of an Economy*. 2d ed. Washington, D.C.: Brookings Institution.

———. and J. Ros. 1999. "Economic Reforms, Stabilization Policies and the Mexican Disease." Pp. In *After Neoliberalism*, Edited by L. Taylor. Ann Arbor: University of Michigan Press.

———, and M. Székely. 1998. "Economic Trends, Poverty and Inequality in Mexico." Mimeo. Washington, D.C.: IDBank.

McLeod, D., and J. Welch. 1992. "El Libre Comercio y el Peso. " *Economía Mexicana (Nueva Época)* 1 no. 1 (January).

Morley, Samuel. 1995. *Poverty and Inequality in Latin America*. The *Impact of Adjustment and Recovery in the 1980s*. Baltimore: Johns Hopkins University Press.

Oks, D. 1992. *Stabilization and Growth Recovery in Mexico: Lessons and Dilemmas*. Washington, D.C.: The World Bank, Latin America and the Caribbean Regional Office.

———. and Van Wijnbergen. 1992. "Mexico after the Debt Crisis: Is Growth Sustainable?" *Journal of Development Economics* 47, no. 1 (June).

Organización de las Naciones Unidas (ONU). 1997. *Informe del Secretario General de las Naciones Unidas: Actividades Operativas para el Desarrollo. Cooperación Técnica entre los Países en Desarrollo: Situación de la Cooperación sur-sur*. Available from ONV homepage [Accessed 2-11].

Ravallion M., and Huppi. 1991. "Measuring Changes in Poverty: A Methodological Case Study of Indonesia during an Adjustment Period." *World Bank Economic Review* 5.

Revenga, A. 1995. *Employment and Wage Effects of Trade Liberalization: The Case of Mexican Manufacturing*. Mimeo. Washington, D.C.: The World Bank.

Ros, J. 1994. "Mercados Financieros y Flujos de Capital en México." In *Los Capitales Externos en la Economías Latinoamericanas*, Edited by J. Ocampo. Mexico City: Fedesarrollo and the IDB.

———. 1995. "Poverty in Mexico during Adjustment." *The Review of Income and Wealth* 41, no. 3 (September): 331–48.

———. and C. Bouillon. 2001. "La Liberalización de la Balanza de Pagos en México: Efectos en el Crecimiento, la Desigualdad y la Pobreza." In *Liberalización, desigualdad y pobreza: América Latina y el Caribe en los 90*, Edited by E. Ganuza, R. Paes de Barros, L. Taylor, and R. Vos. Buenos Aires: United Nations Development Program, (UNDP), CEPAL, and Editorial de la Universidadde Buenos Aires (EUDEBA).

———. and N. C. Lustig. 2001. "Mexico: Trade and Financial Liberalization with Volatile Capital Inflows: Macroeconomic Consequences and Social Impacts during the 1990s." In, *External Liberalization, Economic Performance and Social Policy*, Edited by L. Taylor. New York: Oxford University Press.

World Bank. 1996a. *Mexico: Poverty Reduction: The Unfinished Agenda*. Report no. 15692-ME. Washington, D.C.: The World Bank.

———. 1996b. *Mexico, Rural Poverty*. Report no. 15058-ME. Washington, D.C.: The World Bank.

# 6

# Defending Labor Rights across Borders: Central American Export-Processing Plants

*Mark S. Anner*

As the twentieth century drew to a close, Central American garment workers grappled with the adverse consequences of economic globalization. At times, they joined forces across borders with labor activists in "anti–sweatshop" campaigns designed to improve working conditions in local export-manufacturing plants. This emerging international movement built a broad alliance of civil society organizations, raised public awareness in consumer countries, defended the right to unionization, and proposed novel solutions to the sweatshop problem such as the independent monitoring of corporate codes of conduct by local organizations. While the overall impact of these efforts fell far short of the movement's goal of ending all abusive conditions in export-oriented garment-manufacturing factories, some important gains were made. A few new unions were formed, and conditions improved marginally in some factories. Yet more important, these experiences highlight the complex dynamics of international campaigns to defend workers' rights.

This chapter is about cross-border labor activism in the Americas. It explores the arduous and often conflicting efforts of Central American workers and their allies to respond to neoliberal reforms and the globalization of production. The segmentation of the production process on an international scale has greatly debilitated the capacity of national labor movements to pursue their demands domestically (Tilly 1995). Thus, as Charles Tilly notes, "if workers are to enjoy collective rights in the new world order, they will have to invent new strategies at the scale of international capital" (Tilly 1995: 5). While sustained international labor activism has been the exception and not the rule (Boswell and Stevis 1997), the examples that do exist are worthy of our attention because they provide important insights into how labor has begun to respond to changes in the world economy. Several campaigns pursued by Central American garment workers and their allies, including U.S. labor groups, provide rich insights into the dynamics of cross-border labor activism at the end of the twentieth century.

## *Maquila* Republics

In the aftermath of the violent civil wars of the 1980s,[1] the Central American nations began the tumultuous path toward demilitarization and democratization. The region also began a neoliberal economic transition that engendered an explosion in export-oriented garment-manufacturing plants, known locally as *maquilas*. These plants produce under contract mostly for large U.S. clothing manufacturers and retailers in a shared production system in which materials used in the production process are imported and final products are exported.[2]

Following the oil crises of the 1970s, growing international competition led manufactures to reduce costs by expanding the subcontracting system to low-wage countries in Asia and Latin America. By the 1990s, the Caribbean Basin surpassed Asia as the largest exporter of apparel to the U.S. market. In El Salvador by 1998, the local value added generated by maquila production reached $339 million, surpassing that of coffee, which had been the largest Salvadoran export for over a century.[3] In Honduras—where the business sector boasted of having "the most competitive labor costs in the Western Hemisphere"[4]—from 1990 to 1998, the number of workers in the sector rose from 9,000 to 104,200, and, by 1998, the value of annual apparel exports approached $2.5 billion.[5] In Guatemala, by the mid-1990s, approximately 70,000 workers, 79 percent of whom were women, worked in *maquila* factories (Lievens 1997).

The dramatic growth of this sector was accompanied by an equally dramatic rise in reports of labor and human rights violations. The mostly young and female workforce complained of violations, including forced overtime, high production quotas, sexual harassment, and intolerable health and occupational safety conditions (Valverde 1996). The highly competitive nature of the sector and the low value-added generated by garment production per employee induced employers to keep wages and benefits low and made labor conditions worse than in the traditional industrial sectors (Valverde 1996). Moreover, these factors greatly limited the effectiveness of traditional forms of domestic labor protest. Forced to keep production costs as low as possible, factory owners vigorously fought unionization attempts and occasionally moved production elsewhere when a union was formed. It is in this context that some workers found that international allies and cross-border campaigns could assist them in pursuing their demands.

## Cross-Border Labor Activism in Central America

This chapter explores efforts by local labor unions and nongovernmental organizations (NGOs) in El Salvador, Honduras, and Guatemala to join forces with U.S. solidarity groups,[6] with the goal of ending sweatshop practices. In this chapter I explore two types of campaigns: factory-focused campaigns, which were designed to organize workers and improve conditions at one work center at a time, and industrywide campaigns, which were designed to force all manufacturers to comply with the same set of standards. I argue that, on a factory level, the movement appeared to be most successful in improving conditions when it combined local organizing efforts with effective international campaigns that targeted multinational corporations (MNCs) in their home countries. I measured success in these campaigns by whether a union was formed or strengthened, and by the degree to which wages and benefits increased beyond the average industry level and abusive management practices (such as sexual harassment and forced overtime) ceased. That is, I was interested in improvements in working conditions *and* worker empowerment represented by the ability of workers to collectively defend their interests at the point of production.

In addition to factory-focused campaigns, the movement pursued industrywide campaigns to eradicate sweatshop conditions in garment plants. In this chapter, I specifically explore the campaign for independent monitoring of corporate codes of conduct.[7] Many MNCs had already established a set of basic labor rights standards (covering areas such as child labor, discrimination, the right to organize, etc.) that they summarized in codes of conduct. These standards were then imposed upon all subcontractors. However, the codes were unilaterally established by the MNCs, and often had no enforcement mechanism. The demand of the movement for independent monitoring was to negotiate with the MNCs a standardized code, the compliance of which would be verified by local NGOs in producer countries.

The idea of incorporating local NGOs in this proposal reflected the fact that interest in the sweatshop problem had expanded beyond trade unions. Indeed, the very nature of the rights-abuses occurring in *maquila* plants engendered broad civil society participation in the search for solutions. For example, physical abuse of workers by management entailed the violation of human, and not just labor, rights. In addition, *maquila* production reflects gender-based labor-market segmentation manifested by the extensive use of female workers in these lower-skill-demanding more unstable, and poorly remunerated jobs (Gammage 1999). The facts that, on average, 80 percent of the workforce was female, and that rights-violations included sexual harassment, forced pregnancy testing, and denial of paid maternity leave, induced women's groups to become involved in the issue.

Yet the movement has fallen short of the goal to achieve broad, effective, industrywide, local NGO monitoring of *maquila* plants. I argue that this was due to cross-sector and cross-national differences that made sustainable alliances untenable. Monitoring was conceived of and mostly promoted by U.S. NGOs, making local implementation of monitoring problematic at times. Moreover, the cross-sector alliances became increasingly problematic. Some women's groups felt that male-dominated labor unions were unable and unwilling to address gender forms of discrimination at the workplace, and, hence, they believed that the problems facing female garment workers would be better addressed by women's groups, as opposed to traditional trade unions (Bickham Mendez 1998). Some unionists asserted that women's groups (and other NGOs) knew very little about labor organizing and were trying to usurp the union's role of representing workers at the workplace (Frundt 1998).

While there are important differences in the dynamics of factory-focused and industrywide campaigns, a common trend is also apparent. In both cases, the dynamics of the relationship between local and international organizations had a crucial impact on campaign outcomes. Local actors who were too weak, relative to local elites, to pursue their demands domestically instead developed cross-border ties to international actors to resolve this power imbalance. Yet their domestic weakness meant that they were invariably weaker than their international allies, not only in terms of resources, but also in terms of access to the international arena. This imbalance greatly limited their ability to control the strategy of international campaigns and, consequently, to ensure that the outcomes of these campaigns responded to their local needs.

Cross-border campaigns for social justice are extremely worthy endeavors. Yet they can be problematic, difficult to control, and, at times, conflictive. This may in part explain why, despite the dramatic increase in the globalization of production regimes, sustained international labor rights campaigns are not more common. At the same time, in spite of all these problems, the movement has had a discernible impact on conditions in both specific factories and the industry as a whole. To varying degrees, working conditions have improved in factories that were the sustained target of local and international campaigns. Child labor in Central American *maquila* factories was reduced, most large clothing manufacturers now accept some degree of responsibility for abuses committed by their subcontractors, and U.S. consumers are much more aware of the sweatshop problem.

In this chapter I first explore theoretical considerations regarding the study of cross-border activism. I will develop three case studies of factory-focused campaigns. They involve the Mandarin factory in El Salvador, the Kimi plant in Honduras, and the *Camisas Modernas* facility in Guatemala. These are arguably the three most important factory-focused cross-border campaigns to occur in Central America in the 1990s, and they have been chosen for this reason. The second empirical section focuses on the industrywide campaign for independent monitoring of corporate codes of conduct. This much-debated campaign became the focus of the movement in the 1990s, and greatly influenced the U.S. government–initiated proposal for industrywide monitoring, which later was the subject of negotiations by several concerned parties in the United States, and was then institutionalized into the Fair Labor Association (FLA) in November 1998. The potential long-term implications—both good and bad—and the broad scope of this initiative make it worthy of our attention.

Data for this project were drawn from a variety of sources. I interviewed movement participants in the United States, and in Central America during visits to the region in 1998 and 1999. I also relied on movement publications, newspaper articles, and several secondary sources. In the case of El Salvador, much of my account is written from the perspective of a participant observer. I lived in the country for over seven years (1988–1989; 1991–1996), and, as a representative for the Salvadoran Center for Labor Studies (Centra), I participated in the monitoring of labor conditions at the Mandarin plant.

### Theorizing About Cross-Border Labor Activism

Margaret Keck and Kathryn Sikkink (1998: 12) argue that when domestic actors are blocked from pursuing their demands locally, they may "bypass their state and directly search out international allies to try to bring pressure on their states from outside." They refer to this process as the "boomerang pattern." In a similar vein, Jackie Smith (1997) notes that transnational activism may occur when local activists, unable to find points of access or vulnerabilities in the national political system, find favorable opportunities on an international level.

Since the 1970s there has been a dramatic transformation in the structure of capitalist production in which internationally networked production regimes increasingly replaced traditional mass production systems (Piore and Sabel 1984; Harrison 1994; Gereffi and M. and R. Korzeniewicz

1994). The segmentation of the production process in Central America weakened labor's ability to pursue its demands domestically. Moreover, when unions attempted to act politically and pursue their demands by targeting the state, government officials were of little assistance. First, ministries of labor and workplace inspection were dramatically underfunded (Arévalo and Arriola 1996). Second, even when funds may have been available, political will was often lacking. As one politician succinctly put it: "Let's face it, if we are strict about compliance with our own labor laws, all the foreign *maquila* producers will go elsewhere."[8]

Garment workers in export-processing plants clearly were unable to find or exploit plant-level or national opportunities through which to pursue their demands. Thus, as Keck and Sikkink and Smith suggest, one possible venue would be to develop international alliances through which outside pressure could be brought to bear on local producers and governments. As shown below, *maquila* workers did in fact develop alliances with international solidarity groups (although often it was the international activists who pursued local contacts and not the other way around). These allies discovered that one weak link in the global commodity chain lay in the importance of brand identity and the good image of the retailer's label. As Andrew Ross notes, MNC high profits came with risks, of which "none are greater than the potentially embarrassing exposure of human rights violations in the factories of companies that cannot afford to have the names of their designers, endorsers, or merchandising labels publicly sullied" (1997: 25).[9]

Thus, what Smith posits as a precondition for international activism—vulnerabilities or points of access that lie beyond the confines of the nation-state—did exist in the garment industry. Moreover, the movement found that it could exploit certain international political opportunities. In the United States, political concern about the sweatshop problem allowed for a certain receptivity to the movement's demands. For example, Robert Reich, who was named U.S. secretary of labor in 1995, became personally involved in the sweatshop issue. He initiated an effort to bring together large U.S. garment manufacturers, organized labor, consumer groups, and other concerned NGOs to discuss ways in which to resolve the sweatshop problem. This effort led to the formation of the Apparel Industry Partnership to End Sweatshop Practices (AIP).

The existence of international venues does not imply that movements will be able to pursue their goals unproblematically. Social movement scholars have often noted that movements are seldom able to directly control the outcome of their efforts (Tarrow 1998), and this appears to be particularly true of movements that venture beyond their own borders. First, since movements must frame issues so that they resonate well within a given political culture (Snow et al. 1986), where and how an issue gets framed delimits the range of possible solutions that might eventually be achieved. So while Central American workers might mostly want the ability to organize themselves into trade unions in order to best articulate and defend their interests, U.S. activists might decide that the U.S. public is not particularly receptive to this demand and decide to focus instead on issues involving human rights abuses, such as child labor. The gap between where the problem being addressed occurs and where the issue gets framed is, by definition, greater in international campaigns.

Second, the loose nature of the coalitions that constitute movements makes it very difficult to establish and maintain one set of goals. This problem is particularly acute given the divergent nature of cross-sector (labor, women, and human rights groups working together) and cross-border coalitions.

Finally, movements do not pursue their goals in a vacuum, but rather they do so in political contexts that entail constant interaction with opponents. Cross-border movements involve a myriad of actors (local elites, MNCs, foreign governments), all of whom might respond in different ways to movement demands. In sum, the dynamics of issue framing, ephemeral coalitions, conflicting interests, and elite countermaneuvering suggest that movements will seldom achieve exactly what they purportedly set out to do, particularly in international campaigns.

These factors suggest two important modifications to Keck and Sikkink's boomerang pattern. First, the difficulties in establishing and maintaining cross-sector, cross-border alliances enhance the probability that movement goals will be significantly modified or displaced. Hence, Keck and Sikkink's boomerangs may well begin to take wing, but they may also travel on some very unanticipated trajectories. Second (and as shown below), while an inability to fully pursue demands domestically may make actors more receptive to international alliances, cross-border activism can never completely replace domestic activism. Continued local activism is a needed complement to international pressure, and ensures that domestic actors play a role in establishing goals and implementing solutions.

### Factory-Focused Campaigns

*Mandarin International in El Salvador*

Mandarin International, a Taiwanese-owned factory, began operations in the early 1990s in the San Marcos Free Trade Zone in El Salvador. Forced overtime, lack of adequate drinking water, and other harsh conditions motivated workers to try to organize themselves. The first two attempts to form a union resulted in mass firings. A third attempt was more successful because the unionists worked more clandestinely, and a union leader was able to use his political connections inside the ministry of labor to gain official recognition for the organization. The union was formed with the minimum requirement of thirty-five workers, but to bargain collectively Salvadoran law required over 50 percent of the workforce to be organized. Over the next several months, the union managed to organize 350 workers out of a workforce of 850, and some observers thought that Mandarin might become the first factory in a Salvadoran export-processing zone with a collective bargaining agreement.[10]

However, the company responded once again by firing union members, instigating a cycle of protest and repression. Inside the factory, workers who had not been fired participated in short work stoppages and occasional product sabotage, while outside the factory fired workers organized increasingly contentious activities. The company hired a retired army colonel as personnel manager, and workers responded by carrying spiked clubs during a series of wildcat strikes. Despite the militancy of their campaign, the odds were still against labor. By June 1995, all 350 unionists had been fired and the union leadership was denied entry into the factory.[11] Repeated attempts by the workers to resolve their problem by appealing to the appropriate governmental institutions ended in failure and frustration.

During this period, a grouping of Salvadoran civil society organizations concerned with the growing problems in export-processing plants formed a coordinating body.[12] In response to the multifaceted nature of the *maquila* problem, the group represented a novel attempt to bring together human rights, religious, and women's organizations. This group spoke out against the labor-rights violations taking place at the factory and encouraged The Gap (a clothing retailer) to visit the country and to rectify the situation (Anner 1998). This broad, local civil society alliance played an important role in highlighting the problems in the *maquila* sector and legitimizing the struggle of the *maquila* workers. Yet the Salvadoran government publicly supported the factory owners, and key spokespeople, including then-president Calderon Sol, denounced the labor protesters and their local allies.

News of the conflict spread beyond the borders of El Salvador, reaching the New York–based labor rights group, the National Labor Committee (NLC).[13] When the NLC learned that Mandarin produced for The Gap, it believed that it could assist the unionists by launching a campaign in the United States designed to target the San Francisco–based company. Concretely, the NLC believed that The Gap's desire to protect its public image would provide a useful lever to pressure the company into assuming responsibility for the problems at the factory. The Gap added to its vulnerability by publicly releasing its corporate code of conduct, which allowed for the right of workers to form trade unions. The Gap noted that it had published the code on recycled paper and that it was one of the most progressive codes in the garment industry. The NLC responded that, while the code appeared to be good, it had not been translated into Spanish, much less distributed to factory workers in El Salvador. Indeed, The Gap had no enforcement mechanism to ensure that local contractors complied with the code.[14]

The NLC then invited one of the fired workers, Judith Viera, to conduct a speaking tour in the United States. Viera described the low wages, forced overtime, incidents of corporal punishment, and illegal firings. Columnist Bob Herbert picked up the story and prepared a series in the *New York Times* on the Mandarin case. Schoolchildren supported the campaign. For example, as its annual project, the National Honor Society at one U.S. high school pressured The Gap to end the labor abuses. Soon, consumer and religious groups joined the campaign as well (DeSimone 1998a).

As a result of these efforts, The Gap, in an accord signed with the NLC, eventually agreed to compel the local factory owner to rehire all the union members. In order to ensure compliance with the accord, The Gap's corporate code of conduct, and local labor law, The Gap also agreed to allow independent monitoring of the facility by local human rights, religious, and labor organizations. In El Salvador in March 1996, the union and soon-to-be monitors formalized The Gap/NLC accord into an agreement signed with the owner of Mandarin.

Overall, the campaign appeared to be a success. By October 1996, the union leaders were back at their jobs, and by early 1997 other fired workers were offered the opportunity to return to work. But the union remained weak. In fact, it had never been organized in a very careful, systematic way. For example, union leaders had not received a great deal of trade union training, and, in 1995, many workers had joined quickly, in the heat of the conflict, without knowing much about unions. As a result, union support was wide, but thin. Later, when ex-union rank-and-file members returned to work, many decided not to rejoin the union. At the same time, the owner was able to build and consolidate a promanagement union inside the factory, which presented a serious obstacle for the independent union. While monitoring of the facility by local NGOs ensured that the most egregious labor-rights violations were eliminated, monitoring has not been able to provide sufficient leverage for the independent union to expand its support beyond a core group of workers.

In sum, the Mandarin/Gap campaign represents a case of local organizing coordinated with a strong transnational campaign that effectively exploited a company's vulnerabilities. As a result of the campaign, unionists returned to their jobs and the factory was monitored by local NGOs. This, in turn, ensured that overtime was no longer obligatory, women no longer had to ask permission to go to the bathroom, adequate drinking water was made available, and the ex-army colonel–made-personnel administrator was removed from his post. In a poll conducted in October 1997, over 88 percent of the workforce rated their treatment by their supervisors and management as good or very good.[15] On the other hand, while the union was legalized and inside the factory, it remained weak and unable to negotiate a collective contract. Wages did not improve above the industry average, and individual worker productivity goals remained high. This-less-than-optimal outcome appears attributable to the fact that, while the international campaign was strong, local organizing at this factory was relatively weak. That is, even with the best international campaign, if attention is not given to properly organizing the local union, results will be limited.

### Kimi in Honduras

The Honduran *maquila* sector became the focus of international attention in 1996 when the NLC exposed labor-rights-violations at a factory producing garments for television celebrity Kathie Lee Gifford. Like The Gap, Gifford created her own vulnerability. She advertised on her clothing labels that 10 percent of the proceeds from the sale of her garments would go to poor children. The NLC noted that that was very generous of her, but unfortunately poor children were in fact making her clothing. The NLC then brought Wendy Diaz on a U.S. speaking tour. Diaz was an employee of a Honduras-based factory where she had been making Kathie Lee Gifford clothing since she was thirteen. Diaz testified that she was one of one hundred minors working at the apparel factory (Krupt 1997: 60). The growing attention on underaged girls working in Honduran *maquila* plants forced the local government and export-processing zone administrators to take measures to address this problem.

The attention on Honduras, combined with the fact that the country had become one of the largest exporters of garments to the United States,[16] led the U.S. clothing and textile workers' union, UNITE (Union of Needletrades, Industrial, and Textile Employees), to choose Honduras as a country in which to expand its cross-border organizing efforts. UNITE decided to focus its efforts on organizing Kimi, a Korean-owned factory that produced for The Gap, Macy's, and other U.S. retailers. The NLC was also interested in the factory because, as a result of its campaign in El Salvador, The Gap had agreed to accept monitoring of *all* its facilities in Central America. Thus, the campaign at Kimi had both an organizing component and an international component. However, these two components were not coordinated.

The organizing drive was led by a representative of UNITE who was assigned to Honduras. With his guidance, the union implemented a variety of new organizing tactics, including classifying workers according to their perceived level of support (prounion, middle of the road, or antiunion), and then aggressively targeting the undecided segment by means of house visits in which organizers would directly inform workers about the benefits and importance of joining a union.[17] The tactic paid off; the majority of the workforce voted in favor of the union.

Conditions did not improve immediately, due to extreme management recalcitrance and because the international campaign never reached major proportions. The anti–sweatshop movement never aggressively adopted the Kimi case. That is, it did not establish a *sustained* international campaign to mobilize grass-roots support to improve conditions at the plant and strengthen the union. Consequently, MNCs like The Gap and Macy's were eventually able to terminate their production orders at the factory when the union drive gained ground. A coordinated campaign might have been able to deter the MNCs from fleeing the country and to stay and work with local management and labor to resolve their problems.

As it turned out, J.C. Penney and other clients soon filled much of the void left by The Gap and Macy's (Frundt 1998). Yet, in the hope of encouraging The Gap and Macy's to return, the plant owner invited the NLC to establish a monitoring group similar to the one functioning in El Salvador. The NLC was forced to put the group together quickly and, as a result, the monitors appeared somewhat ill-prepared for their task. On one occasion a monitor took to discussing terms and conditions of employment with management without the union's participation. While the group learned from its mistake, the damage was already done. In March 1998, union leaders Yesenía Bonilla and Sara Guillon openly stated that they did not want monitoring, that it was not helping their situation, and that it in fact had become an obstacle for the union by preventing them from freely and directly negotiating a collective contract.[18] The U.S. union movement, which was already suspicious of nonunion groups getting so involved in labor issues, more openly criticized NGOs' monitoring of sweatshops as attempting to usurp the role of unions.

By February 1999, the monitoring group decided to disband. However, the union remained active in the factory and, by March 1999, managed to negotiate a collective contract. In addition to formalizing the institutional representation of workers by the union, contract provisions included a wage increase of approximately 10 percent, better health benefits, increased vacation time, prolonged maternity leave, and leave for union leaders to attend to union tasks.[19] Yet, even with the wage increase, wages still failed to cover a family's basic needs, and remained among the lowest in the Central American *maquila* sector.

The presence of both a local organizing effort and international pressure provided for a degree of success. The Kimi factory became one of the few unionized plants in the Honduran *maquila* sector, and conditions in the factory improved above the industry average. However, these improvements were only marginal, and eventually were not sustainable. This appears to be due in part to the lack of a sustained and vigorous international campaign and in part to the lack of coordination between the international campaign and the local organizing component. In early 2000, the owners of Kimi moved the plant to another location within Honduras and then, in May 2000, closed the plant, which also highlights the mobility of the sector and the limitations of factory-based campaigns.

### Phillips–Van Heusen in Guatemala

Workers at the *Camisas Modernas* factory in Guatemala achieved the legal recognition of their union in 1992. They did so in the context of a petition on labor-rights violations brought by U.S. labor groups before the U.S. trade representative. However, the union could not get the company to negotiate a collective contract and thus improve employment conditions at the factory. According to Guatemalan (in contrast to Salvadoran) law, 25 percent of the workforce needs to be part of the union in order to oblige the company to negotiate with the union. Union representatives said that they had enough members; the company said that they did not. The matter went to the Ministry of Labor, which, according to the U.S.-based NGO Human Rights Watch, "abdicat[ed] its responsibility and invit[ed] the union and PVH to take their concerns to the labor courts" (cited in DeSimone 1998b: 146). With well over one thousand cases backlogged in the Guatemalan labor-court system at any given time, waiting for a judicial verdict might easily take two or more years.

The factory was owned by Phillips-Van Heusen (PVH), the U.S. shirt maker that sold most of its shirts at J.C. Penney retail stores. Because local unionists were unable to achieve their demands at the factory level or to pursue their demands through Guatemalan institutions, the unionists responded receptively when approached by the U.S. Guatemalan Labor Education Project (GLEP),[20] which proposed an international campaign that would target PVH. GLEP began leafleting PVH outlets and

J.C. Penney retail stores in the United States. It also began a letter-writing campaign directed at PVH management. At the peak of the campaign, U.S. activists joined Guatemalan unionists and participated in simultaneous protest activity that focused on PVH outlets in the United States and the PVH factory in Guatemala.

GLEP then discovered that the CEO of PVH, Bruce J. Klatsky, was also a member of the board of directors of the well-recognized U.S.–based human rights group Human Rights Watch (HRW; see Bounds 1997). As with The Gap and Kathie Lee Gifford, the anti–sweatshop movement had found a vulnerability of yet another large clothing company. GLEP pressured PVH to accept an HRW fact-finding trip to Guatemala. HRW would investigate specifically whether the union had the needed support to obligate the company to negotiate a collective contract. Klatsky found himself having to accept the idea and, a priori, agreed to accept the HRW findings.

HRW traveled to Guatemala in January 1997, and concluded that the union did meet the representation requirements under Guatemalan law. Two months later, PVH agreed to recognize the union and negotiate a collective contract. Negotiations were difficult, and lasted for four months. In the end, workers achieved an 11 percent wage increase the first year and a commitment to a 12.5 percent increase the second year. They also won improved medical care, a grievance procedure, and subsidized transportation to work. Thus, the PVH campaign suggests that a well-coordinated combination of effective transnational activism and local organizing can produce an important degree of success.

Nonetheless, the situation was far from stable. The union never achieved a significant degree of internal cohesion. At the same time, according to the union's secretary general, Marisol López, the union became more inclined to pursue its work independently of the international solidarity movement in order to control the strategy of the campaign.[21] Then, in a move that caught the anti–sweatshop movement by surprise, on December 11, 1998, PVH closed the *Camisas Modernas* plant. While PVH justified the closure because of the loss of a major client, the movement considered the move to be a sign of antiunionism (MSN 1999).

Economic pressures seemed equally responsible. Wages at PVH were much higher than at other *maquila* factories. Thus, the PVH campaign highlights one of the greatest challenges facing the movement; significant success at one plant without the ability to effectively pressure the industry as a whole may lead to the closing of that plant. This experience, like the Kimi experience, highlighted the need for an industrywide strategy.

## The Industrywide Campaign

### *The Campaign for Independent Monitoring*

While the anti–sweatshop movement achieved some success with specific, factory-focused campaigns, movement leaders came to realize that it would be impossible to end sweatshop practices on a plant-by-plant basis. The movement needed a strategy that had the potential to affect the entire industry. In this light, building on the lessons learned from the monitoring experiences in El Salvador and Honduras, the NLC began to explore the possibility of pressuring manufacturers to accept local NGO monitoring of all their facilities. The idea made sense on two counts. First, it had the potential of forcing all companies to accept the same standards, thus limiting the potential for *maquila* owners to compete with one another based on poor working conditions and extremely low wages. Second, it provided a mechanism for nonlabor civil society organizations to join labor unions in the effort to end sweatshop practices.

Yet labor leaders became increasingly wary of allowing nonlabor groups to be too involved in representing workers' interests. By early 1998, international labor leaders were openly questioning any form of NGO monitoring. In a speech delivered at a *maquila* workers' conference in the Dominican Republic, Neil Kearney, secretary general of the International Textile and Leather Workers' Federation (ITLWF) stated emphatically: "Only trade unions can defend their own interests."[22] Yet no one seemed to have an alternate strategy around which the entire movement could rally. Some activists began to pursue the idea of a "living wage" campaign while focused on "corporate disclosure," the goal of which was to get MNCs to disclose where all their clothing was being made, based on the premise that this would force companies to be more careful about letting labor-rights violations committed by their subcontractors go uncorrected.

U.S. clothing manufacturers and retailers took advantage of the confusion within the movement and began to pursue forms of monitoring more to their own liking. Most notably, MNCs began using large auditing firms such as Ernst & Young and Pricewaterhouse to carry out "social" audits. Yet these company-controlled mechanisms presented numerous problems, not the least of which was that they could be used only for public relations purposes.[23] Movement activists denounced this type of monitoring, but were unable to stop it. By 1998, Pricewaterhouse announced that it would be monitoring 5,000 factories throughout the world that year. While no systematic study of the effects of these efforts has been conducted, initial indications suggest that they have fallen far short of resolving the sweatshop issue (Liubicic 1998).[24]

Meanwhile, the Apparel Industry Partnership (AIP) continued discussions to establish an industrywide code of conduct and a monitoring mechanism. The anti–sweatshop movement was surprised in November 1998 when the manufacturing groups within the AIP and the more moderate NGOs formalized an agreement without the participation of the unions and the religious sector. These groups criticized the accord because it failed to include a living wage provision, did not adequately guarantee the right to organize, and gave companies too much control over the monitoring process (see MSN 1998).

By early 1999, the movement appeared divided and frustrated. Campaigns to moderately improve conditions at a few factories took a tremendous amount of time and energy, and even "successful" campaigns often ended in plant closings. Meanwhile, the monitoring idea that was initiated by the movement was becoming increasingly co-opted by the MNCs. Movement leaders began to turn inward, increasingly criticizing each other. By March 1999, concern about the divisiveness within the movement was openly addressed. Medea Benjamin, codirector of the San Francisco–based solidarity group Global Exchange, noted: "We should be collectively celebrating the huge steps we have taken, and pooling our limited resources to become even more effective in the struggles ahead. Instead, it seems that we have suddenly veered off track, wasting time attacking each other over tactical differences. Our infighting threatens to sap the strength of our movement."[25]

Groups like the Canada-based NGO the *Maquila* Solidarity Network (MSN) argued for the need for greater consultation with "southern" partners. MSN stated, "We are particularly concerned that in our efforts to move ahead with Stop Sweatshop campaigning in the North (i.e. in the U.S., Canada and Europe), there has been too little consultation with and involvement of groups actively working on these issues on the local and regional level in the major garment producing countries in Asia and Latin America."[26]

In addition to the apparent inability of weaker partners to significantly influence the movement's strategies, basic forms of information sharing were often lacking. Even crucial documents, such as the AIP agreement, were not translated and distributed to concerned groups in Central America until many months after being signed. Meanwhile, across sectors, labor unions and women's groups increasingly debated who had the right to represent a workforce that was mostly female. Thus, the most promising aspect of the sweatshop issue—its potential to bring together a wide range of social actors within and across countries—also proved to be the movement's greatest liability.

The most positive development in this otherwise difficult period for the movement was a dramatic resurgence in student activism in universities throughout the United States. Led by students at Duke, Georgetown, and the University of Wisconsin, student groups demanded that apparel bearing their universities' names not be made under sweatshop conditions (see Greenhouse 1999a). They held teach-ins, brought in *maquila* workers on speaking tours, petitioned university authorities, and, in several cases, organized sit-ins at university administrative buildings. In an attempt to mitigate student pressure, fifty-six universities announced that they would join the Fair Labor Association (FLA) of the Apparel Industry Partnership (Greenhouse 1999b). The student groups, organized into the United Students Against Sweatshops, harshly criticized the FLA,[27] and established the Worker Rights Consortium (WRC) with the goal of increasing local worker control over the policing of sweatshops.

In sum, while there were growing internal debates and divisions in the movement, there were also several discernible positive results. Some of the worst labor-rights violations were reduced in *maquila* factories, and U.S. consumers greatly increased their awareness of the conditions under which their clothing was made. And there were also other positive developments, most notably the dramatic increase in student activism around this issue. These new actors brought new energy and creative ideas to the anti–sweatshop movement.

### Conclusions

In this chapter I have explored the dynamics and outcomes of campaigns to improve conditions and empower workers in Central American export-manufacturing plants. We have seen how Central American garment workers, unable to fully pursue their demands on a domestic level, formed alliances with actors in other countries. These alliances assisted them in pursuing their demands by targeting the multinational clothing companies that provided the contracts to the factories in which they worked.

Yet, the cases explored here also suggest that cross-border activism, while important, cannot supplant domestic activism. The more fruitful endeavors combined international pressure with local organizing efforts. Indeed, in the most successful campaigns labor built alliances not only across borders, but also with other local civil society groups, among them human rights, religious, and women's groups. However, the Central American experiences indicate that, due to the highly competitive and mobile nature of the industry, it was extremely difficult to achieve sustained improvements in just one factory. Independent monitoring was considered a possible venue for achieving this goal. Yet, these cases suggest that pursuing industrywide monitoring required making and *maintaining* cross-sector and cross-border alliances. This proved to be extremely difficult for the young anti–sweatshop movement. Across sectors, tensions developed most noticeably between women's groups and labor unions, which limited the sustainability of these coalitions.

As the debates in the United States over the movement's strategy and goals became more heated and complex, the *maquila* workers themselves became somewhat marginalized in the movement's strategic decision-making process. This adversely affected the movement because successful campaigns depended on the movement's ability to adequately develop mechanisms of interest representation that effectively and systematically incorporate the ideas and aspirations of the workers whom the movement strived to assist and empower.

Despite the numerous difficulties of these initial campaigns to develop and maintain multisector international coalitions, the movement has shown an ability to recognize its weaknesses and to learn from its mistakes. The incorporation of new actors, such as students, has reinvigorated the movement. While these initial campaigns depict the many unintended trajectories of the boomerangs that they helped to launch, later efforts must display an increased ability on the part of movement actors to join forces more effectively across sectors and borders in order to improve the quality of some of the more precarious jobs that have been created by economic globalization.

### Notes

The author thanks Maria Cook, Matthew Evangelista, Sidney Tarrow, and Lowell Turner for their helpful comments on earlier versions of this chapter.

1. Negotiated solutions to armed conflict were signed in Nicaragua (1990), El Salvador (1992) and Guatemala (1996). Honduras, which mostly avoids direct armed confrontation, but which became enmeshed in the regional conflict as the United States increasingly used the country as a training ground for insurgency and counterinsurgency activity, began a process of demilitarization in the 1990s. Costa Rica was the least affected, but played an active role in the regional peace processes.
2. Caribbean Basin countries benefit from the Harmonized Tariff Schedule of the United States (HTSUS) 9802, under which U.S.–made apparel components are shipped to the region for assembly and then returned to the United States. Duties are only paid on the value added.
3. The value of coffee exports in 1998 was $325 million. *Banco Central de Reserva* (BCR), San Salvador, El Salvador (http://www.bcr.gob.sv/boletin.htm).
4. Author's interview with administrator of the Choloma Free Trade Zone, Honduras, February 1997.
5. *Banco Central de Honduras*; U.S. Department of Commerce, Bureau of the Census.
6. Organizations from many other areas have also assisted *maquila* workers, most notably organizations from Canada and western Europe. Yet, time and space have forced me to limit myself to the work of U.S. labor and solidarity groups.

7. Other industrywide campaigns included the movement's call for a "living wage" for *maquila* workers and corporate disclosure of the names and locations of all factories in which MNCs produced. The independent monitoring campaign was the largest and, to date, the most consequential industrywide campaign.

8. Author's interview with Eugenio Chicas, Salvadoran parliamentarian, San Salvador, El Salvador, October 17, 1995. Chicas was referring to the comment made to him by a representative of the governing ARENA (Alianza Republicana Nacionalista) party.

9. Corporate executives publicly acknowledged as much. In the words of Peter Jacobi, president of global sourcing for Levi Strauss: "The corporate reputations behind the brands have become increasingly important to people when they decide what products to buy. [. . .] If your company owns a popular brand, protect this asset at all costs" (Cited in Nichols 1993: 15–16).

10. Author's interview with Amanda Villatoro, president of the Center of Democratic Workers (CTD), San Salvador, El Salvador, September 1995.

11. Legally, the elected leadership of the union could not be fired. So, the company instructed them to pick up their paychecks each week at the Ministry of Labor, but otherwise not to report to work.

12. The group's full name in Spanish was the *Coordinadora Social para la Dignificación del Empleo en la Maquila* (COSDEMA).

13. The NLC was formed in 1980 by a group of unionists that was concerned about U.S. support for the military regime in El Salvador and AFL-CIO advocacy of that foreign policy. In the aftermath of the Salvadoran civil wars (1980–1992), the NLC began exploring the idea of pursuing labor rights campaigns with workers in the country's export-processing zones. The NLC traveled to El Salvador and, during the heat of the conflict, met with the local union at the Mandarin plant.

14. Author's interview with Charles Kernaghan, executive director of the NLC, New York, April 11, 1997.

15. *Grupo de Monitoreo Independiente de El Salvador*, "Segundo Informe Público del Grupo de Monitoreo Independiente de El Salvador." San Salvador, December 1997 (reprinted in Anner 1998).

16. The value of Honduran apparel exports to the United States in 1997 was $1.69 billion. Honduras followed China (including Hong Kong), Mexico, the Dominican Republic, Taiwan, and Indonesia, but exported more than did several of the world's largest apparel producers, including South Korea (whose apparel exports to the United States totaled $1.66 billion in 1997), India ($1.51 billion), and the Philippines ($1.62 billion). For complete yearly figures for apparel (SITC, Standard International Trade Classification, 84) exports, see the U.S. Department of Commerce: Bureau of the Census (http://tier2.census.gov/sitc/sitcpage.htm).

17. While these were new tactics for Honduras, they are fairly standard procedures in many U.S. organizing campaigns.

18. Yesenía Bonilla and Sara Guillon, interventions at the conference, "Estrategias de Organización de las Zonas Francas (Maquilas)," Santo Domingo, March 16–20, 1998.

19. "Acta de finalización de negociación del primer contrato colectivo de condiciones de trabajo celebrado entre la empresa Kimi de Honduras, S. A. y el sindicato de trabajadores de la empresa Kimi de Honduras S.A. (Sitrakimih)," March 19, 1999. Copy rests with author and is available upon request.

20. GLEP is a U.S.-based labor rights group with an office in Guatemala. GLEP was founded in 1987 by several labor activists in the Chicago area who participated in the international solidarity campaign with Guatemalan Coca-Cola workers in the mid-1980s.

21. Author's interview with Marisol López, Santo Domingo, Dominican Republic, March 18, 1998.

22. From speech by Neil Kearney at the conference "Estrategias de Organización de las Zonas Francas (Maquilas)," Santo Domingo, March 16–20, 1998.

23. For example, when Ernst & Young informed Nike through a confidential report on the poor occupational health conditions in a factory in Vietnam, Nike did little to rectify the situation until the report was leaked to the press.

24. Jill Esbenshade (N.d.), who studied similar monitoring programs in Los Angeles, California, found that, while corporation-controlled monitoring helped, 60 percent of monitored shops were still out of compliance with basic labor rights standards.
25. Medea Benjamin, open letter to anti–sweatshop movement activists, March 23, 1999.
26. *Maquila* Solidarity Movement, open letter to the anti–sweatshop movement, April 10, 1999.
27. Open letter to AIP members, United Students Against Sweatshops, March 16, 1999.

# References

Anner, Mark. 1998. *La maquila y el Monitoreo Independiente en El Salvador*. San Salvador: Grupo de Monitoreo Independiente de El Salvador (GMIES).

Arévalo, Rolando, and Joaquin Arriola. 1996. "El Caso de El Salvador." Pp. 109–58 in *La Situación Sociolaboral en las Zonas Francas y Empresas Maquiladoras del Istmo Centroamericano y República Dominicana*, edited by Organización Internacional de Trabajo (OIT), Oficina de Actividades para los Trabajadores (ACTRAV). Costa Rica: (OIT).

Bickham Mendez, Jennifer. 1998. "Creating Alternatives from a Gender Perspective: Central American Women's Transnational Organizing for Maquila Workers' Rights." Paper delivered at the annual meeting of the American Sociological Association, San Francisco, CA. August.

Boswell, Terry, and Dimitris Stevis. 1997. "Globalization and International Labor Organizing: A World-System Perspective." *Work and Occupation* 24, no. 3: 288–308.

Bounds, Wendy. 1997. "Critics Confront a CEO Dedicated to Human Rights." *Wall Street Journal*, February 24: B1.

DeSimone, Peter. 1998a. "El Salvador: An Experiment in Independent Monitoring." Pp. 281–307 in *The Sweatshop Quandary: Corporate Responsibility on the Global Frontier*, edited by Pamela Varley. Washington, D.C.: Investor Responsibility Research Center.

———. 1998b. "Guatemala." Pp. 113–195 in *The Sweatshop Quandary: Corporate Responsibility on the Global Frontier*, edited by Pamela Varley. Washington, D.C.: Investor Responsibility Research Center.

Esbenshade, Jill. N.d. *Monitoring in the Garment Industry: Lessons from Los Angeles*. Working Paper no. 5-1, Chicano/Latino Policy Project Series. Berkeley: University of California.

Frundt, Hank. 1998. "Cross-border Organizing in the Apparel Industry: Lessons from C.A. and the Caribbean." Author manuscript.

Gammage, Sarah. 1999. "Globalization and the Gender Composition of Manufacturing Employment in Latin America." Paper delivered at the Association for Women in Development (AWID) Conference, Washington, D.C.

Gereffi, Gary, Miguel Korzeniewicz, and Roberto P. Korzeniewicz. 1994. "Introduction: Global Commodity Chains." Pp. 1–14 in *Commodity Chains and Global Capitalism*, edited by Gary Gereffi and Miguel Korzeniewicz. Westport, Conn.: Praeger.

Greenhouse, Steven. 1999a. "Activism Surges at Campuses Nationwide, and Labor is at Issue." *New York Times*, March 29: 14.

———. 1999b. "Student Critics Push Attacks on Anti-Sweatshop Association." *New York Times*, April 25.

Harrison, Bennett. 1994. *Lean and Mean: The Changing Landscape of Corporate Power in the Age of Flexibility*. New York: Guilford Press.

Keck, Margaret E., and Kathryn Sikkink. 1998. *Activists Beyond Borders: Advocacy Networks in International Politics*. Ithaca, N.Y. and London: Cornell University Press.

Krupt, Kitty. 1997. "From War Zone to Free Trade Zone: A History of the National Labor Committee." Pp. 55–77 in *No Sweat: Fashion, Free Trade, and the Rights of Garment Workers*, edited by Andrew Ross. New York: Verso.

Lievens, Karin. 1997. *Las Republicas Maquiladoras: Las Zonas Francas en El Salvador, Guatemala, Honduras y Nicaragua*. Brussels, Belgium: Oxfam.

Liubicic, Robert J. 1998. "Corporate Codes of Conduct and Product Labeling Schemes: The Limits and Possibilities of Promoting International Labor Rights through Private Initiatives." *Law and Policy in International Business*, 30, no. 10 (fall):111–58.

*Maquila* Solidarity Network (MSN). 1998. "Coming Apart at the Seams: Agreement Divides US Apparel Industry Partnership." *Maquila Network Update* 3, no. 4: 1.

———. 1999. "PVH Grinch Steals Christmas in Guatemala." *Maquila Network Update* 4, no. 1: 1.

Nichols, Martha. 1993. "Third-World Families at Work: Child Labor or Child Care?" *Harvard Business Review* 71, no. 1: 12–21.

Piore, Michael J., and Charles F. Sabel. 1984. *The Second Industrial Divide: Possibilities for Prosperity*. New York: Basic Books.

Ross, Andrew. 1997. "Introduction." Pp. 9–37 in *No Sweat: Fashion, Free Trade, and the Rights of Garment Workers*, edited by Andrew Ross. New York: Verso.

Smith, Jackie. 1997. "Characteristics of the Modern Transnational Social Movement Sector." Pp. 42–58 in *Transnational Social Movements and Global Politics: Solidarity Beyond the State*, edited by Jackie Smith, Charles Chatfield, and Ron Pagnucco. Syracuse N.Y.: Syracuse University Press.

Snow, David, E. Burke Rochford, Jr., Steven Worden, and Robert D. Benford. 1986. "Frame Alignment Processes, Micromobilization, and Movement Participation." *American Sociological Review* 51: 464–81.

Tarrow, Sidney. 1998. "Social Protest and Policy Reform: May 1968 and the Loi d'Orientation in France." Pp. 31–56 in *From Contention to Democracy*, edited by Marco G. Giugni, Doug McAdam, and Charles Tilly. Lanham, Md.: Rowman & Littlefield Publishers, Inc.

Tilly, Charles. 1995. "Globalization Threatens Labor's Rights." *International Labor and Working-Class History* 47: 1–23.

Valverde, Oscar. 1996. "Balance Subregional de la Situación Sociolaboral de las Zonas Francas y Maquiladoras en Centroamérica y República Dominicana." Pp. 3–45 in *La Situación Sociolaboral en las zonas Francas y Empresas Maquiladoras del Istmo Centroamericano y República Dominicana*, edited by Organización Internacional del Trabajo (OIT), Oficina de Actividades para los Trabajadores (ACTRAV). Costa Rica: Roxana Marín S.

# 7

# Subversion and Compliance in Transnational Communities: Implications for Social Justice

*Alejandro Portes and Patricia M. Fernández-Kelly*

## Introduction

"Capital is global, labor is local": The aphorism in vogue for almost two decades to portray the dynamics of the world economy carries a dual meaning. Advocates use it to celebrate the virtues of free trade and market rationality. Critics brandish it to mark the demise of proletarian consciousness and national liberation movements. Whatever the outlook, the catchphrase is part of a larger narrative that envisions direct corporate ventures and portfolio investments crisscrossing the earth in search of valorization. The attendant expectation is that international capital, in its wide and voracious sweep, will reduce the capacity of national states to promote economic autonomy and remove the hard-earned prerogatives of workers.

Yet, capital's international impulse is nothing new. Numerous accounts document the centuries-long propensity of merchants and financiers to seek enrichment in foreign lands. Unique at the present moment, however, is the scale, velocity, and vigor of capital mobility (Harrison 1994). Driven by technological improvements, today's investments instantaneously link exchanges in remote geographical points. Designs for garments designed in New York and Los Angeles can be transmitted electronically to plants in Mexico or Taiwan, and the first batches of the product can be received in San Francisco or Miami in a week's time. Such developments mark an unprecedented leap in the scale and character of capitalist operations.

To many observers these processes seem overwhelmingly on the side of groups best able to tap the new technologies and turn globalization into an apotheosis of the market over its adversaries, be they state managers or union leaders. Nevertheless, this all-embracing conclusion should be greeted with skepticism. More than an era of unrestrained capitalism, the revolution that we are witnessing announces a variety of responses and countervailing arrangements. The rise of transnational communities is one such emerging phenomenon.

In this chapter we attempt a twofold objective: to summarize current knowledge about transnational communities and to examine their ramifications for social justice, mainly in Latin America and the United States. Although there is now a promising literature on the subject, an analysis of the effects of transnational communities on resource distribution and social justice has not been attempted. Here we make a step in that direction. We argue that transnational communities are incipient but powerful forces that oppose the more visible manifestations of globalization, including the growing imbalance between capital and labor.[1] In an effort to systematize our discussion, we give attention to the types, origins, and effects of transnational networks.

The increasing integration of the world economy since the late 1960s—when advances in technology and transportation enabled investors to move productive operations from advanced to less-developed countries—dealt a severe blow to workers' organizations on both ends of the geopolitical spectrum (Fernández-Kelly 2000). In poor nations, the establishment of export-processing zones and the implementation of drastic neoliberal policies thwarted workers' attempts to mobilize effectively. In rich countries, like the United States, globalization brought about rapid declines in union membership even as average wages stagnated. Thus, the tendency toward world economic integration is a two-pronged process. From an economic point of view, it contributes to the realization of profit through the reduction of production costs and returns to labor. As a political trend, it represents a massive realignment in the balance of power between capitalists and workers in favor of the former (Fernández-Kelly 1983; 2000).

Attempts to create international trade unions and pressure national governments to impose labor standards on Third World exports have been among the reactions to globalization. Both efforts have proven ineffective because the competitive realities of the world economy undermine fledgling class solidarity along national lines (Portes 1994). Nevertheless, unionization and regulation are only two possibilities in a larger array of responses to capitalist hegemony. At the local level, workers have not remained inert in the face of the onslaught. Instead, they have begun to create a field that sits astride political borders and that, in a real sense, is "neither here nor there," but in both places simultaneously. The economic activities that sustain these nascent communities are grounded on advantage differentials created by the same political boundaries that their members traverse on a regular basis. In that respect, they are no different from multinational corporations, except that they originate at the grass-roots level and their actions are often informal. Thus, capital's tendency to render international borders irrelevant from an economic point of view has paralleled a less-ballyhooed phenomenon entailing workers' strategies. Rapid changes in transportation and communications, as well as new cultural understandings about membership in "the global village," are redefining the migrant condition. With growing frequency, individuals live a divided existence in which home—the place of community and personal validation—and workplace—the locus of subsistence and competition—are separated by international borders.

Some observers warn that the heightened instrumental character of migration will have a deleterious effect on the capacity of the foreign-born to assimilate into receiving societies and become true citizens. Yet it is equally feasible to envision the same phenomenon as the harbinger of new forms of citizenship liberated from the antiquated constraints of the nation-state. In addition, transnational communities may afford vulnerable groups a certain degree of autonomy from the most exploitative aspects of capitalism—what Fernand Braudel calls the *antimarket*—by providing new channels for workers' subsistence and accumulation through commerce and entrepreneurship. Finally, social networks spanning international borders are constructing surprising alternatives to political participation within the nation-state and, in some cases, challenging entrenched structures of privilege. Keeping these ideas in mind, we offer below a conceptual discussion followed by an exploration of the origins and types of transnational communities.

### Origin and Variation

Transnational communities consist of social networks, formed through regular international travel, involving socioeconomic, political, and cultural exchanges required by stable occupations. The concept is emerging within the analytical repertoire with which we must approach the world system. It is also an element in a less-developed but important enterprise: building a midrange sociological theory to account for the everyday behaviors and relationships that form in and around international economic structures. Finally, the definition proposed above is part and parcel of an ongoing dialogue not free of conflict or equivocation. The two words at the center of the debate, *transnational* and *community*, have long assumed various, and sometimes contradictory, meanings. They suffer from ideational overload. The first term has been mostly applied to the activities of corporations, while the second has been used to designate social groups characterized by some degree of cohesion along one or more criteria. Both have been heatedly called into question for distorting as much as clarifying empirical realities.[2] Joining the two words to form a new concept raises new dilemmas.

Qualms about the precise meaning of *transnationalism* have continued to the present. According to a group of social scientists that pioneered inquiry in this field:

> "[T]ransnationalism" [is] the process by which migrants forge and sustain multi-stranded social relations that link together their societies of origin and settlement. We call these processes transnationalism to emphasize that many immigrants today build social fields that cross geographic, cultural, and political borders. [A]n essential element ... is the multiplicity of involvements that transmigrants sustain in both home and host societies. We are still groping for a language to describe these social locations (Basch, Glick Schiller, and Blanc-Szanton 1994: 6).

The statement above reflects not only a concern about terminological accuracy, but also a genuine puzzlement in the face of a wide array of phenomena associated with transnationalism. Here we opt for a limited understanding that focuses on the dual *directionality and regular character* of activities carried out by individuals and groups as they form domains of socioeconomic consequence across international demarcation lines. To understand variations in the characteristics of transnational communities, we also give attention to their *relationship to apparatuses of governance* in countries of origin and reception.

The dynamic character of transnational communities is aptly conveyed by an example offered by Smith (1992). He describes the reaction of members of the Ticuaní Potable Water Committee upon learning that the much-awaited tubing had arrived and with it the final solution to the town's water problem:

> They immediately made plans to inspect the newly installed equipment: On first sight, this is no more than an ordinary civic project. ... Yet when we consider certain other aspects of the scene, the meaning becomes quite different. The committee and I are not standing in Ticuani [Puebla], but rather at a busy intersection in Brooklyn. ... The Committee members are not simply going to the outskirts of the town to check the water tubes but rather they are headed to JFK airport for a Friday afternoon flight to Mexico City from which they will travel the five hours overland to their pueblo, consult with the authorities and contractors, and return by Monday afternoon to their jobs in New York City.

In a few sentences, Smith creates an image of individuals transcending borders as they engage in civic action. Churches and private charities have joined this movement between home country and immigrant communities with an expanding number of initiatives involving both. Such activities, however, would not be possible without the frequent involvement of migrants in binational economic activities. Finally, the phenomenon acquires a cultural dimension as performers, artists, and commentators use expatriate communities as platforms to break into the First World scene and as returnees popularize cultural forms learned abroad. Such are the multiple dimensions of transnational communities.

If conditions confronting today's immigrants were similar to those faced by their U.S.-bound European predecessors at the turn of the century, it is unlikely that they would have moved so decisively in the direction of transnational enterprise as a means of survival and mobility. That earlier period featured two significant conditions different from those existing today. First, a plethora of relatively well-paying jobs in industry; second, costly and time-consuming long-distance transportation. The first condition militated against widespread entrepreneurial ventures and gave rise over time to stable working-class communities. Most Poles and Italians in the United States, to name but two instances, became workers and not entrepreneurs because labor market opportunities in the American industrial cities in which they arrived made this an attractive, and often the only, option. At present, most migrants continue to work in low-skilled menial occupations either in factories or, more typically, in services. Yet the decline of the manufacturing economy has restricted their capacity to increase earnings even as globalization has opened new alternatives to wage labor.

Similarly, at the turn of the century, the state of communication and transportation technology was such as to make it prohibitive for ordinary migrants to span national divides on a regular basis. No commuting across the Pacific was possible. No means were available for Polish peasants to check how things were going at home over the weekend and be back at their New York jobs by Monday. Although some activities that could be dubbed *transnational* did occur among earlier European immigrants, the present moment differs with respect to the quantity and quality of the activities entailed. Airplanes, telephones, fax machines, and electronic mail facilitate contact and exchange among common people on a scale incommensurate with that of the past. Given the multitude of incentives, more immigrants are becoming involved in transnational activities. People from Latin America and the Caribbean, who constitute a growing proportion of migrants to the United States, experience particular advantages because of their proximity and continued familiarity with everything American. Once it begins, transnationalism can become cumulative so that, at any particular time, it can turn into a normative process not only among pioneers, but also among those initially reluctant to follow in their path. Immigrant communities, like the ones formed by the Chinese in Monterey Park near Los Angeles, and some towns in El Salvador and the Dominican Republic are examples of rampant transnationalism.

Not all transnational communities are alike. Peggy Levitt (2000) discusses the diversity of contents and purposes in the activities they promote and calls attention to the distinction between personal intent and communal effect. Individual actors may be transnational with respect to some aspects of their lives and not others. They may earn their sustenance across borders but remain aloof of political participation in either country. They may display loyalty to the institutions and mores of their country of destination but depend mostly for their existence on religious or other cultural demands in their country of origin. They may divide their time evenly between nations in order to finance small businesses in their hometowns. They may opt for a dual citizenship to retain visibility and "voice" in two different political contexts. When a substantial number of individuals sharing common characteristics systematically engages in one or more of such activities, a transnational community is born. It is the patterned effect of these collective actions that matters to theory and empirical research.

The end result of this cumulative process is the transformation of pioneering economic ventures into transnational networks densely woven across space by an increasing number of people who lead dual lives. Members are at least bilingual, move easily between different cultures, frequently maintain residence in two countries, and pursue economic, political, and cultural interests that require a simultaneous presence at home and abroad. The same forces driving large-scale capitalist endeavors nurture this process, but the results at the local level are filled with surprises that can subvert the established economic order. Marx described the proletariat as created and placed into the historical scene by its future class adversaries; in a similar vein, global capitalism has given rise to conditions and incentives to make labor transnational.

A shared nationality and/or ethnic identity are frequently associated with the formation of transnational communities. Nevertheless, other criteria may be involved as well. For example, in her study of Laleli, a commercial district in Istanbul, Hatice Deniz Yenal (2000) notices the vigorous flow of shuttle traders, marked by a multiplicity of national origins but unified by a similar identity, as women engaged in commerce.

Mostly from Russia, but having other Eastern European backgrounds as well, these women perceive themselves, and are perceived by others, as members of the same group. As such, they often depend on one another to build the relationships of trust and reciprocity needed to negotiate transactions in less-than-friendly environments. The elements that create and maintain community cohesion vary from case to case.

The effects of class and gender are equally significant. Whether collective activities spanning international boundaries result in accumulation or mere subsistence depends upon various factors, most significantly the material resources available to individuals and groups, their capacity to forge and deploy personal contacts, and their position within households and collectivities. Thus, the experience of Egyptian entrepreneurs able to finance lucrative earthenware factories in their home country by working half a year as cab drivers in New York contrasts with that of the *Natashas*, studied by Yenal (2000), who must hustle meager profits driven by the economic collapse of the Soviet bloc.

It is important to observe, in addition, that not all immigrants are involved in transnational activities and these do not affect everyone in countries of origin. The sudden popularity of the term could make it appear as if everybody is "going transnational," which is far from being the case. In this sense, little is gained by the relabeling of immigrants as *transmigrants,* since the new term adds nothing to what is already known. As discussed above, it is preferable to use *transnational* for activities of an economic, political, and cultural sort that require the involvement of participants on a regular basis and as a major part of their occupations. It is also pertinent to distinguish at least two categories of transnational migrants: entrepreneurs and those involved mostly in the provision of services. Hence, the Salvadoran merchant who travels regularly back home to replenish supplies or the Dominican builder who comes periodically to New York to advertise among his compatriots are transnational entrepreneurs. The immigrant who buys one of those houses or the one who travels home yearly bearing gifts for his family and friends is not.

Finally, the very existence of transnational communities depends on government's capacity and willingness to regulate economic and political behavior. Particularly enlightening in this respect is Yenal's reminder that transnational activities have always flourished in the interstices of large economic or political structures. For example, the lively trade promoted by the Genoese across the Black Sea in the thirteenth century thrived in between the fragmentation and eventual demise of the Byzantine empire, on the one hand, and the rise of the Ottoman empire on the other. Similarly, the emergence of autonomous trade networks in

Central and South America before the Spanish conquest was related to the waning power of the Aztec and Inca empires (Chase-Dunn 1997). Following Braudel, Yenal observes that genuine capitalist formations rely extensively on the social arrangements imposed by national states. They are, in other words, antithetical to the market as imagined by orthodox economists. Economic integration on a global scale and liberalization policies have begun to reconfigure, if not diminish, the capacity of states to subject workers to the impositions of organized capitalism. Transnational communities, with their propensity to rely on informal economic transactions, may be the most important manifestation of that trend. We further consider the paradoxical connections between transnational communities and their capitalist context in the next section.

## Immigration and Transnationalism

Symbiosis rather than hostility characterizes the relationship between transnational communities and preexisting economic and political structures. Here we argue that: (1) transnational communities are tied to the logic of capitalism itself; (2) they represent a distinct phenomenon at variance with traditional patterns of immigrant adaptation; and (3) because they are fueled by the dynamics of globalization, they have greater growth potential and offer a broader field for autonomous popular initiatives than other ways of dealing with the depredations of world-roaming capital.

The public in advanced countries has been conditioned to believe that contemporary immigration stems from the desperate quest of Third World peoples trying to escape poverty at home. The facts are vastly more complex. It is not the poorest of the poor who migrate.[3] Although it is true that factors internal to sending countries have fueled migration, other external forces have been even more important. For example, the introduction of mechanized agriculture in the Mexican countryside led to the displacement of workers, many of whom ended up seeking jobs in the United States. On the other hand, agricultural firms in California and other states in the West and far South have assiduously recruited Mexicans for more than a century. Mexicans, as well, have been continuously exposed to a barrage of media messages promoting desirable styles of life and consumer expectations. In other words, two major forces rooted in the dynamics of capitalist expansion have driven contemporary immigration: first, the labor demands of First World economies and second, the widespread diffusion in peripheral countries of standards of consumption and cultural patterns generated in advanced societies.

Other contributing factors stemming from advanced countries have played a part as well. A combination of social and historical developments has led to acute labor scarcities in rich nations. Some of the shortages are absolute, as in the dearth of industrial workers in Japan and the deficits in certain professions, like nursing and engineering in the United States. In some instances the scarcities arise from cultural expectations as manifested by the resistance of native-born workers to accept low-paid and menial jobs commonly performed by migrants in the past (Piore 1990; Gans 1992; Portes and Guarnizo 1991). The list of such stigmatized occupations is long and includes, among others, agricultural stoop labor, domestic and other personal services, food preparation in restaurants, and work in sweatshops (Sassen 1989).

Because of trade union and public opposition, the continuation of the immigrant labor flow has often taken place surreptitiously. In the United States, one of the latest episodes in a long and contentious history was the passage of the 1986 Immigration Reform and Control Act (IRCA) in reaction to outcries about increases in the number of unauthorized entries. This piece of legislation reflects with clarity the resilient need for immigrant labor and the enduring power of employer associations. Instead of reducing the volume of immigration, the 1986 law actually allowed its increase through several ingenious loopholes.[4]

By 1990 the foreign-born population of the United States had reached almost twenty million, the largest absolute total in the century (Fix and Passel 1991; Rumbaut 1994). The IRCA's legislated loopholes, in addition to new generous provisions in the 1990 Immigration Act, virtually guarantee that this absolute number, and the proportion that immigrants represent as part of the U.S. population, will increase significantly in the years to come. In Germany and France, despite the official termination of the foreign guest worker program in the 1970s, immigrant communities have continued to grow through a variety of legal ploys and clandestine channels (Zolberg 1989; Hollifield 1994). Today Germany has a foreign population of seven million, or roughly 9 percent of the total, a proportion quite similar to that in the United States (Münz and Ulrich 1995; Bade 1995). Even in ethnically homogeneous Japan, labor scarcity has prompted a variety of lawful subterfuges including the use of foreign company "trainees" and visa overstayers to perform industrial jobs. By 1990 the foreign-born population of Japan numbered about 1.1 million, still an insignificant percentage of the total population, but expected to more than double during the next decade (Cornelius 1992; 1994).

The flip side of the coin entails the effects of globalization on the supply of immigrants. The drive of multinational capital to expand markets in the periphery and, simultaneously, to take advantage of its reserves of labor has had a series of social consequences. Among them are the reconfiguration of popular culture and the introduction of new consumption standards bearing little relation to local wage levels. This process simultaneously socializes future immigrants with respect to expectations of lives abroad, and increases the drive to move across the gap between local realities and imported desires. But not everyone is susceptible to becoming an immigrant. The poorest of the poor remain excluded from networks and environments where pertinent information about, and necessary resources for, migration exist. It is working- and middle-class sectors that are most exposed to marketing messages and cultural stimuli beamed from the centers (Grasmuck and Pessar 1991; Portes and Bach 1985). Thus, migration from poor to rich countries is driven by the structural requirements of advanced capitalist accumulation. As such, the presence of Third World people in cities of the developed world can be confidently expected to endure and expand. Immigrants provide the raw material out of which transnational communities emerge.

De facto open immigration policies and industrial relocation strategies are complementary aspects of contemporary capitalism. The first enable investors to tap into a reserve of pliant, low-cost labor of strategic importance in certain sectors of production in First World countries, especially those requiring rapid handling of products and proximity to local markets. Agriculture, construction, landscaping, and some types of garment manufacture are examples. In other cases, where nearness to consumers is not critical and products can withstand lengthy storage or long-distance transportation, investments move abroad, into regions where other pools of pliable, inexpensive labor are available. Electronics, auto-transport equipment, and certain kinds of apparel are examples.

Whether as migrants away from their hometowns, or as operators in export-processing zones, individuals are not passive objects of exploitation, but agents who can comprehend, use, and try to subvert the social arrangements in which they are enmeshed. José Itzigsohn (1994) shows how workers in the Dominican Republic become informal entrepreneurs in order to assuage drudgery and improve the minimal pay available from jobs in the industrial-export sector. In the Dominican context, the informal economy becomes, paradoxically, a means of popular resistance against the designs of foreign capital.[5] The entrepreneurial impulse is not solely an effect of the new global order, but also a way to upend some of its deleterious consequences. Immigrants, as well, soon become aware that the remuneration and labor conditions in store for them in the advanced world do not go far in promoting their personal economic goals. To bypass the dead-end jobs that the host society assigns them, they activate personal contacts. Immigrant networks display two characteristics generally absent among domestic workers. First, they are simultaneously dense and extended over long physical distances. Second, they tend to generate solidarity by virtue of generalized insecurity.

Exchange under conditions of uncertainty creates stronger bonds than those formed under the auspices of full information and impartially enforced rules. This sociological principle, established both in field studies and experiential observation, applies particularly well to immigrant communities (Kollock 1994). Economic transactions, both internal and with outsiders, tend to occur on the basis of little knowledge about the reliability of buyers and sellers, or the character and dependability of government regulation. Once trustworthiness has been established with a set of partners, incertitude about external actors reinforces the need to "stick together," regardless of tempting outside opportunities that may, nonetheless, present additional costs and dangers.

The reliance of immigrants on social networks is not new. A rich literature, which grew in breadth and insight during the 1980s and 1990s, points to the benefits of sociability among foreign-born populations in various areas of destination. Thick, cohesive, and geographically spread-out, those networks can facilitate economic initiatives and bolster the negotiating potential of individuals and groups. In one such instance, highlighted by Sassen (1994), they led to long-distance labor transactions in which job opportunities in faraway locations were identified and appropriated. In another, described by Min Zhou (1992), they eventuated in the pooling of resources to lower consumption costs and produce enough savings for business or real estate acquisition. In a third case, extensively studied by Light (1984) and his associates (Light and Bonacich 1988), they enabled the creation of informal credit associations where pooled savings were allocated on a rotating basis. A fourth such initiative consisted of appropriating the price and information differentials between sending and receiving countries through the creation of transnational businesses. This fourth strategy—an antecedent of newer forms of transnationalism—is not necessarily incompatible with the others, but is distinct in that it depends on exchanges that occur across political borders. To be feasible, such transactions require highly resilient networks to insure timely supplies, deliveries, and payments under conditions where little or no external regulation exists. In the past, these variegated forms of exchange have been typical of the immigrant experience. Recently, however, they have expanded in frequency and scope.

Grass-roots transnational enterprise benefits from the same set of technological innovations in communications and transportation that underlie large-scale industrial restructuring. A class of immigrant transnational entrepreneurs that shuttles regularly between countries and maintains daily contact with events and activities in the two settings could not exist without these new technologies and the expanded choices and lower costs that they make possible. More generally, this popular response to global restructuring does not necessarily emerge in opposition to broader economic forces, but in an opportunistic relationship to them. Thus, shuttle traders join global commercial circuits imitating and adapting imaginatively to the new economic circumstances.

In the same vein, transnational enterprises are not set up in explicit confrontation to the designs of large banks and corporations. What the world-ranging activities of these major actors do is provide examples, incentives, and technical means for common people to attempt novel and previously unimagined alternatives. By combining their new technological prowess with mobilization of their social capital, former immigrant workers are able to imitate corporate entities by taking advantage of economic opportunities unequally distributed in space.

Nevertheless, the parallel between the strategies of dominant economic actors and immigrant entrepreneurs is only partial. Both make extensive use of advanced technology and both depend on price and information differentials across borders. But, while corporations rely primarily on their financial muscle to make such ventures feasible, immigrant entrepreneurs depend almost entirely on social capital (Guarnizo 1992; Zhou and Bankston 1994). The social networks that underlie such popular initiatives are constructed through a protracted and difficult process of adaptation to a foreign society. Transnational entrepreneurs expand and thicken, in a cumulative process, the web of social ties that makes their activities possible. The internal complexity (texture) of networks and firms grounded simultaneously in two countries eventually leads to a qualitatively distinct phenomenon that represents the terminal point of inquiry in this chapter.

## Building Transnational Communities

The Dominican Republic is literally dotted with hundreds of small- and medium-sized enterprises founded and operated by former immigrants to the United States. They include small factories, commercial establishments of various types, and financial agencies. What makes these businesses transnational is not so much that former immigrants created them, but that their existence depends on continuing ties to the United

States. A study of 113 such firms conducted in the late 1980s found that their mean initial capital investment was only $12,000 (U.S. here and *passim*), but that approximately half continued to receive periodic capital transfers from abroad averaging $5,400. Kin and friends residing in the United States, who were also partners in or co-owners of the firms, issued the remittances. In addition to capital, many firms received transfers in kind, producer goods, or commodities for sale (Portes and Guarnizo 1990: 116).

In the course of fieldwork, Portes and Guarnizo have identified a second mechanism for capital replenishment, namely, owners' periodic trips abroad to encourage new potential immigrant investors. Factory owners and managers use these trips to sell parts of their production abroad. Proprietors of small garment firms, for example, regularly travel to Puerto Rico, Miami, and New York to sell their wares. It is common practice to have a prearranged verbal agreement with buyers abroad, including small clothing stores. On their way back to the Dominican Republic, the informal exporters fill their empty suitcases with inputs needed for business, such as garment designs, fabric, and needles.

In a similar vein, Freeman (1999) describes the class- and gender-based dimensions of transnational communities in Trinidad. Young women, employed in telemarketing offices contracted by U.S. airline companies to process accounts, receive small wages and are subjected to extreme forms of supervision. They are, in every sense, proletarians. Nevertheless, in an effort to upgrade their self-image and dissociate from other factory workers, these women invest heavily in uniforms and suits meant to convey a professional look. Unable to finance their wardrobes with their meager earnings, they borrow the money necessary to travel regularly to New York and acquire garments for later sale in their home country. Their involvement in an informal economy that transcends geographical limits bolsters their participation in formal enterprises and subsidizes the cost of their own reproduction.

The cases sketched above share several features. To the untrained eye, loaded-down international travelers appear to be common migrants visiting and bearing gifts for their relatives back home. In reality, they are engaged in an expanding form of transnational trade that escapes government regulation. The information requirements for this dense traffic are invariably transmitted through kin and friendship networks spanning the distance between places of origin and destination. The men and women who operate firms or trade in clothing and other items are not *return immigrants* in the traditional sense of the phrase. Instead, they make use of their time abroad to build a base of property, bank accounts, and business contacts from which to organize their return home. The result is not final departure from the United States, but a cyclical back-and-forth movement through which the transnational entrepreneur makes use of differential economic opportunities spread across both countries .

The dynamism of transnational enterprise contrasts with prevalent governmental misunderstanding or ignorance of the phenomenon. Accustomed to think about migration as a unidirectional flow from poor to rich countries, and saddled with outdated legislation, public officials in the Dominican Republic and the United States are mostly interested in the size and channeling of immigrant remittances. They seem unaware of, or unable to deal with, the intense entrepreneurial activity they reflect.

Research conducted during the last three years in the capital city of Santo Domingo reveals how returned immigrants have pioneered a number of business lines based on ideas and skills learned in the United States. These include fast food, home delivery, computer software, and video stores. They also sell and rent cellular phones, and detail automobiles among other ventures. Meanwhile, executives of the Dominican construction industry admit that many of their firms could not survive without demand for second homes and business space from Dominicans abroad. Entire new sections of the city, especially in the west and near the international airport, have been built with immigrants in mind.[6] Popular lore has even found a name for this population: *dominicanos ausentes* (absent Dominicans) or Dominican Yorkers (because of their concentration in New York City). By and large, the Dominican state in the past has been indifferent to and generally unaware of these developments (Guarnizo 1994). The contrast between vigorous business transactions and legislative immobility points to the lack of correspondence between economic and political structures in the contemporary world.

Levitt (2000) provides further evidence regarding the extent to which areas in the Dominican Republic have become transnationalized. Migration from the village of Miraflores to Boston, which began in the late 1960s, eventually produced a transnational community. By 1994, over 65 percent of the 445 households in that village had relatives in the greater Boston metropolitan area. Almost 60 percent of those households received at least some of their monthly income from contacts in the United States, and, for nearly 40 percent of them, remittances constituted between 75 and 100 percent of their total income. By contrast, only 31 percent of households in Miraflores depended on money earned solely in the Dominican Republic. Not surprisingly, the avalanche of resources has transformed life at the local level. Many houses have been renovated and filled with the clothes, appliances, toys, and foods that migrants bring back.

Like the Dominican Republic, El Salvador is a country deeply influenced by the transnational activities of its expatriate communities. In this case, out-migration was initially prompted by a violent civil war that sent enough Salvadorans out of the country to decisively alter the country's economic and social fabric. By 1996, remittances had mounted to approximately $1.26 billion, exceeding the sum total of the country's exports (Landolt 1997). The influence of Salvadoran transnational enterprises goes well beyond this figure. Major travel and package delivery firms have grown out of small informal concerns to service the manifold needs of the immigrant community and their counterparts at home. Immigrant capital has funded everything from new Tex-Mex food stands in the capital city of San Salvador to well-stocked computer software and video stores both in the capital and in provincial cities such as San Miguel.[7] In turn, Salvadoran banks and major businesses have come to see the large immigrant concentration in cities like Los Angeles as a new market and a means of rapid expansion. Thus, the *Constancia* Bottling Company, a beer and soft drinks concern, set up a plant in Los Angeles to cater to the needs of the immigrant population. Similarly, the Salvadoran Cámara Salvadoreña de la Industria de la Construcción (Chamber of the Construction Industry, CASALCO) has held real estate fairs in Los Angeles, seeking to expand the already sizable demand for new housing from Salvadorans abroad. As in the Dominican Republic, expatriates have also acquired a new name in Salvadoran culture, *el hermano lejano* (the distant brother). Having access to the solidarity and resources of such "brethren" has become a vital means of survival, not only for families, but also for entire communities.

Because of their origins in a harsh civil war, and perhaps because of their mostly rural backgrounds, Salvadorans abroad maintain strong emotional ties with their hometowns. Dozens of *comités de pueblo* (town committees) have sprung up in Los Angeles, Washington,D.C., and Houston to support the respective communities and advance local development projects. Patricia Landolt (1997: 20) summarizes the significance of such efforts: Akin to the contrast between families that receive remittances and those that do not is the difference in the level of prosperity between municipalities obtaining this "grassroots transnational aid" and those deprived of it. Towns with namesake associations abroad commonly have paved roads and electricity. Their soccer teams have better equipment, fancier outfits, and perhaps even a well-kept field where they practice. In other words, transnational communities can be a powerful mechanism to combat certain kinds of inequalities but can also exacerbate imbalances in the distribution of resources at the local level.

A comparable story, but with a unique cultural twist, is told by David Kyle (1994) in his study of the Otavalan communities in the highlands of Ecuador. Populated by indigenous Ecuadorans, Otavalo has specialized in the production and marketing of woolens, entailing the adaptation of production skills learned long ago under Spanish colonial rule. In the last quarter of a century or so, Otavalans have taken to traveling abroad to market their colorful wares in the major cities of Europe and North America. By doing so, they have bypassed intermediaries, thus pocketing the profits usually made elsewhere by middlemen linking Third World producers and final consumers. After years of traveling abroad, Otavalans have also brought back to their hometowns a wealth of novelties from the advanced countries, including newcomers. It is not uncommon to see European women donning indigenous attire in the streets of Otavalo— they are the wives of transnational traders who met them abroad and took them back to Ecuador from their long-distance journeys.

During the same period, semipermanent Otavalan enclaves have begun to appear abroad. As a distinct feature, their dwellers are not providers of wage labor, or even self-employed. They are, instead, traders of goods produced in Ecuador who maintain constant communication with their hometowns in order to replenish supplies, monitor their *telares* (garment shops), and buy land. The back-and-forth movement required by these exchanges has turned Otavalans into a familiar sight, not only at the Quito airport, but also in street fairs in New York, Paris, Amsterdam, and other large cities. According to Kyle, Otavalans have even discovered the commercial value of their folklore and, in recent years, groups of indigenous musicians have fanned out through the streets of First World cities. The sale of colorful ponchos and other woolen items in tandem with the plaintive sounds of the *quena* flute have yielded large profits, and the effects are visible at the grass-roots level.

Otavalans are unique among indigenous populations in their level of home ownership and conspicuous consumption which reverses the traditional dominance of whites and mestizos. Abroad, their economic success translates into the almost universal refusal to accept wage labor. Although hardly engaged in a deliberate movement to redress inequality, they have used entrepreneurial know-how and community bonds to subvert the predicted effects of globalization.

A final example involves immigrant communities of considerably greater economic power. The very growth of Asian populations in the United States, particularly the Chinese, has created opportunities for moneyed entrepreneurs from Taiwan and Hong Kong to invest profitably in the United States and, in the process, become part of a transnational community. Smith and Zhou (1995) explain how the rapid growth of Chinese home ownership in the New York suburb of Flushing has been largely financed by new Chinese banks established with Taiwanese and Hong Kong capital. The rapidly growing Chinese population, extending to adjacent cities in the borough of Queens, is highly oriented toward home ownership, but lacks the knowledge of English and credentials necessary to seek credit from mainstream institutions. To meet the burgeoning demand for housing loans processed in their own language, entrepreneurs have gone to Taiwan and Hong Kong to pool capital for new banks, and new immigrants have come to the United States bearing the necessary resources. As a result, Chinese-owned banks have proliferated in Flushing. Although small by conventional standards, they simultaneously serve the economic interests of the immigrant community and their overseas investors.

Three thousand miles to the west, the city of Monterey Park, California has been transformed into the "first suburban Chinatown" largely by the activities of well-heeled newcomers. Many Taiwanese and Hong Kong entrepreneurs established businesses in the area less for immediate profit than as a hedge against political instability and the threat of a Chinese Communist takeover. Opening a new business in the United States facilitates obtaining permanent-resident status and many owners bring their families along to live in Monterey Park, while they themselves continue to commute across the Pacific. The activities of the *astronauts,* as these entrepreneurs are dubbed locally, add a new layer of complexity to their transnational community. In this instance, returned immigrants do not invest U.S.-accumulated savings in new enterprises at home, but, rather, immigrants bring new capital to invest in firms in the United States. The birth of a child on American soil guarantees U.S. citizenship and anchors the family definitively in its new setting. As a result of the twin processes of successful investments and citizenship acquisition, Chinese immigrants have moved swiftly from the status of marginal newcomers in Monterey Park to the core of the city's business class.

We have dwelled on these examples at some length as a step to suggest the political ramifications of phenomena that, when initially described, strain the imagination. A multitude of similar examples can be brought forth, as illustrated by the pioneering collection by Linda G. Basch and her collaborators (Basch, Glick Schiller and Blanc-Szanton 1994). The central point is this: once begun, transnationalization acquires a cumulative character expanding not only in numbers, but also in the quality of activities encompassed. Hence, while the original propeller of these activities may be economic and their initiators can be properly labeled *transnational entrepreneurs,* subsequent developments encompass political, social, and cultural events as well. New York's former Mayor

Rudolf Giuliani's tour through the Dominican Republic in the wake of Hurricane George is but one instance of the political consequences of transnationalism, a theme we give further attention in the next section.

### Compliance, Subversion, and the Role of the Nation-State

The ways in which individuals distribute their resources and loyalties between their sending and receiving countries is, in part, determined by the kinds of institutional opportunities available to them (Levitt 2000). Alerted by the initiatives of immigrant entrepreneurs, political parties and even governments have established offices abroad to canvass immigrant communities for financial and electoral support. Not to be outdone, many immigrant groups organize political committees to lobby the home government or, as in the case of multiple Salvadoran and Dominican immigrant initiatives, to influence local municipalities on various issues. Transnational communities, formed by Mixtec Indians, have emerged in Mexico and Northern California and are built around a common ethnic identity and experience of oppression in both geographical settings (Rivera-Salgado 1999). Mexican immigrants in New York City have organized vigorous campaigns in support of public officials in their respective towns or challenged the long-held dominance of the *Partido Revolucionario Institucional*, Mexico's ruling party (Portes 1999).

As a result of these and other developments, governments in sending nations have begun to perceive their expatriate communities not just as sources of remittances, but as a possible fountain of investments, entrepreneurial initiatives, markets, and political representation. Many have initiated or implemented policies to grant citizens abroad dual citizenship as part of efforts to enable their political involvement at home. Seven of the ten countries sending the most immigrants to the United States between 1981 and 1986 now allow some form of dual citizenship. Some seventy nations, including Canada, Italy, Israel, South Africa, and New Zealand, allow their citizens to retain or regain their citizenship or nationality after becoming naturalized in another nation (Levitt 2000). This is in striking deviation from earlier times, when immigrants were seen almost as defectors, and when naturalization in a different country entailed the automatic loss of citizenship in the country of birth.

Equally impressive are the initiatives carried out by Third World governments to reap economic and political benefits from expatriate communities. They range from a specialized ministry of government department in Haiti and Mexico, the granting of dual citizenship and right to vote in national elections in Colombia, to new legislation allowing the election of representatives of the diaspora to the national legislature in Colombia and the Dominican Republic. Consulates of Mexico, Colombia, El Salvador, Guatemala, and the Dominican Republic have sprouted in areas where nationals from these countries concentrate in the United States. Paradoxically, they promote the acquisition of U.S. citizenship or permanent residence as a strategy to establish a firm foothold beyond the Mexican border. In like fashion, some governments have extended their reach in order to support their citizens' claims for political asylum abroad. That is the case of the governments of El Salvador and Guatemala, whose actions are a tacit admission of repression and persecution at home.

Despite the nascent efforts of national states to bring into the fold their expatriate communities, transnational migrants are quick to see and overturn subterfuges. For example, many Mexicans leave their country partly as a result of their frustration with a corrupt and negligent bureaucracy and are therefore unwilling to vow loyalty to the political elite of their country. In fact, transnational migrants may use the new opportunities offered by dual citizenship or the right to vote to express their dissatisfaction with established political orders. The delays in granting Mexicans abroad the right to participate in national elections seem to be related to fears on the part of public officials that their co-nationals in the United States may support opposition parties in Mexico. Thus, the interaction between transnational communities and the attempts at seduction from national states is fraught with potential tensions.

### Conclusion: Limits and Potential of Transnational Communities

In this chapter, we have made a first attempt to consider dimensions of transnationalism that will have an impact on structures of justice and inequality. We have argued that the same forces that have led to a growing integration of the world economic system drive transnational communities. This process, however, is not static but dialectic. Transnational networks maintain an opportunistic relationship vis-à-vis capitalism, taking advantage of interstices in the margins of hegemonic investments and state action. Paradoxically, transnational communities often subvert established orders of inequality by providing immigrants with alternatives to exploitative wage labor. At the same time, the economic and redistributive effects of transnationalism are not unidirectional or self-evident.

The long-term potential of the tranationalization of labor runs not only against growing international inequalities of wealth and power, but also against internal disparities in countries of origin. The process weakens the hegemony of corporate economic elites and domestic ruling classes. That premise, noted at the outset of this chapter, is that labor and subordinate workers should remain local, while dominant groups range globally. So far the process has not run its course to the extent of threatening Third World labor supplies for runaway multinationals or the abundance of immigrant workers for employers in the advanced world. Yet it has gained sufficient momentum to earn the attention of authorities in small nations like El Salvador and in large countries like Mexico, where policies have begun to be designed to control or co-opt these grass-roots ventures.

If, in the short term, transnational enterprise can become an equalizing force, it can also have the opposite effect in the long run. We have noted several reasons for the growing disparities between sending localities that receive a large volume of remittances, or possess civic committees among their migrants, and those that do not. Pioneering transnational entrepreneurs who have become successful favor their own families and perhaps their home communities but, at the same time, seek to restrict competition from others. Similarly, political activists who have mobilized support among immigrants strengthen their own parties at home while trying to prevent others from gaining access to the same resources. Hence, to the extent that the process of transnationalization is short-circuited by the regulatory or co-optive activities of established elites, it may simply incorporate a minority of successful entrepreneurs into the privileged ranks while continuing to exclude others. Inequalities among Third World families and local communities could be exacerbated, not reduced, by the transnational activities of immigrants.

There is reason, however, to be optimistic about the overall effects of this trend. Despite the anticipated, indeed inevitable, co-optive and controlling attempts of sending governments and transnational corporations, the process of capitalist globalization is so broadly based and has generated such momentum as to continuously nourish its grass-roots counterpart. Every new attempt to market wireless telephones, internet access, or cheaper airline tickets in less-developed countries, and every effort of employers in New York or Los Angeles to resupply themselves with new pools of docile migrant labor strengthens this feedback process. The targets of such initiatives are not simply "customers" or "laborers," but individuals capable of reacting creatively to the new situation in which they find themselves.

Multinational elites and national governments may believe that the process of transnationalization from below is still too feeble to pose any significant challenges to the status quo. In reality, the tiger may have left the cage already, and there would be little point in closing it after that.

## Notes

1. The concept of transnationality, like that of globalization itself, presents numerous risks because it threatens to become one of those passing fads that grips popular attention for a short while only to fade into oblivion. We contend, however, that there is enough real substance in the phenomenon at hand to make its use worthwhile.
2. For a more extended discussion of related conceptual issues see Dowd (1978).
3. Sassen (1989) has developed a variant of this argument where runaway industries located in peripheral export-processing zones promote migration by presocializing their workforces in First World cultural practices. Most of the labor force in these industries consists of young women who are routinely dismissed after only a few years. The combination of acquired skills, new aspirations learned during employment, and ejection from the local labor force transforms them into a ready pool of potential migrants. Sassen provides little empirical evidence, but subsequent research in a number of Latin American countries indicates that Sassen's thesis has some validity. See Pérez-Sáinz (1994); Itzigsohn (1994).
4. Some 2.5 million formerly unauthorized aliens were legalized under IRCA. Subsequent legislation contained generous provisions for newly legalized immigrants to bring their relatives. More important, IRCA retained a large loophole allowing for the continuation of the unauthorized flow: it required employers to check prospective workers' documents but not to establish their validity. As may have been predicted, a massive fraudulent-documents industry sprang up to service the new immigrants and their employers (Bach and Brill 1991). More recent legislative attempts to control immigration, such as Proposition 187 in California and a new act implemented by the U.S. Congress in 1996, promise to fare no better.
5. Past analyses of the informal sector in peripheral countries have shown it to be an efficient tool for decreasing costs and increasing flexibility for large formal firms. These studies assumed a regulatory framework, enforced by the state, that protected workers and simultaneously constrained employers. That framework has largely evaporated in the new export-production zones, where workers are subjected to much harsher conditions. It is this surrender of the regulatory powers of the state that is redefining the character and meaning of popular informal enterprise in many Third World cities.
6. This is based on interviews conducted by Alejandro Portes and a research team headed by Professor Carlos Dore of the Latin American School of Social Sciences (Facultad Latinoamericana de las Ciencias Sociales, FLACSO) in the Dominican Republic during the fall of 1996.
7. This brief summary is based on interviews with informants in the Salvadoran communities of Washington, D.C. and Los Angeles and in two major sending cities in El Salvador itself, San Salvador, the capital, and San Miguel. Interviews were conducted by a field team led by Patricia Landolt of Johns Hopkins University and Luis E. Guarnizo of the University of California–Davis in cooperation with the *Fundación Nacional para el Desarrollo* (FUNDE, National Development Foundation), a Salvadoran nongovernmental research organization. The Salvadoran research team was led by Mario Lungo and Sonia Baires. These interviews are part of a comparative project led by Alejandro Portes.

## References

Bach, Robert L., and Howard Brill. 1991. *Impact of IRCA on the U.S. Labor Market and Economy*. Report to the U.S. Department of Labor, Institute for Research on International Labor. Binghamton: State University of New York.

Basch, Linda G., Nina Glick Schiller, and Cristina Blanc-Szanton. 1994. *Nations Unbound: Transnational Projects, Post-Colonial Predicaments, and De-Territorialized Nation-States*. Langhorne, Pa.: Gordon and Breach.

Chase-Dunn, Christopher. 1997. *Rise and Demise: Comparing World-Systems*. Boulder, Colo.: Westview Press.

Cornelius, Wayne A. 1992. "Controlling Illegal Immigration: Lessons from Japan and

Spain." Working Paper, Center for U.S.-Mexico Studies. San Diego: University of California.

———. 1994. "Japan: The Illusion of Immigration Control." In *Controlling Immigration: A Global Perspective,* edited by Philip L. Martin, Wayne A. Cornelius, and James F. Hollifield. Stanford, Calif.: Stanford University Press.

Dowd, Douglas. 1978. "Continuity, Change and Tension in Global Capitalism." In *Social Change in the Capitalist World Economy,* edited by B.H. Kaplan. Beverly Hills, Calif.: Sage Publications.

Fernández-Kelly, Patricia. 1983. *For We Are Sold, I and My People: Women and Industry in Mexico's Frontier.* Albany: State University of New York Press.

———. 2000. "The Future of Gender: Economic Transformation and Changing Definitions." In *Understanding Societies,* edited by York Bradshaw and Joseph F. Healey. Thousand Oaks, Calif.: Pine Forge Press.

Fix, Michael, and Jeffrey S. Passel. 1991. "The Door Remains Open: Recent Immigration to the United States and a Preliminary Analysis of the Immigration Act of 1990." Working Paper, The Urban Institute and the Rand Corporation.

Freeman, Carla. 1999. *High Heels and High Tech.* Durham, N.C.: Duke University Press.

Gans, Herbert. 1992. "Second Generation Decline: Scenarios for the Economic and Ethnic Futures of the Post–1965 American Immigrants." *Ethnic and Racial Studies* 15 (April): 173–92.

Grasmuck, Sherri, and Patricia Pessar. 1991. *Between Two Islands: Dominican International Migration.* Berkeley: University of California Press.

Guarnizo, Luis E. 1992. "One Country in Two: Dominican-Owned Firms in the United States and the Dominican Republic." Ph.D. dissertation, Department of Sociology, Johns Hopkins University.

———. 1994. "Los 'Dominican Yorkers': The Making of a Binational Society." *Annals of the American Academy of Political and Social Science* 533: 70–86.

Harrrison, Bennett. 1994. *Lean and Mean: The Changing Landscape of Corporate Power in the Age of Flexibility.* New York: Guilford Press.

Hollifield, James F. 1994. "Immigration and Republicanism in France." Pp. 143–75 in *Controlling Immigration: A Global Perspective,* edited by Philip L. Martin, Wayne A. Cornelius, and James F. Hollifield. Stanford, Calif.: Stanford University Press.

Itzigsohn, José A. 1994. "The Informal Economy in Santo Domingo and San Jose: A Comparative Study." Ph.D. dissertation. Department of Sociology, Johns Hopkins University.

Kollock, Peter. 1994. "The Emergence of Exchange Structures: An Experimental Study of Uncertainty, Commitment and Trust." *American Journal of Sociology* 100, no. 2 (September): 313–45.

Kyle, David. 1994. "The Transnational Peasant: The Social Structures of Economic Migration from the Ecuadoran Andes." Ph.D. dissertation, Department of Sociology, Johns Hopkins University.

Landolt, Patricia. 1997. "Transnational Communities: An Overview of Recent Evidence from Colombia, Dominican Republic and El Salvador." Report to the Program in Comparative and International Development, Department of Sociology, Johns Hopkins University.

Levitt, Peggy. 2000. "Transnational Migration and Development—A Case of Two for the Price of One?" Working Paper no. 00-02-I. Princeton, N.J.: Center for Migration and Development, Princeton University.

Light, Ivan. 1984. "Immigrant and Ethnic Enterprise in North America." *Ethnic and Racial Studies* 7 (April): 195-216.

Light, Ivan, and Edna Bonacich. 1998. *Immigrant Entrepreneurs: Koreans in Los Angeles 1965–1982.* Berkeley: University of California Press.

Münz, Rainer, and Rolf Ulrich. 1995. "Changing Patterns of Migration, the Case of Germany, 1945–1994." Paper delivered at the German–American Migration and Refugee Policy Group, American Academy of Arts and Sciences, Cambridge, Mass., March 23–6.

Pérez-Sáinz, Juan Pablo. 1994. *El dilema del Nahual.* San Jose: FLACO Editores.

Piore, Michael J. 1990. "Labor Standards and Business Strategies." Pp. 35–49 in *Labor Standards and Development in the Global Economy.* Washington, D.C.: U.S. Department of Labor.

———. 1994. "Bypassing the Rules: The Dialectics of Labour Standards and

Informalization in Less Developed Countries." In *International Labour Standards and Economic Independence*, Edited by W. Sensenberger and D. Campbell. Geneva: Institute for Labour Studies (ILO).

———. 1999. "Towards a New World—The Origins and Effects of Transnational Activities." *Ethnic and Racial Studies* 22, no. 2 (March).

———, and Robert L. Bach. 1985. *Latin Journey: Cuban and Mexican Immigrants in the United States*. Berkeley: University of California Press.

———, and Luis E. Guarnizo. 1991. "Tropical Capitalists: U.S.–Bound Immigration and Small Enterprise Development in the Dominican Republic." Pp. 101–31 in *Migration, Remittances, and Small Business Development: Mexico and Caribbean Basin Countries*, edited by Sergio Díaz-Briquets and Sidney Weintraub. Boulder, Colo.: Westview Press.

Rivera-Salgado, Gaspar. 1999. "Political Organizing across the U.S.-Mexican Border: The Experience of Mexican Indigenous Migrant Workers." Workshop on Comparative Immigration and Integration Program Research. San Diego: University of California.

Rumbaut, Rubén G. 1994. "The Crucible Within: Ethnic Identity, Self-Esteem, and Segmented Assimilation among Children of Immigrants." *International Migration Review* 28: 748–98.

Sassen, Saskia. 1989. "New York City's Informal Economy." Pp. 60–77 in *The Informal Economy: Studies in Advanced and Less Developed Countries*, edited by A. Portes, M. Castells, and L. A. Benton. Baltimore, Md.: Johns Hopkins University Press.

———. 1994. "Immigration and Local Labor Markets." In *The Econimic Sociology of Immigration: Essay in Networks, Ethnicity, and Entrepreneurship*, edited by A. Portes. New York: Rusell Sage Foundation.

Smith, Christopher, and Min Zhou. 1995. "Flushing: Capital and Community in a Transnational Neighborhood." Author Manuscript. New York: Russell Sage Foundation.

Smith, Robert C. 1992. *"Los Ausentes Siempre Presentes*: The Imagining, Making, and Politics of a Transnational Community between New York City and Ticuani, Puebla." Author Manuscript. New York: Institute for Latin American and Iberian Studies, Columbia University (October).

Yenal, Hatice Deniz. 2000. "Shuttles Weave a Transnational Market: Informal Trade Between Turkey and the Former Soviet Union."Ph.D. dissertation, Department of Sociology, State University of New York at Binghamton.

Zhou, Min. 1992. *New York's Chinatown: The Socioeconomic Potential of an Urban Enclave*. Philadelphia: Temple University Press.

———, and Carl L. Bankston. 1994. "Entrepreneurship: An Alternative Path to Economic Mobility for Asian Americans." In *Asian American Almanac*, edited by I. Natividad. Columbus, Ohio: Gale Research.

Zolberg, Aristide R. 1989. "The Next Waves: Migration Theory for a Changing World." *International Migration Review* 23, no. 3 (fall): 403–30.

# part III.

# *Gender, Sexuality, and Social Rights*

# 8

# Guatemaltecas:
# The Politics of Gender and Democratization

*Susan A. Berger*

Between 1978 and 1985, the Guatemalan government destroyed approximately 440 villages, killed some 200,000 citizens, and left over 100,000 children orphaned, 150,000 refugees in Mexican camps, and some one million people internally displaced. Responding to this repression and the ensuing economic crisis, *Guatemaltecas* (Guatemalan women) organized to defend their rights as mothers, wives, and daughters, in accordance with traditional gender roles. They demanded to know the whereabouts of disappeared husbands, fathers, and children; decried forced military recruitment; called for land for the dispossessed; and organized cooperatives to better feed their families (Smith-Ayala 1991: 163). Most of these activist women participated in mixed-gender organizations, *not* women's organizations as such, for they did not actively question the patriarchal order or pursue gender equity.

Beginning with the return of civilian rule in 1986, however, women slowly began to demand a reconfiguration of public and private spheres: they insisted upon their gendered participation in the peace accords negotiations; called for legislative and educational reforms to enhance gender equality; sought the engendering of state policy-making; held forums on domestic violence; and lobbied for the establishment of women's studies programs in the universities.

*Guatemaltecas* began to address a broadened range of concerns for several reasons. First, they had gained new political skills from their participation in mixed-gender organizations during the previous decade. Second, many women had experienced severe gender discrimination and/or violence during that same decade either from the state, the male-dominated society, or from their male colleagues within the social movements. Third, the lessening of authoritarian tactics after 1986 and the signing of the peace accords in 1996 generated a gender-friendly political opening. Fourth, Guatemalan women had increasing contact with foreign women's groups through regional and Latin American

*Encuentros* and international conferences (Saporta Steinbach et al. 1992). Fifth, international nongovernmental organizations (NGOs) became interested in funding women's organizations in Guatemala. And finally, the state's adoption of a neoliberal "modernization" program had the effect, if not the intent, of encouraging women to discuss identity issues.

By the time the peace accords were signed in December 1996, ending a thirty-year war between the government and the *Unidad Revolucionaria Nacional Guatemalteca* (Guatemalan National Revolutionary Unity, URNG), it appeared as if women and women's organizations in Guatemala had actually created a movement. In the process, women shifted their focus from what Molyneux (1985) calls practical concerns to strategic interests as well; that is, from preoccupation with class issues to preoccupation with gender equality.[1]

The evolution of the Guatemalan women's movement is not quite so linear, though. A closer analysis reveals the contradictory nature of women's collective action. *Guatemalteca* organizations, at times, do challenge dominant ideologies, structures, and power relations, but, at other times, they help to strengthen and validate the existing order (Schild 1998: 95). Thus, while the Guatemalan women's movement is participating in the negotiations to redefine political space and citizenship in Guatemala, the movement is also being shaped by the cultural-political manifestations of the state's neoliberal project.

Much has been written about social movements in Latin America during the last decade. When social movements were first spotted on the Latin America landscape, the responses of prodemocratic activists and academics alike were almost unanimously positive: The movements would reinvigorate civil society and advance the conception of democracy by decentering politics and political power and by changing how politics were done. More recent studies, however, have begun to examine the contradictory nature of social movements and the roles of globalization—and two of its Latin American faces, neoliberalism and NGOization—in shaping, strengthening, and delimiting social movements. On the one hand, these trends have opened up new possibilities for social movements by facilitating the exchange of information and promoting supportive global-issue networks (Keck and Sikkink 1998). On the other hand, they have weakened and displaced movements as new definitions of citizenship have been introduced. For example, unlike the "passive" citizen associated with the post–Wold War II period, the neoliberal citizen must be economically self-reliant, participatory (in a procedural kind of way), and individualistic. Neoliberalism, the argument continues, is introducing new relations between government and society, as well as forms of civil society.

The lens provided by a study of the Guatemalan women's movement will help us to better understand what are in fact the complex and contradictory relationships among neoliberalism, NGOization, and social movements. My examination builds upon the complexity of these relationships and focuses on a series of questions: How has the Guatemalan women's movement cultivated spaces wherein different conceptions of citizenship and democracy have arisen? How has the state recruited material and cultural resources from *Guatemaltecas* to help it construct a new state form? How are women's organizations negotiating the social and political spaces carved out or being carved out by neoliberalism? Has the women's movement helped to destablize dominant cultural meanings and redefine issues of gender and citizenship? Are the state and/or the women's struggles advancing alternative concepts of modernity?[2]

### Women Under Military Rule, 1976–1985

Guatemalan women have a long history of public involvement. Such women as Dolores Bedoya de Molina (1783–1853) mobilized women to participate in the independence struggles; Vicente Laparra de la Cerda (1831–1905) edited an early women's newspaper, *La Voz de la Mujer* (The Voice of the Woman); and Ester de Urrutia (1892–1964) founded the *Alianza Femenina* (Feminine or Women's Alliance) between 1944 and 1954. Nonetheless, *Guatemaltecas* did not begin to mobilize in large numbers until the late 1970s and early 1980s. During this period, women initiated or joined mixed gender organizations to confront escalating state repression, the rising cost of living, and land grabbing by elites. Their main objectives were to protect and provide for their families, to meet practical family needs.

Women participated in three main types of organizations at that time: organizations that focused on human rights, economics, and radical social change. Women, for example, took a leading role in organizing human rights groups, demanding to know the fate of disappeared relatives. One such group, the *Grupo de Apoyo Mutuo* (Mutual Support Group, GAM), initially founded in 1984 by mestizas (mixed-ethnicity women) in the capital city, quickly became a more nationally representative mestizo/indigenous organization, with a membership approximately two-thirds Mayan (Schirmer 1988). Women were also active in peasant unions such as the *Comité de Unidad Campesina* (Committee for Peasant Unity, CUC) founded in 1978 to defend the political and economic rights of the peasantry and rural workers. Rigoberta Menchú, who won the Nobel Peace Prize in 1992, became one of its leaders (1998).

Other women helped to organize the Communities of the Population in Resistance (CPRs), which were composed of internally displaced citizens who had been forced to flee their villages when government repression became unbearable. In addition, women organized in the refugee camps in Mexico to improve living conditions. Women also joined the armed revolutionary group the URNG and its affiliates in the late 1970s and early 1980s to fight for social justice (Smith-Ayala 1991; Hooks 1991).

These organizations were clearly the outcome of a society's history. Repudiating authoritarian and hierarchical structures, most organizations set up directive bodies in which decisions were made collectively and offices were regularly rotated. As state repression mounted, the women's groups became increasingly confrontational. GAM members, for example, organized conferences, masses, and demonstrations, and they demanded meetings with the president, occupied the national palace, and directly accused the security forces of kidnapping their family members. On October 12, 1984, they led a 1,000 strong 19-kilometer march to publicize human rights abuses (Americas' Watch 1985). Most organizations began with little outside financial assistance except from the Catholic Church. Church support came in the form of small donations, permission to use Church facilities, training in leadership skills, and technical assistance. GAM, for example, held its first meeting in the home of the archbishop.

Women participated in these groups both as leaders and in the rank-and-file. In either case, the organizations involved both men and women, and subordinated gender to class concerns. Accordingly, they did not focus on specific women's demands. Nevertheless, the involvement of women outside the domestic sphere had political-cultural repercussions. First, women who participated in social movements during this period faced enormous obstacles not only from family members, but also from the state and the movements themselves. The state responded to civil mobilization with intense repression. The army resorted to gender-specific terror in the form of rape and other sexual abuse (Aron et al. 1990). GAM leader Rosario Godoy de Cuevas purportedly was raped before she was assassinated. Such experiences solidified women's opposition to the authoritarian regime and sensitized them to state gender biases.

Women also became incensed by gender discrimination within the revolutionary armed insurgent forces. Female recruits, for example, were initially relegated to domestic chores and prohibited from participating in active combat. One URNG recruit argued, however, "We never accepted that. We rebelled and began to demand other kinds of responsibilities, and the compañeros really let loose on us. They accused us of being comfortable and petit bourgeois, of not valuing domestic work—this was coming from our own compañeros!" (Smith-Ayala 1991: 212). Over time, women revolutionaries forced their male counterparts to distribute tasks more equitably.

In addition, participation in social movements helped to politicize women. Women activists not only learned basic political skills, but they also learned to demand their own rights. One participant in the CPRs noted,

> We've suffered, but we've also learned to solve our problems. And something we women have learned to do is stand up for our rights and be proud. It's something new and it is a little hard to do. Before women felt that because we couldn't read or write, we were only good for the kitchen, to take care of the children and all that. But now in the Communities in Resistance, we've seen a change in ourselves. Now many women are literacy workers, health promotion workers or catechists. Some young women who didn't want to be health workers or teachers, they wanted to work with a machete, so they went to work with the men. (Smith-Ayala 1991: 77)

Thus, while women mobilized during this period to meet practical needs, the boundary between practical and strategic interests was not clear-cut. Even at this early stage of collective involvement, some women questioned the patriarchal definition of citizenship and gender roles. They challenged the very cultural foundations of both state and civil society.

These incipient strains were strengthened by developments in the international arena. NGOs were not yet interested in Guatemalan women's issues, but beginning with the 1975 United Nations World Conference on Women held in Mexico, the Guatemalan government was slowly pulled into a series of international and regional conferences, convened to recommend reforms for the improvement of conditions for women. In 1981, upon the advice of the *Comisión Interamericana de Mujeres* (Interamerican Commission on Women) and the Central American Ministries of Labor, the Guatemalan government formed the *Oficina Nacional de la Mujer* (National Office of Women, ONAM) as the state watchdog on women's issues. Of course, ONAM's powers and financial resources were minuscule. However, the decision by the government to establish such an agency reflects an evolution of domestic and international pressure to "do something" about women. As I show later, women tried with time to utilize ONAM and other state agencies to reform the state from within, for their own ends.

## Democratization and Neoliberalism

In 1986, the military—impelled by the further deterioration of the economy, the expansion of civil discontent, and pressure from the international community—returned the government to civilian rule and began to rethink the relationship between state and civil society.[3] It oversaw the promulgation of a new constitution that pledged the democratization of state–civil society relations and, implicitly, the redefinition of citizenship by addressing gender for the first time. Articles 4, 47, and 52 called for the state to improve conditions for women.

The reconsidering of state-society relations became even more urgent as the Guatemalan state turned to neoliberalism in the 1990s. The state's neoliberal project began in earnest with the 1992 World Bank structural adjustment loan for $120 million (U.S., here and *passim*) and escalated rapidly with the signing of the peace accords. The state is thus attempting to utilize World Bank, Inter-American Development Bank, NGO, and foreign state loans and donations to "modernize" state and society and the relations between the two according to neoliberal dictums. World Bank financing has been obtained for projects in infrastructural privatization, public sector modernization, tax administration, technical assistance, and land administration; while Inter-American Development Bank projects include community development, road rehabilitation, and modernization and urban environmental programs (Ruthrauff and Carlson 1997).

As I show in this section, social movements had to adjust to these changes. The opening of political space allowed for the expansion of the gender debate and the formation of a variety of women's groups. The political opening and adoption of neoliberal reforms, however, also forced social movements in general, and the women's movement in particular, to reassess strategies and goals. Paradoxically, neoliberalism drew the state and the women's movement closer together. Increasingly, leaders of the women's movement became active in institutional politics, and many women's groups, financed by NGOs, began to do work previously done by the state.

The 1986 political opening induced a proliferation of women's groups—some feminist, some not. For example, in 1988 two of the first self-identified feminist organizations in Guatemala were formed: *Grupo Guatemalteco de Mujeres* (Guatemalan Women's Group, GGM) and the *Agrupación de Mujeres Tierra Viva* (Women's Gathering–Living Land). Both organizations were formed by a small number of mestiza middle-class professional women in Guatemala City. Many of the women had participated in prodemocracy social movements during the previous decade, and some of the founding members had exposure to feminism while in the university or in exile abroad. Both *Tierra Viva* and GGM began informally with discussions about women and their concerns. *Tierra Viva* ultimately decided to focus primarily on information gathering and dissemination in an attempt to influence societal understandings of gender issues. *Tierra Viva*, accordingly, runs a women's documentation center and holds conferences on women's health, education, and violence. It also publishes information on issues of concern to Guatemalan women (Pellecer 1998).

In contrast to *Tierra Viva*, the GGM has concentrated on providing services for women. At first, GGM opened a women's center, which offered social welfare, psychological, and legal services, but beginning in 1994, it focused exclusively on domestic violence. It opened one of only two women's shelters for victims of domestic violence in the country. The shelter can accommodate six women and their children, to whom it offers a wide range of material and psychological services. In response to threats against the shelter, GGM leaders became specialists in security issues (Lemus 1998).

While *Tierra Viva* and GGM at first relied on financing provided by their members, with time they both received international-NGO assistance. Unlike earlier mixed gender groups, neither *Tierra Viva* nor GGM received assistance, however, from the Catholic Church. Representatives from both feminist groups contend that the Catholic and Protestant churches impeded their work. GGM, for example, had to return a nine-year-old child who had suffered incest to the abusing father after a priest intervened and requested that the government legislate the return (Lemus 1998).

Other women's organizations evolved from the labor and indigenous movements. For example, in 1986 the labor confederation, the *Unión Sindical de Trabajadores de Guatemala* (Union of Guatemalan Workers, UNSITRAGUA) formed a women's committee composed of the wives of union leaders, called the *Grupo Femenina Pro-Mejoramiento Familiar* (Women's Group for Family Betterment, GRUFEPROMEFAM). The union's male leadership envisioned the committee as a support base for their initiatives. The committee however, had a different vision: it did a study of women in industrial plants; examined the origins of sexual discrimination in the plants; provided training for women workers; and assisted unionization efforts of women *maquila* workers. Ultimately, UNSITRAGUA presented an ultimatum to the committee: "do as we want or you won't get funding" (Rivas 1998). The committee responded by breaking with the union and organizing independently to work for the members' specific gendered labor concerns.

After gaining its independence, GRUFEPROMEFAM obtained financial assistance from a religious organization in the United States for leadership training sessions and other services for women unionists. Women labor unionists, nonetheless, faced many obstacles. Not only do governments and employers have a long tradition of brutally repressing unionism, but feminist labor leaders also faced machismo at home. Many activists lost both their jobs and their spouses. The costs of activism are enormous (Rivas 1998).

Women's organizations also proliferated in the countryside after 1986. Most of these organizations did not consider themselves to be feminist, but they were aware of gender inequities and struggled against them. Indigenous women in the highland province of Quiché, for example, formed the *Coordinadora Nacional de Viudas de Guatemala* (National Coordinator for Widows of Guatemala, CONAVIGUA) in 1988 around the motto: "For the dignity and unity of women, (we are) present in the struggle of the people." CONAVIGUA's stated objectives included:

> For women to participate, for our opinions to be taken seriously, for our dignity and rights as women to be respected. How is that accomplished? By participating in social, cultural and religious actions, and in larger marches and demonstrations called by USAP (Unidad de Acción Sindical y Popular), we show that women must also participate. (Schirmer 1993: 52)

CONAVIGUA fought from its inception for gendered ethnic justice. It did so in conjunction with campaigns against forced recruitment into the military and civil patrols, demands for the excavation of clandestine cemeteries, and programs that it sponsored in literacy training and physical and psychological health for women. CONAVIGUA subsequently demanded that rapes of Guatemalan women during the period of military repression be labeled crimes against humanity.

Many other women's organizations formed during the late 1980s and 1990s as well. The organizations were generally class, ethnic, and/or regionally specific. All of the organizations—feminist or not—tried to decentralize organizational structures and policy-making and initiated novel leadership structures. Collective directorates typically managed the groups, and positions of authority were rotated. In the more open political milieu and availability of international funding, the groups shifted their organizational strategies from confrontational to pragmatic-project politics. Many of the women's organizations implemented specific grassroots projects, such as the running of women's shelters, the providing of legal services to women, the helping of women to form a cooperative, and the construction of women's health clinics. Organizations have also begun to bring women into the political arena to fight for legislative and state policy reforms.[4]

By the beginning of 1990, international NGOs had made important inroads into funding *Guatemalteca* organizations and projects. Most groups were wary of such assistance because of the potential for NGO interference in project formation and implementation. However, they saw no other way to finance their projects, since government and church support was not forthcoming. Consequently, *Guatemalteca* activists contended that they would try to pick out the NGO with goals that best coincided with their own or the NGO that they believe would be the least intrusive. Despite their cautionary provisions, however, NGOs at times have influenced project form, staffing, and regulations contrary to the organization's liking (Lemus 1998; Pellecer 1998; Rivas 1998).

Meanwhile, the civilian state provided no financial assistance and little moral support to the fledgling women's organizations. The government, indeed, began to depend on the women's groups to help implement neoliberal reforms. Authorities, for example, would send victims of domestic abuse to the GGM shelter and rely on CONAVIGUA to offer literacy training to indigenous women, and on other women's rural organizations for development projects. At the same time, the state continued to underfinance ONAM and rejected legislative reforms proposed by the agency. Still, the state relied on ONAM to represent it to the international community and to project a state sympathetic to women. Women's groups responded to the state's use of ONAM by obtaining NGO funding to form the *Proyecto Mujer y Reformas Jurídica* (Project for Women and Legal Reforms). Lawyers who were associated with the *Proyecto* proposed upgrading ONAM from an "office" to a more powerful and autonomous "institute" and have also presented legislative reform bills on topics including education, labor, the civil code, and the penal code (Armas España 1998). Most of these proposals have been rejected by the government.

Until 1994, the women's movement had grown but consisted of many small independent groups, each with its own agenda. The groups came together only to coordinate special events, such as the activities for the International Day Against Violence Against Women. Predictably, factionalism also weakened the movement. The government could deal separately with each organization and sometimes pit the interests of one against those of another. And groups providing comparable services competed for the same limited range of domestic and international funding.

The year 1994 proved a watershed. That year Guatemalan women from diverse socioeconomic and political sectors united to form the

*Sector de Mujeres*, in a search for common ground as women. Representatives from thirty organizations—including *Tierra Viva*, GGM, GRUFEPROMEFAM, CUC, *Convergencia Cívico Política de Mujeres* (Women's Civic Political Convergence), and CONAVIGUA—and eight individuals without organizational affiliations participated in the sector. The sector represented the diversity of Guatemalan society well: indigenous, mestizas, middle class, working class, religious, academic, feminists, and nonfeminists. One of the goals of the Sector was to seek group consensus and to respect diversity (*Sector de Mujeres* n.d.: 3).

The formation of the *Sector de Mujeres* was a by-product of the peace negotiations between the government and the URNG. By the early 1990s, the Guatemalan government was convinced that neoliberal reforms could only be successful if political stability were restored by ending its lengthy war with leftist guerrillas. It agreed to enter into peace negotiations with the URNG in 1991. As peace negotiations progressed, women, along with other groups in civil society, demanded inclusion. Although not allowed to sit at the negotiating table, representatives from diverse social sectors, including youth, indigenous, refugee, peasant, and the working class, together formed the *Asamblea de la Sociedad Civil* (Civil-Society Assembly, ASC). The *Sector de Mujeres* represented women in the ASC. As state/URNG negotiations advanced, the *Sector de Mujeres* made suggestions to the ASC on each topic discussed. The ASC then debated and presented compromise proposals to the formal negotiators. Some of the recommendations were incorporated into the final peace accords. Compromise occurred at every step of the way: in the *Sector de Mujeres*, in the larger ASC, and in the negotiations between the government and the URNG.

Initially both left and right-wing political factions—inside and outside the ASC—questioned the need for a separate women's voice in the peace negotiations. Both viewed the women's movement as a foreign import. The right questioned the relevancy of the movement to "Guatemalan culture," and the left argued that gender issues might divide their supporters at a critical historical moment. Such resistance notwithstanding, *Guatemalteca* activists pressed for the formation of the *Sector de Mujeres* and its participation in the ASC.

The participation of the *Sector de Mujeres* in the ASC and the peace accords ultimately strengthened the women's movement and its causes of concern. It increased the national visibility of the movement, strengthened its internal organization, and helped it develop a multicultural, multiclass gender analysis. The *Sector de Mujeres* put gender-identity politics on the map, and secured a place for gender in the final peace accords, signed in December 1996. The final documents called for gender equality in the receipt of land, credit, and development assistance; the elimination of discrimination against indigenous women; support for gender equality in the home; equal rights for working women; gender equity in education; and opportunities for women in the armed forces. The accords also required the creation of the *Foro Nacional de la Mujer* (National Woman's Forum, FORO) to help "translate the accords into a platform of action that would include and make viable the completion of the compromises reached by the parties who had signed the accords" (Oficina Nacional de la Mujer and Proyecto Mujer y Reformas Jurídicas 1997: 16). Although the accords were sufficiently vague to allow for varied interpretations regarding implementation, many *Guatemalteca* activists saw the accords and the FORO as positive first steps toward achieving improved conditions for women.

While women and state authorities worked together, tensions persisted between them. Debates and political maneuverings that resulted in the formation of the FORO are revealing in this context. While the peace accords called for the formation of the FORO, it specified neither its structure nor how or by whom it would be formed. The women's movement, anxious that the government not be the one to dictate the organization of the FORO, immediately met and held workshops and conferences throughout the country to explain the peace process to women and to get feedback from them. Fearing that the women's movement was getting the upper hand, the government tried to take back the control of forming the FORO by appointing ONAM as the agency in charge of overseeing its formation. Nevertheless, with ideological allies in ONAM, and with a well-organized base, the women's movement and ONAM worked fairly quickly toward a consensus, which, if permitted, would have created a decentralized, participatory FORO structure. This was prevented by rapidly mounted high-ranking government opposition, which quickly substituted Secretaría de la Paz (Secretariat of the Peace, SEPAZ), the state agency charged with implementing the peace accords, as the official organ responsible for establishing the FORO.

Negotiations had to begin all over again. Although women activists felt that the government "was not interested in hearing any of the movement's points of view" (Marroquín 1997: 9), they persisted. Negotiators agreed to form a thirteen-member *Comisión Coordinadora* to design, promote, and organize the FORO, but the government at the last minute approved only a ten-member commission: six representatives from civil society and four from the government. The reduction eliminated representatives from the numerically smaller feminist organizations, which chose to withdraw rather than encourage infighting within the women's movement.

The commission and SEPAZ reached a compromise to organize a FORO based on elected delegations that would work in the country's twenty-two provinces and among twenty-four linguistic communities. Before the inauguration of the FORO, however, the government and SEPAZ installed a new commission, effectively overturning the newly reached agreement. The new commission, nevertheless, designed a FORO that maintained the multicultural component of the original plan. Six thousand women participated in local meetings that selected regional assemblies, from which delegates for the national assembly were selected. Inaugurated in November 1997, the FORO began a tedious process of reviewing state policies and legislation, and presenting to the government suggestions for improving conditions for women. The FORO has no mandated authority, and can only recommend changes for the executive branch to consider.

The unity gained by the women's movement during the peace negotiations helped sustain it through these arduous debates and numerous political maneuverings. The government was not, however, monolithic. Not all government representatives on the commission were anti–civil society or antifeminist. While some officials supported an antifeminist stance, others did not.

Still, from a feminist perspective, the process and outcome were disappointing. For one, representatives of feminist organizations were removed from FORO leadership. Second, the government's rigid antifeminist line prohibited the FORO from utilizing gender analysis or gender discourse (Moran 1998). Third, the government's deliberate tactics to stall the establishment of the FORO put the women's movement at a calendar disadvantage. According to the original accord implementation timetable, the accords were to be fully implemented by the year 2000, at which time all accord-related institutions, including the FORO, would be dismantled. Many women activists correctly believed that the FORO could not complete its tasks by that time. Subsequent changes in implementation deadlines have extended the life of the FORO, but the institution continues to lag behind completing stated tasks (Moran 1998).

While many *Guatemalteca* activists, especially feminists, quickly became disillusioned with the FORO, some have continued to work with it. They argue that the FORO represents the first official "space" that women have obtained, and that women must take it and mold it to their advantage (Moran 1998). They also contend that the FORO can continue to strengthen the women's movement, raise consciousness about gender inequities, and improve socioeconomic and political conditions for women (Moran 1998).

## Conclusion

The Guatemalan women's movement, in sum, demonstrates contradictory tendencies within the movement itself and in its relations with the government. As the government changed, so too did the movement. Democratization served not only to broaden, strengthen, and consolidate the movement, but also to contain and regulate it. With democratization, the government turned increasingly to legislative and bureaucratic structures to manage civil society, with mixed results for the women's movement. The government opened political space for the expansion of women's organizations and gender debates. Women, in the process, redefined gender rights, but government authorities have largely ignored women's legislative proposals.

At the same time, neoliberalism has had the unintended effect of generating new but controversial opportunities for women's groups. As the state tightened its fiscal belt, international funding for women's groups increased. Relying on NGO support, women's groups began to provide a range of social services on which the government, in turn, has come to rely. Women's groups in due course shifted from a strategy of confrontation to one of conciliation. They promoted information dissemination, project implementation, and political participation. Some women's constituencies also sought political and administrative office, contending that they could thereby best serve the development of civil society in general and of women in particular. By the end of the century, however, women remained underrepresented at all levels of government.

Disappointments and shortcomings of the movement notwithstanding, the analysis illustrates the symbiotic relationship between state and social-movement dynamics. Government structures and policies influenced the Guatemalan women's movement, but so too did women's groups influence state activity. Women have helped lay the bases for a multiclass and multicultural gender consensus for the future.

### Notes

1. While I refer here to collective actions of *Guatemaltecas* as a movement, I do recognize the problems in doing so. The Guatemalan women's movement is neither homogeneous nor united behind a single objective. It is factionalized by projects, ethnicity, class, and locale (Mijangos 1997). Still, I maintain that in the Guatemalan context it is appropriate to define these actions as a movement using Alberto Melucci's (1998: 424) conceptual framework that social movements are "always the outcome of a society's history, and in their empirical reality they are a highly heterogenous mixture of diverse patterns and levels of action."
2. This study relies heavily upon author interviews with Guatemalan women's activists, the publications of Guatemalan women's organizations, and the personal and organizational archives of movement activists. The author would like

to thank all the *Guatemaltecas* who so freely shared their experiences and records for this study.

3. Jane Jaquette (1991) notes that transitions from military dictatorships to democratic governments typically offer new opportunities, but set new constraints too.

4. The *Convergencia Cívicoa de Mujeres*, for example, was formed in 1994 to "encourage the involvement of women from various ideological perspectives, life and work experiences, skills and residences, in existing socio-political organizations or that such organizations be formed that meet the specific demands of women" (Agrupación de Mujeres Tierra Viva et al. 1996: 17).

# References

Agrupación de Mujeres Tierra Viva, et al. eds. 1996. *Poder, Liderazgo y Participación Política de las Mujeres*. Guatemala City: Tierra Viva.

Americas' Watch. 1985. *Guatemala: The Group for Mutual Support*. New York: America's Watch Committee.

Aron, Adrianne, Shawn Corne, Anthea Fursland, and Barbara Zelwer. 1990. "The Gender Specific Terror of El Salvador and Guatemala: Post Traumatic Stress Disorder of Central American Refugee Women." *Women's Studies International Forum* 14, nos. 1–2.

Hooks, Margaret. 1991. *Guatemalan Women Speak*. London: Catholic Institute for International Relations.

Jaquette, Jane, ed. 1991. *The Women's Movement in Latin America: Feminism and the Transition to Democracy*. Boulder, Colo.: Westview Press.

Keck, Margaret, E. and Kathryn Sikkink. 1998. "Transnational Advocacy Networks in the Movement Society." Pp. 217–38 in *The Social Movement Society*, edited by David Meyer and Sidney Tarrow. Lanham, Md.: Rowman and Littlefield Publishers.

Marroquin, Mafia Dolores. 1997. "Cumplimiento de los aeuerdos de paz en 10 relativo alas mujeres existen avances?" *Ut'z'ilal': Organo Informativo Asamblea de la Sociedad Civil* no. 2 (29 dieiembre): 9.

Melucci, Alberto. 1998. "Third World or Planetary Conflicts?" Pp. 424–29 in *Cultures of Politics/Politics of Cultures*, edited by Sonia Álvarez, Evelina Dagnino, and Árturo Escobar. Boulder, Colo.: Westview Press.

Menchú, Rigoberta. 1998. *Rigoberta: la nieta de los Mayas*. Madrid: Aguilar.

Mijangos, Eugenia. 1997. "La Organización de Genero y sus Perspectivos." *Debate* 1, no. 4: 29–31.

Molyneux, Maxine. 1985. "Mobilization Without Emancipation: Women's Interests, the State and Revolution in Nicaragua." *Feminist Studies* 11, no. 2: 227–254.

Oficina Nacional de la Mujer, and Proyecto Mujer y Reformas Jurídicas. 1997. *Las Obligaciones Legislativas a Factor de las Mujeres Derivadas de los Acuerdos de Paz*. Guatemala City: Proyecto Mujer y Reformas Jurídicas.

Ruthrauff, John, and Teresa Carlson. 1997. *A Guide to the Inter-American Development Bank and World Bank: Strategies for Guatemala 1997*. Silver Spring, Md.: Center for Democratic Education.

Saporta Sternback Nancy, Marysa Navarro-Aranguren, Patrieia Chuehryk, and Sonia Alvarez. 1992. "Feminisms in Latin America: From Bogota to San Bernadino." In *The Making of Social Movements in Latin America: Identity, Strategy, and Democracy*, edited by Arturo Eseobar and Sonia Alvarez. Boulder Colo.: Westview Press.

Schild, Veronica. 1998. "New Subjects of Rights? Women's Movements and the Construction of Citizenship in the 'New Democracies.'" Pp. 93–117 in *Cultures of Politics/Politics of Cultures*, edited by Sonia Alvarez, Evelina Dagnino, and Arturo Escobar. Boulder, Colo.: Westview Press.

Schirmer, Jennifer. 1993. "The Seeking of Truth and the Gendering of Consciousness." Pp. 30–64 in *Viva: Women and Popular Protest in Latin America*, edited by Sarah Radcliffe and Sallie Westwood. London: Routledge.

———. 1998. "'Those Who Die for Life Cannot Be Called Dead': Women and Human Rights Protests in Latin America." *Harvard Human Rights Yearbook* 1.

Sector de Mujeres. (N.d.) *Mujeres Construyendo la Paz*. Guatemala City: Programa de Mujeres.

Smith-Ayala, Emilie. 1991. *The Granddaughters of Ixmucane: Guatemalan Women Speak.* Toronto: Women's Press.

United Nations Development Fund for Women-United Nations Children Fund (UNIFEM -UNICEF). 1994. *Políticas públicas con perspectiva de genero en Centroamérica.* Guatemala City: UNIFEM-UNICEF.

————. 1996. *El sexismo en los textos escolares en Centroamérica.* Guatemala City: UNIFEM-UNICEF.

## Interviews

Armas España, Malvina, Proyecto Mujer y Reformas Jurídicas, May 19, 1998.

Asturias, Laura, editor, *La Cuerda*, May 20, 1998.

Cofiño, Ana Maria, editor, *La Cuerda*, May 20, 1998.

Lemus, Giovanna, Grupo Guatemalteco de Mujeres, May 20, 1998.

Montenegro, Nineth, chair of Comisión de la Mujer, el Menor y la Familia; member of Foro Nacional de la Mujer (FORO); and founder of Grupo de Apoyo Mutuo (Mutual Support Group, GAM), May 22, 1998.

Moran, Sandra, Sector de Mujeres, May 18, 1998.

Pellecer, Carmen Lucia, Tierra Viva, May 19, 1998.

Rivas, Olga, Grupo Femenina Pro-Mejoramiento Familiar (GRUFEPROMEFAM), May 22, 1998.

Rodriguez, Edna, Proyecto Mujer y Reformas Jurídicas, and Convergencia Cívico Política de Mujeres, May 19, 1998.

Sanchez, Blanca, Fundación Guatemala (FUNDAGUATE), May 21, 1998.

# 9

# Adjustment with a Woman's Face: Gender and Macroeconomic Policy at the World Bank

*Cynthia A. Wood*

The World Bank's policies for structural adjustment have been consistently criticized for the unequal distribution of their negative effects, or "social costs." Two major strands of this criticism are the poverty critique, articulated in UNICEF's (United Nations Children's Fund) *Adjustment with a Human Face* (Cornia, Jolly, and Stewart 1987c; 1988), and the gender critique, put forward in *The Invisible Adjustment: Poor Women and the Economic Crisis* (UNICEF 1989; see also Commonwealth Secretariat 1989).[1] However, the World Bank has responded to these critiques very differently. The Bank's many published analyses of the social costs of adjustment since 1987 deal almost exclusively with the poor. Gender inequalities in the costs of adjustment have not been addressed. While the poverty and gender critiques have much in common, they are not identical. The Bank's different responses to them thus have important implications for policy.

Because the Bank has shown increasing commitment to issues of gender and development in other areas of policy, the persistent lack of attention to gender in its analysis of structural adjustment requires an explanation. Much of this explanation must come from institutional and political analyses of the Bank that are beyond the scope of this chapter (see O'Brien et al. 2000: 24–66; Women's Eyes 1997).[2] However, such analyses are not enough; conceptual issues must also be addressed. I argue in this chapter that criticisms of the social costs of adjustment are given credence by macroeconomic policy makers at the Bank only to the degree that they can be framed in terms of the neoclassical economic paradigm that has dominated Bank lending for many years (Kapur, Lewis, and Webb 1997; Murphy 1995: 35). Arguments in *Adjustment with a Human Face*, which were so framed, were quickly addressed in official discussions of adjustment. In contrast, the gender and adjustment critique is not framed in neoclassical terms, and suggests instead that the paradigm is problematic. Consequently, the Bank disregards this literature even in its discussions of social costs and of compensatory measures to ameliorate those costs. The few Bank documents that discuss gender in the context of structural adjustment generally present only issues compatible with the paradigm and do not refer to the gender critique.

With continued pressure from critics, gender is beginning to enter Bank analysis of structural adjustment. However, many gender inequalities resulting from adjustment emerge in areas likely to be marginalized in neoclassical economics. I focus on one such area—unpaid domestic labor (or housework)—to show that the failure to consider issues excluded by the paradigm makes it likely that future macroeconomic policies emerging from the Bank will continue to be gender biased.[3] Furthermore, without attention to unpaid domestic labor and other issues incompatible with neoclassical theory, compensatory programs are unlikely to counter many gender inequalities in the effects of structural adjustment, and may worsen them in some cases. As long as the neoclassical paradigm domi-nates macroeconomic policy-making at the Bank, institutional changes and political pressure that encourage greater attention to gender will not, by themselves, eliminate gender bias in adjustment policies.

I base my argument on an examination of publicly available World Bank documents—formal publications, technical notes, and material on the Bank's external website—analyzing structural adjustment, the social costs of adjustment, and gender. I also analyze Bank documents that men-tion gender in the context of adjustment and other publications that demonstrate the Bank's position particularly well. My goal is to present an accurate picture of the Bank's analysis of structural adjustment and social costs using documents that together constitute its public discourse on the topic.[4]

After a description of structural adjustment policies, I briefly review the gender and adjustment literature. Next, I document the absence of gender in Bank analyses of structural adjustment and social costs, including a review of exceptions to this rule. I then illustrate the overall lack of discussion of adjustment in the Bank's gender analyses until the publication of *Engendering Development* (World Bank 2001b). I explain the Bank's failure to incorporate gender into macroeconomic policy-making through an exploration of the neoclassical paradigm, focusing on its exclusion of unpaid domestic labor. Finally, I discuss the success of the poverty critique in attracting Bank attention and implications for the future of gender analysis in Bank macroeconomic policy.

## Structural Adjustment and Compensatory Programs

From a neoclassical economic perspective, the problems faced by less-developed countries beginning with the debt crisis in the early 1980s were due to long-term interference with the market by individual governments (Mosley, Harrigan, and Toye 1991: 4–9; Commonwealth Secretariat 1989: 19–22). "Structural adjustment" was the process of correcting these market imbalances (Mosley, Harrigam, and Toye 1991: 23). Successful adjustment was signaled by market criteria: low inflation, competitive exchange rates, reductions in government spending, and a "microeconomic environment that is favorable to new investment" (World Bank 1990: 11).

Policies to achieve macroeconomic "stabilization" devalued exchange rates, cut consumption and government spending, and tightened monetary policy. The World Bank made loans conditional on changes in national economies, which increased the role of the market through trade liberalization, privatization, reduction of state involvement in the economy, and elimination of exchange-rate controls and subsidies on consumer goods and services (Mosley, Harrigan, and Toye 1991: i, 34). From the Bank's perspective, short-term recessional effects resulting from adjustment policies were transitional costs necessary to achieve the conditions needed for long-term growth (World Bank 1987: 6).

Rising unemployment, falling wages, widening income inequality, and increasing morbidity and mortality rates devastated countries that applied structural adjustment policies during and after the 1980s. Many argue that the long-term effects of these policies will be equally damaging (see Cornia, Jolly, and Stewart 1987c; 1988; Oxfam Policy Department 1995; SAPRIN 2001). In response to criticisms such as these, the Bank developed "compensatory programs," such as social emergency funds, which were designed to accompany adjustment and compensate vulnerable groups through targeted provision of income and social services (Vickers 1991; Benería and Mendoza 1995). The Bank eventually made social protection a condition of further loans (World Bank 1996). However, gender is not yet a factor in Bank evaluations of the social costs of adjustment, despite a substantial literature on the topic.

### Gender Critiques of Adjustment

Numerous presentations, articles, and books on gender and adjustment have appeared since 1987, several published by respected international agencies.[5] Most authors of these works are development practitioners or hold Ph.D.s in economics at universities, international agencies, or nongovernmental organizations (NGOs). Overviews of the literature highlight a few major points (see Cagatay, Elson, and Grown, 1995; Sparr 1994; Blackden and Morris-Hughes 1993; Vickers 1991: 15–42): (1) Structural adjustment policies are biased against women in conception, implementation, and evaluation; (2) the invisibility of this bias to policy makers at international agencies, such as the World Bank, is part of the problem and is reflected in the paucity of statistical data on the issue; (3) evidence consistently shows that women suffer more and gain less than men from adjustment policies.

At the conceptual level, many argue that the neoclassical underpinnings of adjustment policies are a major source of gender bias. There are many threads of this argument that I will be unable to discuss here. I focus on unpaid domestic labor because I believe that, in defining economic analysis in market terms, neoclassical theory is particularly resistant to the inclusion of such labor as an economic activity (see Wood 1997).

Critics argue that because neoclassical economics does not include unpaid domestic labor in its definition of economic activity, the effects of adjustment on such labor are invisible to Bank policy makers. Yet this labor is an important household resource, and must be considered if the effects of adjustment are to be understood fully. The substitution of unpaid domestic labor for market income and social services, in particular, is a major factor in the "success" of structural adjustment policies as defined by neoclassical policy makers (see Elson 1989: 57–58). This substitution occurred routinely as a direct result of structural adjustment policies in the 1980s and after; poor households used all available resources to adapt to worsening economic conditions. Since unpaid domestic labor is defined socially as "women's work," this particular effect of adjustment was not gender neutral. Women's workloads increased more than men's.

Quantitative data are difficult to find on unpaid domestic labor. Since it is not considered an economic activity, it is not measured in conventional economic surveys.[6] However, case studies and anecdotal evidence from NGOs and other sources suggest that adjustment increased the quantity and intensity of unpaid domestic labor. Women compensated for falling income by spending more time on day-to-day management of the household and by substituting unpaid work for commodities they could no longer afford. Searching for lower prices and cheaper substitutes to make a smaller income go further, women in Argentina, Mexico, and elsewhere went to more shops or markets, shopped more frequently, traveled farther from home, and spent more time checking prices (Feijoó and Jelin 1989: 39; Benería 1991: 175). Time spent seeking out loans or selling assets such as jewelry in response to lower income also increased (Moser 1989: 149; Stewart 1991: 1853). Women worked longer hours to produce what they could once buy, and had a lower quality of domestic equipment (Feijoó and Jelin 1989: 39; Benería 1991: 175; Waylen 1992: 158). They bought food that was less processed, which required that the processing be done at home, and spent more time gathering firewood and water (Commonwealth Secretariat 1989: 65). Repairs not made on items such as refrigerators increased cooking time (Benería 1991: 175; Moser 1989: 148).

Many adjustment policies directly increased women's domestic labor by cutting government funds to social services. Decreasing public expenditures on water, sanitation, and sewage made the search for potable water and the disposal of waste more difficult (Rocha et al. 1989: 27). As a result, illness became more common. Since many countries also cut spending on healthcare and subsidies on food as part of their adjustment program, women spent more time caring for the sick (see Cornia, Jolly, and Stewart 1987c; 29, 39; Commonwealth Secretariat 1989: 42; Waylen 1992: 159–60). Cutting clinic hours or shutting down clinics meant that women spent more time traveling or waiting in line with sick children. Raising or introducing charges for clinic visits meant that many could not afford to go at all.

Poor women found innovative ways to cope with reduced income and social services, such as communal kitchens in Peru, but these also often required increases in unpaid domestic labor (Jacobs 1991; Waylen 1992: 170–71; Commonwealth Secretariat 1989: 42). Even outside assistance to address the effects of structural adjustment on the poor increased women's unpaid work (Moser 1989: 158). Increases in adult women's workload overall resulted in girls staying home from school to take on domestic labor (Moser 1989: 154–55; Cornia, Jolly, and Stewart 1987c: 40).[7]

While the breadth and complexity of gender critiques of adjustment cannot be pursued here, this summary is enough for an examination of the World Bank's treatment of gender in its evaluation of structural adjustment policies. Almost without exception, Bank policy makers evaluating structural adjustment and their social costs do not measure, or even recognize, the effects of adjustment on women described in these critiques.

### Gender in the Bank's Analysis of Structural Adjustment

The Bank has not addressed gender critiques of its policies in publications devoted to adjustment or social costs. It fails for the most part even to acknowledge the existence of these critiques, in stark contrast to its response to *Adjustment with a Human Face*. Gender itself is marginal to the Bank's discussions of structural adjustment, as even some within the Bank have noted (Blackden and Morris-Hughes 1993: 16).

Consider a paper on "The Structural-Adjustment Debate," given in 1993 by Lawrence Summers, then chief economist of the World Bank.

According to Summers and his co-author, the paper "distill[s] the main lines of criticism levied against structural-adjustment programs to four critiques and assess[es] the validity of each" (Summers and Pritchett 1993: 383). Summers discusses the poverty critique, but does not refer either to gender or to the literature criticizing adjustment's effects on women. Since Summers was a major figure in the development of Bank policies for structural adjustment at the time, the absence of gender in his presentation is especially significant. His lack of attention indicates the Bank's general position.

A review of more recent Bank publications on structural adjustment and social costs demonstrates the continued failure to address gender in this area of analysis. In the overview *Structural and Sectoral Adjustment: World Bank Experience 1980–92*, there is only one brief reference to women (Jayarajah and Branson 1995: 177). The study *Social Dimensions of Adjustment: World Bank Experience, 1980–93*, supposedly a review document on social costs, "looks at all the evaluated adjustment operations supported by the Bank. . . . and tracks what happened to poverty and income distribution" (Jayarajah, Branson, and Sen 1996: xi). The review never refers to gender in the context of structural adjustment, nor does it analyze gender in terms of social costs. It mentions women only briefly in isolated comments (see 107, 111, 114, 118). While it is difficult to document the absence of attention, I have found no Bank analysis of adjustment or the social costs of adjustment that makes more than a passing reference to gender, with the exception of the documents discussed below.

The first exception is Paul Collier's (1993) work, which explains the impact of adjustment on women in terms of the constraints they face in earning income and differences in their consumption of certain public services. Collier's essay is significant in defining a legitimate space for gender in the World Bank's structural adjustment literature, as demonstrated by its appearance in a publication edited by senior economists, but this space is telling for what it excludes. He does not refer to the literature on gender and adjustment, which is important because it allows him to define both the problem and the solution to it in neoclassical terms, as I discuss below.

The second exception is an Africa Region Technical Note by C. Mark Blackden and Elizabeth Morris-Hughes (1993) entitled *Paradigm Postponed: Gender and Economic Adjustment in Sub-Saharan Africa*. Blackden and Morris-Hughes not only refer to gender critiques of adjustment, but also take this literature (and feminist economic theory) as their primary frame of reference in analyzing policies for structural adjustment. Research and policy recommendations of the multidonor Special

Program of Assistance for Africa (SPA), including a pilot Structural Adjustment and Gender in Africa (SAGA) initiative funded by the World Bank, are based in part on *Paradigm Postponed* (World Bank 1996; Blackden 1998).

However, no other publication in the Bank's literature on adjustment and social costs to date refers to *Paradigm Postponed*, nor does it appear in a collection or series indicating general acceptance among Bank economists responsible for macroeconomic policy, as Collier's work does (see also O'Brien et al. 2000: 56). Even *Adjustment in Africa, Reforms, Results, and the Road Ahead*, a formal Bank publication produced by the office of the chief economist in "close collaboration with the World Bank's Africa Region," fails to cite Blackden and Morris-Hughes, and makes only two brief comments on gender in the context of structural adjustment (World Bank 1994a: xv, 167–68, 174). In light of these indications of marginality, I consider *Paradigm Postponed* an "outlier" in the Bank's analysis of structural adjustment. Nevertheless, it is important as a published alternative to Collier's approach to gender and adjustment appearing within the Bank, and the application of this work by the Africa Region and the SPA models innovative macroeconomic analysis responsive to the gender critique of adjustment (see Blackden 1998).

Examining the exceptions to the general absence of gender in the Bank's macroeconomic analysis runs the risk of overstating their importance. The Bank's overviews of adjustment and social costs cite neither Collier's work nor *Paradigm Postponed* (e.g., Jayarajah and Branson 1995; Jayarajah, Branson, and Sen 1996; World Bank 2001a). Even combined with the work of the Africa Region and the SPA, these documents were not enough to bring about the incorporation of gender into the Bank's overall analysis of structural adjustment.

At the United Nations' 1995 Fourth World Conference on Women held in Beijing, James D. Wolfensohn, president of the World Bank, stated:

> A priority concern must be to ensure that women are not hurt by structural adjustment programs. I am well aware of the wide criticism of the Bank on this subject. I believe that a macroeconomic plan is crucial to development, but I will be vigilant and more sensitive to arguments which relate to disproportionate adverse social impacts on women. (Wolfensohn 1995)

Wolfensohn is known to be concerned with the social costs of adjustment and "is regarded by gender equity advocates both within and outside the Bank as a tremendous positive resource for change" (O'Brien et al. 2000: 53). Nevertheless, some years after the Beijing conference, there is little evidence that macroeconomic policy makers are paying serious attention to the effects of structural adjustment on women, except in the Africa Region, where interested and committed staff responded very early to the gender critique (see Women's Eyes 1997; O'Brien et al. 2000: 24–26).

## Structural Adjustment in the Bank's Analysis of Gender

Corresponding to the absence of gender from the Bank's analysis of structural adjustment is the lack of discussion of adjustment in its now-extensive work on gender. Bank staff working on gender are not directly involved in macroeconomic policy-making, so this is the less important of the two in the design of policies for structural adjustment. However, pressure exerted by staff interested in promoting or mandated to promote gender issues at the Bank could, at least theoretically, affect macroeconomic policy.[8] Unfortunately, serious pressure to incorporate gender into the Bank's analysis of structural adjustment is not obvious in Bank publications on gender. While unpublished internal pressure certainly exists, to date these efforts have failed to "engender" macroeconomic policy at the Bank. The recent publication of its Policy Research Report *Engendering Development* (World Bank 2001b) actually undermines the impetus to do so.

The Bank's literature on gender is devoted almost exclusively to project-based lending in areas of "social development," such as education, population, and health, so much so that adjustment policy must be seen as outside the purview of gender analysis as defined by the Bank, at least until *Engendering Development* (see Buvinic, Gwin, and Bates 1996: 2–4). In two World Bank studies, Josette Murphy reviews the Bank's "record of incorporating gender issues in the operations it supports" and discusses a total of eight hundred projects either implemented or approved between 1967 and 1996 (1995: xi, 1; 1997: 1). Neither study considers macroeconomic lending, and, other than a brief comment on the work of the SPA, Murphy does not mention structural adjustment (1995: 54; 1997: 15–16). Indirectly, she suggests that gender and macroeconomics are mutually exclusive: "The Bank's shift toward macroeconomic policy during the early 1980s made such issues as poverty alleviation and gender less immediate Bank concerns" (1995: 35).

A few exceptions to the general absence of structural adjustment in Bank discussions of gender exist before *Engendering Development*. In 1994, the first World Bank Policy Paper on women appeared: *Enhancing Women's Participation in Economic Development* (World Bank 1994b). Policy papers must be approved by the Bank's Board of Executive Directors and represent the Bank's official position, so it is especially significant that this document explicitly addresses the effects of structural adjustment on women: "In some countries and situations, . . . short-term adverse effects [of adjustment policies] may fall disproportionately on women" (World Bank 1994b: 66–67). It also states that "the beneficial effects of adjustment may be slow in reaching women" (68). These remarks constitute the Bank's first acknowledgment in an official document that adjustment may have adverse effects on women. Coupled with the statement that "[g]ender issues will be systematically addressed . . . in the design and implementation of lending programs, including adjustment operations" (13), they justify and even mandate analysis of gender and adjustment. Unfortunately, follow-through on this particular aspect of the policy paper has not been forthcoming. Even the Operational Policy statement accompanying the paper summarizes recommended policy changes without mentioning structural adjustment (World Bank 1994c).

Two Bank publications prepared for the United Nation's Beijing conference mention macroeconomic policy in the context of gender, but neither comments on actual or potential negative effects (see World Bank 1995a; World Bank 1995b). A progress report following Beijing devotes a section to "integrating gender into adjustment operations and economic reform" (World Bank 1996). This report acknowledges the gender critique of Bank policies, and suggests that "the design and implementation of [economic reform] programs . . . should take gender differences in needs, constraints and resources into consideration." However, the SPA's work is the only concrete example offered to support the assertion of Bank progress in this area. The majority of this section discusses poverty.

Again, documenting exceptions to the general absence of adjustment in the Bank's gender analysis makes them appear more important than they are. The Bank itself does not take these exceptions seriously. In *Mainstreaming Gender and Development in the World Bank: Progress and Recommendations*, Caroline N. Moser and her coauthors do not refer to structural adjustment in their comments on the documents analyzed above (Moser, Tornqvist, and van Bronkhorst 1999).[9]

The most recent publication on gender, *Engendering Development*, presents several pages on gender differences in the effects of structural adjustment, finally breaking the silence on this issue in gender analysis at the Bank (World Bank 2001b: 212–19). However, despite several promising suggestions for engendering macroeconomics and a call for more research, it seems likely that policy makers will find ample reason to ignore gender in the design and evaluation of adjustment policies in this statement: "While there is evidence to support both sides of the debate about the impact of structural adjustment, on balance the evidence suggests that females' absolute status and gender equality improved, not deteriorated, over the adjustment period" (215).

Further investigation is necessary to understand how the authors of the report came to a conclusion so contrary to the negative effects "exhaustively documented" in the existing gender and adjustment literature (World Bank 1998). It seems to be based primarily on the Bank's own research conducted for purposes of the report. [10] Despite acknowledging the existence of a debate and the legitimacy of many of its arguments, the report does not actually respond to specific gender critiques of adjustment. This is certainly due in part to the Bank's consistent dismissal of qualitative research as legitimate evidence (see World Bank 2001b: xiv). The conclusion bears scrutiny, in any case. For example, while the report finds that changes in women's life expectancy and girls' school enrollments over the adjustment period were more positive for adjusting than for nonadjusting countries, it assumes that these positive outcomes resulted from adjustment policy. Other potential explanations would suggest that these outcomes occurred despite, rather than because of, adjustment.[11]

### Explaining the Absence of Gender in the Bank's Analysis of Structural Adjustment

Why does the Bank fail to consider gender or the gender critique in its analysis of structural adjustment and social costs? My answer to this question is based on an analysis of the economic paradigm dominating macroeconomic policy-making. Neoclassical theory excludes or marginalizes issues central to a complete understanding of the effects of adjustment on women. As a result, even Bank economists committed to the elimination of gender inequality will produce gender-biased macroeconomic policies. Further, they will be unable to recognize that their policies are gender biased. This not only explains the absence of gender in the Bank's discussions of structural adjustment throughout the 1990s, but also predicts the outlines of gender bias in future macroeconomic policies that do recognize gender as a topic relevant to discussions of adjustment.

According to the World Bank charter, "it must lend only for productive purposes and must stimulate economic growth in the developing countries where it lends" (World Bank 1985: 3). The apparent neutrality of this goal obscures the implicit assumption of market criteria for defining legitimate boundaries for economic analysis and policy evaluation. In practice, for policy-making and lending at the Bank, "economic growth" refers to growth in the market sector, and market indicators are the only evidence necessary for measuring economic advance or decline. Neoclassical approaches to macroeconomics assert that free prices are the most efficient and desirable means to policy goals (World Bank 1991: 1). This approach has not been altered by the Bank's recent attention to poverty reduction and sustainable development, both of which it sees as defined by and best achieved through the market.

In light of gender critiques of the neoclassical paradigm, an evident problem with this focus on the market is that it ignores or marginalizes nonmarket economic activity such as unpaid domestic labor in the creation and evaluation of policy. Since the Bank defines productivity and economic growth in market terms, attention to unpaid labor in Bank policy would be incompatible with its goals. The emphasis on "getting prices right" also ensures that such labor remains invisible to policy makers. Macroeconomists do not look at unpaid domestic labor in their analyses of economic policy except in a few cases as a noneconomic factor explaining market behavior, because the paradigm does not allow them to do so.

Institutionalized attention to women in the analysis of development and policy does not prevent this exclusion. According to Nüket Kardam (1991: 79), policy makers within the Bank who wish to promote policy benefitting women have "taken care to make WID issues acceptable by framing them within economic rather than social welfare and equity arguments" (see also Razavi and Miller 1995: iv-v, 40; Murphy 1995: 44; Buvinic, Gwin, and Bates 1996: 73; Women's Eyes 1997; O'Brien et al. 2000: 48).

Gender research at the Bank is thus devoted to proving that there are economic (market) benefits from those projects targeting women or taking gender into account. For example, in 1992, Chief Economist Summers spoke at the Bank's annual meeting on the importance of girls' education in the process of development (1994). Summers suggests that "investment in girls' education may well be the highest return investment available in the developing world" (1).[12] However, the focus of this analysis is still the market, since "education is positively correlated with overall economic growth, with one year of schooling . . . leading to as much as 9 percent increase in GDP for the first three years of schooling" (Summers 1994: v). A primary argument in *Engendering Development* is that "[g]ender inequalities undermine the effectiveness of development policies" and that gender inequality "diminishes an economy's capacity to grow" (World Bank 2001b: xiii, 11).

If gender achieves legitimacy at the World Bank by being made acceptable to neoclassical economists, it follows that gender analysis that is not framed in neoclassical terms will be excluded. The theoretical framing of much of the gender and adjustment literature requires analysis of unpaid domestic labor as an economic activity. Since the neoclassical paradigm assumes a market definition of economic activity, discussions that analyze unpaid domestic labor in economic terms (i.e., as itself an economic activity rather than subsidiary to economic activity) will be marginalized.[13] Both because it is critical of the neoclassical paradigm and because it focuses on nonmarket issues, the gender critique is necessarily excluded from the Bank's analysis of structural adjustment.

More telling, perhaps, is the absence of gender itself. This absence cannot be completely explained by hostility to the gender and adjustment literature, because the topic could be discussed without reference to the literature. But if, as many gender critiques suggest, understanding the effects of structural adjustment on women requires a look at unpaid domestic labor, economic analyses of adjustment based on the neoclassical paradigm are hard-pressed to address the topic at all.

The few Bank documents that look at gender in the context of adjustment do not refer to unpaid domestic labor. In keeping with neoclassical economic analysis, these documents focus almost exclusively on the market repercussions of adjustment, differentiated by gender. According to *Enhancing Women's Participation in Economic Development*, for example, "[a]djustment policies typically remove price distortions and restore profitability of certain crops and activities, but women may not be able to take advantage of such beneficial changes unless their particular constraints are removed" (World Bank 1994b: 68). Similarly, most of Paul Collier's work analyzes the impact of adjustment on women in terms of the market (1993: 185–93). He looks at unpaid domestic labor only as it affects the allocation of women's time to market work, and gives no indication that structural adjustment has any effect on unpaid domestic labor itself (193–96). In its discussion of structural adjustment, *Engendering Development* refers to domestic labor only in terms of the impediments such labor imposes on women's ability to "participate fully in longer term economic opportunities associated with adjustment" (World Bank 2001b: 214).

While it is important to look at the market effects of structural adjustment policies on women, gender critiques highlight the centrality of unpaid domestic labor to understanding gender bias in adjustment. In this context, the absence of any reference to such labor in the Bank's few analyses of gender and adjustment is striking. Even if Bank policy makers believe these critiques to be flawed, their analyses should at least address the effects of adjustment on unpaid domestic labor, if only to give solid reasons for dismissing the importance of these effects.

*Paradigm Postponed* suggests that, for the Bank, "[t]he critical question is whether the distribution of costs (and benefits) of adjustment between men and women . . . is sufficiently important to make a difference to economic outcomes and prospects" (Blackden and Morris-Hughes 1993: 16). In other words, the Bank will show serious concern for gender inequality in the effects of adjustment only if an economic justification for such concern is provided. Since *economic* in a neoclassical context refers to the market, Bank statements to the effect that "the effective integration of gender concerns into the design and implementation of reform measures can lead to improved performance outcomes" do not imply that the Bank will consider the effects of adjustment on unpaid labor, except perhaps as instrumental to improving market indicators (World Bank 1996). To the degree that the gender bias of structural adjustment policies derives from their effects on unpaid domestic labor or some other topic excluded from neoclassical economics, future policy will thus remain gender biased.

### Adjustment with a Human Face

The World Bank addressed the poverty critique of structural adjustment policies almost immediately, and in most ways the social-cost literature can still be seen as defined by that critique. How can this difference in reception be explained? According to Joan Nelson (1989: 95), *Adjustment with a Human Face* "focused and legitimized concerns that had been mounting in many quarters." For the Bank's macroeconomic policy makers, legitimization entailed making concerns over the effects of adjustment policy on the poor consistent with neoclassical economic theory.

*Adjustment with a Human Face* was intentionally framed to appeal to a neoclassical perspective: "From the start, it was clear that practical advance toward adjustment with a human face would only be possible if it attracted the understanding and support of those in the mainstream of economic policy-making" (Cornia, Jolly, and Stewart 1987a: 3). The authors did not question the need for structural adjustment, and they highlighted the "economic" reason for their concern—the long-term and irreversible damage to "human resources" that occurs with increasing poverty (Cornia, Jolly, and Stewart. 1987a: 5–6). Concern over the social costs of adjustment from this perspective is legitimized by the potential for falling rates of growth resulting from lost (human) resources.

However, criticisms of structural adjustment policy that were not translated into the neoclassical economic paradigm were not addressed. The Bank never took seriously, for example, the argument that "the appropriate adjustment may not be . . . in the national economies where the major and unsustainable imbalances emerge, but in the international conditions which give rise to them" (Cornia, Jolly, and Stewart 1987b:

133). From the Bank's perspective, *Adjustment with a Human Face* was a warning about the dangers of disinvestment in human capital, a warning that demanded no more than minor changes in the design of adjustment policy. This is the only aspect of its analysis that had "economic" significance within the neoclassical paradigm.

Many policy makers see no problem with discussing the social costs of adjustment exclusively in terms of poverty, since policies that benefit the poor necessarily benefit women (e.g., World Bank 1996). This argument ignores issues crucial to understanding gender inequality in the effects of structural adjustment. An analysis of gender bias in compensatory programs will illustrate this point further.

### Compensatory Programs

Because the World Bank's analysis of social costs does not currently incorporate gender, compensatory programs are designed without attention to gender inequality, and are themselves gender biased.[14] The neoclassical paradigm establishes theoretical constraints on the evaluation of policy, which make it likely that gender bias in structural adjustment will persist despite greater emphasis at the Bank on addressing social costs, even as this comes to include attention to gender (e.g., see World Bank 2001b: 227).

Safety-net and social-emergency programs have reduced the negative effects of adjustment on vulnerable groups, but, while women tend to benefit from income and employment programs designed for the poor, they do not necessarily benefit equally. Lourdes Benería and Breny Mendoza (1995: 65) argue that gender inequality in Emergency Social Investment Funds (ESIFs) in Honduras and Nicaragua can be explained in part by (neoclassical) conceptual biases that ignore gender issues in income distribution (see also Buvinic, Gwin, and Bates 1996: 64).[15]

The exclusion of unpaid domestic labor from economic analysis is a less-obvious source of gender inequality in compensatory programs. In accordance with the neoclassical paradigm, the Bank's analysis of social costs is limited to market effects. *Protecting the Poor during Periods of Adjustment* asserts that "[a]nalyzing the effects of a policy change on the poor involves assessing the effect of that change on real purchasing power by determining the impact on the disposable income of the group and the prices and quantities of the goods and services the group consumes" (World Bank 1987: 36). From this perspective, decreases in market consumption define the possible negative effects of adjustment, and directing monetary income to households is the best compensation. Again, changes in unpaid domestic labor (or in nonmarket consumption derived from such labor) resulting from structural adjustment policies or compensatory programs will not be visible to policy makers in this context, nor they will be compensated for in future policies.

In one World Bank Living Standards Measurement Study (LSMS), Paul Glewwe and Gillette Hall (1995) report that during the late 1980s, female-headed households in Peru were no more vulnerable to macroeconomic shocks produced by structural adjustment than male-headed households. These results are "contrary to the common assertion that female-headed households, and women per se, are one 'vulnerable group' in periods of . . . structural adjustment" (31). It follows from Glewwe and Hall's report that attention to gender in adjustment policy is not justified even on the basis of equity.

But this report, like most LSMS studies, measures household welfare strictly in terms of market consumption (Glewwe and Hall 1995: 5). Female-headed households in Peru may have maintained their market consumption by increasing not only paid labor time, but also the intensity of time spent on unpaid domestic labor. Or, time spent on food preparation, repair of clothes, and childcare at home may have increased in intensity or been shifted onto young daughters. Other than the increase in paid labor time, none of this would be captured by an LSMS survey. How valid, then, is Glewwe and Hall's conclusion? Evidence of structural adjustment's effects on unpaid domestic labor suggests that it is at least problematic. Policy will nevertheless be based on this conclusion, which ignores a persistent source of gender inequality. Glewwe and Hall argue that while "similarity in structural adjustment policies across many countries may produce the same 'vulnerable' groups in those countries, . . . in principle, these groups can be made 'invulnerable' by corresponding policy changes" (3). This is true only if neoclassical policy makers recognize and measure all aspects of vulnerability. Since they do not, it is unlikely that women will be made "invulnerable" to the negative effects of structural adjustment by future policy changes.

The relationship between unpaid domestic labor and social services is another potential source of gender bias in Bank policies that is unlikely to be addressed in compensatory programs, again because issues outside the neoclassical paradigm are not considered. For example, a cut in subsidies decreases the number of days spent at the hospital by increasing costs to the consumer. According to the neoclassical paradigm, fewer scarce resources are used as a result of the increased price. However, Diane Elson (1991: 178) points out that "in reality there has been a transfer of the costs of care for the sick from the paid economy to the unpaid economy of the household. The financial costs fall but the unpaid work of women in the household rises. This is not a genuine increase in efficiency. . . ."

Due to the effects of policy on unpaid domestic labor, compensatory programs that increase household income will not necessarily compensate women for cuts in social programs that do not have affordable and readily available market substitutes. Cutting clinic hours in rural areas is likely to increase women's unpaid domestic labor (by increasing waiting time at the clinic, travel time to another clinic, or time spent caring for the sick), whether or not her household has been compensated with increased income to cover the higher cost of healthcare elsewhere. Supplementary feeding programs, a common component of compensatory programs, may also increase unpaid domestic labor by requiring women's direct involvement in providing food (see Vilas 1996: 24).

Structural adjustment policies shaped by neoclassical economics produce gender inequalities likely to be invisible to policy makers. Compensatory measures, which also derive from neoclassical theory, fail to address these gender inequalities, and may actually compound them, whether or not gender is accounted for in implementation. Conformance with the neoclassical paradigm limits the potential both for adjustment policies to be gender neutral and for compensatory programs to correct the policies' gender biases.

## Conclusion

There is no doubt that over the past ten years the World Bank has increased its commitment to gender issues in development. That its attention to the social costs of adjustment increased simultaneously only highlights the lack of intersection between these two areas of policy-making. Macroeconomics at the Bank remain devoid of gender analysis, despite gender critiques of adjustment. Because Bank lending continues to focus on policies for structural adjustment, the failure to incorporate gender into its analysis of adjustment and social costs is likely to affect women in economies in the process of being "reformed" for years to come.

The Bank is likely to include gender as a component of macroeconomic evaluations of "reform" relatively soon.[16] However, my analysis of the reasons for the absence of gender in the design and evaluation of policies for structural adjustment suggests that the terms of this incorporation are predictable, and will be limited by the neoclassical paradigm. The Bank will continue to consider only market aspects of gender differences in the effects of structural adjustment, and to ignore or marginalize nonmarket effects, especially those on unpaid domestic labor. Other issues incompatible with neoclassical economics but vital to gender analysis of macroeconomics will also be excluded, and any conflict between market growth and women's welfare will be decided in favor of the market. Under these conditions, it is doubtful that "engendering" macroeconomics on the Bank's terms will eliminate gender bias in adjustment policies.

The implications of this analysis go beyond the Bank. The shared approach to policy defined by the "Washington consensus" of mainstream economists in the U.S. government and international financial institutions suggests that gender is similarly absent in macroeconomic policies promoted by the International Monetary Fund (IMF), the U.S. Agency for International Development (USAID), the Inter-American Development Bank (IDB), and other agencies affiliated with, influenced by, or dependent on these institutions (see Williamson 1996). It follows that economic policies prescribed by these agencies are no less gender biased than the Bank's, and for similar reasons.[17]

If the neoclassical paradigm is a primary source of gender bias in policies for structural adjustment, then improved training for policy makers and increased accountability on gender issues will not be enough to eliminate gender inequality from macroeconomics at the Bank and elsewhere. The economic theory on which policy is based must be transformed. Feminist economists underscore the sweeping changes necessary for new economic paradigms to include gender as a fundamental category of analysis. Women's nonmarket activities must be recognized as economic and valued equally with market aspects of the economy. Differences in household organizations of production, and conflicts over distribution not governed by the market, must be built into the theory as well. Method can challenge or reinforce fundamental concepts, so traditional approaches to how economics is done must also be interrogated. These ideas are difficult to grapple with, but essential to explore if gender equity in economic policy is to be achieved.

## Notes

Thanks to Derek Stanovsky, Kay Smith, Susan Eckstein, and Jay Wentworth for comments, and to Daryl Sink for assistance in researching this chapter.

1. UNICEF published the first edition of *The Invisible Adjustment* in both English and Spanish in 1987, the same year as the first volume of *Adjustment With A Human Face*. Note that, while this chapter emphasizes academic and development practitioner critiques of Bank policies, grass-roots opposition stimulated these critiques and has been vital in bringing pressure to bear on the Bank to reevaluate structural adjustment.
2. See Devish Kapur, John P. Lewis, and Richard Webb (1997) and Paul Mosley, Jane Harrigan, and John Toye (1991) for histories of the World Bank.
3. I use the term *unpaid domestic labor* to refer to those unremunerated activities performed in maintenance of households and their residents, such as cooking, cleaning, and childcare. Other activities such as childbirth, emotional caretaking, and sex should possibly be included as well. However defined, unpaid domestic labor is predominantly women's work. See Cynthia A. Wood (1997)

for an analysis of the importance of definitions and first-world bias in how such labor is conceptualized.

4. The World Bank is a large and complex institution, with internal conflicts that are not necessarily reflected in public documents. There are Bank professionals currently working to promote gender analysis in macroeconomic policy. There is also external political pressure to do the same. While these are very important, I believe that the Bank's public documents reflect who is "winning" struggles over the direction of its policies for structural adjustment.

5. In addition to UNICEF (1989) and Commonwealth Secretariat (1989), see Haleh Afshar and Carolyne Dennis (1992); Ingrid Palmer (1991); Jeanne Vickers (1991); Lourdes Benería and Shelley Feldman (1992); Pamela Sparr (1994); Isabella Bakker (1994); Diane Elson (1989; 1991; 1998); and Nilüfer Cagatay, Elson, and Caren Grown (1995). There are differing approaches among these authors, which should not be overshadowed by my brief literature review.

6. Feminist activists and development practitioners working on gender have sought the inclusion of unpaid domestic labor in official data for well over two decades, with little success (see Benería 1992).

7. Women's paid labor force participation also increased more than men's (Cornia, Jolly, and Stewart 1987c: 22; Stewart 1991: 1853; Moser 1989: 144–47, 153; Benería 1991: 172–73).

8. See Josette Murphy (1995); Women's Eyes (1997); and Robert O'Brien et al. (2000) for accounts of the evolution of Bank approaches to gender.

9. This is especially significant because, before her tenure at the Bank, Moser was a prominent critic of Bank policies. Attributing many of the negative economic changes in a barrio of Guayaquil, Ecuador, directly to structural adjustment, her work focused on the effects of these policies on women (1989). In another study done for the Bank, Moser discusses the economic changes in Guayaquil only in terms of "external shocks" and "economic crisis," with no comment on the relationship between structural adjustment policies and the worsening economic environment (Moser 1996).

10. The Bank often uses its own data to support arguments, and ignores critical external research. For example, the Structural Adjustment Policy Initiative (SAPRI) was a joint World Bank/civil society project. A Bank SAPRI report was positive in its evaluation of adjustment policies (World Bank 2001a). The final SAPRI summary, in contrast, "present[s] evidence from studies in which the Bank was involved of the negative impacts of its policies," and suggests that systematic Bank resistance to the SAPRI process demonstrates "the disingenuousness of claims that they are interested in engaging civil-society groups in meaningful endeavors to attend to the issues that have driven so many to the streets" (SAPRIN 2001: 3).

11. Less positive results for life expectancy in nonadjusting South Africa, for example, might result from civil war, transitional governance, or the escalating AIDS epidemic among women during the "adjusting period."

12. Summers' speech on girls' education was given the year before his talk on structural adjustment, which omitted discussion of gender. This reinforces my argument that the Bank's failure to analyze gender in the context of adjustment cannot simply be explained as a lack of knowledge or commitment to gender issues generally.

13. Economists do discuss some forms of unpaid labor such as subsistence agriculture. However, the System of National Accounts, which ostensibly measures all forms of economic activity, explicitly excludes unpaid domestic labor. See Wood (1997) for an analysis of causes and implications of this.

14. Issues of implementation are also important to understanding gender bias in compensatory programs. See Benería and Beny Mendoza (1995). Note that a rising commitment to social protection has not altered structural adjustment policies substantively. Compensatory programs are meant to counter policies that are otherwise unproblematic (World Bank 1987; 1994b: 68; Razavi and Miller 1995).

15. For example, 75 percent of jobs created through the ESIF funded by the World Bank in Honduras went to men (Benería and Mendoza 1995: 58). Income directed toward men is unlikely to be distributed equally within households or to compensate fully for an equal amount of income lost to women due to adjust-

ment policies, since men tend to keep a proportion of their income for personal use (see Dwyer and Bruce 1988; Benería 1992).

16. There are many indications of this. In July 1999, for example, Blackden ran a session on "tools for engendering adjustment" for the Bank's Poverty Reduction and Economic Management (PREM) network, which is directly involved in macroeconomic policy-making (personal communication, June 18, 1999). The Bank's recent SAPRI report commented on the negative effects of adjustment cuts in public-sector employment on women (World Bank 2001a: 27). In addition, an upcoming *World Development Report* will be devoted to gender, in anticipation of the United Nations' Fifth World Conference on Women to be held in 2005 (O'Brien et al. 2000: 47). Pressure on the Bank to demonstrate some change in response to demands made at Beijing to address the disproportionate effects of structural adjustment on women will be very high.

17. The same argument applies to the rising "post–Washington consensus," which is only a refinement of neoclassical approaches to policy and will not contribute to the incorporation of gender in macroeconomics (see Stiglitz 1998).

## References

Afshar, Haleh, and Carolyne Dennis, eds. 1992. *Women and Adjustment Policies in the Third World*. London: Macmillan.

Bakker, Isabella, ed. 1994. *The Strategic Silence: Gender and Economic Policy*. London: Zed Press.

Benería, Lourdes. 1991. "Structural Adjustment, the Labor Market and the Household: The Case of Mexico." Pp. 161–83 in *Towards Social Adjustment: Labor Market Concerns in Structural Adjustment*, edited by G. Standing and V. Tokman. Geneva: International Labour Office.

———. 1992. "Accounting for Women's Work: The Progress of Two Decades." *World Development* 20, no. 11: 1547–60.

———, and Shelley Feldman, eds. 1992. *Unequal Burden: Economic Crises, Persistent Poverty, and Women's Work*. Boulder, Colo.: Westview Press.

———, and Breny Mendoza. 1995. "Structural Adjustment and Social Emergency Funds: The Cases of Honduras, Mexico and Nicaragua." *European Journal of Development Research* (Spring): 53–76.

Blackden, C. Mark. 1998. "Integrating Gender into Economic Reform through the Special Program of Assistance for Africa (SPA)." Paper delivered at symposium, "Économie et Rapports Sociaux entre Hommes et Femmes," January 28–29, Geneva. Available from: http://www.unige.ch/iued/new/information/publications/pdf/yp_silence_pudique/8-Eco-Blackden.pdf [Accessed January 11, 2002.]

———, and Elizabeth Morris-Hughes. 1993. *Paradigm Postponed: Gender and Economic Adjustment in Sub-Saharan Africa*. Africa Technical and Human Division (AFTHR), Technical Note no. 13. Washington, D.C.: The World Bank.

Buvinic, Mayra, Catherine Gwin, and Lisa M. Bates. 1996. *Investing in Women: Progress and Prospects for the World Bank*. Policy Essay no. 19. Washington, D.C.: Overseas Development Council.

Cagatay, Nilüfer, Diane Elson, and Caren Grown, eds. 1995. "Gender, Adjustment and Macroeconomics." Special Issue. *World Development* 23, no. 11.

Collier, Paul. 1993. "The Impact of Adjustment on Women." Pp. 183–97 in *Understanding the Social Effects of Policy Reform*, edited by Lionel Demery, et al. Washington, D.C.: The World Bank.

Commonwealth Secretariat. 1989. *Engendering Adjustment for the 1990s*. Report of a Commonwealth Expert Group on Women and Structural Adjustment. London: Commonwealth Secretariat.

Cornia, Giovanni A. 1987. "Economic Decline and Human Welfare in the First Half of the 1980s." Pp. 11–47 in *Adjustment with a Human Face*. Vol. I, *Protecting the Vulnerable and Promoting Growth*, edited by Giovanni A. Cornia, Richard Jolly, and Frances Stewart. Oxford: Clarendon Press.

———, Richard Jolly, and Frances Stewart. 1987a. "Introduction." Pp. 1–8 in *Adjustment with a Human Face*. Vol. I, *Protecting the Vulnerable and Promoting Growth*, edited by Giovanni A. Cornia, Richard Jolly, and Frances Stewart. Oxford: Clarendon Press.

————. 1987b. "An Overview of the Alternative Approach." Pp. 131–46 in *Adjustment with a Human Face*. Vol. I, *Protecting the Vulnerable and Promoting Growth*, edited by Giovanni A. Cornia, Richard Jolly, and Frances Stewart. Oxford: Clarendon Press.

————, eds. 1987c. *Adjustment with a Human Face*. Vol. I, *Protecting the Vulnerable and Promoting Growth*. Oxford: Clarendon Press.

————, eds. 1988. *Adjustment With a Human Face*. Vol. II, *Country Case Studies*. Oxford: Clarendon Press.

Dwyer, Daisy, and Judith Bruce, eds. 1988. *A Home Divided: Women and Income in the Third World*. Stanford, Calif.: Stanford University Press.

Elson, Diane. 1989. "The Impact of Structural Adjustment on Women: Concepts and Issues." Pp. 56–74 in *The IMF, The World Bank and African Debt*, Vol. 2, edited by B. Onimode. Atlantic Highlands, N.J.: Zed Books Ltd.

————. 1991. "Male Bias in Macro-economics: The Case of Structural Adjustment." Pp. 164–90 in *Male Bias in the Development Process*, edited by Diane Elson. New York: Manchester University Press.

————. 1998. "The Economic, the Political and the Domestic: Businesses, State and Households in the Organisation of Production." *New Political Economy* 3, no. 2: 189–208.

Feijoó, María del Carmen, and Elizabeth Jelin. 1989. "Women from Low Income Sectors: Economic Recession and Democratization of Politics in Argentina." Pp. 29–58 in *UNICEF, The Invisible Adjustment: Poor Women and the Economic Crisis*. Santiago: UNICEF, The Americas and the Caribbean Regional Office.

Glewwe, Paul, and Gillette Hall. 1995. "Who Is Most Vulnerable to Macroeconomic Shocks? Hypotheses Tests Using Panel Data from Peru." Living Standards Measurement Study no. 117. Washington, D.C.: The World Bank.

Jacobs, Beryl K. 1991. "Lima's Communal Kitchens." *Women in Action* 2: 16–17.

Jayarajah, Carl, and William Branson. 1995. *Structural and Sectoral Adjustment: World Bank Experience, 1980–92*. Washington, D.C.: The World Bank.

————, and Binayak Sen. 1996. *Social Dimensions of Adjustment: World Bank Experience, 1980–93*. Washington, D.C.: The World Bank.

Kapur, Devish, John P. Lewis, and Richard Webb, eds. 1997. *The World Bank: Its First Half Century*. Vols. 1 and 2. Washington, D.C.: Brookings Institution Press.

Kardam, Nüket. 1991. *Bringing Women In: Women's Issues in International Development Programs*. Boulder, Colo.: Lynne Rienner Publishers.

Moser, Caroline O. N. 1989. "The Impact of Recession and Adjustment Policies at the Micro-Level: Low Income Women and Their Households in Guayaquil, Ecuador." Pp. 137–66 in *UNICEF, The Invisible Adjustment: Poor Women and the Economic Crisis*. Santiago: UNICEF, The Americas and the Caribbean Regional Office.

————. 1996. *Confronting Crisis: A Comparative Study of Household Responses to Poverty and Vulnerability in Four Poor Urban Communities*. Washington D.C.: The World Bank.

————, Annika Tornqvist, and Bernice van Bronkhorst. 1999. *Mainstreaming Gender and Development in the World Bank: Progress and Recommendations*. Washington, D.C.: The World Bank.

Mosley, Paul, Jane Harrigan, and John Toye. 1991. *Aid and Power: The World Bank and Policy-based Lending*. Vol. 1, *Analysis and Policy Proposals*. New York: Routledge.

Murphy, Josette L. 1995. *Gender Issues in World Bank Lending*. Washington, D.C.: The World Bank.

————. 1997. *Mainstreaming Gender in World Bank Lending: An Update*. Washington, D.C.: The World Bank.

Nelson, Joan. 1989. "The Politics of Pro-poor Adjustment." Pp. 95–113 in *Fragile Coalitions: The Politics of Economic Adjustment*, edited by Joan Nelson. Washington, D.C.: Overseas Development Council.

O'Brien, Robert, Anne Marie Goetz, Jan Aart Scholte, and Marc Williams. 2000. *Contesting Global Governance: Multilateral Economic Institutions and Global Social Movements*. Cambridge, U.K.: Cambridge University Press.

Oxfam Policy Department. 1995. *A Case for Reform: Fifty Years of the IMF and the World Bank*. Oxford: Oxfam Publications.

Palmer, Ingrid. 1991. *Gender and Population in the Adjustment of African Economies: Planning for Change*. Geneva: International Labour Office.

Razavi, Shahra, and Carol Miller. 1995. *Gender Mainstreaming: A Study of Efforts by the*

*UNDP, the World Bank and the ILO to Institutionalize Gender Issues*. Geneva: United Nations Research Institute for Social Development.

Rocha, Lola, Eduardo Bustelo, Ernesto López, and Luis Zuñiga. 1989. "Women, Economic Crisis and Adjustment Policies: An Interpretation and Initial Assessment." Pp. 9–27 in *UNICEF, The Invisible Adjustment: Poor Women and the Economic Crisis*. Santiago: UNICEF, The Americas and the Caribbean Regional Office.

Sparr, Pamela, ed. 1994. *Mortgaging Women's Lives: Feminist Critiques of Structural Adjustment*. London: Zed Press for the United Nations.

Stewart, Frances. 1991."The Many Faces of Adjustment." *World Development* 19, no. 12: 1847–64.

Stiglitz, Joseph. 1998. "More Instruments and Broader Goals: Moving Toward the Post-Washington Consensus." (Available from: http://www.wider.unu.edu/stiglitx.htm [Accessed August 13, 1999]).

Structural Adjustment Participatory Review Initiative Network (SAPRIN). 2001. "The Policy Roots of Economic Crisis and Poverty: A Multi-Country Participatory Assessment of Structural Adjustment." Washington, D.C.: SAPRIN. (Available from: <http://www.saprin.org/SAPRIN_Synthesis_11–16–01.pdf> [Accessed January 11, 2002].)

Summers, Lawrence H. 1994. *Investing in All the People: Educating Women in Developing Countries*. EDI Seminar Paper no. 45. Washington, D.C.: The World Bank.

———, and Lant H. Pritchett. 1993. "The Structural-Adjustment Debate." *The American Economic Review* 83, no. 2: 383–89.

UNICEF. 1989. *The Invisible Adjustment: Poor Women and the Economic Crisis*. Santiago: UNICEF, The Americas and the Caribbean Regional Office.

Vickers, Jeanne. 1991. *Women and the World Economic Crisis*. London: Zed Books.

Vilas, Carlos M. 1996. "Neoliberal Social Policy: Managing Poverty (Somehow)." *NACLA Report on the Americas* 29, no. 6 (May/June): 16–25.

Waylen, Georgina. 1992. "Women, Authoritarianism and Market Liberalisation in Chile, 1973–1989." Pp. 150–78 in *Women and Adjustment Policies in the Third World*, edited by Haleh Afshar and Carolyne Dennis. London: Macmillan.

Williamson, John. 1996. "Lowest Common Denominator or Neoliberal Manifesto? The Polemics of the Washington Consensus." Pp. 13–22 in *Challenging the Orthodoxies*, edited by R. M. Auty and John Toye. New York: St. Martin's Press.

Wolfensohn, James D. 1995. "Women and the Transformation of the 21st Century." Address to the United Nations' Fourth World Conference on Women. (Available from: <http://www.worldbank.org/gender/how/womenand.htm> [Accessed July 8, 1999].)

Women's Eyes on the World Bank–US. 1997. "Gender Equity and the World Bank Group: A Post-Beijing Assessment." Washington, D.C.: Oxfam America.

Wood, Cynthia A. 1997. "The First World/Third Party Criterion: A Feminist Critique of the Production Boundary in Economics." *Feminist Economics* 3, no. 3: 47–68.

World Bank. 1985. *The World Bank Annual Report*. Washington, D.C.: The World Bank.

———. 1987. *Protecting the Poor during Periods of Adjustment*. Washington, D.C.: The World Bank.

———. 1990. *World Development Report 1990*. Washington, D.C.: The World Bank.

———. 1991. *World Development Report 1991*. Washington, D.C.: The World Bank.

———. 1994a. *Adjustment in Africa: Reforms, Results, and the Road Ahead*. Washington, D.C.: The World Bank.

———. 1994b. *Enhancing Women's Participation in Economic Development: A World Bank Policy Paper*. New York: Oxford University Press.

———. 1994c. "The Gender Dimension of Development." World Bank Operational Policy 4.20. (Available from: <http://www.worldbank.org/gender/how/termr2.htm> [Accessed July 8, 1999].)

———. 1995a. *Advancing Gender Equality: From Concept to Action*. Washington, D.C.: The World Bank.

———. 1995b. *Toward Gender Equality: The Role of Public Policy*. Washington, D.C.: The World Bank.

———. 1996. "Implementing the World Bank's Gender Policies." (Available from:

<http://www.worldbank.org/gender/how/report.htm> [Accessed July 1, 1999].)

————. 1998. "Selected Comments on the Concept Note from External Readers." (Available from: <http://www.worldbank.org/gender/know/comment.htm> [Accessed July 8, 1999].)

————. 2001a. "Adjustment from Within: Lessons from the Structural Adjustment Participatory Review Initiative." (Available from: <http://www.worldbank. org/research/sapri/> [Accessed January 7, 2002].)

————. 2001b. *Engendering Development*. Washington, D.C.: The World Bank.

# 10

# Literary Representations of "Maids" and "Mistresses": Gender Alliances across Class and Ethnic Boundaries?

*Judith Morganroth Schneider*

The history, practice, and representation of domestic service and, in particular, of the "maid-mistress" relationship have received more attention from social scientists than from literary critics, even though the theme figures significantly in fictional and testimonial literature written by Latin American and U.S. Latina women. During the past fifteen years, studies by social scientists have emphasized the problematic implications of the institution of paid household labor for those concerned with issues of social justice and feminism (Chaney and García Castro 1989; Gill 1994; Romero 1992). The employment of women household laborers by middle- and upper-class Latin American and U.S. women who identify themselves as "feminists" has brought the contradiction between class interests and gender solidarity not only into the "private" sphere of the home, but also into the public sphere of feminist debate.[1] The issue of the exploitation of some women (usually of a subordinate class, nationality, race, or ethnicity) by other women (usually of a society's dominant class, nationality, race, or ethnicity) has provoked intense polemics within women's movements in Latin America, such as the frequently cited confrontation at the 1975 Conference on the International Year of the Woman between Domitila Barrios de Chungara, head of a Bolivian miners' wives' committee, and a Mexican woman politician from the *Partido Revolucionario Institucional* (Institutional Revolutionary Party, PRI) (Castro-Klarén, Molloy, and Sarlo, 1991: 95). One response to the class/gender contradiction that some Latin American and U.S. Latina intellectual feminists have chosen is to expose and critique the injustices of domestic service and traditional maid-mistress relations in literary representations. The Mexican novelist and essayist Elena Poniatowska (1983: 47) points out that middle- and upper-class intellectual women "mistresses" sometimes become the privileged recipients of their "maids'" narratives of poverty, abuse, and abandonment by parents and/or male partners. In some instances, the role of empathetic inter-

locutor has lead Latin American and U.S. Latina women writers to trans-
pose into fiction or transcribe into life stories the oral histories of their
own household laborers.

While recognizing certain gender commonalities, Poniatowska nevertheless underscores the contradiction between class interests which separate female employers from female domestic workers, and common
gender concerns, which may create female bonding in the intimacy of
the maid-mistress relationship. In her introduction to *Se necesita muchacha*
(maid needed) (Gutiérrez 1983), a collection of testimonial narratives
recorded from Peruvian maids, the Mexican feminist unequivocally
states that the division of class precludes the construction of gender
alliances between women employers-employees: "A real mistress-
servant relationship does not exist. How could it if the mistress leaves
everything she does not want to do for the maid?" (Poniatowska 1983:
54).[2] The writer personalizes her argument by emphasizing the gap that
separates her from her maid, echoing the mind/body division of labor
and the classical feminist view of the monotony of household labor:
"While I write, María, in the kitchen, warms the milk for my children's
breakfast ... I am probably considered at the top of the cultural world.
María will probably be found once more in front of the stove ...
watching the pot of boiling milk, so she can give the children breakfast
number 17159374628430000" (Poniatowska 1983: 54–55). Yet, within this
same text, as Cynthia Steele (1989: 311) notes in her seminal essay on the
maid-mistress relationship in Mexican women's literature, Poniatowska
also insists upon affinities between women of all classes with respect to
their traditional responsibility for house and children, as well as their
position of subjugation in patriarchal societies. Thus, Poniatowska (1983:
56) describes the subordinate condition of Mexican middle- and upper-
class mistresses, who are caught in the double bind of dependence on
the institution of domestic service, which allows them to avoid household labor, and dependence on patriarchal social norms that assign the
responsibility for household labor uniquely to wives: "She [the mistress]
realizes ... that above her stands her husband, her sacrosanct spouse,
her house, her slippers, her handbag, her decency, her responsibility,
God, the Virgin of Guadaloupe, her children, society."

Social scientists investigating domestic labor and concerned with
women's issues have similarly focused on the contradiction between
class and gender interests that characterizes traditional maid-mistress
relations. *Muchachas No More*, the landmark study of domestic service in
Latin America and the Caribbean compiled by Elsa M. Chaney and Mary
García Castro (1989: 197–270), contains a section entitled "Questions for
Feminism" in which Isis Duarte's study (1989: 197) critiques the hypoth-

esis of the generality of the "double day" as elaborated by feminist organizations in the Dominican Republic (Duarte 1989: 197), while Mary
Goldsmith (1989: 238) reports the skepticism of organized Mexican
household workers toward the notion of "feminist sisterhood."
Goldsmith quotes from a leaflet published by the Mexican organization
*Hogar de Servidores Domésticos* (Domestic Servants' Home) that states:
"Until domestic service ends, there will be no possibility of solidarity
among women." In like manner, Leslie Gill's (1994: 15) study of Aymara
women, who are continuously forced into migration because of socioeconomic changes in the Bolivian countryside and pushed into domestic
service because of the paucity of other opportunities for indigenous
women in La Paz, problematizes the contradiction between any feminist
notion of "the general subordination of women" and the fact that "some
women, who usually define themselves as members of a superior class or
ethnic group, hire others to carry out the domestic duties that are typically assigned to women." On the other side of the Latin American–U.S.
border, in an analysis of interviews with Chicana domestics in Denver,
Colorado, Mary Romero (1992: 15) also underscores the "challenge to
any feminist notion of 'sisterhood'" implicit in the refusal of some
middle- and upper-class feminist academics to view private household
labor as equivalent to equitable wage labor agreements made outside the
home (Romero 1992: 44).

Sociologists have not only investigated the psychological and material conditions of paid household labor in Latin America and the United
States, but have also advocated solutions to the injustices commonly
attached to the occupation. Chaney and García Castro (1989: v) make
their position clear by dedicating *Muchachas No More* to the "organized
household workers of Latin America and the Caribbean," whose efforts
toward obtaining social justice are documented in several essays
included in the collection. Ana Gutiérrez (1983: 95) presents her compi-
lation of testimonies of Peruvian female domestic employees who
formed the *Sindicato de Trabajadoras del Hogar del Cuzco* (Cuzco
Houseworkers' Union) as an invitation to household workers
throughout Latin America to organize themselves into unions as "un
inicio de solución a la explotación." Other sociologists have stressed the
need to transform the personal relationships between women employers
and employees through which the former commonly demand from the
latter excessive physical and emotional labor as well as enhancement of
the employer's status through attitudes of deference (Rollins 1985: 120,
156, 162). Romero (1992: 44), on the contrary, argues for the need to redi-
rect sociological investigation away from "narrow psychological views"
and toward a consideration of domestic service within the general con-

text of labor practice, and advocates a restructuring of the material conditions of informal arrangements of household labor along the lines of the industrial model of a fair-wage labor contract. In the capitalist context, her study also mentions an alternative solution toward which some Chicana domestics are moving, one that involves a small business arrangement of selling specifically defined services to clients rather than working for hourly wages (Romero 1992: 147). In a socialist context, the documentary video *From Maids to Compañeras*, directed by Jean Weisman and Belkis Vega (1998), features three former Cuban maids in Havana whose testimonial narratives suggest that domestic service necessarily results in reinforcing class and race privileges, and that the occupation of private household laborers must be abolished in order to eliminate oppression of poor women, especially women of color.

Meanwhile, the so-called vanishing institution of domestic service survives in the capitalist societies of the Americas due to internal and external migrations as well as economic depression, deindustrialization, and growing poverty south of the U.S. border (Steele 1989: 297; Gill 1994: 6). Changes in Latin American societies have affected the material conditions of domestic service but have by no means eliminated the phenomenon. The traditional pattern—whereby domestic servants continue in the service of a single family and its offspring for the course of the servant's lifetime—is disappearing, and a shift has been noted away from live-in toward live-out domestic employment (Steele 1989: 322; Gill 1994: 80). Even so, the greater autonomy that results from the fact that contemporary domestics tend to work for more than one employer does not necessarily lead to improved working conditions, fairer wages, or respect for the occupation (Steele 1989: 301; Gill 1994: 81). While it is the case, at least in Bolivia, that younger female employers who work outside of the home tend to control their employees less strictly than do nonwaged housewives and that many employers find themselves "renegotiating relationships" with more independent-minded employees (Gill 1994: 92, 79), middle- and upper-class women in Latin America and the United States remain the primary supervisors of their female household workers. Furthermore, the number of dual-career families seeking private household workers has increased in the past two decades in both Latin America and the United States (Gill 1994: 6; Romero 1992: 167), and Romero (1992: 68) reports that "a recent estimate indicated that 43 percent of employed women [in the United States] hired household workers." This fact, coupled with political and economic crises in Mexico, Central America, and the Caribbean, accounts for the transnational expansion of the occupation and the growing number of legal and illegal Latina immigrants working as household laborers in the United States.

Sharing the goals of social justice and transnational feminist solidarity articulated by some Latin Americanist sociologists, Latin American and U.S. Latina women writers have likewise drawn attention to the injustices underlying domestic service, and have suggested solutions in works that explore the thematics of the maid-mistress relationship. As Steele (1989: 298) argues with respect to Mexican women writers, these women intellectuals, who write from the dominant side "of the power dialectic," have manifested, both through fiction and oral histories, "female solidarity across lines of class and ethnicity." In concordance with Steele's judgment, Debra A. Castillo's (1992: 12) groundbreaking study of Latin American women writers, which elaborates Latin Americanist-feminist–reading strategies, also stresses the importance of the theme of the "multiply vexed relation between the two housewife figures—the wife and servant" and points out the need for more profound studies of the complex maid-mistress relationship in women's texts (Castillo 1992: 12).

Prompted by Castillo's suggestion, I examine four literary works in which the problematic maid-mistress relationship figures as either the focal point of the text or as a crucial secondary theme. Since testimonial literature has received a great deal of critical attention from Latin Americanists, my study focuses on the less-studied area of fiction, and includes the interpretation of three novels and a play. Continuing in the direction mapped out in Steele's essay, and using the previously cited sociological studies as frames of reference, my textual analysis examines the insights—provided by these Latin American and U.S. Latina literary productions—into the possibilities and pitfalls of constructing fictional gender alliances across class and ethnic barriers. My study points out the direct and oblique ways in which these literary portrayals of the maid-mistress relationship attack and subvert the subordination of women for reasons of class, gender, and ethnicity.

Before entering into the details of my interpretations, I should provide an overview of these works. *Balún-Canán*, the first novel discussed in this chapter, was the first novel published by the Mexican author Rosario Castellanos (1957/1961). The text exemplifies the modernist ideological position of feminism in the mid–twentieth century, in which, as Raquel Olea observes, "feminism projected itself as a movement for the emancipation and liberation of women that was interior to (or in alliance with) ideologies that sought a transformation of the mode of production—in particular, those of socialism" (Olea 1995: 195). Set in rural Chiapas during the period of social reform promulgated by President Lázaro Cárdenas (1934–1940), Castellanos's semiautobiographical novel draws a parallel between the injustices attached to the traditional maid-mistress relationship in a Ladino, land-holding family and other manifestations of oppression in a rigidly patriarchal, capitalist Mexican society. Castellanos's *Balún-Canán* not only underscores the fact "that woman as historical subject was absent from the project of modernity" (Olea 1995: 196), but also corrects this omission by giving a female narrator, female characters, and gender relations prominent positions in its representation of the final decade of the Mexican Revolution.

Thirty years later, Laura Esquivel (1989/1990), contemporary Mexican novelist, continues Castellanos's project of inscribing women in history by placing traditionally marginalized female characters—an unmarried daughter, an illegitimate daughter, indigenous domestic servants—at the center of her novel of the Mexican Revolution, *Como agua para chocolate* (Like Water for Chocolate). However, the strategies Esquivel employs differ from those of Castellanos's earlier work; the contemporary novel is aesthetically and ideologically marked by postmodernist forms that followed and engulfed the 1970s wave of feminism. As Olea (1995: 198) states, "the egalitarian and rights-oriented feminism produced by modernity has given way in the last twenty years to a more all-embracing theoretical-political questioning of the structures of power." This transformation is exemplified by Esquivel's deconstruction of the fixed subject positions of maid and mistress and her use of parody both to revalorize and critique conventionally labelled "feminine" practices. Esquivel creates fictional relations among female subjects that bridge class and ethnic divisions, while at the same time her writing questions the possibility of "thinking about our utopia (is feminism a utopia?) when one of the signs of postmodernity is the end of utopias" (Olea 1995: 192).

The third and fourth literary works analyzed in this chapter incorporate themes arising from the growing migration of poor Latin American women across the U.S. border into the homes of middle- and upper-class families, where they assume the roles of maid, nanny, and/or cook. These texts grow out of the diasporic consciousness of two U.S. Latina writers based in the suburbs of New York. In *Noticias de suburbio*, the Argentinian-born playwright Nora Glickman (1997) stages a gender alliance between two Latin American women of disparate class and ethnic backgrounds who are drawn to each other because of their common immigrant status, use of the Spanish language, shared Hispanic customs, and common gender concerns. Glickman's maid and mistress forge hybrid cultural identities that evade the fixed "position of oppression and victimization" (Olea 1995: 199) that is attacked, yet ultimately preserved, in Castellanos's mid-twentieth-century Mexican novel. Underlying Glickman's play of multiple subject identities is a utopian vision of female bonding comparable to Esquivel's, as well as an affirmation of the ideology of the American Dream that is reinforced by the characters' fulfillment of their immigrant expectations of socioeconomic advancement.

In contrast to Glickman's play, the ironically entitled novel, *El sueño de América* (*America's Dream*) by the mainland Puerto Rican writer Esmeralda Santiago (1996), represents immigrant aspirations with considerable ambivalence. In spite of the novel's postmodernist aesthetic of combining elite and popular discursive forms, Santiago's narrative remains neorealist in style, situating its female subjects in relatively fixed classes and ethnic positions that negate the possibility of constructing gender alliances across social barriers. Santiago's viewpoint is closer to the modernist-feminist position of Castellanos, whose work connects the struggle for gender equality to social movements that seek an end to multiple forms of racial and class oppression, than it is to the utopian perspective informing the texts of her contemporaries Esquivel and Glickman.

Set in the Mexico of the 1930s, *Balún-Canán*, Castellanos' (1957/1961) autobiographically inspired novel, creates in the character Zoraida an archetype of the oppressive mistress, who, in spite of her superior position in the social hierarchy of class and ethnicity, is also represented in the text as a subordinate woman. Of lower-middle-class origins but married, or more precisely "sold"—Zoraida refers to herself as a "bought chicken" (Castellanos 1957/1961: 91)—to a wealthy landowner, the mistress of the Argüello hacienda treats her indigenous servants with arrogance, and often with cruelty. Thus, Castellanos (1957/1961: 229) has the mistress address the nanny disdainfully, using racial insults: "You frightened me. The habit you and your race have of walking without making any sound, of spying, of turning up where you are not expected. Why did you come in? I didn't call." In contrast to Zoraida's hostility, the servant is depicted as a loyal employee seeking emotional support from her employer, whose family she professes to love in defiance of the laws of her own people (Castellanos 1957/1961: 16). While attacking the harsh exploitation of one woman by another inherent in the traditional maid-mistress relationship, the novel at the same time demonstrates the general subordination of women in Mexican society by revealing commonalities between the situation of Zoraida, the upper-class wife, and that of Juana, the spouse of Felipe, the indigenous leader of a revolt of poor farmers against the landowning Argüello family. Felipe, ironically, is a Cárdenas revolutionary who leads a fight for social justice while demanding absolute obedience from his subjugated wife (Castellanos 1957/1961: 182). Through the representation of Juana's fantasies of liberation that culminate in a small gesture of rebellion, the narrative gives voice to the character's resistance to the will of her husband. Zoraida, the domineering mistress, is likewise represented as subordinate to the whims of her authoritarian husband. For example, she rushes to the kitchen to refill the coffee pitcher, after her husband remarks reproachfully in the presence of a guest that the coffee is cold (Castellanos 1957/1961: 100). By juxtaposing this manifestation of Zoraida's subservience with other scenes in which the same character expresses racial animosity and condescension toward indigenous farmworkers, Castellanos foregrounds the parallelism between the subordination of women and the oppression of other marginalized groups in Mexican society.

Although the subservient female subjects of *Balún-Canán* remain essentially fixed in their positions of victim, Sandra Messinger Cypess (1985) has shown that the novel represents some oppressed characters as incipient agents beginning to seize discursive control from their oppressors, a reading that Cypess finds consistent with the historical setting of the work in a period of struggles for indigenous rights and agrarian reform. While Cypess' (1985: 2) analysis of the novel's Foucauldian "shifts of power from patriarchal oppressors to the traditional marginalized figures" does not specifically include the figure of the domestic servant, it is evident that her interpretation applies to the mistress-maid relationship as well. In fact, the novel shows that the nanny exercises a modicum of power, albeit limited, through her relationship with the mistress' daughter, the child narrator to whom the nanny transmits powerful myths about the expropriation of indigenous lands by the conquistadores and their criollo descendants. The female indigenous servant further demonstrates a measure of power over the Argüello family when she recounts the prophesy of the destruction of its male heir by the witches of her indigenous community (Castellanos 1957/1961: 230). It is the nanny's foretelling of this act of revenge that provokes Zoraida's physical attack on her servant, an attack that the nanny resists, at least verbally, by asserting the injustice of her mistress' abuse of power and by invoking her own human rights. Zoraida, nevertheless, retains the authority derived from her class and ethnicity in the Chiapas of the 1930s and proceeds to beat her servant's head with her comb and then fire her on the spot (Castellanos 1957/1961: 232). Castellanos implies that social justice is on the side of the victim by having the child protagonist approach her nanny as she lies on the floor "defeated and abandoned like a worthless object" (Castellanos 1957/1961: 232). In spite of the fact that the female child narrator of *Balún-Canán*, who is the least powerful of the characters belonging to the dominant social group, forms reciprocal bonds of affection with her nanny, the novel ends, as Steele (1989:

310) has demonstrated, with the daughter's being "incorporated into oligarchic power relations and ideology." Even so, Castellanos, as author, manifests her own position of solidarity across social barriers by revealing the harsh mistreatment of indigenous domestic servants in Mexican society during the period in which President Cárdenas sought major social reforms. The novel implies a collectivist solution to the social subtext of the maid-mistress dilemma by foregrounding not only the oppression, but also the rebellion of characters belonging to marginalized social groups. This reading is compatible with Olea's (1995: 195) hypothesis that the feminism of modernity envisioned the liberation of women in alliance with "ideologies that sought a transformation of the mode of production—in particular, those of socialism."

The contemporary novel by Esquivel (1989/1990), *Como agua para chocolate*, whose setting is the Coahuila-Texas border during the Mexican Revolution and its aftermath, exhibits a number of thematic similarities with *Balún-Canán*, including the foregrounding of the triangular relationship between the mother, nanny, and daughter. The figures of the mistresses in the two novels are similarly oppressive (and repressed); both Zoraida in Castellanos' narrative and Mamá Elena in Esquivel's novel are in marriages of convenience rather than passion, transmit to their daughters the role of submission, and treat their domestic workers harshly. The characterizations of the unmarried, childless nanny in both novels illustrate the history of domestic servants in Latin America from colonial times through the 1970s, a history in which the occupation was "almost inevitably incompatible with marriage and childbearing" (Kuznesof 1989: 31). The observation John Sinnigen (1995: 115) has made regarding Esquivel's contemporary novel, stating that "it represents a voice from the margins which articulates a specific female perspective on revolutionary events," would be equally applicable to Castellanos' earlier novel, in which the social movements of 1930s Mexico are represented through the viewpoints of a female child narrator and other marginalized female characters. In *Como agua para chocolate*, the devalued daughter, like the female child of *Balún-Canán*, struggles against her mother's oppressive authority. Moreover, each of these subjugated middle- or upper-class *criolla* protagonists turns for support in her rebellion against maternal power to the symbolic figures of the nanny and other female household servants associated with indigenous, pre-Hispanic knowledge.

In spite of these similarities, the representation of the maid-mistress relationship in the fiction of Esquivel differs significantly from that of her predecessor, in particular in the construction of shifting female subject identities. Unlike the socially positioned child narrator of *Balún-*

*Canán*, whose "love for the nanny leads the girl to become aware of her insertion in the class structure" (Steele 1989: 317), Tita, the middle-class daughter in *Como agua para chocolate*, subverts the asymmetry of the traditional relationship by working side by side with Nacha, her nanny, in an idealized kitchen until the death of the servant. Even after Tita completes her revolt against her tyrannical, bourgeois mother in order to gain sexual freedom, and even after her mother's death, Esquivel shows her female protagonist's willingness to remain in the role of family cook and housekeeper. The representation of Tita as an egalitarian mistress transposed into the setting of early-twentieth-century Mexico contrasts sharply with the depiction of traditional mistress figures, such as Castellanos' Zoraida and Esquivel's own Mamá Elena. The protagonist's egalitarian behavior toward family servants, moreover, contradicts the testimonies of actual Mexican servants, such as Poniatowska's (1969/1994: 245) Jesusa Palamares (a pseudonym for Josefina Borquez), who describes her real Mexican female employers as "despots." Tita, on the contrary, is shown to treat Chencha, her servant, as a comrade, politely asking her to help with preparations for a dinner party and thanking her for "her great assistance" (Esquivel 1989/1990: 160). In traditional maid-mistress relationships, which continue to exist in many parts of Latin America, employers typically confide in domestic workers, while the latter "are not encouraged to discuss themselves and their problems in a similar way" (Gill 1994: 71). In the fictional world of *Como agua para chocolate*, these roles are reversed; it is Chencha who dominates exchanges with her mistress (Esquivel 1989/1990: 140), and Tita who tries to coax her servant out of a state of depression (Esquivel 1989/1990: 156). Esquivel's projection of a democratized relationship between Tita and her servants, as well as her vision of a utopian "community of women" (Ibsen 1997: 113), may be interpreted as a manifestation of the writer's own desire for gender solidarity across class and ethnic boundaries and as an oblique way of recommending to her readers the restructuring of the unequal social relationships still surrounding domestic service.

Another way in which Esquivel's postmodernist literary strategies operate against the traditional marginalization of maids is by undoing the socially determined stigma that characterizes household labor in Latin American society. The bonds established in the narrative between the middle-class Tita and her poor indigenous maids, Nacha and Chencha, are based on a system of shared domestic values and shared space: "the kitchen, from which men are traditionally excluded ... an area in which women may assert a small measure of control," which is denied them in the "public" sphere (Ibsen 1997: 113). As Sinnigen points out, the quasi-magical pre-Hispanic recipes that link Esquivel's mistress and maid are associated with a subordinate indigenous culture in the throes of rebellion, and that association is used by the narrative to support the daughter's revolt against the (maternally transmitted) patriarchal order (Sinnigen 1995: 122). Yet, paradoxically, while fomenting revolt, Esquivel's narrative valorizes the cult of domesticity that historically has been used to promote women's subordination to that same patriarchal order. In *Como agua para chocolate* the narrator semiseriously exalts household labor to the level of ritual, representing tasks like setting the table or disinfecting mattresses (Esquivel 1989/1990: 158, 160) with the solemnity and precision of a religious sacrament. Critics have discussed the playful way in which the narrative uses parody simultaneously to appropriate, revalorize, and subvert "popular discourse, with its emphasis on such 'feminine' values as nurturing and selflessness" (Ibsen 1997: 113). By reaffirming the creative aspects of traditional feminine roles, Esquivel's narrative, in effect, argues against the stigmatization of both paid and unpaid household labor and the negative evaluation of those who perform such work—whether maids or housewives—as "uninteresting, worthless people" (Romero 1992: 20). In the final chapter of *Como agua para chocolate*, the novel takes a paradoxical turn by obliterating the idealized community of women projected in its preceding pages. The narrative leaps forward in time, and Tita's grandniece, who, as it turns out, has been the narrator of her family's matriarchal history, is represented alone in the kitchen with no mother, no nanny, no servants, only her grand-aunt's book of recipes. It is as if the anachronistic issues of domestic service and the relationships of maids and mistresses had faded into the pages of history. With respect to the narrative's subtext of the exploitation of women by other women, the novel's final passages imply an individualistic response (as well as nostalgia for the communal collaboration across social barriers evoked in earlier chapters) to the housework dilemma. The image of the middle-class woman alone in her modern kitchen may imply a solution to the injustices of domestic service proposed by some feminists concerned with social justice, a solution that Romero (1992: 167) considers "utopian," that is, the elimination of domestic service by having each person clean up her own mess.

*Noticias de suburbio*, Glickman's (1997) contemporary play set on the other side of the Latin American–U.S. border, follows the northward movement of poor women to the metropolis, where they hope to obtain decent living and working conditions, money to send home to their families, social services, and, in some cases, more equitable gender relations. *Noticias de suburbio* shares with *Como agua para chocolate* a postmodernist aesthetic and ideology that blurs the boundaries between elite and popular culture while destabilizing the fixed positions of class and ethnic identities. Like Esquivel's novel, Glickman's play creates "a proposal of communion among women" (Schiminovich 1997: 458) in which gender solidarity diminishes rather than masks class and ethnic interests, a fictional solidarity that contrasts with sociological evidence presented by Romero ( 1992: 95). The character of Alicia, a native of Argentina, is a middle-class U.S. citizen established in the suburbs of New York City who is experiencing downward mobility due to her recent divorce. Consequently, she is forced to look for work outside the home and for a household worker who will also take care of her children. Alicia hires Magdalena, a recent Ecuadorian immigrant, to work on a live-in basis in her home. In the course of the play's action, the diasporic identities of the Argentinian "white" and Ecuadorian "indigenous" protagonists become intertwined. The female characters form bonds reinforced by shared experiences of immigration and dislocation, common linguistic and cultural components, and hopes for their "economic independence and the realization of the *American Dream*" (Schiminovich 1997: 460). Emphasizing the hybridity of their new cultural identities, Glickman (1997: 445) has Magdalena revive Alicia's connection to her Hispanic heritage: "The decor of the house has become more tropical and Hispanic: flowering plants, canaries, strings of garlic." And Alicia initiates Magdalena into the U.S. middle-class habitus of driving a car, seeking legal assistance from a woman lawyer, and taking courses in English and business administration. Glickman's play constructs a feminist alliance, or "politics of location," an alliance that allows them to resist "multiple patriarchies" and "scattered hegemonies," to borrow terms from Inderpal Grewal and Caren Kaplan (1994: 17). Thus, Alicia triumphs over the business world, which typically discriminates against women who return to the labor force after working for several years as housewives. Concurrently, she manages to break off her relationship with a cheating lover whose indifferent behavior kept her in a state of constant frustration. For her part, Magdalena survives both the blackmailing attempts of a bogus husband, contracted in marriage in order to obtain a green card, and the manipulations of a fraudulent lawyer contracted for the same purpose. To emphasize the common subordination of women across class and ethnic divisions, and of Latina immigrants in particular, Glickman devises the strategy of fusing the character of Alicia's cheating lover with Magdalena's cheating immigration lawyer.

The shifting, transcultural identities constructed by Alicia and Magdalena destabilize various binaries that have been used to fix definitions of female subjects within and across different ethnic and socioeconomic groups. For instance, the patriarchal distinction between feminine "private" and masculine "public" space becomes blurred as the home gradually turns into a space of business for both women: "The living room space now also serves as an office: desk, blackboard, filing cabinets, calendar, computers, telephones, Fax" (Glickman 1997: 445). Like Esquivel, Glickman uses parodic humor to undermine stereotypical representations. In a playful inversion of stereotypes, Glickman portrays Alicia, the nearly "gringa" Argentinian employer, as disorganized and technologically impaired, while endowing Magdalena, the newly emigrated indigenous Ecuadorian employee, with the ability to master the computer. In contrast to the "position of oppression and victimization" emphasized in the modernist discourse of mid-twentieth-century feminists (Olea 1995: 199), exemplified by Castellanos' representation of household servants in *Balún-Canán*, the Latina maids in Glickman's suburban setting are portrayed as articulate and autonomous. Finally, through the creation of the Alimagda enterprise—a Hispanic grocery supply company that Alicia and Magdalena manage jointly—the play, as Flora Schiminovich (1997: 460) states, "emphasizes the union between women of different social classes."

Glickman's representation of a contemporary collaborative maid-mistress relationship, like Esquivel's portrayal of Tita's idealized relationship with Nacha and Chencha in the historical period of the Mexican Revolution, creates an attractive, yet probably unrealistic, image of the structure of domestic service. Undoubtedly, social change has improved some aspects of the socioeconomic condition of women north and south of the Mexican-U.S. border, including that of some female household laborers, yet Romero's interviews with chicana household workers provide a societal subtext of continuing exploitative conditions that contradicts Glickman's literary vision. The inequality that characterizes actual mistress-maid relations, as described by chicana household laborers in the U.S. Southwest, includes expectations of deference or traditional demeanor imposed on employees; affirmations of ethnic superiority on the part of employers; demands of "invisibility" for the domestic worker; instances of detailed supervision of the employee; and maternalistic rituals, such as the giving of useless or dilapidated gifts, practiced by the employer (Romero 1992: 101, 114, 118, 103,109). In *Noticias de suburbio* Magdalena indeed provides emotional labor in some of the ways traditionally expected of servants (Glickman 1997: 453); however, in contrast to the traditional situation, this emotional labor is reciprocal (Glickman 1997: 455; Romero 1992: 108). While the play alludes to many of the social problems confronted by Latina domestics in the United States, such as the lack of documentation, dependent children or relatives left in their countries of origin, unwanted pregnancies, and unavailability of healthcare, the playwright focuses on the resilience and courage with which the female employees confront these obstacles rather than the social injustices that create them. The question remains as to how Glickman's *Noticias de suburbio* articulates solidarity with Latina household workers whose labor in U.S. society is generally exploited (Romero 1992: 97–133). While a fictional work should not be required to elaborate an explicit ideological or socioeconomic program, a disturbing gap in the drama is the absence of an explanation of the financial arrangements involved in the Alimagda partnership. The playwright herself gives voice to this self-criticism through Magdalena's young Colombian friend, María, who refuses to join in the enterprise, protesting to Magdalena: "She will always be the boss, not you. And if you have a fight and she fires you, then, where will you go? And what happens to me?"(Glickman 1997: 456) On the other hand, if we were to consider the play's underlying strategy of a business partnership between employer and employee as a proposed solution to the injustices of domestic service in the United States, then we might imagine women employers providing their immigrant employees with the sort of educational and training opportunities offered on stage by Alicia to Magdalena. In that case, individual household labor might be viewed as a bridging occupation leading to a better job, although it should be noted that studies of domestic service both in the United States and Latin America show that thus far there exists no evidence pointing toward the actual existence of such a bridging function (Gill 1994: 100; Kuznesof 1989: 31; Romero 1992: 27). More convincingly, Glickman's *Noticias de suburbio* manifests the writer's sense of solidarity across social barriers through her reconstruction of Latina diasporic identities that break with class, national, and ethnic stereotypes, notably the construction of subaltern Latin American women as passive victims. In fact, her optimistic vision is consistent with some recent studies that conclude that the experiences of immigration and transculturation have decreased the subordination of many women within Hispanic families in the United States (Poggio and Woo 2000). According to Sara Poggio and Ofelia Woo (2000: 135), many Mexican and Salvadoran female immigrants, a high percentage of whom are engaged as household laborers, report decreasing material and emotional dependence on male family members and a concurrent increase in their own self-esteem and autonomy.

Set in the same suburban county and contemporary time period as *Noticias de suburbio*, the novel *América's Dream* by Esmeralda Santiago (1996), a writer who migrated from Puerto Rico to New York City at the age of thirteen, represents a less optimistic image of domestic service in the United States. The narrative tells the migratory story of América Gonzalez, a Puerto Rican woman who works first on the cleaning staff of a hotel on the island of Vieques; then as a live-in maid in Westchester County, New York; and finally on the cleaning staff of a hotel in Manhattan. Narrated primarily from the point of view of the subordinate woman, the novel suggests multiple meanings for its title by alternately alluding to the protagonist's lack of concrete goals for self-fulfillment, to her developing sense of self-realization, and to positive and negative connotations of the broader cultural myth of the American Dream. Although the predominant social subtext referred to in the novel is domestic violence—América comes to the mainland in an attempt to escape from the brutality of Correa, the abusive lover who is also the father of their adolescent daughter—the themes of domestic service and the maid-mistress relationship provide secondary themes crucial to Santiago's portrayal of the process of consciousness raising that brings the protagonist to an awareness of her subordinate condition and to the valorization of her own personal worth.

In contrast to the idealized working conditions of domestic service in Glickman's *Noticias de Suburio*, Santiago's representation of individual household labor foregrounds the same excessive demands documented in Romero's study: Hispanic domestics are paid lower wages than white housekeepers (Santiago 1996: 229; Romero 1992: 95); the ill-defined tasks of childcare and cleaning overlap imprecisely in their work schedule (Santiago 1996: 255; Romero 1992: 101); hours are long with breaks unspecified (Santiago 1996: 207; Romero 1992: 127); days off and free time are impinged upon by employer's unexpected requests for additional hours (Santiago 1996: 284; Romero 1992: 127); and finally, employers devalue the feelings and judgments of Latina immigrant maids through racial and ethnic slurs (Santiago 1996: 227; Romero 1992: 132). "It's like they need us ... but they don't want us," remarks one of the Hispanic household workers portrayed in the novel after she runs to help an anglo child who has fallen from a playground swing, only to find herself disdainfully reproached by the child's mother (Santiago 1996: 240).

Unlike the mutually supportive gender alliances formed by maids and mistresses in the works of Esquivel and Glickman, Santiago's representation of the employee-employer relationship shows no signs of common concerns reaching across class and ethnic boundaries. Karen Leverett, América's white anglo employer, is depicted as blond, tall, slim, professional, and perpetually stressed due to her efforts to balance the demands of her marriage, her home, her children, and her career as a hospital administrator. While she is far from being represented as the tyrannical figures of Zoraida or Mamá Elena, and even though Karen is occasionally shown to express understanding toward the difficulties of transculturation that her employee is experiencing, the novel's evaluation of the employer overwhelmingly emphasizes her ethnocentrism and egocentrism. For example, Karen thoughtfully meets América at the airport with a winter coat and hat, but the critical look that she casts on the young woman's elegant dress and high heels, her ironic "You look so nice!", her commanding way of carrying América's luggage through the snow to the car, and her shocked silence upon learning that América became a mother at the age of sixteen are all signs that communicate to the reader the employer's assumption of her own cultural superiority and dominant status (Santiago 1996: 130).

Like Romero's study *Maid in the U.S.A.*, Santiago's fictive world shows the home as a *"site* of class struggle" (Romero 1992: 44). Condescension rather than contemptuousness characterizes Karen's style as an employer, and Santiago portrays her exploitation of América as a more subtle, contemporary version of Zoraida's overt mistreatment of the nana in *Balún-Canán*. Santiago's narrative demonstrates that, for this live-in Latina maid in the United States, the conditions described by Mary García Castro (1989: 116) as characteristic of domestic service in Latin America may be reproduced on the other side of the border: "Her workplace is the home of the *patrones* and she is always on call; given that, the time when her labor is *potentially* at the service of the patron is actually work time." Santiago stages a confrontation between employee and employer by having América protest that she has been working a thirteen- to fifteen-hour day instead of the eight-hour day agreed upon in the informal arrangement. When the employee requests a raise, the novelist has her employer refuse and condescendingly retort with the misrepresentation that América has six free hours in the mornings, while the children are in school (Santiago 1996: 255). After portraying this unsuccessful attempt to obtain higher wages, the narrative represents América's growing sense of *ressentiment*, a feeling characteristic of exploitative maid-mistress relationships (Rollins 1985: 227). Through the increasing allusions to class differences in the protagonist's interior monologues—América is shown to increasingly resent the fact that her employer pays fifteen dollars a piece for twenty pairs of underwear and thirty dollars a piece for fifteen brassieres, but refuses to pay twenty dollars more a week to the woman who takes care of her children (Santiago 1996: 256)—Santiago critiques the materialistic values of the upper middle class in U.S. society.

While *América's Dream* reveals many of the injustices facing Hispanic immigrants employed as household workers in the United States, and points toward the possibility of constructing a community of Latina women workers, Santiago stops short of elaborating collectivist solutions similar to those that have been advanced by women's movements in Latin America (Chaney and García Castro 1989). Shortly after América's arrival in Westchester County, a sign reading *"OFICINA HISPANA"* makes the protagonist aware of the existence of other speakers of Spanish in the vicinity (Santiago 1996: 162). The narrative subsequently describes América's tentative contacts with other Latina maids who talk together while they watch the children for whom they care play in the park. Santiago depicts the attractions and repulsions connecting these mainly undocumented Hispanic women who have come from a variety of educational, social, and national backgrounds to the same occupational position in the United States. In particular, the narrative emphasizes an incipient feminist consciousness developing in these women, as well as an awareness of the negative differential in the treatment given to domestic workers "of color" in comparison with that of white household laborers. América begins to find support within this community of working Latina women and makes a hesitant gesture of solidarity toward Frida, a former schoolteacher, who offers to lend her a book on machismo written, as Frida points out, in Spain by a Latin American woman. However, the sudden appearance in New York of Correa, her abusive lover, causes América's withdrawal from this circle of women and into solitary feelings of shame and desperation (Santiago 1996: 293).

Ultimately, Santiago's novel provides an individualist solution to its subtext of the exploitation of Latina maids in the United States. In its final chapter, as a result of her extraordinary, single-handed battle to survive an attempt on her life by her ex-lover, the protagonist obtains a modest version of the American Dream and the feminist ideal of a room of one's own. The narrative stresses América's contentment with her small apartment in a Puerto Rican neighborhood of the Bronx, where she gets up in the morning, prepares her toast as she likes it, and drinks her coffee in peace. She prefers her new job in a large downtown hotel to domestic service, because it gives her more money and less work and includes overtime pay and medical insurance (Santiago 1996: 322). Whereas materialistic norms may perceive América's shift in employment as a simple move from a low-status occupation in the periphery to the same job in the metropolis, the evaluative stance of Santiago's novel, which is articulated through the protagonist's point of view, represents the change of jobs and geography as a move toward autonomy and self-realization. The profound lesson learned by the protagonist in this story of feminist consciousness-raising is expressed by a maxim that América often repeats to herself. On the opening page of the novel, this statement is tinged with resignation, but by the end of the narrative it sums up

América's newly acquired self-determination and her individualist phi-losophy of life: "It is, after all, her life, and she's the one in the middle of it" (Santiago 1996: 325).

Finally, in what ways does *América's Dream* demonstrate the author's solidarity with Latina domestic workers? First of all, by foregrounding the exploitative conditions that frequently structure their employment in middle- and upper-class U.S. households. Second, by implying that the stigma of household work is socially determined, and that cleaning house, as Romero (1992: 44) has argued, is not "naturally" demeaning. The novel's evaluative stance with respect to the occupation is expressed in the words of the protagonist: "It's a job like any other ... There's no shame in it" (Santiago 1996: 219). Without romanticizing household labor in the manner of Esquivel, Santiago's text nevertheless works against the stigmatization of domestic work and domestic workers by representing her protagonist as "intelligent, hard-working, enterprising and sensitive" (Olazagasti-Segovia 1996/1997: 55), a household worker who takes pride in her housekeeping skills (Santiago 1996: 262) and invents strategies that make her workday more meaningful. Echoing an idea of resistance sim-ilar to that of Castellanos in *Balún-Canán*, Santiago (1996: 30) shows the protagonist turning her intimate knowledge of her employers' lives and habits into a limited form of empowerment: "She knows more about them than they will ever know about her." Another manifestation of Santiago's solidarity with the struggle of domestic workers is her depic-tion of the protagonist's refusal to accept the negative evaluation imposed upon her by some members of the dominant class and ethnicity. Thus, in spite of the construction of her "invisibility" by hotel clients in Puerto Rico, the narrative shows that América is convinced of her own subjective identity: "She feels herself there, solid as always, but they look through her, as if she were a part of the strange landscape" (Santiago 1996: 3). Like Castellanos, Santiago depicts women household laborers as subject to patriarchal abuse and economic exploitation that are rein-forced by ethnic discrimination. And yet, like Esquivel and Glickman, she allows her protagonist to shift her identity position from that of victim to resister, if only slightly with respect to socioeconomic class, most decidedly in the arena of gender relations.

Based on my analysis of representations of the thematics of the maid-mistress relationship in contemporary works by Esquivel, Glickman, and Santiago—texts that I have examined in comparison with the modernist feminist treatment of the theme by Rosario Castellanos—it is evident that Latin American and U.S.-Latina women writers, using a variety of lit-erary strategies, continue to manifest solidarity with other women across class and ethnic boundaries. While Castellanos' *Balún-Canán* directly exposes injustices historically associated with domestic service, and points toward a socialist transformation that would eliminate multiple facets of oppression, Esquivel's *Como agua para chocolate* uses the traditional image of the oppressive mistress as a starting point from which to launch a postmodernist deconstruction of class, gender, and ethnic barriers and to valorize, albeit parodistically, both paid and unpaid household labor. By setting her novel in the period of the Mexican Revolution, Esquivel obliquely suggests that, within the restricted sphere of female influence, the subversion of traditional patriarchal values was already occurring. Glickman's *Noticias de suburbio,* even more optimistically reconstructs victimized female subjects as resilient agents who transform the traditional roles of the oppressive mistress and the oppressed maid through an unusual gender alliance. Finally, Santiago's representation of the subaltern female subject in *América's Dream* is somewhat ambivalent. Her evaluation of the novel's protagonist vacillates between Castellanos' realist portrayal of the domestic servant as victim, a point of view that concords with the feminism of modernity, and Esquivel and Glickman's questioning of the structures of power, a questioning that is indexical of postmodernist feminist discourse.

Nevertheless, with respect to the social subtext of the exploitation of women by other women and the solutions that have been proposed in feminist sociological studies, these literary representations of the maid-mistress relationship remain problematical. On the one hand, we might argue that Esquivel and Glickman's optimistic representations correspond to neither the historical nor the recent experiences of private household workers in Latin America and the United States, as reported in testimonial works and sociological studies, such as Poniatowska's (1969/1994) *Hasta no verte Jesús mío* (Here's to You, Jesus) and Romero's (1992) *Maid in the U.S.A.,* and that the solutions implied in these contemporary literary texts are utopian. On the other hand, Glickman's empowerment of the fictive figures of household workers is consistent with the findings of Poggio and Woo (2000), who demonstrate the increased autonomy of some Latina women in the United States as a result of their migratory experience. Santiago's more direct critique of the hierarchical structure of the maid-mistress relationship and of the exploitative conditions of domestic service is consistent with the reality described by domestic workers interviewed by Romero (1992). At the same time, Glickman's novel reproduces some of the pessimism of Castellanos' earlier work without reproducing Castellanos' implied solution of democratization to be brought about by progressive social movements and legally mandated social change. Santiago's emphasis on an individualist solution might even be viewed as an abrogation of efforts by household workers engaged in collective struggles for better working conditions. Considered conjointly, these four works remind readers of the obstacles that will continue to confront feminist intellectuals who attempt to reconcile contradictions between gender, class, and ethnicity through fictional writing, as long as gender alliances across the boundaries of class interests and ethnic identities are rarely constructed in social relations beyond the limits of literary representation.

## Notes

1. In this chapter, I use the terms *feminist* and *feminism* in the sense of Amy Kaminsky's (1989: 223) general working definition: "'Feminism' recognizes and seeks to redress the subordination of women, which it sees as culturally determined." I assume that the expression *culturally determined* encompasses social, political, and economic forms of determination.
2. All translations from the original Spanish are mine.

## References

Castellanos, Rosario. 1957/1961. *Balún-Canán*. Mexico City.: Fondo de Cultura Económica.

Castillo, Debra A. 1992. *Talking Back: Toward a Latin American Feminist Literary Criticism*. Ithaca, N. Y.: Cornell University Press.

Castro-Klarén, Sara, Sylvia Molloy, and Beatriz Sarlo, eds. 1991. *Women's Writing in Latin America*. Boulder, Colo.: Westview Press.

Chaney, Elsa M., and Mary García Castro, eds. 1989. *Muchachas No More: Household Workers in Latin America and the Caribbean*. Philadelphia: Temple University Press.

Cypess, Sandra Messinger. 1985. "*Balún-Canán*: A Model Demonstration of Discourse as Power." *Revista de Estudios Hispánicos* 19, no. 3: 1–15.

Duarte, Isis. 1989. "Household Workers in the Dominican Republic: A Question for the Feminist Movement." Pp. 197–220 in *Muchachas No More: Household Workers in Latin America and the Caribbean*, edited by Elsa M. Chaney and Mary García Castro. Philadelphia: Temple University Press.

Esquivel, Laura. 1989/1990. *Como agua para chocolate*. Mexico City: Planeta.

*From Maids to Compañeras*. 1998. Directed by Jean Weisman and Belkis Vega. Distributor: Jean Weisman.Videocassette.

García Castro, Mary. 1989. "What Is Bought and Sold in Domestic Service? The Case of Bogotá: A Critical Review." Pp. 106–26 in *Muchachas No More: Household Workers in Latin America and the Caribbean*, edited by Elsa M. Chaney and Mary García Castro. Philadelphia: Temple University Press.

Gill, Leslie. 1994. *Precarious Dependencies: Gender, Class and Domestic Service in Bolivia*. New York: Columbia University Press.

Glickman, Nora. 1997. "Noticias de Suburbio." Pp. 425–57 in *Antología Crítica del Teatro Breve Hispanoamericano 1948–1993*, edited by María Mercedes Jaramillo and Mario Yepes. Medellín, Colombia: Editorial Universidad de Antioquia.

Goldsmith, Mary. 1989. "Politics and Programs of Domestic Workers' Organizations in Mexico." Pp. 221–44 in *Muchachas No More: Household Workers in Latin America and the Caribbean*, edited by Elsa M. Chaney and Mary García Castro. Philadelphia: Temple University Press.

Grewal, Inderpal, and Caren Kaplan, eds. 1994. *Scattered Hegemonies: Postmodernity and Transnational Feminist Practices*. Minneapolis: UMP.

Gutiérrez, Ana. 1983. *Se necesita muchacha*. Mexico City: Fondo de Cultura Económica.

Ibsen, Kristine. 1997. "On Recipes, Reading, and Revolution: Postboom Parody in *Como agua para chocolate*." Pp. 111–22 in *The Other Mirror: Women's Narrative in Mexico, 1980–1995*, edited by Kristine Ibsen. Westport, Conn.: Greenwood Press.

Kaminsky, Amy. 1989. "Lesbian Cartographies: Body, Text, and Geography." Pp.

223–56 in *Cultural and Historical Grounding for Hispanic and Luso-Brazilian Feminist Literary Criticism*, edited by Hernán Vidal. Minneapolis: Institute for the Study of Ideologies and Literature.

Kuznesof, Elizabeth. 1989. "A History of Domestic Service in Spanish America, 1492–1980." Pp. 17–36 in *Muchachas No More: Household Workers in Latin America and the Caribbean*, edited by Elsa M. Chaney and Mary García Castro. Philadelphia: Temple University Press.

Olazagasti-Segovia, Elena. 1996/1997. "*El Sueño de América: Sobrevivir la pesadilla.*" *The Latino Review of Books* 2, no. 3: 54–55.

Olea, Raquel. 1995. "Feminism: Modern or Postmodern?" Pp. 192–200 in *The Postmodernism Debate in Latin America*, edited by John Beverley, Michael Aronna, and José Oviedo. Durham, N.C. and London: Duke University Press.

Poggio, Sara, and Ofelia Woo. 2000. *Migración Femenina hacia EUA: Cambio en las Relaciones Familiares y de Género como Resultado de la Migración*. Mexico City: EDAMEX.

Poniatowska, Elena. 1969/1994. *Hasta no Verte Jesús Mío*. Mexico City: Ediciones Era.

———. 1983. "Presentación al Lector Mexicano." Pp. 7–86 in *Se necesita muchacha*, edited by Ana Gutiérrez. Mexico City: Fondo de Cultura Económica.

Rollins, Judith. 1985. *Between Women: Domestics and their Employers*. Philadelphia: Temple University Press.

Romero, Mary. 1992. *Maid in the U.S.A.* New York and London: Routledge.

Santiago, Esmeralda. 1996. *América's Dream*. New York: HarperCollins.

Schiminovich, Flora. 1997. "Nora Glickman: una Propuesta Utópica de Comunión Entre Mujeres." Pp. 458–62 in *Antología Crítica del Teatro Breve Hispanoamericano 1948–1993*, edited by María Mercedes Jaramillo and Mario Yepes. Medellín, Colombia: Editorial Universidad de Antioquia.

Sinnigen, John H. 1995. "*Como Agua para Chocolate*: Feminine Space, Postmodern Cultural Politics, National Allegory." *CIEFL Bulletin* (Hyderabad, India), n.s., 7, nos. 1–2: 111–31.

Steele, Cynthia. 1989. "The Other Within: Class and Ethnicity as Difference in Mexican Women's Literature." Pp. 297–328 in *Cultural and Historical Grounding for Hispanic and Luso-Brazilian Feminist Literary Criticism*, edited by Hernán Vidal. Minneapolis: Institute for the Study of Ideologies and Literature.

11.

# Sexual Orientation, AIDS, and Human Rights in Argentina: The Paradox of Social Advance amid Health Crisis

*Mario Pecheny*

In 1984, the *Comunidad Homosexual Argentina* (Argentine Homosexual Community, CHA) was founded. It was the first gay organization that was able to endure and consolidate itself as an institution in Argentina. CHA was a pioneer in the sexual minorities' movement, which has been growing and diversifying ever since. Simultaneously, Argentina was hit by the Acquired Immunodeficiency Syndrome (AIDS) epidemic. Since the onset of the first case of AIDS in 1982, the epidemic has moved forward without pause, totaling an estimated 20,000 cases by the end of 2001. This chapter analyzes the evolution of social and political responses to the AIDS epidemic in Argentina, ranging from the initial response of ignorance, stigmatization, and prejudice to the gradual creation of discourse about, and legislation governing, tolerance and protection for people living with the human immunodeficiency virus (HIV) and AIDS. This analysis suggests that the AIDS epidemic and some of the responses it brought about have actually helped redefine the social status of homosexuality and the rights of sexual minorities. I also argue that discrimination and social recognition operate at different societal levels and, therefore, that no necessary congruence between them will necessarily exist.

The outbreak of AIDS created the fear that infected persons would suffer discrimination, especially exacerbating such treatment of those who appeared as the main victims of infection: homosexual males.[1] Nevertheless, those fears did not materialize as expected when the epidemic began. Instead, there emerged a discourse of tolerance and even acceptance concerning "that which can be said or believed" regarding both people living with HIV/AIDS and homosexuals.

On the whole, however, it cannot be said that discrimination against these persons has disappeared from Argentina. If we analyze different social arenas—from intimate spaces to public political space—we find no neat correspondence between them. Even though the law is protective or nondiscriminatory, the level of discrimination experienced at the hands of "significant others"—namely relatives, partners, friends, coworkers, and neighbors—generally prevents people from asserting their positive rights, where applicable. The reason is clear: *Legal* rights are difficult to exercise if such acts entail revealing a *socially* stigmatized trait of one's identity. In these cases, beyond the matter of HIV itself, there is also the possible fear of revealing stigmatized practices, such as homosexuality, or even illegal practices, such as consumption of illegal drugs.

These considerations are pertinent to the general analysis of social movements and the possible emergence of a gay movement. The visibility of the members of a social category is one of the core aspects that turns that social category (merely defined by some common property) into a social group. Becoming a true social group is a prerequisite to envisioning any collective action or social movement activity. Visibility is particularly important when we analyze movements made up of individuals belonging to "stigmatizable" (or "discreditable") categories, that is, individuals who possess a quality considered socially inferior yet not instantly observable (Goffman 1963/1989). The capacity to conceal allows the management of the stigma in such individuals: to make it public or not, depending on the particular social spaces and interlocutors with which they are coacting. Therefore, a category constituted by stigmatizable individuals is not a priori a social group, which implies a modicum of visibility and communication among its members and toward nonmembers.

The development of the Argentine gay movement occurred within a framework of macroconditions that favored its growth, such as political liberalization after 1983 and the formal and informal transnational networks that rose to defend and advocate human rights and nondiscrimination (Keck and Sikkink 1998). On the other hand, globalization has accelerated "international flows" (Badie and Smouts 1992) and what Anthony Giddens (1991) calls "the mediated experience," that is, the intrusion of distant events into people's daily consciousness through the media. Both phenomena allow individuals to virtually share situations that happen in other parts of the world and thus expand the universe of possible lifestyles, including different ways of experiencing sexuality. Since the early 1980s, therefore, homosexuality has begun to emerge from its social invisibility, thanks to the action of the gay community and movement, but also in reaction to AIDS, which forced the government and society to publicly discuss the topics of homosexuality and sexuality in general.

### The AIDS Epidemic in Argentina

We know that the first AIDS case in Argentina was diagnosed in 1982 and, by the end of 2001, the number of accumulated cases was 20,000, third place in Latin America after Brazil and Mexico. The male/female case ratio, which is decreasing, is 3.2 to 1. The average age in infected males is 28 and in females 24. The epidemic is an urban one, mainly concentrated in Buenos Aires and its environs. The number of HIV positives is impossible to accurately calculate, given that there is no systematic notification to the HIV infected; thus, the typical person does not know his or her HIV status, and the published figures constantly vary. Different estimates made in Argentina have yielded a figure between 80,000 and 160,000 infected people.

Until 1987 sexual transmission between men accounted for 75 percent of all cases. After 1990 intravenous drugs became the main mode of transmission (Pecheny 1999). Both modes combined account for 70 percent of all AIDS cases in adults declared before 2001. In 1996 heterosexual transmission overtook homosexual transmission in a number of new cases per year. These changes in the epidemic profile parallel a social and demographic change: AIDS increasingly affects people who are younger and poorer.

### Social Reaction to AIDS

*AIDS: From Marginalization to Tolerance*

The AIDS epidemic appeared when, at least in the Western world, medicine had largely been able to control infectious diseases, and the major life-threatening diseases had become individual and nontransmittable, for example, cardiovascular diseases and varieties of cancer. Within this context, HIV resurrected the old ghosts and social fears associated with the deadly infectious and contagious diseases of the past.

Even when, in modern-day Argentina, there are recurring outbreaks of cholera, tuberculosis, and measles, the underlying (and true) explanation of them is that these outbreaks are engendered by a weak, inefficient public health system and by the inadequate socioecomic welfare of too many persons, not by medical shortcomings. These diseases are viewed, all in all, as ills of the past that adequate and consistent health policies could easily eradicate.

AIDS appeared instead as an incurable affliction that medicine could scarcely control. Moreover, the new ailment did not seem to attack at random: in countries where the first cases were detected (and in Brazil and Argentina) the first victims were mostly homosexual males, later to be joined by intravenous drug users. According to predominant social representations, these *risk groups,* as epidemiological science calls them (Oppenheimer 1992; Grmek 1995; Kornblit et al. 1997), were separable from the general population by boundaries pertaining to different lifestyles or to geography.

Historically, a common social reaction to epidemics and plagues has been the search for scapegoats. In the early 1980s, the birth of a contagious, lethal disease of mysterious origin, associated with stigmatized behavior, and attributable to groups presumed different and identifiable, foreshadowed social reactions inclined to segregating these groups and the victims of infection (Herzlich and Adam 1997). Voices were raised to express fears that discrimination and stigmatization might spread. Many of the initial attitudes toward AIDS, based on prejudice and fear, confirmed the apprehension: requests for massive and mandatory blood tests, proposals for an "AIDS sanatorium," quarantines, files on HIV positives, persecution of homosexuals and prostitutes, institutions and health workers repeatedly denying HIV patients their due treatment, banishment from families, tests of job candidates before hiring, firing employees, and social ostracism in general.

It is interesting to note that, with AIDS, phrases that had been notorious in times of military dictatorship (referring to victims of repression) again became current: "They must have done something, there must be a reason." The counterpoint to such catchphrases was "it can't happen to me." The victims are blamed for their "punishment," while oneself is innocent and perceived as invulnerable.[2] As far as AIDS is concerned, this attitude implies discrimination toward those afflicted by the disease. It also conveys a propensity to feel free from risk and therefore leads people not to take preventive measures. Even in the testimony of some patients there is evidence that they feel a need to assert their "innocence" regarding sexual issues ("I'm not a homosexual"; "I'm not promiscuous"), drug issues, or both (Pecheny 2001).

Social reactions to AIDS constitute a contradictory process. On the one hand, as mentioned before, the epidemic triggered a return of many ancient fears and prejudices about "others" considered different (gays, drug users, the promiscuous, foreigners, etc.). On the other hand, a unique situation emerged wherein some of these (heretofore invisible) others are now integrated into these new discourses and public action. They thus partially contribute—by means of their publicity—to filling the gap that allowed such others to remain simply an abstract notion in the eyes of other Argentines. The suffering of AIDS victims, regardless of such real or imaginary differences, made the abstract others become concrete others. Death and disease played a universalizing role (we are all equal in the face of the suffering that the disease brings and we are all equal in loneliness, etc.) and aided in the social recognition of the victims' human rights.

### AIDS and Redefining the Status of Homosexuality

Early social research on homosexuality in Argentina (Jáuregui 1987; Sívori 1994; Salessi 1995; Sebrelli 1997; Vujosevich, Kornblit, and Pecheny 1998) concurs on a double-sided truth: On the one hand, a genuine "homosexual world" had developed, especially in Buenos Aires, yet that world existed in "historic invisibility." In fact, the core issue has long been such invisibility more than homosexuality as a practice.

AIDS destabilized the place in our social order that homosexuality had traditionally been assigned, in other words, a place of discreet behavior, which was a condition for its tolerance. This social order may be labeled *hypocritical* because it accepts homosexuality only as long as it remains nonvisible: confined to privacy, without being able to express itself publicly as a loving and affectionate bond (Sullivan 1995).

Since 1813, when the holy office was abolished, legislation has not outlawed same-gender consensual sexual relations in Argentina. Discretion is all that is asked of homosexuals in return. The national constitution of 1853 and subsequent judicial sentencing expressed it clearly: whatever belongs to the private realm of individuals is allowed, as long as it does not affect the public domain. Problems arise when private boundaries are crossed and homosexuality becomes publicly visible.

Since the nineteenth century and during most of the twentieth, public discretion remained the main characteristic of most homosexuals, who have had to lead different lives and take on identities according to their social spheres and connections. The situation is more difficult outside of Buenos Aires and other important urban centers, because if people are openly homosexual, they could take on the roles of town characters or scapegoats. Otherwise, their double lives may result in their migrating to the capital city and/or dreading potential blackmail.

In the first half of the twentieth century, homosexuals began to be persecuted and repressed, especially via police guidelines, which had originally been intended to punish minor crimes.[3] Such police interdictions—used to penalize, for instance, "inciting or soliciting carnal acts" in public and "wearing garments pertaining to the opposite sex"—were abolished in 1996. Also in the 1940s some "homosexual scandals" were featured prominently in the press: an alleged orgy involving military school cadets and the expulsion from Argentina of Spanish performer Miguel de Molina.

Toward the 1970s, the lives of homosexuals continued in relative tranquillity, periodically interrupted by harassment from the police, who used interdictions to repress and extort homosexuals on the streets. Twenty-four-hour detention of presumed homosexuals and sex workers constituted a source of (illegal) income for police precincts. Profiteering aside, however, it is difficult to understand the logic behind such arbitrary detention as a method of dissuasion or repression. The detention and fear in revealing one's homosexuality are not efficient means for ending homosexual activity, but instead promote a type of social interaction that favors disassociating sexuality and affection, searching for maximum efficiency in the "pickup," creating codes and subcultures, and learning to pretend (Vujosevich, Kornblit, and Pecheny 1998).

The repression of homosexuality worsened during Juan D. Perón's administration (1973–1974) and in his wife Isabel's term (1974–1976), when police and parapolice forces were cleared to carry out repressive actions. The coup d'état of March 24, 1976, did nothing but worsen matters. During the ensuing military dictatorship (1976–1983), repression singled out not only any political and ideological opposition, but also any suspicious behavior related to personal appearance, any cultural and artistic innovation, and so forth. Thus, in the first months after the coup, the few surviving gay bars and discotheques were closed by the police. In particular, right before the Soccer World Cup of 1978, which Argentina hosted, the government carried out a "cleansing" campaign enlisting the police and its Moral Brigade. After the World Cup, the more or less clandestine homosexual clubs were reopened and managed to function (in spite of frequent police raids), thanks to bribes paid systematically to police precincts (Perlongher 1983a; 1983b; Rapisardi and Modarelli 2001).

After the 1980s and the return of democracy, the homosexual situation began to change. Political liberalization and the aftermath of the pro–human rights movement that arose during the dictatorship created a favorable context to advance the cause for achieving new rights and developing new participants, such as the women's movement (Chejter 1996) and sexual minorities' movement (Brown 1999).

### The Contemporary Gay Movement and the Fight Against Discrimination

Discrimination against sexual minorities is not only a question of individual, private attitudes, but also fundamentally a social problem of human-rights violations. In this sense, we speak of discrimination when the government, society, a social group of people, or an individual separates, excludes, expels, or even kills a certain person or group, attacks their dignity, and/or removes or keeps them from exercising their rights, based on the single fact that this person or group possesses a characteristic that is different—either real or imaginary—from what is established as *normal*. Social discrimination implies uneven relationships of power. The search for social recognition implies, then, that the groups and individuals who are discriminated against try to increase their relative power, for which (among other things) they have created their own organizations.

The analysis of sexual minorities' organizations must attempt to explain the social stigma homosexuality still endures, keeping in mind the distinction that Goffman (1980/1992) makes between stigmatized individuals and stigmatizable individuals. In stigmatized individuals, the features that make them different are known or immediately perceptible, while in stigmatizable individuals the difference is not seen immediately. In the latter case (which corresponds to the situation of most gays and lesbians), the problem is deciding how to manipulate information about their difference: whether or not to expose it or disguise it, and, in either case, how, when, and to whom. Dealing with concealment is a protective recourse (Zempleni 1984) that many stigmatizable individuals can exploit; the problem is that this recourse becomes a liability for political participation and consequent public exposure. This makes visibility a key issue in gay politics, as well as for HIV-positive people.

How individuals participate in organizations may be analyzed in terms of costs and benefits. The cost refers to time and effort that one must dedicate to public action. For an individual, according to this analysis, the rational thing to do is wait for others to take on the cost of participating for the common objective, in case the object sought is a common good (nondiscrimination, for instance). Evidently, in the event that the common good is achieved, he or she will still benefit and become a so-called free rider (Olson 1966/1978). The famous "free-rider problem" in social movement theory is that, if each individual follows the free-rider logic, the common good is never obtained.

The price individuals pay for joining the struggle to obtain a common good like sexual rights may be too high. The price is linked not only to time and effort, but also to the issue of visibility, since "coming out" may entail further costs. Therefore it is appropriate to ask why some individuals do, in fact, face the onerous cost of joining in collective action, despite the risk. One possible answer to this question comes from "New Social Movement" theory, where the analysis is reframed to focus on issues of identity and symbolic struggle (Melucci 1989). In the cases with which this chapter is concerned, the benefits for the participants in collective action are not necessarily material, but are actually advances in terms of personal identity. These benefits may involve self-esteem, enthusiasm for standing among one's peers, the enjoyment of participating in a common struggle, and so on. On the other hand, AIDS has cast many into a tragic situation, in the sense that personal identity is not the only issue at stake, but the very quality and duration of life for oneself and/or one's loved ones is also at stake. As Hannah Arendt points out in *Men in Dark Times:* "One can only resist in terms of the identity which is under attack."

There are two precursors to today's sexual minorities' movement in Argentina: the feminist organizations of the 1960s (Chejter 1996), and the *Frente de Liberación Homosexual* (Homosexual Liberation Front, or FLH), which operated almost without abandoning its clandestine status. In 1976 feminist and gay political activities were interrupted because of repression under military rule. Like many other Argentines, many gay (and feminist) activists of the time were forced into exile.

Unlike the FLH of the 1970s, most gay and lesbian movements of the 1980s and 1990s have not presented homosexuality as a form of transgression, but rather as a lifestyle choice as legitimate as any other. In keeping with the spirit of the times, the language of *liberation* is replaced by that of *rights*. The corresponding community and contemporary gay-lesbian movements also attempted to redefine homosexual identity in terms of gay identity.

If in the developed countries the gay movement was the first to take on the fight against AIDS (Altman 1994), in Latin American countries like Argentina, the organization of a movement for the rights of sexual minorities was parallel to the development of the AIDs epidemic (Roberts 1995). In 1983, with political liberalization, bars and nightclubs were reopened. The Coordinator of Gay Groups was formed, and it organized the first conference on AIDS. The coordinator was dissolved the following year. In response to a police raid on a bar in March 1984, over 150 people attended an assembly in a discotheque, deciding to found the CHA. The subsequent public presentation of CHA, conceived as a human rights organization, was made in the newspaper *Clarín* in May of the same year, by way of a petition "against discrimination and repression." That same month CHA was approved as a Civil Association and then decided to apply for legal status. In December 1989, the Inspector General of Justice denied CHA its legal status. Inspector General Alberto González Arzac argued that the goals of CHA "are not in concurrence with those of the common good, as an expression of public interest or welfare" because, according to the National Academy of Medicine, homosexuality "is treated as a deviation from normal sexual instinct" and "prevents forming a family and therefore threatens it." In April 1990, CHA appealed, with the support of numerous human rights organizations. The Court of Appeals confirmed the resolution of the Inspector. CHA then appealed to the Supreme Court. In November 1991, the Court, by six votes to two, declared that CHA's appeal lacked merit.

According to the Argentine legal system, its Supreme Court had the final word on these matters. Yet, CHA was finally able to obtain legal status, thanks to a political decision by President Carlos Menem, who was pressured by gay activists during a presidential visit to the United States. In Washington, on being questioned on the issue, Menem publicly announced that CHA's legal status would be granted. The executive, using the discretion that the court recognizes in administrative affairs, ordered the new inspector general to reopen the case, and CHA obtained legal status in January 1992 (Verbitsky 1993). This is a typical case of what Margaret E. Keck and Kathryn Sikkink (1998: 12) call the "boomerang pattern": If a government ignores its pleas, a country's nongovernmental agents can pressure their own government through the action of a more powerful foreign or international nongovernmental organization (NGO) from another state or from an intergovernmental organization and thus succeed where normal domestic political avenues have failed.

CHA was the first organization of sexual minorities formed after the transition to democracy, and from it others were formed. In the 1980s CHA's main activities worked toward political and symbolic status and community integration. It also participated at the most important demonstrations for justice and human rights. In the beginning, CHA did not consider the need to carry out AIDS campaigns focused on the gay community, but in 1988, in light of the advance of the epidemic, it decided to launch the Stop-AIDS campaign with the support of the Pan American Health Organization (PAHO). Indeed, CHA has decided to change direction and location many times. One of its presidents, Alejandro Zalazar, served as undersecretary of the ministry of the interior for some time, which elicited criticism from leaders of other organizations. In 1997 CHA was "refounded" without formal leadership and made up of representatives of different parts of the movement.

Another mixed organization, the *Sociedad de Integración Gay-Lesbica Argentina* (Gay-Lesbian Integration Society of Argentina, SIGLA), has been active since 1992. SIGLA carries out activities of community integration and assistance, and also runs campaigns on AIDS prevention. For several years SIGLA had a weekly radio show. On his own personal initiative, Rafael Freda, president of SIGLA, obtained from his insurance company medical coverage for his life-partner, thus setting one of the precedents for social protection of homosexual couples.

In the late 1980s AIDS became the almost exclusive axis of gay political action. Some activists, wanting to distance themselves from this core and suggesting that the rights of sexual minorities go beyond AIDS issues, founded new organizations, which gave a fresh impetus to the budding social movement. Gays and Lesbians for Civil Rights, the most important group in this regard, carried out its main activity between 1993 and 1996, when Carlos Jáuregui, its main leader, died of AIDS. This group took on the legal defense of victims of discrimination and violence, in sexual-orientation and AIDS-related matters. Jáuregui received a good deal of media exposure, and took numerous initiatives, such as suing the archbishop of Buenos Aires, Monsignor Antonio Quarracino, for making discriminatory remarks. Although the lawsuits were never heard in court, each accusation prompted discussions about discrimination and the acceptance of sexual minorities in the news media. Jáuregui was the main gay leader to ensure that the issue of homosexual rights and nondiscrimination became part of the public debate.

In the 1990s the Argentine press began to deal with the issue of sexual minorities from a different point of view, shifting from a sensationalist and stigmatizing tone to one of respect. The media began to tell stories of the everyday lives of gays and lesbians, and to denounce acts of discrimination. This change in attitude stemmed from different sources than previous changes had: Gays and lesbians had become more visible, the press had evolved more, and society in general had become more receptive. In fact, at the time, some voices were heard telling of gay life in the first person, and at once the media realized that framing gay issues in these terms also "sells."

Since 1993 the Nexo group has edited *N/X* magazine, which has a large readership among gay men. For the first time in Argentina, a gay magazine is sold at newsstands on a regular basis. Nexo also owns facilities where it holds courses and cultural activities. Since 1997 Nexo has also offered companionship, self-help, and assistance to gay people living with HIV/AIDS.

Among lesbian groups are *Convocatoria Lesbiana* (Lesbian Convocation), *Las Lunas y las otras-La Fulana* (The "Moons" [i.e., lesbian feminists] and others), La Fulana), and *Lesbianas a la Vista* (Lesbians in Full View). *Convocatoria Lesbiana* was formed from a television appearance by Ilse Fuskova, a leader hailing from feminist circles. This small group participates in different activities organized by the others and it especially shows up when called on by television programs where issues of interest to it are discussed. *Las Lunas*, a group of lesbian feminists, has met since 1990. It considers itself a closed group of women and owns a home that it uses for its meetings. *Lesbianas a la Vista* speak not only of the specificity of lesbian issues, but also of the need not to retreat and remain in hiding. There are other, less visible groups, and there are those organized only for certain circumstances, such as the Lesbian Mothers or the Group for Lesbian Integration.

Lesbian militants are typically linked to feminist organizations and women's movement organizations. They participate in seminars and publications of such organizations, like the massive National Encounter of Women, (*Encuentro Nacional de Mujeres*), which has met in different Argentine cities since 1986. In the second (1987) Encounter of Women, in Córdoba, the first workshop on lesbianism was held. Since then the Encounter of Women has featured lesbianism workshops in which lesbians and heterosexuals exchange experiences and overcome (although not without difficulty) their mutual distrust.

A phenomenon peculiar to the Argentine case is the existence of several organizations specific to transvestites and transsexuals. The problems that they face are police repression—not always related to prostitution—and the issue of legal identity. Since the late 1980s, there have also been numerous centers—not political but cultural or communitarian—like *Casa de las Lunas (House of the "Moons")*, *Encuentro Gay (Gay Encounter)*, the Nexo group center, and *Lugar Gay de Buenos Aires (The Gay Place of Buenos Aires)*, where there are workshops and cultural and leisure activities. Academic and cultural institutions have been created; one operates in the *Centro Rojas* (Rojas Center) of the University of Buenos Aires. And there are even gay athletic institutions, such as the *Deportistas Argentinos Gays* (Argentine Gay Athletes), which participated in the Amsterdam Gay Games of August 1998.

The manifestations of pride that have been held annually since 1991 attract a growing, but still small, number of participants, never more than 2,500 to 3,000 people. Since 1995 there have also been National Encounters of Lesbians, Gays, Transvestites, Transsexuals, and Bisexuals. What's more, at least four periodicals addressing gay issues can be purchased in Buenos Aires.

In short, the first gay organization, CHA, was created in 1984 with the premise that sexuality is a human right. Since then, sexual minority organizations have multiplied and diversified. Toward the late 1980s, if the issue of nondiscrimination remained the common banner for all such groups, the AIDS question became the main and almost exclusive concern of gay men's organizations. By contrast, the lesbian organizations were more inclined toward the feminist and women's movements, denouncing repression based on both sexual orientation and gender. For the gay organizations, fighting the disease became the main objective, and through that struggle they acquired certain "citizen's rights." Furthermore, fighting AIDS naturally led to some unusual convergences, since it entailed new cooperation between hetereogeneous actors, such as public officials, politicians, epidemiologists, physicians, gay and AIDS activists, and patients.

Since 1992 and 1993, not only as a response to the consequences of the AIDS epidemic—and given the visibile inequalities suffered by people with different sexual orientations regarding access to social security, health treatments, inheritance, and so on—but also in an attempt to disentangle gay issues from AIDS, a debate has grown in Argentina about the positive rights of sexual minorities, for example, legal recognition of same-sex unions, adoption, and so forth. In 1996 the constitutional assembly of the city of Buenos Aires revoked the rights of police interdictions that served to legitimize police persecution of gay people. The new city constitution, approved in August of that same year, acknowledges "the right to be different" and condemns "discrimination that tends to segregate due to race, ethnic background, gender, sexual orientation, age, religion, ideology, opinion, physical traits, social, economic, psychological and physical condition, or any other circumstance that entails difference, exclusion, restriction or derision."

AIDS helped to make visible issues not previously discussed publicly, such as homosexuality—or indeed, sexuality—and to make them an inevitable part of the public agenda, and a necessary one. The public emergence of homosexuality and homosexuals that AIDS brought about has had the effect of breaking down the hypocritical order mentioned earlier (see page 255). AIDS also acted as a catalyst for the consolidation of the homosexual movement, the demand for rights, and public debate about these issues. Thus the AIDS experience created, paradoxically, a context for redefining the subordinate status of a stigmatized practice that had been relegated to the private space of discretion, and it precipitated public concern over discrimination and the civil rights of sexual minorities entering the public scene. Because of AIDS, different forms of sexuality were discussed in public, not only in terms of sexual relations, but also in terms of love, public displays of affection, and social and civil rights. In particular, the AIDS epidemic accelerated the debate on the legal status and social protection of unmarried and gay couples. The public model of tolerance and a glimmer of social acceptance are due, among other factors, to the action of the united gay movement and its fight against AIDS, the predominance of epidemiological strategies that emphasize individual responsibility over social surveillance, the hegemony of the liberal values of respect for individual rights, and pressure from international organizations like the World Health Organization.

## The Rights of People Living with HIV/AIDS and the Ambiguity of State Policy

In the 1980s, people living with HIV/AIDS found themselves legally unprotected in the face of discrimination. The state did not get involved, and the first initiatives were taken instead by the nascent organizations dedicated to fighting AIDS, together with the gay movement and some health professionals. The AIDS organizations were not only pioneers in assisting the afflicted and launching prevention campaigns, but they were also the first to denounce discriminatory attitudes (which came from the government and the ministry of health, among others) and to push for antidiscriminatory campaigns.

In the mid-1980s, the first AIDS organizations were created. Some arose from circles of friends with HIV/AIDS who were convinced that something had to be done. Others originated from existent homosexual organizations, and yet others were founded by health professionals confronted with the hostility of public health officials and even hospitals. In the 1990s in Argentina, and in Buenos Aires in particular, a genuine nongovernmental movement to fight AIDS was formed, mainly composed of two types of NGOs. On the one hand, NGOs or foundations linked to health institutions (*Huésped* and *Fundai*) of greater economic power focused on assistance and prevention. On the other hand, there were the smaller NGOs, community help and self-help groups, dedicated to localized prevention, patient care, and antidiscrimination. NGOs have formed networks that have seriously criticized the wisdom of government action (and inaction) on many occasions.

In spite of limited resources and difficulties in contacting the afflicted, AIDS groups have contributed considerably to improving the social response to AIDS. Most associations take on the health issue as well as the human rights issue. In particular, these associations have been able to redefine the social, political, and legal context of AIDS. They have helped the sick with their paperwork in hospitals, courts, and offices. They have contributed to the improvement of medical care and hospital infrastructure. They play a part in controlling the government, hospitals, and doctors. They have created places that help keep HIV/AIDS patients from becoming isolated and lonely. They have made visible a group of people whom society had forced into an extremely dramatic role while simultaneously denying them their tragedy. Last, they have fostered a public culture wherein a less negative attitude toward the disease now prevails.

The government's response came too late and halfheartedly. Due to national and international pressure, the Argentine parliament approved a national law for the fight against AIDS (Law 23,798) only in 1990. The law attempted to guarantee individual rights, even in the face of alleged considerations of public health. The priority given to individual rights underscored the view that prevention is the responsibility of the people infected and of each member of the community. The basic principles of the law are as follows (Puccinelli 1995):

a. The respect for the autonomy of free will; that is, each individual has the right to make his or her own vital decisions. Hence, the law guarantees informed consent for blood tests and treatment.
b. Confidentiality, that is, physician-patient confidentiality and coded test results.
c. Nondiscrimination against virus carriers.
d. Information and education on all aspects relating to AIDS and its transmission.

The law went into effect in 1991. The provincial legislatures, many of them repressive and/or persecutory, began to adapt to the national law. That same year, the National Program against AIDS was created in order to come up with national strategies for prevention and control of HIV infection, to coordinate public campaigns, and to establish the basis for agreements with the provinces, among other goals.

The Ministry of Health has since developed very few campaigns for prevention in general, following an orientation of "abstinence."[4] Until the mid-1990s, the use of condoms was not clearly specified, nor was the danger of sharing needles when using intravenous drugs explained. The campaigns instead took on a moralizing tone. Only in 1997 and 1998 did the Ministry (with World Bank funds) begin to finance AIDS prevention campaigns together with NGOs, among which were some gay organizations, such as Nexo and SIGLA. The Ministry of Education has not yet (as of early 2002) implemented any type of campaign for the educational system as a whole.

In 1994 Law 24,455 compelled union *obras socials* (health maintenance organizations, HMOs) to cover AIDS treatments. In 1996, the same was asked of private HMOs. The HMO law, justified from the point of view of nondiscrimination, manifests the government's will to transfer responsibility and the cost of AIDS care to these two other sectors of the healthcare system, due to its current policy of decentralization and budget cuts (Belmartino 1995). The Ministry of Health covers total medication costs for patients who prove they cannot afford them. Although supplying medication, including combination therapies, is one of the few activities the Ministry carries out effectively, it is interrupted periodically. The reasons cited (even by the Ministry's own representatives) include the negligence of government officials and of vendors. It is a well-known fact that interrupting these treatments brings about devastating consequences in patients' health as well as in fighting the virus in general, given the risk that the virus may become resistant to new drugs.

In short, the government concerned itself with AIDS, but with the least conflictive aspect from an ideological point of view (supplying medication). The public campaigns have been and continue to be vague, erratic, and faulty by omission: rarely have they mentioned condom use or harm-reduction related to drug use. Notwithstanding, thanks to the active participation of NGOs and the media, the population has an adequate level of knowledge about AIDS. There are laws to protect HIV/AIDS patients, and they undeniably represent an advance over the previous decade. Nevertheless, certain employment-related, nondiscrimination laws are poorly enforced in many cases, for example in preemployment and on-the-job testing. Companies, including state-owned companies, continue to fire or not hire people who have tested positive for HIV.

In Argentina, difficult access to justice in general, with its slowness and inefficiency, discourages many citizens from exercising their civil rights. In the case of an individual living with HIV/AIDS, this exercise is also fundamentally constrained by the conditions of stigmatization and discrimination regarding people close to their affections, whether real or only perceived. These conditions worsen when knowing the mode of transmission implies revealing an identity and/or practice that is not publicly accepted, particularly homosexuality or drug use. Yet, very often when homosexuality and/or HIV status is revealed, such feared discrimination from family, friends, partners, and so on does not manifest itself. However, fear of discrimination operates by having the individual prefer to be secretive to protect him/herself, even to the point where the situation becomes unsustainable, instead of becoming visible and sharing the experience.

## Concluding Remarks

Discrimination found in situations of such hidden subordination may be transformed by novel movements that open outward, toward the public space. Since the transition to democracy initiated in 1983, a sexual rights movement has formed in Argentina. Whenever there are actors who claim rights in the public arena, new issues are liable to be debated, new relations to be questioned, and new spaces to become grounds for political action. This may result in novel "dynamics of human rights," the conflict and debate about such rights now taking place in the public arena of a democratic society (Lefort 1986). These open-ended dynamics allow legitimate rights to be extended in two ways: (1) including new identities (subjects) as claimants to rights recognized previously for others, and (2) including new rights themselves. The first case has been witnessed in extending suffrage to women, to illiterates, and to nonlandowners, and in extending the right of marriage to two people of the same sex. The second case corresponds to the claims for new rights in the public arena—generally in the reformulation of rights already present. Incorporating new subjects to rights, as in the paradigmatic case of women, is expressed in two ways that oppose and complement each other. First, in pursuing equality, equals are seen to deserve identical rights, while, second, the equal recognition of difference implies that different individuals deserve specific approaches, since formal universal treatment suppresses the specifics that constitute each identity.

The claims of sexual minorities also fall under this double reasoning, that of equality and that of recognizing differences/specifics. The early tendency in sexual minorities' goals was to pursue equality: first, demanding rights equal to those of heterosexuals (social rights derived from marriage, participating in public institutions, and so forth); second, and as a counterbalance to the first demand, the right to privacy, that is, the right to do whatever the individual wants to do in private, as long as no harm comes to others (i.e., to be left alone). The epidemic and the fight against AIDS put many of these rights on the main agenda of both the government and the social movement. Another trend in the pursuit of rights, addressed the issues of social recognition and the exercise of formal rights. The Argentine movement among sexual minorities that arose in the 1980s has demanded such rights. And the AIDS epidemic, with all the suffering and harm it has brought—far from increasing homosexuals' ostracism and segregation—has instead, and ironically, contributed over the years to an ever-greater visibility for their social movement and to a host of claims that, until the era of AIDS, had been historically invisible.

## Notes

I would like to thank Mariana Alcañiz and Timothy Wickham-Crowley for their great help in translating this chapter from the original Spanish.

1. During the 1980s, sex among men was the predominant way of transmission in North America and Western Europe, as it was in Brazil, Mexico, and Argentina.

2. In this respect, reactions to AIDS reveal authoritarian social mechanisms that go beyond the dread of the disease. (Inversely, AIDS has also revealed attitudes of empathy, overcoming those of fear and isolation.)

3. There are no detailed historic studies that attempt to explain why repression was unleashed at the time. However, it may be pointed out that toward the end of the nineteenth century, an urban subculture of men was formed in Buenos Aires, men who had sex with other men and men who dressed as women. This subculture would clash with moral and "hygienic" values that were being imposed on a budding nation (Salessi 1995; Guy 1994).

4. In order to prevent HIV transmission, the orientation of "abstinence" prescribes sexual abstinence or monogamous fidelity among HIV positives. Regarding intravenous transmission, the prescription is total interruption of drug use. On the contrary, the "realistic" or "risk reduction" orientation proposes using condoms, and also not sharing needles in the event that one cannot or will not halt intravenous drug use.

# References

Altman, Dennis. 1994. *Power and Community: Organizational and Cultural Responses to AIDS*. London: Taylor & Francis.

Badie, Bertrand, and Marie Claude Smouts. 1992. *Le Retournement du Monde: Sociologie de la Scène Internationale*. Paris: Presses de la Fondation Nationale des Sciences Politiques.

Belmartino, Susana. 1995. "Transformaciones Internas al Sector Salud: La Ruptura del Pacto Corporativo," *Desarrollo Económico* 137: 83–103.

Brown, Stephen. 1999. "Democracy and Sexual Difference: The Lesbian and Gay Movement in Argentina." Pp. 110–32 in *The Global Emergence of Gay and Lesbian Politics: National Imprints of a Worldwide Movement*, edited by Barry D. Adam, Jan Willem Duyvendak, and André Krouwel. Philadelphia: Temple University Press.

Chejter, Silvia. 1996. *Feminismo por Feministas: Fragmentos para una historia del Feminismo Argentino 1970–1996*. Buenos Aires: Documentos del CECYM (Centro de Encuentros Cultura y Mujer).

Giddens, Anthony. 1991. *Modernity and Self-Identity: Self and Society in the Late Modern Age*. Cambridge, England: Polity Press.

Goffman, Erving. 1963/1989. *Stigmate: Les Usages Sociaux des Handicaps*. Paris: Ed. de Minuit.

Grmek, Mirko D. 1995. *Histoire du Sida: Début et Origine d'une Pandémie Actuelle*. Paris: Payot.

Guy, Donna J. 1994. *El Sexo Peligroso: La Prostitución Legal en Buenos Aires 1875–1955*. Buenos Aires: Sudamericana.

Herzlich, Claudine, and Philippe Adam. 1997. "Urgence Sanitaire et Liens Sociaux: L'exceptionnalité du Sida?" *Cahiers internationaux de Sociologie* 102: 5–28.

Jáuregui, Carlos L. 1987. *La Homosexualidad en la Argentina*. Buenos Aires: Tarso.

Keck, Margaret E., and Kathryn Sikkink. 1998. *Activists Beyond Borders: Advocacy Networks in International Politics*. Ithaca, N.Y. and London: Cornell University Press.

Kornblit, Ana Lía et al. 1997. *Y el Sida está Entre Nosotros: Un Estudio Sobre Actitudes, Creencias y Conductas de Grupos Golpeados por la Enfermedad*. Buenos Aires: Corregidor.

Lefort, Claude. 1986. "Les droits de L'homme et l'Etat-providence." Pp. 31–56 in *Essais sur le politique*. Paris: Seuil.

Melucci, Alberto. 1989. *Nomads of the Present: Social Movements and Invidividual Needs in Contemporary Society*. Philadelphia: Temple University Press.

Olson, Mancur. 1996/1978. *La Logique de L'action Collective*. Paris: Presses Universitaires de France.

Oppenheimer, Gerald. 1992. "Causes, Cases, and Cohorts: The Role of Epidemiology in the Historical Construction of AIDS." Pp. 49–83 in *AIDS: The Making of a Chronic Disease*, edited by E. Fee and D. Fox. Berkeley: University of California Press.

Pecheny, Mario. 1999. "Consumo de Drogas, Discriminación y Prevención del Sida: Consideraciones Generales, con Referencias al caso Argentine."In *Pour un XXIe siècle libéré des drogues*, edited by Sonia Bahri. Paris: Unesco.

———. 2001. *La Construction de L'avortement et du Sida en Tant que Questions Politiques: Le Cas de l'Argentine*. Lille, France: Presses Universitaires du Septentrion.

Perlongher, Néstor. 1983a. "La Represión del Homosexual en Argentina." *El Porteño* 22: 8–9.

———. 1983b. "La represión del Homosexual en el Proceso." *El Porteño* 24: 16.

Puccinelli, Oscar Raúl. 1995. *Derechos Humanos y Sida*. Buenos Aires: Depalma.

Rapisardi, Flavio, and Alejandro Modarelli. 2001. *Fiestas, Baños y Exilios: Los Gays Porteños en la última dictadura*. Buenos Aires: Sudamericana.

Roberts, Matthew W. 1995. "Emergence of Gay Identity and Gay Social Movements in Developing Countries: The AIDS Crisis as Catalyst," *Alternatives* 20, no. 2: 243–64.

Salessi, Jorge. 1995. *Médicos maleantes y maricas: Higiene, criminología y Homosexualidad en la Construcción de la Nación Argentina (Buenos Aires, 1871–1914)*. Buenos Aires: Beatriz Viterbo.

Sebrelli, Juan José. 1997. "Historia Secreta de los Homosexuales de Buenos Aires." Pp.

275–370 in *Escritos Sobre Escritos, Ciudades bajo Ciudades*. Buenos Aires: Sudamericana.

Sívori, Horacio. 1994. "Rehearsing Morality at the Margins: Contexts of Gay Interaction in a Provincial City of Argentina." Master's thesis. Department of Anthropology, New York University.

Sullivan, Andrew. 1995. *Virtually Normal: An Argument about Homosexuality*. New York: Alfred A. Knopf.

Verbitsky, Horacio. 1993. *Hacer la Corte*. Buenos Aires: Planeta.

Vujosevich, Jorge, Ana Lisa Kornblit, and Mario Pecheny. 1998. *Gays y Lesbianas: Formación de la identidad y derechos Humanos*. Buenos Aires: La Colmena.

Zempleni, Andras. 1984. "Secret et Sujétion: Pourquoi ses 'Informateurs' Parlent-ils à L'ethnologue?" *Traverses* 30: 102–15.

# part IV.

## *Racial and Ethnic Rights*

# 12

# Under the Shadows of Yaruquíes:
# Gaining Indigenous Autonomy in Cacha, Ecuador

*Amalia Pallares*

Between small everyday acts of resistance and revolution lie dramatic breaks in the social order. I delineate below how such breaks occur. Unlike weapons of the weak (Scott 1976; 1985), which require no formal organization and gradually tinker at the margins of hierarchical relations, this type of resistance involves a collective critique of dominant understandings, direct confrontation, and high political risk. Unlike revolutions, however, these movements do not seek to replace the state. By focusing on contemporary indigenous resistance in Cacha, Ecuador, this study seeks to analyze how such breaks in order are made possible. The Cacha case is optimal because it involves a dramatic transition from an order of domination and labor control to one of political, religious, and legal autonomy. The Cachas discovered a common past, created a common semantic and physical space, and pursued political autonomy. Together, these factors facilitated the invention of a "Cacha" ethnic identity that served to confront racial subordination and form a distinct political entity.

In order to explain resistance, it is important to explain or problematize lack of resistance. In his discussion of the Nicaraguan Meskitu, Charles Hale (1994) argues that populations that fail to rebel are not passive, but are engaged in negotiation or adjustment. However, while concepts such as small acts of resistance and negotiation correctly undermine the notion of a passive peasantry, they do not reflect the broad range of possibilities contained within the realm of acquiescence. While the possibility of negotiation necessitates people's awareness of alternatives, in more rigid situations these so-called alternatives are not visible to social actors. The analysis of these latter situations can be facilitated by applying Pierre Bourdieu's (1977) concept of *doxa*, defined as a realm in which social arrangements are not questioned. Doxa involves a strict correspondence between social structure and mental structures. It is a situation in which the relation of order "which structures both the real world and the thought world" is accepted as self-evident (Bourdieu 1984: 471). Doxa is "that which goes without saying" because there "is a quasi-perfect correspondence between the objective order and the subjective principles of organization" (Bourdieu 1977: 166).

In Cacha, domination was rendered natural. Its inhabitants willingly participated in practices that, despite their exploitative nature, were the only ones considered possible. The transition from doxa to what Bourdieu (1977) calls *heterodoxy* (in which alternatives are visible) involves a transformation of meanings such that the "natural" order of dominance is questioned. Alternatives that were not previously visible require, according to Bourdieu, both an objective change or crisis and the transformation of subjective perceptions of such reality. Hence, the dominated must have both the material and symbolic means required for change.

### Domination and Resistance in Highland Ecuador

Since the conquest, highland indigenous communities in Ecuador have experienced a long history of colonial and postcolonial social control. Mid-twentieth-century communities were part of a closed, corporate system in which landowners along with priests and local officials controlled zones of *huasipungos*, or small land plots, that Indians could work in exchange for labor in the haciendas. While indentured workers, or *huasipungueros*, and their relatives depended on the hacienda, dwellers of free communities faced another set of power relations. In zones such as Cacha, where most Indians were small landholders, local merchants and *caciques* (political bosses) dominated with a more dispersed, but nonetheless significant, political and economic control.

The 1930s witnessed the institutionalization of indigenous resistance, as local cooperatives and unions eventually formed the *Federación Ecuatoriana de los Indios* (Ecuadorian Federation of Indians, FEI), under the auspices of the Communist Party. These unions and cooperatives obtained ownership of a few public haciendas in the northern highlands, and fought for improvements in wages and working conditions in all haciendas. Becuase the FEI focused primarily on disputes within haciendas, the organization rarely supported free communities' struggles for land and water rights.

International pressure, the struggles of rural and urban social movements, and the initiatives of certain landowning elites led to the land reform laws of 1964 and 1973. While the 1964 law abolished the *huasipungo* and gave former *huasipungueros* alone access to hacienda lands, the 1973 law allowed neighboring communities to demand expropriation of haciendas, due to demographic pressure. Through land reform and related rural development projects, the state became a direct presence in the lives of Indian communities (both free and former hacienda ones). It expanded its previous role as police authority and occasional regulator of disputes between landowners and peasants to become a more constant and invested participant. The state engaged in the explicit and detailed regulation and oversight of land and water conflicts, as well as in the institutionalization of economic and legal resources that could be used by indigenous peasants to challenge landowner power.

The democratic transition of 1979 led to further changes in the relationship between the state and Indians. First, the expansion of the vote to illiterates extended citizenship to many indigenous peasants previously excluded. Second, the *neo-indigenismo,* initiated by the Jaime Roldós regime and continued by the Hurtado (1981–1984) and Borja (1988–1992) administrations,[1] involved the further expansion of the state to include indigenous bilingual education and rural development. As the national government wrested economic and political power away from local elites and encroached further into rural policy, it provided indigenous activists with unprecedented access to policy and state officials. This *neo-indigenista* state encouraged the creation of indigenous organizations, created policies and programs designed to uphold and support Indian language and culture, and made several attempts to create governmental units focused on indigenous policy.

*Neo-indigenismo,* the expansion of the state presence in the countryside, the weakening of landowner control over local resources, the increased access to education, the economic expansion and modernization that accompanied oil exploration in the 1970s, and the development of the Christian left and of Liberation Theology are all factors that promoted an increase in indigenous activism in the 1970s and the development of new local and national organizations with sole indigenous leadership and a distinct indigenous agenda. In the 1980s, the local and provincial organizations were consolidated into three major regional federations: Confederación de Nacionalidades Indígenas de la Amazonia Ecuatoriana (National Federation of Amazonian Indians, CONFENAIE), Coordinadora de Organizacione Indigenas de la Costa Ecuatoriana, (Coordinator of Coastal Indians of Ecuador COICE), and The Ecuadorian Indian Awakens (ECUARUNARI). In 1986 these new Indian organizations coalesced with lowland provincial organizations to form one national organization, Confederación de Nacionalidades Indígenas del Ecuador (National Confederation of Indigenous Organizations, CONAIE). The CONAIE, in conjunction with the efforts of regional and local organizations, generated an unprecedented uprising in 1990 and subsequent uprisings in 1992 and 1994. It is in the context of this twenty-year history of national mobilization that local resistance in Cacha took place.

## Methodology

In field research conducted in 1992, 1993, and 1998, I studied the contemporary history of Cacha, a zone located in the central highland province of Chimborazo. I interviewed current activists, public officials, and organization leaders as well as several elders. Current organization leaders were able to discuss the current political and social processes at work, and offer insights into the contemporary political uses of reconstructed history. The elders' memories, by contrast, presented a more nuanced and complex picture of mestizo political domination and social control, as well as the Cachas' consent to and participation in it. In addition, I interviewed Cachas in the nearby city of Riobamba, and mestizos from the old prominent families in Yaruquíes, as well as priests and nuns who had worked in the area.

## Consent and Coercion: The Structure of Social Control

Contemporary Cacha consists of twenty-three indigenous communities located within a mountainous region surrounding the small town of Yaruquíes. Until the 1970s, what is today known as Cacha consisted of three distinct *anejos*, or annexes, of the Yaruquíes parish: Cacha, Amulag, and Querag. The main sources of income are migrant work and commerce, while needlework production and agricultural production are also important (Arrieta 1984). Yaruquíes is directly in the path between Cacha and the city of Riobamba. Riobamba is the political and economic center of the province of Chimborazo. Until 1981, the only form of transportation to Riobamba was by foot or donkey. Since all the small trails required crossing Yaruquíes to get to Riobamba, Yaruquíes was a necessary rest stop.

The town of Yaruquíes and the roads that connected it to the indigenous communities were literally and symbolically sites of racial domination and confrontation. The white-mestizo Yaruquíes dwellers secured their domination over the indigenous Cachas through the obligatory use of Yaruquíes space for indigenous cultural and material reproduction. The Cachas' visit to Yaruquíes were of two general types: those that involved passing through Yaruquíes on the way to Riobamba and those in which the town was the object of the visit. The indigenous Cachas had to pass through Yaruquíes to reach Riobamba, the site of the weekly major *feria*, or market, where they could buy and sell agricultural goods or pursue work opportunities. Whenever they passed Yaruquíes, they were strongly pressured to engage in commercial exchange in the town, instead of in Riobamba. Given the lack of large haciendas in the area, economic reproduction of the mestizo economy hinged on the Cachas' demand for Yaruquíes. The second type of visit, an exclusive trip to Yaruquíes, was usually made on Sundays and religious holidays to celebrate religious rituals, or on weekdays to conduct affairs in public offices.

In both types of visits, white-mestizos expected indigenous deference. While the indigenous were a very large demographic majority, constituting approximately 93 percent of the population by 1982, they were a political minority. Until 1960, Yaruquíes was a rural parish[2] with complete political authority over Cacha. Until the early 1970s, Yaruquíes exercised de facto political and economic control over the entire zone. Cachas were under the authority of mestizo power-holders and public officials from the town. They had to register their marriages, births, and deaths in the Yaruquíes civil registry. They were also controlled by the town's *teniente político*, the local policing authority with a mandate to settle disputes and ensure order.

The Indian communities in the periphery framed the whiteness of Yaruquíes at the center. The physical distance and topographical difference in altitude served as markers of an existing racial barrier. The ritualization of racial interaction and the maintenance of physical barriers promoted racial distance. In a racialized social hierarchy the Cachas had an ascribed status that was not only characterized or embodied in cultural difference, but also underscored by prevalent understandings of their racial inferiority. Yaruquíes dwellers considered the indigenous ignorant, childlike beings who were incapable of defending their own interests, and therefore had to be protected from the laws and institutions of the state by the white-mestizo local elites. The Cachas confronted this racial barrier every time they passed through the town; and they could even symbolically transgress it during the religious fiestas that were celebrated in the town. These exchanges, however, were ritualized and controlled. They involving a constrained contact that was limited to certain times of the year and specific public places.

The *cacique* system of local rule helped mantain this unequal relationship between the indigenous and mestizos. In the colonial period, *caciques* were Indians of a noble lineage who secured Indian tribute and allegiance to the crown in exchange for land concessions and dispensation from forced labor activities. By the mid-twentieth century, there had been dramatic changes in their ethnic identity and administrative role. While some were the mestizo descendants of original caciques who had intermarried, others were mestizos of less-known descent. Their former monopoly of power had given way to a greater dependence on the *teniente político's* ability to make Indians comply. Each *cacique* oversaw the local administration of one annex, considered to be under his exclusive control. The *cacique* did not rule directly, but appointed indigenous *alcaldes*, or mayors, who supervised communities. The Cachas complied with the *caciques'* orders in exchange for the *caciques'* protection within the town limits, and intervened with mestizo authorities when necessary. When conflicts could not be resolved within a community or family, Cachas would frequently visit their *caciques* in Yaruquíes and rely on the *cacique* to admonish and physically punish the guilty party.

As in many experiences of social domination, the naturalization of hierarchical relations in Cacha involved a combination of consent and coercion. Violence coexisted with what Michael Jimenez (1989) called a close identification between the dominant and the subordinate groups' views of social relations in Cacha. The indigenous vested the *caciques* with authority while identifying closely and personally with them. The Cachas' consent and participation in this social order was possible because of a profound and culturally reinforced intertwining of their own livelihoods and those of *caciques* and other mestizo notables. One's compliance with town and *cacique* authority, and friendship with mestizos of status became yardsticks with which Indians measured their own positions in their communities.

Close identifications were reinforced in the religious fiestas[3] that served as agents of socialization and domination. The match between the subjective and objective structures that characterizes doxa was most evident during these celebrations in which indigenous resources were literally "redistributed" to the pueblo and its dwellers. Every January 1, in a ceremony called "the passing of the baton," Yaruquíes *caciques* appointed several indigenous men to the position of *alcaldes*, who were responsible for coordinating the fiestas. The *alcalde de doctrina*, or *ordinario*, was the highest position, overseeing all the fiestas. In addition, an *alcalde* was appointed for each of the three annexes. The appointed *alcaldes* were usually men who had demonstrated great generosity as captains in previous fiestas. Most of them had given the *caciques* and *teniente político* sizable gifts beforehand.

The *alcaldes*, in turn, appointed the *priostes* (captains) in each annex. A *prioste* shared the financial responsibility for the fiestas. Becoming a *prioste* was an honor, and tested a community member's capacity for leadership as well as his generosity toward the *caciques* and the town.

The costs, however, were significant. *Priostes* had to provide three day's worth of food and drink for the entire town of Yaruquíes. Because the position served as a marker of status and differentiation, *priostes* were very competitive amongst themselves. Instead of sharing the expenses of a band, for example, each *prioste* paid for a different one. In their effort to establish a good name and outdo each other, they purchased large quantities of food from Yaruquíes mestizo vendors as well as barrels of *chicha* (a fermented drink made of corn frequently consumed in the Andean highlands[4]) from mestizo *chicheros* (vendors of *chicha*) Furthermore, because these celebrations catered to the *cacique, teniente político,* and governor—who were the guests of honor—the fiesta food was expected to be of an acceptable quality. This involved the purchase of expensive food items that the indigenous did not produce in their lands. The need for cash led to frequent borrowing from *chulqueros* (money-lenders) who would charge excessively high interest rates. The Cachas were often forced to offer their land or harvest as collateral and, not infrequently, forfeited property when unable to pay loans.

While coercive strategies occasionally played a role in the acceptance of these appointments,[5] on most occasions societal expectations were sufficient sources of pressure. Because compliance with *caciques* and *alcaldes* established status in the community, families expected their members to fulfill this duty. The fact that there was no fundamental contradiction between families' expectations and those of Yaruquíes authorities suggests a tight fit between the mentalities of some of the indigenous and the objective structure that reinforced the domination of the mestizos over them. The societal pressure of one and all helped to mantain doxa, as each community member constrained and imposed on others in the same way in which he or she was constrained.

The fiestas acted as a differentiating force on two levels. Among Cachas, the fiestas allotted prestige and power, and established distinction. They also reproduced power inequalities between mestizos and Indians. While the fiestas did create nonmonetary distinctions among the indigenous, they also perpetuated their subordination by widening their distance from town mestizos. The purported "ideal" intent of the fiesta—redistribution among community members—was counteracted by the continuous and ritualized transfer of resources from Cacha to Yaruquíes.

The fiestas were particularly powerful mechanisms of domination because they were considered the creation of the indigenous, events they organized and controlled,[6] even though the mestizos determined who would be *alcaldes,* what food would be served, where Indians could purchase *chicha,* and which saints would be revered. Everyone considered them an indigenous, and not a mestizo, cultural production. This factor has contributed to contemporary Cacha inhabitants' bafflement with their ancestors' willingness to carry out the fiestas. Looking back, they usually attribute it to ignorance, mystification, self-deception, or some form of false consciousness that kept them ignorant of the real objectives of the fiesta.

But the fact that the fiestas made sense to the Cachas underscores the existence of a realm of doxa in which the objective and the subjective are so deeply intertwined that they cannot be separated or questioned. There were at least two important ways the fiesta made sense. First, by reproducing indigenous notions of equality, reciprocity, communal obligation, and mutual respect, the fiestas mitigated the Cachas' exclusion from the Yaruquíes social and political life. The most crucial equalizing mechanism was the *compadrazgo*, the process by which an indigenous parent would have a Yaruquíes mestizo be the godparent of his child. The *compadrazgo* established an important bond between Indian and mestizo adults. The mestizo became part of the Indian's social circle of mestizo *compadres* (godparent to one's children), mediators, advisors, and friends. In this context, fiestas were an opportunity to celebrate, reform, solidify, and demonstrate to other Cachas the interpersonal relationships between Indians and mestizos.

These relationships were crucial because white-mestizos served as intermediaries between the indigenous and public officials. For the indigenous, interactions with the state were very complex and difficult, both because of language differences—most Cachas spoke primarily or only Quichua—and because of the authorities' routine abuse of the indigenous. Public offices were notorious for serving mestizos before indigenous, making indigenous wait, or refusing them altogether. Language was the main barrier monolingual Cachas had to confront, since Spanish was the only official language used in public offices. Additionally, Indian Spanish speakers were likely to be illiterate[7] and unable to adequately defend their interests in the official realm. Thus, the Cachas never approached authorities directly. Instead, they routinely relied on intermediaries (*quishqueros*)[8] to intervene for them in public offices, as well as in churches for the arrangement of marriages, and in deaths or legal disputes. These intermediaries could be *caciques* themselves, *chulqueros, chicheros*, or members of the wealthiest Yaruquíes families who also employed several indigenous as field workers and house servants. This need for mediation made the careful selection and pleasing of *quishqueros* a central preoccupation for the Cachas.

Second, the fiestas made sense because of the conflation of religious and political authority. Once elected to conduct the fiesta, indigenous *alcaldes* were responsible for governing their particular annex all year.

They controlled community issues, settled disputes, and ensured that the indigenous fulfilled their forced labor obligations. The *alcalde* reported to the *teniente político*, who was therefore able to maintain control without entering into the communities. *Alcaldes* watched over the morality of the communities, resolved problems of inheritance, and neighbors' fights; organized large *mingas* (work details) for public maintenance of the streets, the cemetery, and the church; and organized the fiestas in the annexes.[9]

While indigenous consent and participation in the reproduction of mestizo power was prevalent in the fiestas, it was absent in other areas. As in most of the Ecuadorian highlands, Yaruquíes authorities believed the Cachas owed them servile labor of both a public and a private nature. *Caciques*, the *teniente político*, the governor assisting the *teniente político*, and the priest all used their public authority to implement forced labor practices. As a condition for marriage, for example, an indigenous groom was obliged first to work in the house of the *teniente político* and in that of the priest by carrying out menial tasks for a period of two weeks. Indians also maintained the public grounds, city parks, and streets in order to earn the privilege to use town facilities. As a condition for attending mass, for example, they swept the church floor and cleaned the church square. These practices were not only considered humiliating, but also produced economic hardships by depriving the Cachas of their labor time. In some cases, they led to job loss when employers became impatient with unexpected absences. They were racialized practices, affecting only Indians. Poor mestizos were not called on to participate in these activities.

The use of coercion to ensure compliance was common. When an *alcalde* failed to secure labor in the communities because of indigenous reluctance, he was imprisoned, or his family members were compelled to work. In addition, there was an alternative way of ensuring compliance: On their way to Riobamba, the Cachas had unexpected encounters with the *teniente político*, who held them for a day or more to carry out forced labor. Coercion was also used in daily interactions and commercial exchange. When Cachas transported livestock and produce to Riobamba, they were often stopped by townspeople. The towspeople would engage in *arranche*, the common practice of seizing a product first and then underpaying the owner. The *arranche* prevented Cachas from selling at a more advantageous price in the Riobamba market and gave town mestizos access to goods below market price.

In both cases of coercion and consent, the Cachas' literal distance from Yaruquíes not only justified subservience, but also reproduced it. Yaruquíes white-mestizos ruled almost every aspect of the Cachas' lives.

In contrast to even the poorest of town mestizos, Indians had to undergo coerced labor, obey *cacique* rule, and pay extraordinarily for public services. In the political and administrative realm, Yaruquíes *quishqueros'* roles as mediators relied on the maintenance of rigid boundaries between mestizo and Indian worlds and on the perpetuation of Indian ignorance.[10] Yaruquíes housed the Cacha dead and ruled the living. The Yaruquíes civil register recorded Cacha births, marriages, and deaths, and the *teniente político* controlled their movements and had the power to punish or imprison them in order to obtain their labor. Relationships that were considered reciprocal were actually balanced favorably toward mestizo vendors. Yaruquíes *caciques* appointed fiesta organizers, and Yaruquíes vendors profited greatly from these ventures. The indigenous, on the other hand, repeatedly spent resources they did not have to engage in the fiesta as a public spectacle. In doing so, ironically, they were made responsible for what mestizos considered the moral degradation of the town. In the words of one mestizo informant, the system was not an "improvised" one.[11]

### Leaving Yaruquíes: Resistance and the Quest for Autonomy

In his discussion of doxa, Bourdieu refers to a moment of crisis in which objective relations are transformed and a critique lays the route for new alternatives. Cacha experienced such a break and crisis after several developments disrupted the preexisting order. While the 1964 and 1973 national land reform laws did not restructure land ownership patterns in Cacha, agrarian modernization played a strong role in the political and economic transformation of the zone. Throughout the highlands, the state became more receptive to indigenous communities' claims and more capable of meeting their demands through the recently acquired rights to repossess land and control all water sources.

The freeing of labor and subsequent massive migration to the coast, particularly to Guayaquil, had two important effects. First, it provided many Cachas with more labor opportunities outside of Yaruquíes. This decreased dependence on agricultural labor arrangements with Yaruquíes landowners and exposed many Cachas to labor-organizing experiences in the cities that proved valuable for rural organizing upon their return. Second, the dramatic growth of Guayaquil gave Riobamba an increasingly important role as a food supplier for the city. As it grew, Riobamba consolidated its resources and annexed the adjoining Yaruquíes in 1960, changing its status from rural to urban parish. The eventual consequence of this annexation was the abolition of the Yaruquíes civil registry and of the *teniente político's* office in the 1970s, since these offices were granted only to rural parishes. Yaruquíes fell under the authority of the Riobamba police commissioner and civil registry. This freed the Cachas from the tight authority of the local offices, and initiated a dramatic breakdown in local authority.

The *teniente político*'s departure facilitated the legal development of indigenous communities as well as intercommunal activism. Without fear of reprisal, young activists were free to develop a political alternative. Communities in different annexes began to circumvent *alcalde* authority and to organize in defense of their socioeconomic rights by applying for the status of legalized communities[12] and presenting demands directly to the national government. Disregarding or replacing the authority of the *alcaldes*, these new community activists began focusing on other needs such as schools, community centers, and irrigation projects. They also began targeting state agencies and international nongovernmental organizations (NGOs) to fund projects. These new community activists were joined by several literacy coordinators. Together they formed a cadre of activists who did not owe their power to the dutiful fulfillment of fiesta rituals. They began holding discussion sessions to reflect on their socioeconomic needs and to plan political strategies.[13]

By the mid-1970s Catholic activism overturned the last legitimating source of the eroding order. This religious activism was rooted in a new, theologically grounded movement within the Catholic Church known as Liberation Theology, associated organizationally with the formation of *pastorales indígenas* (Christian Base Communities) and focused on consciousness-raising among the indigenous poor in the highlands. This movement was represented at the local level for the first time by Father Modesto Arrieta, who began working in Yaruquíes in 1972. Arrieta opposed white-mestizo domination in the town, and supported indigenous communities' struggles for water rights. Using a methodology designed to raise consciousness, Arrieta promoted the open discussion of Cacha's needs in pastoral meetings. The Cacha participants analyzed their own socioeconomic subordination, focusing particularly on the unjust and un-Christian nature of the fiestas and on the abuse by authorities. They reached the common conclusion that the fiestas were a form of exploitation and should be eliminated.[14] Arrieta joined some organized communities that were already campaigning to end the fiestas and encouraged them to air their complaints to higher religious authorities.[15] In 1975 Arrieta suppressed the baton ceremony. This act undermined the authority of the *caciques* by eliminating their last remaining function: the appointment of the *alcaldes*.

With the Church's withdrawal of support for the fiestas, the match between the social and the normal, or natural, was broken. Absent the cultural and religious authority that provided the institutional support for these festivities, the economic hardship they entailed was no longer buttressed by religious ideology. Gradually, even in the most traditional communities, popularly elected *cabildos* (town councils) began to assume the roles and responsibilities previously carried out by the *alcaldes* and their assistants.

Arrieta's activities in the town also threatened to undermine the well-established organization of space. He planned to build in Yaruquíes a center designed to teach handicrafts and manual-manufacturing techniques to the indigenous and the mestizo poor. This was considered a threat by many townspeople, who claimed that this was an unsolicited use of their town space, an invasion of Indians. Soon after the money for the handicraft project was secured from the Catholic Church, Arrieta was accused of stealing sacred figures and selling them in order to fund projects for the Indians.[16] A group of Yaruquíes notables asked for Arrieta's removal from Yaruquíes, calling for an investigation into the alleged pilfering from the Church. Finally, once their written appeals failed, the organized townspeople expelled Arrieta by force on January 30, 1977. Arrieta's warning that he was not abandoning the cause but merely relocating to Cacha angered Yaruquíes mestizos, who believed he was the only one responsible for "opening the eyes of the *verdugos.*"[17]

Ironically, Yaruquíes' opposition to the cancellation of the fiestas and the push to impede a handicraft center for Indians were simultaneous campaigns. Not coincidentally, the expulsion of Arrieta occurred exactly eight days after a group of indigenous Cachas asked the bishop in Quito to end the fiestas. The *Yaruqueños* were not necessarily opposed to an Indian presence per se, since the town benefitted greatly from the managed presence of the fiestas; they opposed one that was outside their control and did not produce a profit. Hence, the handicraft school was barred before it was ever opened. Until this point, Yaruquíes mestizos had preordained and regulated the indigenous presence in the town. Arrieta, the indigenous Catholics, and the newly organized communities were threatening this order. Arrieta's persecution was both retribution for threatening the old forms of control as well as deterrence against any further "opening of the eyes." Once Arrieta moved into community territory, the lines of conflict were spatially demarcated: Arrieta, his supporters, and indigenous activists belonged in Cacha, the mestizos belonged in town.

What the *Yaruqueños* did not anticipate was how this demarcation would be used by Cachas to excise themselves much further than

Yaruquíes dwellers had ever desired. By the time Arrieta arrived in Cacha, the leaders of the most recently politicized and legalized communities had created a pre-federation of communities. They had decided that intercommunal organization was necessary in order to promote social and economic development and undermine dependence on Yaruquíes. This Pre-Federation of *Cabildos de Cacha*, later to be called Federación de los Cabildos Indigenas de la Parroquia de Cacha (Federation of Indigenous *Cabildos* of the Cacha Parish, FECAIPAC), sought the empowerment of communities, autonomy from Yaruquíes, and the creation of a separate parish. Initially created with fourteen communities, by 1994 it had twenty-three affiliated communities. Together, Arrieta and the new activists planned a transformation of power relations in three main steps: the construction of an automobile road that led directly to the city of Riobamba, the elimination of the fiestas, and the establishment of Cacha as an autonomous parish.

Since racial hierarchies in Cacha were spatially configured, FECAIPAC activists believed that altering the use of space could transform the power relationship. They believed that, while it was not possible to avoid crossing through Yaruquíes, it was possible to divest the crossing of its previous significance. Hence, the first project was the completion of an automobile road that would connect Cacha to Yaruquíes. This would allow the Cachas to pass quickly through Yaruquíes on their way to Riobamba, instead of encountering *chicheros* and other Yaruquíes merchants. This project was attacked by the townspeople, who attempted to discredit it in front of public authorities by accusing the FECAIPAC of destroying individual property, by telling their indigenous *compadres* that it was all a hoax, and by blocking the road when indigenous workers were scheduled to work. While they were unsuccessful in blocking the construction, the *Yaruqueños* were correct in intuiting the road's larger significance of depriving them of commercial control over the zone. The direct transportation to Riobamba led to the proliferation of stores within Cacha and to its eventual commercial independence from Yaruquíes.

The second goal was the elimination of the fiestas held in Yaruquíes. By the late 1970s, some organized communities had already received permission from national Church authorities to suspend their fiestas. After the suppression of the baton ceremony, the fiestas were increasingly questioned and gradually banned. Fearing town reprisal, the Cachas decided first to cut time in the activities. On one occasion they did not arrive in Yaruquíes until the actual morning of the *fiesta*. This deprived the town of the liquor and *chicha* profits traditionally obtained from indigenous consumption on the eve of the fiesta celebration. On another occasion, approximately eighty *priostes* and hundreds of indigenous held a procession, purposefully marching to a hill right before Yaruquíes, where they could be seen by the townspeople. However, they never proceeded down to Yaruquíes. While Yaruquíes vendors were opposed to this cancellation, retribution against the Cachas was difficult. Several physical confrontations with Cachas kept mestizos away from the communities. Instead, they deliberately harassed the Cachas by rejecting their presence in the town and barring the Cachas' use of the town cemetery to bury their dead. This issue was finally resolved with the construction of three cemeteries in the Cacha zone, but until this occurred, there were several confrontations between indigenous people carrying bodies and mestizos physically blocking their way to the burial grounds.

The final objective of the FECAIPAC was to create its own rural parish with Indian authorities. This was an unprecedented move in the history of Ecuadorian indigenous organizing. FECAIPAC activists believed this would ensure political autonomy and legitimate their territorial independence. In February 1980 the FECAIPAC solicited the mayor of Riobamba to establish the political parish of Cacha with its own civil registry and *teniente político*.

While it provoked the ire of local townspeople, the parish project appealed to the national government's *neo-indigenista* policy. The Cachas targeted the government by arguing that an Indian parish would match the state's new multicultural agenda. When targeting political and civil authorities, they used cultural difference as the main reason for wanting a separate parish. They argued that having their own parish would enable them to preserve their cultural legacy and facilitate their incorporation into the state. Cacha was declared a parish on August 19, 1980, by the cantonal council of Riobamba in a document that emphasized ethnic and cultural values. The culminating point was the inauguration of the parish in April 1981, attended by then-President Roldós, who arrived in Cacha by helicopter. In one of his last public acts before his death, Roldós delivered an emotional speech in which he lauded the Cachas for preserving their customs and cultural identity and referred to the historical importance of the zone.

With the establishment of the parish, Cacha released itself from all formal dependence upon Yaruquíes. Since 1980 Cacha has ruled itself and has operated its own institutions. The inauguration of the parish was soon followed by the creation of a new indigenous civil registry and an elected Indian *teniente político* office that rendered the parish official.[18] By managing all civil procedures and resolving most local disputes, the Cacha parish has permanently eliminated the white-mestizo intermediary in both commercial transactions and public affairs.

### Subjective Conditions: Ethnic Identity
### and the Politicization of History

The break between the ghosts of the old system and the new one is so great that it is often difficult for young Cachas today to understand how their ancestors ever participated in such an exploitative system. When thinking back on these times, Cachas try to explain the reasons behind these practices by attributing them to ignorance and a lack of education.

> Even I went [to a fiesta]. But those people [the elders] didn't know. The elders did not know much. Now, with schools, we know more ... now even the poor know.[19]

> We did not realize, we did not realize.[20]

It is not, however, the process of formal education alone that explains the difference between Cachas then and now, but a particular knowledge of something previously amiss. What did Cachas not realize back then? What does the knowledge consist of and how was it acquired? This realization was not a sudden opening of the eyes, but a complex transition of a mode of consciousness and action in which the learning of history played a central role.

Activists relied on the recovery of pre-Columbian and colonial histories of noble grandeur and ethnic resistance to achieve changes in the status quo. In 1980 a number of activists, along with the priest, organized workshops to familiarize Cachas with the history of the Cacha dynasty, which played a central role in the creation of the Ecuadorian Inca lineage.[21] These workshops not only taught Cachas the lineage and specific ethnic heritage of the Cachas, but also provided attendants with a sense of Cacha as a spatial unity. In nightly sessions, Arrieta and local activists held discussions about elements that were distinctive to the Cachas: the Cacha dynasty that married into Inca nobility, and the momentous Daquilema rebellion in the nineteenth century. Paralleling the history of many other nationalist groups, the Cachas were posited as a distinct and distinctive ethnic group with an important tradition of resistance.

The effects of this teaching and learning of history have included the legitimization of the FECAIPAC's activities and the promotion of the new parish. Most activists agree that before the workshops were held, most of the indigenous had no knowledge of Cacha history. No one remembered the Duchicela dynasty or spoke of Fernando Daquilema and his rebellion. The absence of memory allowed for selective representations of historical moments that underscored important connections between the Cachas of the past and of the present: a shared geography, a shared oppression, and a shared struggle to resist this oppression.[22]

A second important effect of this education was the introduction of the concept that the entire area of indigenous communities had once been one political entity called *Cacha*. Before the workshops and the early efforts of the FECAIPAC to promote unprecedented intercommunal meetings, most Cachas lacked any sense of the zone as one unit; instead, they considered it as consisting of three different annexes of Yaruquíes: Querag, Amulag, and Cacha. Now they were learning that Cacha had once been a highly populated political and geographical entity in its own right, until an earthquake destroyed it in 1640, while Yaruquíes, ironically, had been a mere appendix. This knowledge encouraged Cacha activists to propose the idea that the three annexes should join into one; it reminded the Cachas that in doing so, they were not breaking away from tradition, but continuing it.

In a long process that began with the workshops and continued through the inauguration and political practices of the parish, the sense of being "from Cacha" became ingrained. This new "knowledge" highlighted the existence of a distinct ethnic construction that differed greatly from a stigmatized, generic Indian identity. Hence, Cacha's identity proved to be a powerful source of collective affirmation and pride. While contemporary Indians were considered to be ignorant, drunken, and childlike, the Cacha *cacique* Daquilema had headed the largest Indian rebellion in colonial history. While Indians were considered subhuman and inferior to whites and mestizos, a Cacha princess had initiated the Ecuadorian Inca lineage. The Cachas redefined their identity not by reinterpreting the broader meaning of Indianness itself (as occurred in other highland areas), but by constructing a distinct identity as Cachas that highlighted their positive aspects vis-à-vis non-Cachas. The workshops as well as the ongoing political education by activists provided the zone with a sense of history and place, crucial in an area where geography and race were intertwined so deeply. The creation of Cacha as a political and geographical unit—a place distinguished by a unique and rich (if once forgotten) heritage, a pueblo—provided the tools to construct a political alternative not previously available, to move from doxa to heterodoxy. It was now possible to remain in Cacha, to retain one's cultural identity, and to improve one's socioeconomic status as a collective. In the words of one woman who attended a local political conference: "Now we know that we had great consciousness. One day we were big, why not today?"[23]

## Conclusion

Resistance in Cacha involved the securing of political autonomy through spatial excision and administrative control. The new activists in Cacha had a project: the spatial, political, and cultural break from Yaruquíes as a precondition for self-rule and empowerment. Instead of demanding to be incorporated into mestizo society, Cacha secured a space for cultural, political, and economic reproduction. Cacha has relied on state institutions to make the state its own; it is reformulating the practice of politics as distinct and distinctively Indian politics, located at what now appears to be an irreconcilable distance from its former dependence on Yaruquíes.

The creation of an intercommunal organization is representative of a larger trend in the country. However, in many ways, Cacha and the FECAIPAC's experience is unique, unparalleled in Ecuador in terms of its effectiveness in separating the local mestizo and indigenous political spheres, and pioneering in its creation of a solely Indian parish. In many other Ecuadorian towns, indigenous intercommunal organizations have had to alternate power with mestizo elites, and maintain a strong market and labor interdependence with town mestizos. Because excision is not feasible or, in many cases, is undesirable, local politics and everyday interactions remain infused with interracial struggles in which the Cachas no longer engage.

Nevertheless, both empirically and theoretically, the Cacha experience also has relevance to the study of other indigenous and social movements. Studies of contemporary Andean resistance have primarily focused on former hacienda communities. The study of dispersed power relations in free communities, by contrast, presents new theoretical and methodological challenges. In distinction from former hacienda communities, there is no central node of power or source of information, and the sites of domination and resistance are more varied. With its focus on space and its social meaning, religious rituals, everyday racial relations, and the politicization of history, this analysis aims to provide some direction for future research sites beyond land conflict.

Finally, by using doxa as a theoretical tool, this study underscores the joint role played by objective changes and subjective interpretations in both acquiescence and resistance. The Cachas experienced both coercion and consent, but the latter was more important in maintaining racial domination. The Cachas faced seemingly inescapable objective conditions, but they also participated in and helped reproduce some of the necessary subjective conditions through religious rituals and interpersonal relationships. The intricate intertwining of power and culture is evident in the naturalization of domination as well as in the inability of contemporary Cachas to understand how such domination could be allowed by their ancestors. In this context, the analysis of dramatic "breaks" from the past requires understanding that the interpretations of realities may be as important as or more important than the objective realities themselves, and further, that the realizations that stem from a changing political consciousness deeply shape the construction of political alternatives.

### Notes

1. The administration of Leon Febres Cordero (1984–1988), a right-wing conservative from the Partido Social Cristiano (Social Christian Party, PSC), was characterized by the freezing of most policies targeted toward the indigenous, but not an absolute reversal. The Instituto Ecuatoriano de Reforma Agraria y Colonización (Institute for Land Reform and Colonization, IERAC) continued, as did other programs, even though many were seriously diminished in size and in budget.
2. A *parroquia* is a territorial parish, the smallest division of local government. Ecuador has twenty provinces, each divided into cantons, which in turn are divided into several parishes. Rural parishes' local governments consist of a *teniente político* and a civil register, which records births, marriages, and deaths.
3. A *fiesta* is a generic term that refers to most indigenous celebrations. Fiestas are usually held to celebrate a religious holiday or mark the harvest season. A fiesta usually lasts several days and involves a number of symbolic rituals of evolving social meaning and political significance. In Cacha the most important fiestas were Cacha-fiesta in November; *la fiesta de Pascua* on Easter weekend; *la fiesta de Alajahuán*, or that of Corpus Christi, in March; and the *fiesta de carnaval* in February.
4. The *chicheros* were mainly mestizos who owned *chicherías* in the town as well as on the roads between the communities and Yaruquíes. Burgos (1977) states that in the early 1970s it was still possible for a poor young mestizo couple to open a *chichería* (chicha bar) and make a very good living. The biggest problem the indigenous encountered in *chicherías* were *chicheros* taking advantage of their illiteracy or their highly inebriated state and grossly overcharging them.
5. One example of coercion is the kidnaping of the bride. The reigning *alcaldes* would kidnap a woman who pleased a Cacha so that he could wed her, later "encouraging" the groom to whom the favor had been granted to become a *prioste* in the following fiestas.
6. The idea that they "owned" the fiestas gave the Cachas a sense of control over their cultural reproduction; it also enabled *Yaruqueño* racial constructions of the indigenous as avid fiesta-makers and drunkards who misspend their money irrationally on lavish preparations.
7. According to the Ecuadorian census, in 1982 only 37.62 percent of Cachas over ten years of age were literate, compared to a 78.2 percent literacy rate in the province of Chimborazo. By 1990 the literate population had increased to 55.78 percent.
8. Commonly known in the area as *quishqueros*, intermediaries are more generally known as *tinterillos*. The *tinterillo* is not just a translator, but is also often considered something more akin to a lawyer: someone who will intervene in favor of the indigenous and use his knowledge to help them adequately conduct their affairs. Because they needed to understand both worlds, it was not uncommon for *tinterillos* to be recent descendants of indigenous people, who had become educated and used their knowledge of language and local culture.
9. The *alcalde* system was the only form of community government until the late 1970s. The *cabildos*, or communities of self-elected governments, were nonexistent or nonfunctional until the mid-1970s.

10. According to several indigenous and mestizo informants, vendors and *chul-queros* were usually those most interested in keeping the indigenous as uneducated and isolated as possible. They would spread rumors that the military was going to seize children who went to school or that all children who went to school would leave their communities or be taken by the state. In addition, according to Modesto Arrieta (1984), one attack of Cachas against vaccinators in an inoculation campaign was instigated by mestizo vendors, *quishqueros*, and other *compadres*.
11. Interview with Héctor Lovato (November 1993—Riobamba).
12. While all Ecuadorian communities have been eligible to apply for legal status since the 1937 *ley de comunas*, many communities were not even aware of the potential advantages of this status until the 1970s. It could also be argued that until the 1970s, the advantages to be gained by becoming a legalized community were few, since it was only in this decade that the state pursued rural development aggressively.
13. Modesto Arrieta (1984); Agustina Asqui and José Janeta (1993); Pedro Morocho (1993); Pedro Vicente Maldonado (1993); Manuel Janeta (1993).
14. Arrieta (1984).
15. Arrieta (1984); Asqui and Janeta (1993); Manuel Vallejo (1993).
16. Upon consultation with several sources and despite the existence of a formal investigation, it appears that these claims were never verified.
17. *Verdugo* means "executioner." It is a derogatory term used to refer to Indians in the Chimborazo province. It signifies the representation of Indians as violent and prone to attack mestizo pueblos. Documentation in the 1960s reveals that the term was already used then, and its origins might be located much earlier.
18. The *teniente político* position, however, did not become a state-paid position until six years later. Pedro Morocho, the first *teniente político*, occupied the position without receiving compensation during this entire period.
19. Manuel Janeta (1993).
20. Asqui and Janeta (1993).
21. According to some historical accounts, the Duchicela family of Cacha was a noble dynasty that intermarried with Inca nobility, founding the Ecuadorian Inca dynasty. In addition, Cacha was the site of the largest uprising in nineteenth-century history. The uprising was headed by a local *cacique*, Fernando Daquilema.
22. Unexpectedly, the Duchicela dynasty was soon given a contemporary life-form. In the mid-1980s Cacha was visited for the first time by alleged descendants of the last Inca emperor, Atahualpa. The family had emigrated to the United States a generation earlier and was now in Cacha to bury its father. While the descendants had never been to Cacha and actually had trouble finding it, they were soon declared Cacha royalty; Felipe was crowned and his sister was married in Cacha-Machángara. While the Duchicelas had no real power in the community, many people attended the ceremonies, which played an important role as symbols of the historical and cultural heritage of Cacha.
23. Arrieta (1984: 60).

## References

*Books and Articles*

Arrieta, Modesto. 1984. *Cacha: Raíz de la Nacionalidad Ecuatoriana*. Quito: Ediciones del Banco Central del Ecuador-Foderuma.
Bourdieu, Pierre. 1977. *Outline of a Theory of Practice*. Cambridge, England and New York: Cambridge University Press.
———. 1984. *Distinction: A Social Critique of the Judgement of Taste*. Transl. Richard Nice. Cambridge, Ma.: Harvard University Press.
Hale, Charles. 1994. *Resistance and Contradiction: Meskitu Indians and the Nicaraguan State*. Stanford, Calif.: Stanford University Press.
Hobsbawm, E. J., and Terence Ranger. 1983. *The Invention of Tradition*. Cambridge, England: Cambridge University Press.
Jimenez, Michael F. 1989. "Class, Gender and Peasant Resistance in Central America,

1900–1930." In *Everyday Forms of Peasant Resistance*, edited by Forrest D. Colburn. Armonk, N.Y.: M. E. Sharpe.

Scott, James. 1976. *The Moral Economy of the Peasant*. New Haven, Conn.: Yale University Press.

———.1985.*Weapons of the Weak: Everyday Forms of Peasant Resistance*. New Haven, Conn.: Yale University Press.

Zamosc, Leon. 1995. *Estadística de las Areas de Predominio Étnico de la Sierra Ecuatoriana*. Quito: Abya-Yala.

## Interviews

Asqui, Agustina, and José Janeta, Cacha-Obraje, November 7, 1993.

Janeta, Manuel, Cacha, November 3, 1993.

Lovato, Héctor. Riobamba, November 1993.

Maldonado, Pedro Vicente, Cacha, November 10, 1993.

Morocho, José, Cacha-Machángara, November 1, 1993.

Morocho, Pedro, Cacha-Machángara, November 3, 1993.

Tiopul, Tomás, Cacha-Machángara, November 7, 1993.

Vallejo, Manuel, Yaruquíes, November 12, 1993.

# 13

# Social Justice and Reforms in Late Colonial Peru: An Andean Critique of Spanish Colonialism

*Alcira Dueñas*

Part of the understanding of social movements and political culture in colonial Latin America is the study of the intellectual practices that colonized subjects developed in contexts parallel to rebellions and riots proper. In the midst of a prolonged social crisis in eighteenth-century Andes, protest writing developed as a noticeable contribution of subordinated groups to the late colonial culture. Andean intellectuals engaged in elaborating and presenting their ideas of social change and political reform in representations, letters, and petitions in an attempt to end the injustices of colonialism during times of impending rebellion. This chapter explores Andean writers' elaboration of social justice and native power in mid-eighteenth-century Peru, as it became part of the Andean thought and anticolonial resistance of that time. I argue that, in an effort to effect social change, Andeans elaborated notions of social justice and ethnic power by challenging canonical truths and proposing a new arrangement of their political relationships with the colonial state. They disputed colonial officials' authority by questioning their behavior as Christians. Andeans also challenged the royal power's legitimacy and justified Amerindians' social and political advancement by reinterpreting the history of the Spanish empire in favor of the social inclusion of Andeans as members of the Catholic Church with full ecclesiastical rights.

Scholarly interest in Andean intellectuals of the colonial period has focused only on such authors as Felipe Guaman Poma de Ayala, Inca Garcilaso de la Vega, Santacruz Pachacuti Yamki Salcamaigua, and Titu Cusi Yupanki. Since the 1980s, historians, anthropologists, and scholars in cultural and postcolonial studies have developed works on those Andeans, which have mostly focused on identity and cultural resistance of the colonized subjects as well as their historical consciousness, interpretation, and cultural mediation (Adorno 1986: Castro-Klaren 1995; Zamora 1990; Rappaport 1990). Rarely, however, have the voices and thoughts of native and mestizo writers of late colonial Peru been revealed. By identifying the political and philosophical views of social justice and resistance to colonialism in the eighteenth century, this chapter provides historical explanations and background for understanding contemporary forms of popular resistance and notions of social justice based on Christian ideas in Latin America.

I take as my focus a section of the 180-folio manuscript "Representación verdadera"[1] (shortened title), a text written in 1748 by the Franciscan Fray Calixto de San José Túpak Inca. After discussing the manuscript with the *caciques* (Indian chiefs) of the Lima and Cuzco provinces, he journeyed clandestinely to Spain and handed it to King Ferdinand VI on August 23, 1750 (Loaiza 1948: 69–70). Using historical and textual analysis, this chapter identifies distinctive elements that characterized Andean thought and consciousness in eighteenth-century Peru at the time of the Andean rebellions preceding the Túpak Amaru rebellion. In writing a critique of colonialism, Fray Calixto positioned himself as a representative of the the natives and mestizos before the king. He described Andeans' experiences of colonial subordination and reclaimed participation in the colonial administration, while seeking the acquiescence of the king by a sophisticated use of religious truths. Drawing on the Bible and Spanish law, the "Representación verdadera" erodes the religious and philosophical foundation of colonialism, questions the legitimacy of imperial policies, and reformulates colonial Christianity in Andean terms.

According to Homi K. Bhabha (1994), any discourse—or "cultural performance"—incorporates a linguistic difference that is revealed in the split between the subject of enunciation and the content of enunciation itself. In order to produce new cultural meaning, these two elements mobilize into a "third space" of enunciation in which "cultural knowledge is customarily revealed as an integrated, open and expanding code." This is an ambivalent process that constitutes "the discursive conditions of enunciation that ensures that even the same signs can be appropriated, translated, rehistoricized and read anew" (Bhabha 1994: 36–37). Fray Calixto as a colonial subject of enunciation—a Franciscan and mestizo intellectual—and the interpretation of native subordination embodied in the "Representación verdadera" moves toward such an "inbetween space" to produce a cultural translation, an Andean realization of colonialism that contests the dominant colonial discourse. This discourse was apparent in the corrupt practices of the *corregidores* (magistrates and administrators of Indian communities), priests, and judges who more directly contributed to the obliteration of Indian societies and cultures in colonial Peru. Such a rendition—the production of Andean notions of power, justice, and cultural meaning—articulates, negotiates, and reformulates elements proper of colonial discourse, such as colonial Christianity and colonial history, in order to advance the positions of Andeans under colonialism, thus locating itself in a space in-between the Andean and Hispanicized worlds.

In doing so, Andean scholars' discursive strategy conforms to what Bhabha (1994) refers to as "hybridity as camouflage," a relocation of sub-altern agency (political self-assertion) in a "third space." Bhabha's notion points to the forms of resistance in which the subaltern subject seizes the signs, ideas, and cultural symbols of the colonizer's culture and displaces them to change their meaning in favor of his own ideas and projects. It is such a notion of resistance that illuminates the way Andeans dealt with colonialism on the intellectual and political level. Bhabha (1994: 193) defines this notion of political agency as follows:

> [T]here is a contestation of the given symbols of authority that shift the terrains of antagonism. The synchronicity in the social ordering of the symbols is challenged within its own terms, but the grounds of engagement have been displaced in a supplementary movement that exceeds those terms. This is the historical movement of hybridity as camouflage, as a contesting antagonistic agency functioning in the time lag of sign/symbol, which is a space in-between the rules of engagement.

The "Representación verdadera" used various elements of the colonial discourse of Christianity and subtly questioned them, while reaffirming Andeans' acceptance of basic principles and assumptions of this religious doctrine. The hidden agenda of this strategy was intended as a form of ideological negotiation to secure the reader's acquiescence.

Although the text has been available to contemporary scholars in a publication from 1948, it has received only scanty attention. During the *Indigenista* movement in Peru in the 1940s and 1950s, some scholars unearthed and reprinted the document and regarded it as a precursor of the Peruvian nationalist movement, presenting it as *reformista* (reformist) (Loaiza 1948; Bernales Ballesteros 1969). John Rowe (1954: 3–33) placed the "Representación verdadera" in the context of the "Inca nationalist movement," a series of peaceful campaigns and rebellions during the eighteenth century in which elite Amerindians attempted to restore the Inca dynasty by creating an independent Inca state, which would resemble not the old Inca state but the Spanish monarchy. The proposal of social justice in the manuscript is, however, one of Amerindians participating as equals with Spaniards and mestizos within the judicial and political administration of the colonial state. It is unlikely, then, that this text could support an Inca nationalism of any sort.

In *Power and Resistance: The Colonial Heritage in Latin America*, Sakari Sariola (1972) regards the author as part of a "new mestizo intelligentsia" in colonial Latin America, which at times wrote to protest colonial domination, as a form of "latent resistance from below." He noticed that the demands Túpak Amaru raised to colonial authorities in 1780, had been elevated by Fray Calixto in the "Representación verdadera" one generation earlier. For Sariola, the manuscript's notion of an "Indian 'nation' demanding its rights" reflected the existence of a supportive network of Amerindians united by their common subordination. Fray Calixto's demand for sharing political power assumed that the king, as the ultimate power-broker, could use his authority to attack those interest groups entrenched within the colonial system (Sariola 1972: 196).

More recently, Victor Peralta (1996: 67–88) assessed the relevance of the "Representación verdadera" as a product of the Scholastic tradition of the Franciscans, and the meaning of the proposals for social reform as a mere attempt on their part to gain the king's favor in order to counterbalance the power of the Jesuits and the viceroy at the local level. Peralta suggests that the text was a response of the Scholastic Franciscans to the modernizing efforts of the Bourbon reformers. Unfortunately, Peralta delves more into the Scholastic views of the Franciscans in Peru and does not fully develop his hypothesis to show how the manuscript contested the Bourbon reforms. The influence of the Scholastic idea of the state as a *corpus politicum mysticum* (a political body bound by ties of reciprocity) indeed underlies the text, is noted below when analyzing Fray Calixto's use of Jeremiah's Lamentations as a philosophical and literary format. But the way in which the "Representación verdadera" subverts the content of such ideas to both delegitimize the imperial rule of Spain in the Americas and give political power to natives and mestizos distances itself from the Scholastic tradition. Peralta devotes little attention to the text itself and to the proposals of judicial and political reform, which present the more radical tone of the text. He used a seventeen-page version reproduced and reviewed by Jorge Bernales Ballesteros (1969: 5–35), as opposed to the 180-folio original manuscript, a copy of which stands at the *Biblioteca del Palacio Real* (Library of The Royal Palace, BPR) in Madrid and which I have used here.

A careful historical and textual analysis of the "Representación verdadera" allows one to grasp its complexity. The various voices that speak in the text, the subtle meanings and turns that Andeans gave to the dominant colonial discourses of the time, the conceptualization of social justice and philosophical and political views of Andeans preceding the Túpak Amaru rebellion, and the roles of priests and writings of protest in the rebellions of mid-eighteenth-century Peru are but some of the issues that emerge when one views the text in its full cultural, textual, and historical dimension. Before examining the terms of the textual strategies in the manuscript, we need to understand the historical conjuncture of mid-eighteenth-century Peru to more appropriately assess the relevance of the text and its ideas of social justice and Indian power.

## Social and Political Order in Mid-Eighteenth-Century Peru and the "Representación Verdadera"

The dawn of the Bourbon era in 1700 inaugurated a period of rapid socioeconomic and political changes in colonial Latin America. State policies were intended to adjust the colonial economy and society to the needs of an empire that struggled to survive in the midst of growing competition from neighboring imperial powers and increasingly powerful creole elites. Tax increases on Amerindians, changes in commercial policies, and royal attempts to centralize administrative and political control triggered a wave of rebellions throughout the colonies.

Official corruption at various levels set the tone of the state politics in late colonial Peru. At the local level, *corregidores* tied their demands to Amerindians, while stressing the system of *repartimiento de comercio* (forced distribution of goods among Amerindians). They frequently charged excessive tax rates to Amerindians, who became increasingly indebted both in cash and labor, while violence became a method to collect debts. Most poorly paid *corregidores*, in turn, were indebted to merchants for their costly posts. Since they monopolized cash, merchants from Lima charged high interest rates and utilized *corregidores* to secure the *repartimiento de comercio*. For *corregidores*, the transfer of tribute revenues to the Crown was barely a secondary concern, and defrauding to the royal treasury thus became a common practice (Moreno Cebrián 1983). Thus, corrupt *corregidores* and judges in colonial Peru were major targets of criticism in the "Representación verdadera." They, after all, incarnated colonial despotism in Indian towns and rural parishes.

Concomitantly, conditions of labor in *mitas* (cyclical forced labor), *obrajes* (textile workshops), and *haciendas* (estates), became particularly harsh. Amerindians were badly paid, and their wages were often unjustifiably withheld. In the mission areas, such as the *Cerro de la Sal* (in the north-central Peruvian Andes, where Fray Calixto worked as a missionary), complaints about priests charging excessive fees for religious services and disapproval of the mistreatment and overexploitation of Amerindians in *obrajes* justified native rejection of the civilizing activities of missions.

A cycle of Andean peasant uprisings against fiscal policies erupted in northern Peru in 1730. From 1742 to 1753 in the Peruvian north-central sierra, Juan Santos Atahualpa led an extensive rebellion, challenging the power of the viceregal army and Franciscan missions. Preceded by an aborted conspiracy against the viceroy Conde de Superunda in Lima in 1750, an insurrection broke out in Huarochirí (north of Lima). The viceroy, accusing Fray Calixto of being involved, claimed that the rebels "destroyed bridges, and wrote letters . . . promoting rebellion in the towns and rural areas," referring directly to the impact of the "Representación verdadera" (Moreno Cebrián 1983: 248). Further uprisings ensued in the Peruvian towns of Ferrafañe, Carabamba, Huaniarcas, Piura, and Otuzo for mistreatment of Amerindians in *obrajes* and missions.

### The Author and His Activities

A native of Tarma, Fray Calixto professed to be a descendant of Túpak Inca Yupanki (Loaiza 1948: 65, 69), a former Inca ruler. Before Fray Calixto was ordained a lay priest in 1751 in Spain, he had held ecclesiastical appointments in Lima and Jauja in 1748. He was also posted to the missions of the Quillabamba Valley in 1749 (Loaiza 1948: 70; Vargas Ugarte 1956: 243). Upon his return to Peru, he appeared involved in political activities with Amerindians of Lima and Huarochirí, which caused him to be expelled to Spain in 1756, where he remained jailed in a Franciscan convent in the province of Granada (Loaiza 1948: 92–93).

Although the viceroy Conde de Superunda initially attributed the manuscript's authorship to the Franciscan Antonio Garro, he later exonerated this friar and placed all the responsibility on Fray Calixto (Loaiza 1948: 88). Nevertheless, one must not dismiss the possibility that Garro may have collaborated with Fray Calixto in composing part of the "Representactión verdadera." The initial accusation of the viceroy led some historians to believe that Garro was the author (Bernales Ballesteros 1969: 11). A number of historians and documents indicate, however, that Fray Calixto was in charge of composing the final draft (Polo 1879; Rowe 1954: 20; Loaiza 1948; Medina 1905; Sariola 1972).

Fray Calixto apparently worked in association with a network of local *caciques* and Indian governors with whom he was tied by kinship and friendship (Loaiza 1948: 69). They entrusted Fray Calixto with composing the final draft, which would be submitted to the *caciques* for final scrutiny before handing it directly to the king in Spain. Fray Calixto, Garro, and other sympathizers of the movement who composed similar documents acted as mediators between the Amerindians and royal power. Fray Calixto's role of mediator originated in his activities as missionary in *Cerro de la Sal* and the province of Cuzco, where he was able to placate Amerindians on the verge of rebellion (Loaiza 1948: 70). His fluency in the Quechua and Spanish languages and his cultural proximity to Amerindians and mestizos enabled him to perform this role, which, in turn, allowed him to advance the Amerindians' interests, particularly those of the Mestizos and of the descendants of the Inca nobility.

## The "Representación Verdadera" and Jeremiah's Book of Lamentations

The manuscript is structured in twenty sections glossed with Latin headings taken from chapter 5 of Jeremiah's Lamentations. The subtitles seek to associate the grievances that the prophet Jeremiah raised to Jehovah with the complaints that Andeans addressed to Ferdinand VI. The Book of Jeremiah is a compendium of sermons, oracles, autobiographical sketches, and history. The Hebrew prophet served as minister of Judah in the last forty years of its existence as an independent state, before falling captive to the Babylonians (Holbrook 1994: 5). The Lamentations, in particular, was a poem of yearning and grief for the decadence of the nation of Judah after the siege of Jerusalem (the Holy Land) in 586 B.C. Although Jeremiah expressed his sadness as a personal sorrow, present in the background is "national suffering" for the demise of the independent state of Israel (Holbrook: 1999: 119). Hebrew prophets incorporated satire in preaching, and their narrative strategy was to question someone or something subtly without openly confronting the reader. They looked for agreements between the audience and speaker about the "undesirability of the object of criticism" (Adorno 1986: 123).

In chapter 5 of the Lamentations, the prophet prayed loudly, reminding God of the oppression Hebrews experienced under the foreign rule of Chaldeans: "Remember, O Jehovah, what is come upon us: behold and see our reproach. Our inheritance is turned unto strangers, our houses into aliens. We are orphans and fatherless" (Saphier 1921). With nearly the same words, Fray Calixto admonishes: "Lord your inheritance is turned strange and unto strangers. We are pupils and fatherless orphans." *"Señor, vuestra herencia está en los extraños y extranjeros. Somos pupilos y huérfanos sin padre"* (BPR Sign II/2823: f. 119). According to Exodus, to "remember" something, in terms of biblical language, means to "do" something immediately to resolve an anomalous situation (Holbrook: 1994: 126). Just as Jeremiah prompted Jehovah to save his people, the "Representación verdadera" urged the king to restore social justice in the Andes. Lamentations finishes with somberness: "[b]ut thou hast utterly rejected us; Thou are very wroth against us (Saphier 1921, 5: 1–3). Following Jeremiah, the "Representación verdadera" paraphrases this statement: "You have cast scorn on us and raged mightly against us" *"[d]espreciándonos nos arrojásteis y os airásteis grandemente contra nosotros"* (BPR Sign II/2823: f. 132v). In short, Fray Calixto legitimated the Amerindians' lamentations by utilizing the Hebrew metaphor of the "chosen people," bringing it to the Andean present as a way of liberating Amerindians from Spanish enslavement.

### Discursive Strategies and Andean Renditions of Social Justice

From the outset, the use of monarchic discourse of the kingdom as a symbolic family appears as one of the missionary's most effective rhetorical formulas, inextricably connected with Jeremiah's text. In this discourse of social harmony, the king—the father—and the subjects—the Amerindians, his children—are bound by ties of reciprocity, mutual duties of protection, and tribute. Criticizing royal negligence, Fray Calixto laments: "We are pupils and orphans. . . . Where is honor for us, your children, obedient, docile, and humble children?" (BPR Sign, II/2823: f. 119v). On occasion, the friar projected the discourse of social harmony onto the Church, where the king would be the oldest brother— the heir—and the Amerindians the minor brothers, the subjects, and the true inheritance was the home that God bequeathed to the king. Paraphrasing Jeremiah's Lamentations, Fray Calixto admonishes: "Your inheritance, Lord, that belongs to you as the oldest son of the Catholic Church, has been taken away by strangers. . . . Your home has been taken away by foreigners. . . . Lord, the Indians in this New World are your vassals . . . [but] only the Spaniards hold the secular and ecclesiastical positions" (BPR Sign, II/2823: f. 119).

Drawing on such Scholastic renditions of social harmony and on Jeremiah's narrative, Fray Calixto manipulated a language of sarcastic insinuation about Spanish rule and the Spanish "foreigners" who monopolized ecclesiastical and secular positions, symbolically separating the Amerindians from the *corpus politicum mysticum* represented by the Crown and Church: "They have alienated themselves from us, regarding us as strangers although we are your natives here" (BPR Sign II/2823: f. 132v). Thus, the author placed the responsibility of the disorder in the kingdom upon the colonial officials in an effort to differentiate them from the king himself and to gain his favor.

Subtly, the priest introduced the first element of criticism, asserting that, although the monarchs had given well-intentioned laws, none had been enforced. He then infers that "from what has been practiced, it seems that you care only for the Spaniards . . . since everything here is going against the law; that is why we weep and wail" (BPR Sign II/2823: f. 119v). Furthering his critique, the Andean priest wanted to make the king aware of his disruption of the pact of reciprocity, since, as the kingdom's father, he had not provided the spiritual food for his children—the indoctrination, the "spiritual bread"—which the missionary reformulated as *"ciencias y letras"* (sciences and letters). Proclaiming that "we are fasting from this bread, because our father the king does not know whether it is imparted to us" (BPR Sign II/2823: f. 119v-120), the Andean priest demanded education for indigenous elites. By using the verb *impart*, Fray Calixto equated spiritual food to knowledge; Andeans were as avid for knowledge as they were hungry for the spiritual bread. The friar claimed that their right to education should be enforced, since it was already legally established by the Spanish king. Thus, social justice was first rendered as enforcement of the law that entitled Andeans to education, which was seen as a path to advance their social position in late colonial times.

Advancing a second formulation of social justice, the "Representación verdadera" claims that Amerindians must be allowed to hold positions of power in the Church, religious orders, and secular government. This demand is repeatedly reiterated throughout the letter, using different circumstances to fix it in the king's mind. The insistence of this point raises doubts as to the extent to which this was a popular concern among all Amerindians; entering the convent and participating in the ecclesiastical administration were mostly preoccupations of such elite Andeans as Fray Calixto Túpak Inca. In interpreting the rationale of Andean rebellions, Sakari Sariola maintains that a primary concern of Andeans was to share the realm of spiritual power with the colonizer (Sariola 1972: 183). This expedient could also help to explain the referred insistence and the author's demands to reform the ecclesiastical administration.

Negotiating with the cultural stereotypes that Europeans used to fix the identities of Amerindians, the Franciscan writer incorporates the biblical argument of Jeremiah that idolatry was the cause of God's rejection of the Hebrew people, thus directing the king's attention to the injustice suffered by eighteenth-century Amerindians. Fray Calixto admitted that his ancestors sinned by practicing idolatry. To elude charges of idolatry, however, he detached his generation from that of his Inca ancestors and professed a new Christian affiliation: "Our forefathers sinned ... for their prolonged and multiplied idolatry; it is true; but they are no longer our fathers, and they and we still bear such iniquities. Are not thou, Lord, our Father, our Lord and our King? How long should we pay for someone else's idolatry, bearing such an affront upon us?" (BPR Sign II/2823: f. 120v). In this case, the Andean accommodated his ethnic origin to his current needs, whereas in a second letter, Fray Calixto presented himself to the king as a descendant of Inca nobles to authorize his *"pureza de sangre"* (purity of blood) and be heard (Loaiza 1948: 65).

To portray an egalitarian notion of social justice, the "Representación verdadera" positioned Andeans and Spanish administrators at the same social level, as subjects of the same king with equal privileges: "Oh Lord, you must know that Indians, your vassals, are equals to your Spanish vassals, and the noble [Indians] are equals to noble [Spaniards]; so, Indians must be allowed as priests and nuns and they must be eligible for judges too" (BPR Sign II/2823: f. 127v). The friar refused to acknowledge the subordinated position of Andeans to Spanish officials in America, meaning that subjects must not be governed by subjects, but by the king himself. What the text presents here is, ultimately, a new notion of social hierarchy in colonial Spanish American society. He suggested that the place of Spaniards and Andeans be determined by their relationship to the Crown as the head of the symbolic family of the kingdom, ignoring the racial assumptions underlying colonial culture and discourse, thus according more power to Andeans.

The way Andeans perceived themselves and their fellow colonized subjects, however, is permeated by European racist stereotypes and elitist notions of social hierarchy, which introduce tensions in the Andean discourse:

> All that has been done so far is only that the kingdom gets crowded by stranger people from [E]thiopia, Blacks, mulattos and *zambos* [racial mixing between blacks and whites] ... *those atrocious, indomitous, swine, and outrageous people that have brought vices, evil, sodomy and burglary.* Is it fair that they be set free and can pass to Spain, whereas we the Indians, even the noble ones, are subjects and *mitayos* [mita workers] of your servants? (emphasis mine) (BPR Sign II/2823: f. 162r–162v)

This ironic tone regarding blacks is used in the passage to deplore that Andeans had lesser status than blacks in terms of political and social rights. The text introduces a new element in the discussion of social hierarchies among the subaltern by suggesting that, among all Indian subjects, the noble Andeans deserve a higher status.

Advancing Andean criticism of colonialism, the text denies historical legitimacy to the Spanish empire by drawing on such historical examples as the captivity of the Hebrews by the Egyptians and the subjection of the Spanish under the Moors. The author argues that, even in those cases, in which the rulers were "infidels," the vanquished were always allowed to govern themselves by their own laws and representatives.

Conversely, Andeans under Spanish-Christian rule were prevented from maintaining their own political regime, despite the fact that they embraced the conqueror's religion. In short, Fray Calixto assigned to the Spanish empire an inferior position in comparison to the "infidel" empires in terms of the treatment of vanquished peoples. The Spanish Crown literally broke the laws of imperial dominion in America:

> Then, there is no other history that can be compared with that of the Christian Indians ... which is different in that they surrendered easily to the yoke of Christ; they submitted loyally to the Catholic King of Spain, and served humbly the Spaniards, enriching them with abundant treasures ... thus Indians becoming degraded. (BPR Sign II/2823: f. 165v)

The assumption is that Christianity and the socioeconomic institutions of colonial rule are the sources of all evil oppressing Andeans. The author inadvertently posed that passive submission to Spaniards was an error on the part of Amerindians; thus his critique of the colonial system takes on more radical overtones.

Fray Calixto crafted his discourse carefully to avoid implicating himself with the prior insurrections of Juan Santos Atahualpa in *Cerro de la Sal* from 1742 to 1753. He denied having met Juan Santos Atahualpa, and attributed little importance to the uprising. It was a simple "noise," limited in geographical scope, in which, after having been harassed, the Amerindians "resisted and ultimately killed some, and then hid themselves in the deepest forests ... where undoubtedly they will die" (BPR Sign II/2823: f. 124). Fray Calixto described the "rebellion" of Juan Santos Atahualpa as a deliberate exaggeration made by Spaniards who sought to justify disproportionate, military expenditures. He strove— against much evidence about the widespread support that Amerindians, mestizos, and blacks lent to Santos Atahualpa—to deny Amerindians' participation in the insurrection: "[T]here was not a single Indian, among the millions of Indians and mestizos living in the Kingdom and the highlands, who have raised even a finger to support this Rebellion, not one absentee, nor a single one has gone to follow the Rebel" (BPR Sign II/2823: f. 124r–124v). In any case, Fray Calixto held the Spanish and creole bureaucrats responsible for the insurrection because of the ill treatment they inflicted upon the indigenous peoples of the area. What is revealing here, nevertheless, is that, although Fray Calixto was cautious in not openly supporting the rebels' ideals or actions, he did not adhere to the colonial discourse of power condemning this rebellion either. He reduced the problem to the existence of an isolated rebel fighting in the jungle with the support of only a handful of Amerindians.

### An Andean Power Proposal from Within the Colonial System

Consciously aware of the forces driving colonialism, the friar used rhetorical tools drawn from Fray Bartolomé de las Casas' writings to propose an implicit negotiation to gain the king's acquiescence. If reform took place, Andeans would show the Crown where to find new sources of wealth and riches that they had hidden for many years:

> [W]e will say that if all those errors are fixed ... a great many benefits will follow; and if not ... the discovery of innumerable riches, great treasures, gold and silver mines, hidden by the ancestors, as well as immense quantities of gold, silver and precious stones that they extracted and hid, will be prevented ... and then they will be lost, as the Illustrious Bishop Casas asserts. Because the [I]ndians see that showing these riches represents more work and affront for them ... imitating in this the Spaniards, who, when conquered, hid their riches so that the Romans could not enjoy them (as Dr. Solórzano points out). (BPR Sign II/2823: f. 163r–163v)

Fray Calixto crafted this section masterfully, authorizing his proposal with the words of Bishop Las Casas and the work of the Spanish juridical scholar Juan de Solórzano. Given his condition as a subject negotiating social reforms with the king, the urgency of his rhetorical approaches becomes understandable. The friar proceeded to cite other scholars, such as the Maestro Meléndez and Garcilaso de la Vega, only to reassert that Amerindians had always been willing to embrace Christianity, and, if some had rejected it, "it is not because of their foolishness, rusticity, or ignorance, but because the Spaniards, since the beginning, have treated them worse than donkeys, and more dejected than dogs" (BPR Sign II/2823: f. 163v-164). Once Fray Calixto refuted such stereotypes of Amerindians, he reinforced his charge by displaying his own knowledge of political thought and history to condemn colonialism, assessing Spanish rule as Machiavellian:

> Is not this practice of Machiavellism, a policy that the Catholic government has insensibly introduced in Spain, whose slogan is: "the Sovereigns who pretend the absolute rule of their domains, should exclude the original dwellers from offices, titles, and power positions; and if they show sentiments for this affront, the sovereigns must destroy them and sweep them all?" (BPR Sign II/2823: f. 164)

The missionary infers that Machiavelli's maxims fomenting factionalism inspired Spaniards to introduce distinctions among Europeans, creoles, Amerindians, and mestizos, thus creating enmity and disunity. The prelude to the reforms ends with an arresting reformulation of the Christian postulate of punishment for sinners after death. The author maintained that there would be not only divine punishment for Spanish officials and priests after death, but also an earthly one in this life for the violence and expropriation they inflicted upon Amerindians: "And since God is an honest and just judge, he will punish them here, apart from the punishment that in the other life, precisely, awaits them for the atrocious and inhuman crimes ... that people subjugated by other nations have suffered" (BPR Sign II/2823: f. 165). In other words, colonialism falls into the category of sin, an unusually weighty sin that deserves double punishment. Amerindians would, then, be redressed through Christianity, a reformulated Christianity, which functioned as their notion of true social justice.

The first three proposed reforms of justice intended the restitution of legal procedures in ecclesiastical and secular matters that benefited Andeans. Enforcing the law was also connected with the need for having Indian representatives in the judicial system to secure true justice. "[A]nd if it is found that some [laws] are not convenient, they must be reformed and other [laws] must be made according to the present time, *commanding that they be enforced*, as it was intended at the beginning" (emphasis mine) (BPR Sign II/2823: f. 166). Andeans wanted the removal of restrictions for them to obtain passage to Spain since they deemed themselves able to present their complaints directly to the king. They wanted Amerindians to be recognized as agents capable of modifying their society through the use of the legal system. The reforms questioned the concentration of power by Spaniards and even the very notion of Spaniards governing Amerindians: "With these [reforms], we all will be saved and everyone, both Spaniards and Indians, will have peace, Spaniards governing Spaniards and Indians governing Indians" (BPR Sign II/2823: f. 168). This is a reformulation of Spanish attempts to separate Amerindians and Spaniards into two republics, by reasserting Indian self-government. This idea, however, is nuanced with the proposal of Indian representation, which implied sharing judicial power with Spanish officials.

A fourth point brings up the crucial issue of actualizing the notion of equal rights for Amerindians and Spaniards as subjects of the same king. The text calls for Indian ownership rights over their own goods and their right to carry out trade. Some other Andean claims are freedom to administer their estates, *cofradías* (brotherhoods), and communities, as well as the *cajas de censos* (mortgage deposits) and tributes. In short, the text calls for a more comprehensive Indian autonomy to manage and govern the indigenous social organizations under colonialism. In the fifth demand, Andeans proposed the abolition of the *alcabala* (sales tax) for indigenous peoples, to further their equality of status with Spaniards.

Other important demands were articulated: access of Amerindians to education (not only the learning of the basics, but also the study of sciences and literature); admission to the religious orders for Indian and mestizo women and men; and eligibility for positions of power in the ecclesiastical and secular administration of the colony, especially in the judicial system. Andeans also proposed that the *mita* be extended to idle Spaniards and mulattos, free blacks, and *zambos* who must be feared for being "ferocious and willful people" (BPR Sign II/2823: f. 167v), thus making apparent prejudices against blacks, mulattos, and *zambos*, as well as contempt for Spaniards.

One of the central proposals was the abolition of the *corregidor* post and its replacement by Indian judges and Indian *corregidores*. Andean scholars reformulated their subordinate position in the colonial society by stating that Amerindians owed allegiance only to the king and viceroy in worldly matters and to the bishops in spiritual ones. They denied subjection to colonial administrators and ecclesiastical appointees, because those positions could legitimately be held by Amerindians.

> [A]nd as the [K]ings of Spain have dominated in Naples, Sicilia, Milan, Flanders and Portugal, only the [V]iceroys and [G]overnors have been Spaniards, and as for the rest of the subaltern positions, they were never taken away from the natives. The same policy must be maintained with the Indians, they must be their own corregidores, and the Spaniards should not interfere with them. (BPR Sign II/2823: f. 167v)

Having Indian officials manage tribute would avoid delays in both rendering tax collection to the Crown and payment of the *curas doctrineros* (parish priests). Andean management would avoid the usury that resulted from Amerindians' increasing debt to *corregidores*. It would also save money for *caciques* who were heavily indebted to *corregidores* not only for the *repartimiento*, but also because they were charged higher tax rates than the official ones. Amerindians would also render their accounts punctually since they would not be indebted.

To enforce these proposals, the Andean authors of the "Representación verdadera" suggested setting up a new tribunal of justice that

> depends directly on your Majesty, and that [the tribunal] be made up of one, two or more bishops and other noble people ... very respectful of God

and faithful servants of your Majesty, in conjunction with noble Amerindians and mestizos, the knights of the Spanish and Indian Nation." (BPR Sign II/2823: f. 168v-169)

Thus, Andeans negotiated their participation in the colonial administration by proposing an organization of justice tied directly to the king himself and in which representatives of Spaniards, Amerindians, mestizos, and the Church would share judicial power. In their view, this governing body would guarantee the proposed social and economic reforms and also dignify the lives of the subaltern indigenous peoples under colonialism. Given the stratified and segregated nature of colonial society in America, this sharing of judicial power between colonial elites and a group of subaltern subjects was a proposal too challenging to even be considered by the Crown. Radical as they appear, however, these proposals acknowledge no place or representation for a large sector of nonelite, colonized Amerindians, let alone the vast sector of black and mulatto women and men, whom Fray Calixto perceived as inferior to Amerindians themselves. None of them were included as representatives in the proposed tribunal of justice. These factors make apparent, once again, the ambiguities and tensions of these Indian-mestizo discourses of Andean power.

## The "Representación Verdadera": A Cultural Text for Asserting Andean Power

The manuscript under consideration shows the ways in which subaltern scholars in eighteenth-century Peru articulated their projects of social justice and change. The discursive strategies of the Andean intellectuals participating in this collective project of combative scholarship show one of the distinctive features of subaltern agency in the colonial Andes: the use of the intellectual skills that Andean literates learned from their Hispanicized culture, along with their own knowledge of and experience with being subaltern under colonialism, which assisted them in demanding social change. Indian and mestizo scholars of colonial Peru took from colonialism the intellectual tools of literacy and education to intervene in society for the reconstruction of a future for their Andean descendants.

The use of the Old Testament and narrative strategies of prophets stemmed from Fray Calixto's experience and knowledge as a Catholic priest. The text is filled with historical allusions that the priest may have learned in his religious education, but the way those examples contest imperial practices of Spain in America is a contribution of Andean scholarship, intending to enhance Amerindians' positions before the Spaniards, thus justifying Andeans' claims for political and social representation.[2] The ability to present in a pragmatic fashion the economic and political advantages that an Andean administration would have for the Crown indicates the incisive vision of those who crafted the text, and adds further distinctiveness to these Andean views of the mid-eighteenth century. Their contact with legal and administrative literature and their personal dealings with colonial authorities enabled them to use their experience and knowledge for their own benefit.

Writing discourses of protest and social justice went hand in hand with diffusion of such writing among the subaltern. This activity was associated with a deep commitment to political action, and the constant recourse to the legal system to advance Andeans' petitions and projects of change. This process, which I term combative scholarship, was one of collective scholarship in which the primary input came from the *caciques principales*, Indian and mestizo scholars, teachers, and sympathetic priests, who provided their skills, experience, and knowledge for the advancement of subaltern discourses and positions of power. Fray Calixto stands as just one example of Andean activism, integrating his actions as missionary and his knowledge to foster it.

The manuscript identifies changes in Andean religious views and imaginary in the eighteenth century. Andeans undertook a whole reformulation of colonial Christianity in Andean terms at a time when one could easily perceive the advent of the modern era and the increasing precedence of colonialism. The text manipulates the Christian discourses of "justice," "sin," "compassion," and "love," as well as the European codes of imperial rule, to construct a distinctive Andean discourse of power that fosters the position of Amerindians and mestizos in the colonial world. Degrading colonialism to the category of sin, and, assuming that it will have terrestrial punishment, as opposed to the afterlife punishment for sins the official Christian doctrine admitted, also challenges the canon while reasserting a new notion of divine justice, a kind of social justice that works in the earthly present of daily life to redress Amerindians. While endorsing some central notions of the existence of the Christian God and the observance of Christian practices, sometimes even without questioning the role of the missions, the "Representación verdadera" moves beyond colonial Christianity, speaking through the words of Jeremiah in tones that at times raise doubts about the existence of God, a god who seems to have forgotten to grant social justice to Andeans. In the "Representación verdadera," we are no longer listening to evocations of a golden age of the Inca past—proper of Andean imaginary expressed in ideologies of rebellion at that time and in 1781—

or even to the foretelling of the restoration of the Andean cosmic order. Rather, the "Representación verdadera" witnesses the implementation of a reformulated colonial Christianity that seeks social benefits for Andeans as they move to a modern future.

The reinterpretation of indoctrination as education in "Sciences and Letters," equating the need for knowledge with the need for spiritual food (the spiritual bread) makes apparent Andeans' understanding of social justice in the new times Amerindians envisioned as well as the influence of Enlightenment ideas in Andean thought of the eighteenth century. Fray Calixto, Garro, and the unknown Andean contributors of the "Representación verdadera" thus reformulated colonial Christianity as a strategy of resistance. Their eager defense of the free admission of Amerindians and mestizos into religious orders may be seen as an act of deep Christian conviction. But, judging from Fray Calixto's own experience, his ordination to the priesthood was also the avenue for his social ascent. This interpretation of Christianity appears to be a rather pragmatic reformulation, which enabled Andeans to adapt to a society where ecclesiastical hierarchies were indeed positions of power.

Like all discourses and counterdiscourses of power, the "Representación verdadera" contains tensions and ambiguities. These ambiguities attest to the intercultural influences on the colonized subjects participating in the production of the text. Thus, cultural values regarding race and gender permeate the manuscript as the construction of subalternity unfolds. Racial stereotypes against blacks, mulattos, and *zambos*, as well as representations of indigenous women as pure, docile, and potential models of spiritual perfection, stand as testimony to the European mores incorporated in the Andean imaginary. The idea of subaltern power unravels the elitist bias of the scholars contributing to this project. The proposal of Andean participation in positions of power allowed for representation only of the elite sectors of Indian and mestizo segments of the population.

Finally, as the previous analysis of the "Representación verdadera" demonstrates, open rebellion was certainly not the only avenue for protest and social change in the colonial Andes. Writing to present alternative interpretations of the dominant religious and political views and proposing reforms of the colonial administration was a peculiar form of resistance in the Andes, whose history goes back to the very moment of the Spanish conquest. During that time, Father Las Casas elaborated his harsh denunciation of the injustices that *encomenderos* (holders of labor grants) committed against Amerindians based on Christian principles to advance the evangelization project. In the late sixteenth and early seventeenth centuries, Andean native and mestizo scholars such as Felipe

Guaman Poma de Ayala, Inca Garcilaso de la Vega, Titu Cusi Yupanki, and Santacruz Pachacuti Yamki Salcamaigua further developed this type of intellectual resistance to validate the position of natives and mestizos in the colonial world, a trend that Andeans such as Fray Calixto de San José Túpak Inca and his Andean collaborators continued in complex forms in the mid-eighteenth century. The "Representación verdadera" still resonates consistently in twentieth-century Latin America as we look at the historical roots of some popular movements in terms of their ideological inspiration. Liberation Theology is an intriguing contemporary philosophy and practice that not only rethinks the role of the Church in Latin American society, but also redefines interpretation of Christianity and Catholic social action. The experience of some popular movements and organizations influenced by Liberation Theology since the late 1970s in such countries as Brazil, Chile, Nicaragua, El Salvador, and Guatemala, among others, shows that Christian Base Communities used Christian philosophy and doctrine to theoretically support their struggles for social change and social justice under the dictatorships that desolated their countries, and continue to do so in the present in ways that resemble those of their colonial Andean counterparts.

## Notes

1. "Truthful Representation, and Surrendered and Deploring Exclamation, of the Whole Indian Nation to the Majesty of the Lord King of Spain and Emperor of the Indies, Lord Don Ferdinand VI, Begging His Attention and Help in Redeeming Them from the Outrageous Affront and Dishonor They Suffer Since More Than Two Hundred Years Ago. Exclamation From the American Indians, Using the One That the Prophet Jeremiah elevated to God in Chapter 5 and Last of His Lamentations" (Biblioteca del Palacio Real [hereafter BPR]: Sign II/2823, folio [hereafter f.] 119). All translations from Spanish hereafter are mine. In its original form, this manifest appeared anonymously. However, some indications, discussed below, demonstrate Fray Calixto's authorship. The text comprises two differentiated sections. The first one, which is the sole focus of this chapter, is 'interrupted' by a whole dossier ("The Breve y Compendiosa Satisfaccion") that inserts a theological counterpoint with the Church councils of Lima. The first section continues in the final pages of the manuscript with the Andean proposal of social and political reform.
2. In this sense, this document bears a striking resemblance to the rhetorical structure of Felipe Guaman Poma de Ayala's (1615) *Nueva corónica y buen gobierno* (New Chronicle and Good Government). In his (1609) *Comentarios Reales de los Incas* (Royal Commentaries of the Incas), Inca Garcilaso de la Vega also uses European history and political culture as a basis for his defense of the Inca culture, although not to delegitimize Spanish rule, as both Fray Calixto and Guaman Poma did.

## References

Adorno, Rolena. 1986. *Guaman Poma: Writing and Resistance in Colonial Peru*. Austin: University of Texas Press.

Bernales Ballesteros, Jorge. 1969. "Fray Calixto de San José Túpak Inca." *Historia y Cultura* 3: 5–36.

Bhabha, Homi K. 1994. *The Location of Culture.* London and New York: Routledge.

Holbrook, Frank B. 1994. *Faith Amid Apostasy/Jeremiah.* Ontario: Pacific Press Publishing Association.

Loaiza, Francisco A. 1948. *Fray Calixto Túpak Inca: Documentos Originales, y en su Mayoría, Totalmente Desconocidos, Auténticos, de este Apóstol indio, Valiente Defensor de su Raza, Desde el Año de 1746 a 1760.* Lima: Imprenta D. Miranda.

Medina, José Toribio. 1905. *La Imprenta en Lima 1584–1824.* Vol. 3. Santiago, Chile: Author's ms.

Moreno Cebrián, Alfredo, ed. 1983. *Relación y Documentos de Gobierno del Virrey del Perú, José A. Manso de Velasco, Conde de Superunda (1745–1761).* Madrid: Consejo Superior de Investigaciones Científicas.

Peralta, Victor. 1996. "Tiranía o Buen Gobierno: Escolasticismo y Criticismo en el Perú del Siglo XVIII." Pp. 67–88 in *Entre la Retórica y la Insurgencia: Las Ideas y los Movimientos Sociales en los Andes, Siglo XVIII,* edited by Charles Walker. Cuzco, Peru: Centro de Estudios Regionales "Bartolomé de las Casas."

Polo, José Toribio. 1879. "Un Libro Raro." *Revista Peruana* 1, no. 8: 625–634.

Rappaport, Joanne. 1990. *The Politics of Memory: Native Historical Interpretation in the Colombian Andes.* Durham, N.C., and London: Duke University Press.

Rowe, John. 1954. "El Movimiento Nacional Inca del Siglo XVIII." *Revista Universitaria Cuzco* 93, no. 2: 3–33.

Saphier, William, ed. 1921. *The Book of Jeremiah Including the Lamentations With Fifteen Drawings in Black and White.* New York: Nicholas L. Brown.

Sariola, Sakari. 1972. *Power and Resistance: The Colonial Heritage in Latin America.* Ithaca, N.Y., and London: Cornell University Press.

"Truthful Representation, and Surrendered and Deploring Exclamation, of the Whole Indian Nation to the Majesty of the Lord King of Spain and Emperor of the Indies, Lord Don Ferdinand VI, Begging His Attention and Help in Redeeming Them from the Outrageous Affront and Dishonor They Suffer Since More Than Two Hundred Years Ago. Exclamation From the American Indians, Using the One That the Prophet Jeremiah elevated to God in Chapter 5 and Last of His Lamentations." Biblioteca del Palacio Real (BPR): Sign II/2823, fols. 118–69.

Vargas Ugarte, Rubén. 1956. *Historia del Perú Virreinato (Siglo XVIII) 1700–1790.* Lima: Vicaris Generalis.

Zamora, Margarita. 1990. *Language and Authority in the Comentarios Reales de los Incas.* Cambridge, U.K.: Cambridge University Press.

# 14.

# The Musical Expression of Social Justice: Mexican *Corridos* at the End of the Nineteenth Century

*Catherine Héau*

## The Problem

Looking at recent history it is easy to see that people's struggles (whether armed or not) for justice and liberty have always generated their own insurgent poetry or (virtually the same thing) rebellious songs.[1] Throughout the history of Mexico, this remarkable link between social struggles and rebel songs has been particularly visible, and a singular characteristic of Mexican insurrectionary songs is their recourse to an enthusiastically accepted genre: the *corrido*.[2] As a result, since the Mexican Revolution of 1910, the *corrido* itself has become an almost obligatory symbol of the struggles and endeavors of the people; there is a kind of metonymy in the nation's collective memory that automatically associates the *corrido* with such struggles. Even today one can observe the *corrido* and its ever-present guitar in the most diverse episodes of popular nonconformity, for example, among the indigenous peoples of Chiapas (Héau Lambert and Giménez 1997: 221–44).

Studies published in Mexico concerning popular culture frequently do not go beyond an ethnographic and descriptive level, and ignore the underlying historical processes that affect peasant culture as a whole. For many years, most research on the *corrido* has been limited to an endless discussion of its origins; the result is a series of unsystematic and imprecise compilations from writers lacking sociological and anthropological perspective.

The present study is based on a historical and cultural anthropology in which the *corridos* are considered not as pieces of popular folklore, but as documents and sources of information so that we can study networks of sociability, political ideologies, and the collective memories of peasant communities at the end of the nineteenth century and the beginning of the twentieth century in south-central Mexico. To be more precise: This chapter traces the nucleus of collective representations about social justice and social rights that are embedded in a little-known collection of *corridos*[3] that express the sociopolitical demands of peasants confronting landholders and President Porfirio Díaz (whose dictatorship lasted from 1876 to 1911), considered to be the patron and protector of those peasants.

For those who may ask why I have used the *corrido* to explore the sociopolitical views of the rural populations of that time, the answer is simple: Since tenant farmers have left little direct written testimony concerning their passage through history in comparison with other social groups (except in legal archives related to problems of land ownership), the researcher must resort to the only source that shows in a direct and consistent manner significant aspects of their sociopolitical worldviews, that is, their songs. Naturally, the validity of such singular documents rests upon a realization of their central importance in representing a means not only of community self-expression, but also of sociopolitical protest in a society whose culture was chiefly oral.

In the texts of the *corridos* lies one critical idea of social justice, which centers on the community's recovery of land; paradoxically, this theme is linked to the Liberal Party of the period, which, in its official, urban version, promoted the *dissolution* of the villagers' communal property when it enacted laws forcing the private sale of communal lands.[4] The texts show that tenant farmers redefined the then-dominant liberal ideas, submitting them to a drastic re-elaboration according to the villagers' local interests and ancestral memory.[5] This revision and ideological adaptation—which implied a radical alteration of the essence of a liberal ideology that barely deserved that title—would not have been possible without the intervention of a group of "village intellectuals," probably members of the liberal clubs of the region. I believe that the collective work of these anonymous intellectuals, and the ideas they generated locally regarding topics such as justice, the village, legality, and reform, must be considered one of the ideological-political precedents of the Mexican Revolution, at least in the south-central region, which is the very region dominated by the personality of Emiliano Zapata, the best-known figure of the peasant wing of the revolution.

The so-called southern region, which includes the present state of Morelos and part of the neighboring states of Mexico, Puebla, and Guerrero, is of vital importance in the history of Mexico. This area was a resistance stronghold during the wars for independence and later the cradle of *Zapatismo*, the great peasant movement of the Mexican Revolution. The South has always been fertile soil for the defense of municipal autonomy (i.e., for federalism) and thus for the fatherland. The South put up spirited resistance to the invading armies of Spaniards,

North Americans, and French; battles were fought by guerrillas belonging to the National Guard, a popular militia that helped fill in the gaps left by the inefficiency of the federal army. The participation of the South in great national events has forged for it an historical identity associated with the memory of such figures as Miguel Hidalgo, Jose María Morelos, and Vicente Guerrero (heroes of independence), and Juan Álvarez and Benito Juárez (Liberal luminaries), all leading finally to the remarkable figure of Zapata.

### A Brief Historical and Political Review

In order to understand the struggles for justice and for village autonomy, one must first understand the economic-political setting of the time, which will help make sense of the sociopolitical demands of the peasantry in that era and region. During the colonial period, the Indian villages were organized for administrative purposes into "Indian Republics," which enjoyed a certain political and cultural autonomy, importantly retaining control of their communal lands, the basis for their community's livelihood. The Indian village was autonomous in establishing its tribute responsibilities, its collective work force, and its finances through a cooperative system. The internal positions of authority—mayor, councilman, constable, and officers in charge of religious pageantry—were filled by individuals chosen from inside the community (Ortiz Peralta 1993: 156).

After independence, these villages acquired a new political status when they were transformed into municipalities, ever more pluriethnic, in which neither traditional political rights nor the collective forms of land ownership could fit well, since the communitarian culture of the Indians was in direct contrast to the world of mestizos and Spaniards, strong defenders of private property. In 1856 the Liberal government, fresh from its victory over the dictator Antonio López de Santa Anna and soon to triumph over the conservatives in the Three-Year War, passed the so-called Lerdo Law (*Ley Lerdo*), thus opening up a period of liberal reforms that in Mexican history is known by the generic term *La Reforma*. This law decreed, among other things, the expropriation and privatization of corporately held properties, for example, those of the Church and the Indian villages. Within the old communitarian regime, lands were not sold but were periodically assigned to new users, always with an eye to keeping them inside the community. In theory, land could only be transferred or ceded to someone in the community. The Lerdo Law led directly to the social disintegration of the villages, since the law suppressed the very material and ideological bases of subsistence—

communal landed property—and replaced this with individual property ownership (Mallon 1995).[6]

In 1857 a new constitution decreed liberty of religion and of education, reaffirmed the universal vote, and divided political power between the legislative assembly and the federal executive. A strong Conservative reaction to this constitution loosed a civil war called the Three-Year War or the War of the Reform (1858–1861). The Liberal Party found itself obliged to seek help within the indigenous communities, who, in turn, were given the promise of respect of their common lands. One year after winning this civil war, the liberal government of President Juárez (a Zapotec Indian with a degree in law) was faced with French intervention (1862–1867). Once again, he sought the support of the villages with a "liberal tradition"—that is, those who had backed the liberal faction in its war with the Conservatives—and in exchange for their support, he stopped championing the process of land division and land sales in order to concentrate all his forces upon resistance to the invaders. Responding wholeheartedly to the call of Juárez, the villages organized themselves into guerrilla bands and provided troops for the National Guard. This group differed from the federal army in that its recruits formed into groups according to their place of origin, and chose their own commanding officers. Their democratic structure strengthened the ideological links connecting municipality with autonomy, liberalism with patriotism. In effect, for these villages of the liberal tradition, to be *liberal* also meant being patriotic, with the ensuing obligation to defend their own region (*patria chica*) as well as their native land (*patria grande*).

After the French had been defeated, the National Guard demobilized, and the republic restored, the privatization of communal land recommenced and was carried out on a very broad scale. In 1876 General Porfirio Díaz ascended to the presidency and stayed in power until he was overthrown in the Mexican Revolution. During the period of his rule, the *Porfiriato* (1876–1911), the legal struggles of the southern villages for their autonomy and for their rights to community land ownership proved ineffectual against the spreading invasions of land by the great estates, the haciendas. Two consequences followed in turn: the ever-increasing spread of peasant rebellions in the South, and a wave of repression in response.

Apparently defeated by the power of the national government, the peasants opted for low-profile resistance while widening their political bases. In this way they were extending their political-ideological activism on two fronts: On the one hand, they were widening the foundations for the disadvantaged in the government system, which allowed them to include in their faction those elements of the rural middle classes that had been forced out of local political power by the figureheads who represented the great landowners; on the other hand, they were creating and deepening an alternative solidarity network, one based on an ideology they generated and created themselves. The traces of this have remained embedded in the political "plans" that preceded the popular uprisings, and in the numerous *corridos* of opposition to the government of Porfirio Díaz. I explore these *corridos* from the end of the nineteenth century in order to trace the ideas of autonomy, legality, and justice expressed in them.

### Perceiving the Protagonists: The "Indian Republic" Versus "Spanish Invaders"

Before examining the actual content of the cause in question—the defense of village-oriented social justice—we must mention the way in which the defendants of this cause identified themselves and also the way in which they identified their adversaries. We face the ideological phenomenon Karl Marx (n.d.) noted in *The Eighteenth Brumaire*: In periods of social struggles, the combatants "tend to conjure up in their support the spirits of the past" in order to represent "the new scenario of history."[7]

We shall begin with the discriminatory and racist manner with which colonists regarded the ancient Indian peoples. Spanish colonization coined the generic term *Indian* to designate the autochthonous inhabitants of Mesoamerica. On the one hand was the Spanish community, divided among those born in Spain, Creoles,[8] and some mestizos, and on the other hand there were the "Indians," who, despite the colonists' vigorous and coercive homogenization efforts, fought to maintain the ethnic-cultural diversity inherited from their ancestors. Both communities shared the same spaces but had knitted together diverse forms of coexistence and were organized around their own social institutions, generating their own forms of interaction and solidarity. The cultural divergence between the two communities immediately took (in the eyes of the Spanish) the form of a dichotomy both discriminatory and grossly racist: On the one side, there was the "superior race"—as the Spanish thought of themselves—and on the other, the "inferior race," as the Iberians termed the indigenous populations.

Until the end of the nineteenth century, the idea of racial superiority seemed to the colonizers to express the "scientific" (i.e., positivist) world-view of the era and was considered to be a natural law, of divine origin. From this conception stemmed a social order based on a strict hierarchy, one, however, that became blurred around the edges, given the unusual status and ideological needs of the Creole populace. In effect, although they were looked down upon by those who were born in Spain (the *peninsulares*), the Creoles felt themselves to be *Americans* and so obliged to appropriate for themselves the grandeur due to their illustrious "American history." To achieve this distinction they drew upon the pre-Hispanic past, which then became their "historical memory." In the version of the Creoles, the Americans built pyramids as the Egyptians had done, and even had early access to the true religion, due to the arrival of the Apostle Thomas, who came to evangelize America and whom the natives of Mexico had called *Quetzalcóatl*.[9] Today, even though Moctezuma[10] may be exalted, the native Indian is still looked down upon, which produces the first paradox of Mexican history: The pre-Hispanic pyramids were used as an ideological basis for the Creole recovery of independence, although in fact the Creoles felt a profound scorn for the Indians.

After its independence from Spain, it was logically necessary for New Spain to be rebaptized with a name that, besides cancelling all memory of the colony, would establish a bridge with the pre-Hispanic past. For this reason the mestizos wished to baptize the young nation with the name of *Anáhuac*. The Creoles, however, did not wish to completely erase the colonial memory, and opted for the Creole name that had supplanted Tenochtitlán: *México*, a toponym that, besides its colonial connotation, implicitly incorporated the name of the Mexican race. The choice of the name *México* instead of that of *Anáhuac* for the new country is symptomatic of the forfeiture of a supposed common memory on the part of the Creoles. In effect, the name *México* represents the great Creole city, while the name *Anáhuac* evokes the land of the Indians; that is why the first name was chosen. From now on the new country would be Creole or nothing.

Toward the end of the *Porfiriato*, the mestizos from the southern countryside took back for themselves the preferred indigenous term for origin as a means of ethnic identification in their continual contest against their adversaries, also identified generically as *Spaniards*. Thus we see, in numerous *corridos* of resistance to the government, that the names *Anáhuac* and *Tenochtitlán* recur again and again to scorn Spaniards and their protector, Porfirio Díaz. We can see this in verses 10 and 16 of the *Corrido a Porfirio Díaz* (author unknown):

> Lo que ambicionabas, Calígula, se cumplió,
> Tributario tienes al gran suelo del Anáhuac,
> Y ésta es la recompensa que el pueblo recibe hoy,
> La que le prometiste en las Lomas de Tecoac.

[ . . . ]

*Sigue tu calvario, preciosa Tenochtitlán,*
*Que tiempos felices tal vez llegarán a ti,*
*Si no hay otro Hidalgo que tenga de ti piedad*
*Cual una Betanía encontrarás tu ángel al fin.*

That which you sought, Caligula, has come about,
You receive tribute from the great soil of Anáhuac,
And this is the reward that the people receive today,
That which you promised them on the Hills of Tecoac.
                              [ … ]
Proceed with your Calvary, precious Tenochtitlán,
Perhaps happy days will yet arrive for you,
If there is no other Hidalgo to take pity on you
As in Bethany you will find your angel at last.

The southern rebels considered themselves preservers of tradition and
part of a mythical and enigmatic "Indian Republic," opposed to the
"Spanish Nation," which was now viewed as an invading power come to
oppress the rights of the peasant population. A new revolution for independence was therefore necessary. The following stanzas are from
*Corrido a la Patria* (Corridor for the Fatherland), compiled in Morelos in
1909, which explicity express these ideas:

*Tú ya no eres República Indiana,*
*Hoy colonia te vas a nombrar;*
*Vas a ser sojuzgada de España*
*Y tus hijos esclavos serán.*

*Cura Hidalgo, si resucitarás,*
*¡Qué dijeras en esta ocasión,*
*al mirar la República Indiana*
*gobernada por un español!*

You are no longer the Indian[11] Republic,
Now you are going to be a colony;
You are going to be subdued by Spain
And your sons will be slaves.

Father Hidalgo, if you were to be reborn,
What would you say now,
Seeing the Indian Republic
Governed by a Spaniard!

It is well known that the expression *Indian Republic* was first coined by Juan Álvarez, the popular commander of the war for independence and a companion of generals Morelos and Guerrero. *República Indiana* may be considered a slogan of the first great indigenous and mestizo movement in the south of Mexico in the second half of the nineteenth century. In the past, indigenous resistance movements were characterized by their millenarian side, that is, by their socioreligious demands oriented toward a kind of theocratic society. Now embodying the term *Republic*, the character of this new movement was clearly civil and secular, even to the point of incorporating the tones of anticlericalism so typical of the reform period. The concept of the *Indian Republic* was becoming secularized, completely abandoning the idea of the millenarian utopia.

The term *República Indiana* in the memory of rural southerners sounded like a faraway echo of the lost autonomy of their *Repúblicas de Indios* of the colonial years, rooted in the communal lands of that era. Perhaps for this reason the term served to secure commitment of the people of the South to the liberal ideology and also to revalorize the indigenous race, both of which led to a resurgence of ethnic pride in confronting the Spanish oppressor, who was now reincarnated in the persons of the hacienda owners and their protector, Porfirio Díaz. Numerous *corridos* of the period epitomize this rediscovered ethnic pride, or inverse racism. We can observe, for example, the following stanza from *Corrido a Porfirio Díaz*, sung in Morelos:

> *No inclines tu frente, República mexicana*
> *Ante el hijo ingrato que se señorea de ti;*
> *Noble descendiente de uno de los reinos de Asia,*
> *País de Moctezuma, Cuauhtémoc y Cuauhtemoczin.*[12]

> Do not bow your head, Republic of Mexico,
> Before the ungrateful son who is lording it over you;
> Noble descendant of one of the kingdoms of Asia,
> Country of Moctezuma, Cuauhtémoc and Cuauhtemoczin.

There is an interesting aspect to such views. The writers of the *corridos* conceived the struggle of the villages for their political and social rights during the *Porfiriato* to be, on the one hand, a continuation or reemergence of the wars for independence against the Spanish conquerors; on the other hand, they saw this struggle as an ethnic conflict between Mexicans, the heirs of the Indian Republic, and the "Spaniard Invaders."

The composers of the *corridos* of the era used the generic terms *Iberos, Hispanos,* or *Españoles* to denote the owners of the haciendas and their overseers. Consider, for example, the tenor of the following anonymous *Corrido a la Patria:*

> *Al mirar que ya los españoles*
> *Son los dueños de este patrio suelo,*
> *Son las pruebas de que estos señores*
> *Vendrá tiempo en que nos peguen fierro.*
>                 *[. . .]*
> *Se halla el territorio mexicano*
> *Invadido por esa nación;*
> *Los primeros son los hacendados*
> *Que nos tienen en gran confusión.*
>
> *El supremo gobierno permite*
> *El que gocen de sus garantías,*
> *Y que a los mejicanos les quiten*
> *El derecho de sus correrías.*[13]

> When we see that the Spaniards
> Are the owners of this fatherland,
> It is proof that these gentlemen
> Will soon be branding us.
>                 [ . . . ]
> The Mexican territory finds itself
> Invaded by that nation;
> The principals are the landlords
> Who hold us in great confusion.
>
> The supreme government permits
> Them to enjoy its guarantees
> And takes away from the Mexicans
> The right of free movement.

Perhaps we may conclude that—owing to the not-so-distant memory of the war of independence; to the effectively Spanish origin of a great number of the landowners and their overseers; and, above all, to the stubborn persistence of the idea of "Indian Republic" promoted by Álvarez in the collective memory of the southern populations—these composers had at their disposal only ethnic categories with which to characterize their fight for social justice and municipal autonomy. It was not yet possible for the cultivating classes (*campesinos*) to conceive of this struggle in terms of social classes, as did the Magonist workers' movement in the cities.[14]

### The Peasantry's View of Social Justice

What was really at stake in this persistent conflict between the villages and the haciendas (the latter backed by federal power), identified ethnically as *Indians* and *Spaniards*, respectively? The peasants' conception of social justice pivoted on the rights of the whole population to those benefits and services required to assure their subsistence and a minimum level of social well-being.[15] Of course, the expression *social justice* is not found literally in our texts. These speak only of "justice," "rights," "law," and, at times, the "legal code," but the context is the same. "Homeland, justice, and law" went the old *Zapatista* theme before being replaced by "Land and Liberty." There is a *corrido* by Elías Dominguez[16] entitled *Nueve Años* (Nine Years) that expresses this theme even more clearly:

> *Los pueblos lo que quieren son buenas garantías,*
> *Que se juzgue arreglado al código legal;*
> *Rigiendo bien sus leyes mucho agradecerán,*
> *Respetando el derecho, así se hará la paz.*

> What the villages want are good guarantees,
> To be judged according to the legal code;
> The fair rule of laws would be much appreciated,
> Respect for one's rights would ensure peace.

For peasants, social justice fundamentally meant communal ownership of land and free access to essential resources such as water, wood, grasslands, and parcels for cultivation. It should be this way because in a rural subsistence economy the land constitutes the ultimate foundation of social well-being, insuring the social and economic reproduction of a community. Based on a long tradition traceable to the Indian Republic of the colonial period, the southern farmer populations considered communal property of the land not only a natural right, but a legal right as well, because their claims were backed by legal titles of ownership from the colonial authorities (seen as an inherent right of all villages). Thus, villages, and not individuals, are the true subjects of social justice considered here, and the term village—*el pueblo*, which could mean *people* in other contexts—signifies within itself a common culture based on reciprocity, including systems for assignment of offices, collective work, economic solidarity through community funds, and so forth. To the villagers, it was not private property sanctioned by the power of the state that would permit them access to and use of the land, but the fact that the lands *belonged to the community*.

Along with land-centered elements of social justice, villagers considered *self-government*, that is to say *municipal autonomy*, an almost natural right, once again based in village tradition. As a political right, autonomy was considered an indispensable means of effecting social justice, that is, of guaranteeing free access to the land and to the available resources that this entailed. In the view of the villagers, municipal autonomy was the necessary political tool that assured them the subsistence and well-being of the entire community. Thus, in the villagers' collective memory, the term *free municipality* signified the old autonomy of the *Repúblicas de Indios* and not the pseudoliberal municipalities formed by Creole governing bodies in the independence period.[17]

The villagers of Morelos denounced the continual violation of their rights by hacienda owners, ranchers, and *caciques*,[18] who were supported by local political bosses chosen by Porfirio Díaz himself. From all this social tension there emerged what Barrington Moore (1996: 17) calls "the feeling of injustice," and it is precisely this sentiment that becomes apparent in *corridos*, with their long litany of objections and complaints related to the plunder of lands (above all) and to the repression, abuses, and general arbitrariness of the local political chiefs, whom Díaz imposed on the villages in his effort to control villagers and curtail their autonomy. The people knew very well that such impositions by the authorities gave the authorites a key way to dispossess the villagers of their lands.

As an example following are two verses from a *corrido* by Ignacio Trejo,[19] entitled *La Toma de Cuautla* (The Siege of Cuautla), with its lament over the seizure of land in the city of Cuautla by the sugar plantations that surrounded it:

> *Cierto es que te encuentras rodeada de ingenios,*
> *Pero esa es tu mayor ruina.*
> *Según unos cuentan que allá en otros tiempos*
> *Tu extensión era más digna.*
> *Hoy veo que sujeta te halláis en terrenos*
> *Y reducida en tus líneas.*
> *Ciudad predilecta ¿Qué sucede en esto?*
> *Despierta si estáis dormida.*

*Tanto así llegan a odiarte*
*Según sus ecos declaran,*
*Que quisieran contemplarte*
*Como el desierto de Sahara.*
*Estéril, siendo un oasis,*
*Donde las aguas del Teara*
*Se transmiten abundantes.*

True that you are now surrounded by sugar mills,
But that is your greatest misfortune.
It is told that in other times
Your domain was much greater.
Today I see you fenced in,
Reduced in your area.
Beloved city, what is happening to you?
Awake, if you are asleep.

Have they come to hate you so
As it is echoed about,
That they would wish to see you
Just like the Sahara desert.
Sterile, while really an oasis,
With the waters of the Teara
Flowing generously about you.

In response to such violations of political rights, the popular *corridos* responded by reaffirming the "sovereignty" of the villages;[20] defaming Porfirio Díaz with slander such as "Calígula," "ungrateful son of the homeland," "traitor," "cruel governor," and so on; and denouncing political assassinations such as that of General García de la Cadena, to which we refer below.

### Competition for Land and Threats to Village Autonomy

In truth, offenses against the communal and political rights of the villages had begun much earlier, from the moment in which the *República de Indios* was transformed into a *municipio* (municipality or, roughly, county) from 1822 on. The municipality included not only Indians, but also ranchers, merchants, muleteers, and some neighboring mestizos, and permitted their participation in the municipal administration. Soon these managed to control the government of the municipality by fraudulent means and to make decisions concerning the use of the communal land, which, meanwhile, had come to be considered "municipal land," and which constituted a real bone of contention among Indians and non-Indians alike. As a counterbalance to offset the abuses of the mestizos, many communities managed to appoint judges to represent the Indian interests, which enabled them to bring long legal suits against local *caciques*, haciendas, and ranchers trying to obtain the communal lands (Guardino 1996). To undermine this legalistic resistance by the villages, in 1836 the government of Santa Anna promulgated a central code called *Seven Laws*, which decreed that all communities were obliged to obtain the approval of their municipal council before initiating any legal action.

Yet the cruelest stab at the rights of the Indian pueblos was the proclamation of the Lerdo Law (1856), which established the privatization and legalization of all corporately held assets, as noted above. This law provoked great discontent among the indigenous populations, since they felt that if they lost their holdings they would also lose their traditions of self-government. The villages were deprived of large areas of land, even though for a short time these could continue to be held and cultivated upon paying a rent. In addition, the internal organization of the villages began to suffer from the interference of the political chieftains named by the federal government in its efforts to control the rural communities.

The devastating effects of the Lerdo Law were mitigated and even retarded to a certain extent when liberals sought the backing of the peasant villages as they struggled, first against the Conservatives and then against the French (1862–1867). In both cases the politicians and liberal governments invariably promised the rural villages that their communal lands would be returned and their traditions of self-government would be respected. Perhaps these promises explain why the villages became "staunch Liberals," paradoxically aligning their hopes of self-government and the return of their lands with the Liberal Party. The promises would also explain why, in the *corridos*, the government of Porfirio Díaz was constantly being reproached for breaking promises and being resented for the grave injustice of having done so:

> *Traidor, tu día se ha cumplido;*
> *Recuerda que te pedían*
> *Justicia y no diste oído*
> *Esa voz que te decía:*
> *Velardeña y Tehuixzingo.*[21]

> Traitor, your time has come;
> Remember when they asked you for
> Justice and you didn't listen
> To the voice saying to you:
> Velardeña and Tehuixzingo.

Far from becoming fewer, however, confiscations of land and seizures of political control in the villages became intensified during the Porfirio Díaz years, and the villagers' feelings of injustice and frustration became stronger and stronger. From these roots, the multiple manifestations of resistance in the region advanced gradually from being more or less implicit to becoming more and more overt until finally they burst into flames in the great blaze of the Zapata revolution.

There certainly exists sufficient evidence of such implicit forms of resistance that, during the period of greatest repression, functioned in the ways described by James C. Scott (1990: 4) as "hidden transcripts." By singing *corridos* about brave men (*valientes*)[22] in bars and at fairs, and ridiculing the arbitrary and harmful measures the authorities inflicted on them, the populace fought back as best they could. This is the case in an 1886 *corrido* of the period that conceals, in the story of an innocent joke, a bitter protest against constraints upon liberties. The *corrido, La camisa metida* (The Tucked-in Shirt), makes reference to an edict that obliged the peasants of a village in Morelos to wear their shirts *inside* their pants—probably to avoid their hiding a weapon under a loose shirt. Morevoer, animal fables, often with an underlying double meaning, and *corridos* with nicknames for real persons were understood by everybody in Nahuatl-speaking regions, for nicknames are very popular there.

Sometimes the resistance was more open, spilling over into numerous village rebellions, which were then punished by greater repression. It came to be considered legitimate, although not legal, to steal from the rich to give to the poor (e.g., in the classic *Corrido de Heraclio Bernal*). The rural populace perceived that theirs was a legitimate battle to recover benefits of which they were unjustly despoiled, which added to the feeling that the community had reached the limit of its economic survival. This began to convince the villagers to take justice into their own hands as they fought to recover the use of, if not the actual possession of, the properties that had been taken from them. The communities became more and more rebellious as they defended their political traditions and struggled to assure their economic survival.

Another manner of resistance, more open but still indirect, was the protection of local bandits. The villages began to shield fellow citizens accused of being cattle thieves (*bandoleros*), because in many cases haciendas in search of secure water sources had appropriated the common grazing lands of the community (where traditionally herds were allowed to wander freely). Some haciendas now tried to charge a tax on each head of livestock. Such was the case of the hacienda of Atlihuayan, a property of the Escandón family, which openly confronted the town of Yautepec, which, in turn, was incensed because it considered itself perfectly within its rights to use the lands that had been confiscated. Acts like these, directed toward ensuring a minimal level of economical survival for the communities and considered by them to be perfectly legitimate and based on ancestral custom, constitute what E. P. Thompson (1979: 62) called the "moral economy of the people." In the aforementioned case the villagers argued that they had the right to pasture their animals on the old lands that belonged to them legitimately, although not legally. The *corrido* entitled *Historia de los Tres Manueles* (Story of the Three Manuels), from the state of Morelos in 1896, narrates the sad end of two villagers[23] who were accused of rustling cattle and later murdered precisely because they considered themselves entitled to do this.

As we can see, the protection extended to the rustlers by the villagers constituted dual acts of civil resistance: first is robbery based on the "moral economy" of the poor, in Thompson's sense; second is opposition to authority when villagers protect a man pursued by the government. The protection given to outlaws who defied the government would thus acquire the significance of an indirect and symbolic manifestation of resistance to the government on the part of the people.[24]

### Conclusion

I have tried to let the *corridos* tell their own stories, as they are documents of an oral tradition that directly reflects the social and political ideas of *los de abajo* (the underdogs), and these acts and musical compositions must be read in their sociohistorical context. I started from the premise that, in a culture strongly marked by oral tradition—which in our case overwhelms the written tradition—folk songs, and in particular the *corrido*, function as a living archive of collective memories and thus as a firsthand testimony to a vision of the world, that of the social ethics and sentiments about justice prevailing in rural communities. No doubt this approach defies the tendency of some historians to trust only the official documents in their archives and to relegate to folklore most oral testimonies.

The study of popular folk songs has been fruitful in that it has allowed the discovery of a version of liberalism both rural and localized, one constitutes an ideological predecessor to the period just before the Mexican Revolution, at least in its southern manifestation.[25] The musical versions of political events, until now largely unnoticed by historians, contradict many studies of liberalism that conclude too rapidly that liberal thought only revolved around ideas of individualism and private property. Such views ignore the popular side of Mexican liberalism, in that it also (and differently) signified patriotism (as a reflection of its role during foreign invasions), municipal self-government (as opposed to political centralism), communitarian *igualitarismo* (with equal oportunities for all), and a kind of communal democracy (through consensual election). This sui generis form of liberalism was embodied in *corridos* that reveal the silent ideological efforts of village intellectuals assembled in liberal clubs all around the region who opposed Porfirio Díaz.

Highly relevant to our understanding of the *corridos* is the way in which *campesinos* employed them to re-elaborate and redefine liberal ideology. Liberalism in its popular version was used as a political banner in a struggle whose protagonists wore ethnic masks, that is, Indians against Spaniards. Surprisingly, however, these "Sons of Anáhuac" and the Indian Republic itself also became "patriots" and staunch Liberals, while their adversaries, that is, the hacienda owners, ranchers, and local chieftains, became "Spaniards," who were conservatives, invaders, and enemies of the Mexican *patria* (fatherland). This bizarre mixture of the political with the ethnic became even more complicated by a curious anachronism that intermingled historical time periods. In the *corridos* the struggle of villagers against hacienda owners and the government was conceived to be a prolongation of the war for independence, and this allowed the figures of Hidalgo, Morelos, Álvarez, and Juárez, among others, to become superimposed within the same framework.

Hidden beneath the mantle of what I have called *popular liberalism,* we can detect a set of principles in the *corridos* studied here, ones that correspond to what today we would call *social justice*—principles centered around the belief that there exist ancestral rights (natural and at the same time legal) of communal access to the land that inhere in Indian villages and that, even today, are worth fighting for. This is a vision that considers land as an essential resource to ensure what natural-law scholars would call the *common good*, that is, survival, economic well-being, and a minimum level of collective prosperity. But the right to land also implies the right to political autonomy (versus the central government), because it is the only way to ensure control and communal administration of this precious resource. In the peasant perception, all rights converged and rested upon the sacred right to land. Indeed, it is possible to say that through time the history of the Mexican *campesinos* has been one permanent struggle for the land.

The peasant idea of social justice comprises certain peculiar characteristics. In the first place, the *corridos* show that justice is not expressed in individual terms but in collective ones: The individual counts as part of a community, but one that identifies itself in ethnic terms. Thus social justice becomes linked to a communal culture based on reciprocity. In the second place, it seems that social justice cannot be separated from the political rights of the pueblos, especially when questions arise about autonomy, electoral liberty, and territorial rights. The direct antagonist is often the state government, which is supposed to be responsible for these rights. When visions of social justice finally appeared in the *corridos*, they set off a conceptual domino effect among the related ideas of peace, equality before the law, justice, and legality. Peace and tranquility were the supreme goals, perceived as basic conditions for work, production, and the normal course of daily life. But peace presupposed legal equality, which could not exist without justice; and there could be no justice without legality, without obedience to the legal code, which was identified with the precepts of the constitution of 1857 in the minds of those who composed the *corridos*. The idea of social justice seems to have taken on a syncretic and multidimensional form in the eyes of the liberal southern rural population, and it comprised elements that were at the same time communitarian, ethnic, political, and legal.

In conclusion, I must mention that these ideas of autonomy and justice in indigenous movements of Mexico and Latin America have not died, despite the encroaching world of economic neoliberalism. They are ancient ideas still profoundly anchored in the conscience and in the memory of the Indian peoples. In Mexico, for example, one of the central objectives of the indigenous movement in Chiapas waged by the *Ejército Zapatista de Liberación Nacional* (Zapatista Army of National Liberation, EZLN), is the reestablishment of the autonomy and, indeed, of the entire rights of the communities (Le Bot and Marcos 1997). And the present impasse in the negotiations between the Mexican government and the EZLN derives from the refusal of the former to recognize the full autonomy of the indigenous pueblos.[26] The ancient question of village self-government and the autonomous management of its lands and of its territory are still, today as yesterday, in the center of the most important ethnic conflict in Mexico. It is as if the ideals for which Zapata fought were continually being reborn from their ashes. And these ideals are precisely those expressed in the verse of a *Zapatista corrido* that even today is being sung in the Chiapas rain forests:

*Ay, ay, ay, renacerás*
*bajo el cielo que amaste,*
*donde vive tu frase*
*de tierra y libertad.*

Ay, ay, ay, you will be reborn
under the sky that you loved,
where still lives your phrase
of land and liberty.

## Notes

1.  One remembers, for example, the political literature popular during the French Revolution and other civil wars and, of course, the protest songs directly or indirectly connected with Latin American guerrillas in the 1960s and 1970s.
2.  The *corrido*, often called the Mexican ballad, is usually rhymed; the music serves as a base, a support for the narration. It is commonly sung in outdoor places (in the plaza, at village celebrations, at fairs, and nowadays in bars). It has inherited traces from the *décimas* (the ten-verse poems of Spain) and from the broadsheets of popular romances sung by blind poets there; from the *valonas* of eighteenth-century France; and from ancient Aztec songs taken from the Nahuatl culture in south-central Mexico—a remarkably mixed provenance. Its composers and "publicists" are ordinary peasants, common people distinguished only by their ability to write verse and strum the *bajo quinto* (a guitar peculiar to the southern region of Mexico). As in all societies based on oral tradition, the songs, together with folk stories and legends, fit into the heart of popular literature (see an ample discussion of this theme in Héau de Giménez 1991).
3.  This is a collection of *corridos*, all written before the Mexican Revolution, which were played and sung in the southern region of Mexico in the last decade of the nineteenth century and the beginning of the twentieth. We have compiled the greater part of these during field trips carried out in the states of Morelos and Guerrero between 1985 and 1995. Their publication will form part of a book now in preparation, *Nuevos Estudios sobre el Corrido*.
4.  The *Ley Lerdo* of 1856, which will be explained later.
5.  Therefore there is no basis, at least in this case, for the historical prejudice, shared equally by Karl Marx and the disciples of Alexis de Tocqueville, proclaiming the scanty politicization of the peasantry and reducing rural movements to brutal *jacqueries*—small revolts or simple, conservative reaction to all processes of modernization.
6.  Florencia E. Mallon (1995) documented the political resistance to the laws of reform in the state of Puebla, resistance very similar to that of south-central Mexico.
7.  Here we encounter what Marx (n.d. [1852]: 9) himself called "the weight of dead generations on the minds of the living." According to Marx, this recourse to the past frequently results only in parody and farce: but not always. In some cases "the resurrection of the dead" serves to glorify the new struggle and not to parody the old, to exaggerate the fantasy of the outlined mission and not to turn back before realizing this, to find the new spirit of the revolution and not to force its specter into idleness.
8.  Creoles are persons of Spanish ancestry born in the Americas.
9.  "*Quetzalcóatl* literally means 'feathered serpent,' but in this context came to signify (figuratively) 'precious twin,' and it appeared as a synonym for the Greek *Tomé*, which also means 'twin'—thus the translation of Quetzalcóatl for *Santo Tomé* or *Tomás*. Thus philology aided the ritual, the beliefs, and representations of the ancient polytheistic religion of Mexico. Quetzalcóatl soon began to bear the characteristics of an apostle of Christ or of a Spanish evangelist" (Lafaye 1977: 227).

10. Moctezuma was the last Aztec emperor.
11. There is no better translation of *Indiana*, yet it remains flawed; I especially do not wish to imply a threat of caste war in this region. This "Republic" might therefore include not just the indigenous peoples, but also certain Creoles and mestizos, with each community respecting the rights of the others.
12. Pride of ethnic origin is also present in the *Corrido a la Raza* (Corrido of the Race) by Felix Cruz, a country troubadour from Guerrero at the beginning of the century, whose initial stanzas are as follows:

> *Público presente que reunido estás,*
> *dígnate escuchar bondadoso a la vez;*
> *porque en esta historia les voy a explicar,*
> *de mi ascendencia les diré cuál es.*
> *Vivo desterrado aquí en este reino,*
> *el que ahora se nombra Patria Mexicana;*
> *mis antiguos padres aquí me trajeron,*
> *pero sí mi reino es Huehuetlapala.*

> Those here present, gathered together,
> deign to listen kindly at the same time;
> because in this story I am going to explain,
> and I will tell you about my origin.
> I live banished in this kingdom
> the one that today calls itself the Mexican Fatherland;
> my ancient ancestors brought me here,
> but my real kingdom is Huehuetlapala.

13. Another *corrido*, dating from the period of the election for the state governor in 1909 in Morelos, and bearing the title *¡Que viva México! Corrido a Leyva* (Long Live Mexico! Corrido for Leyva) —Leyva was running against the official candidate and lost— expresses with even greater clarity this transfiguration of a political-social conflict into the terms of an ethnic conflict:

> "*Esos españoles y dueños de fincas*
> *han hipotecado bastante dinero,*
> *no han querido ver sentado en la silla*
> *a ese señor Leyva, rey del extranjero.*
> *República Indiana yo ya me despido;*
> *¿Dónde estarán esos hombres guerreros,*
> *los que defendieron la patria mejicana*
> *sin interesarse en ningún dinero?*

> These Spaniards and ranch owners
> have mortgaged a lot of money,
> not wanting to see sitting in the [governor's] chair
> this man Leyva, lording it over the foreigners.
> Indian Republic, I now say good-bye;
> Where can those warriors be,
> those who defended the Mexican land
> without thinking about money?

14. Ricardo Flores Magón was one of the most lucid ideologists of the prerevolutionary period. In 1900 he founded the newspaper *Regeneración*, whose editorials, initially reformist, became anarchistic in response to repressive attacks by the Porfirian government.
15. In the traditions of natural law, social justice (which differs from distributive justice and commutative justice) is based upon those rights related to the "common good" of society, its groups, and its social classes, and is relevant to the

redistribution of what is produced in the community. It is a concept that evolved at the beginning of the nineteenth century, and pertains to the so-called social question raised by the rise of workers' movements (Messner 1952: 216)

16. Dominguez was an illiterate country composer born in Los Hornos, Morelos.

17. In another paper (Héau 1997) I have demonstrated the historic quid pro quo that linked two different municipal traditions under the same heading of municipio libre (free municipality) Even today the free municipality of the Indians from Chiapas and the free municipality that has become a slogan of the *Partido de Acción Nacional* (National Action Party, PAN) do not have the same meaning.

18. The term *cacique* at first meant Indian chief and then was used to mean the most influential local personality of the village.

19. Ignacio Trejo was a country balladeer from the end of the nineteenth century. He was born in the south of Morelos but lived in Mayanalán, Guerrero.

20. Here are several: (1) "Los pueblos son soberanos/y acérrimos liberales ..." from Trejo, *Sitio de Cuautla* (Siege of Cuautla); in English: "Our pueblos are sovereign/and staunch liberals ..." (2) "Soberano suelo manchado de sangre/de liberales patriotas ..." from *Corrido a Leopoldo Baena*, 1897; in English: "Sovereign soil stained with the blood/of liberal patriots" (3)"Lo que ambicionabas, Calígula, se cumplió ..." from *Corrido a Porfirio Díaz*; in English: "What you asked for, Calígula, you received" (4) "No inclines tu frente, República mexicana/ante el hijo ingrato que se señorea de ti/" from *Corrido a Porfirio Díaz*; in English: "Do not bow your head, Republic of Mexico,/before the ungrateful son who is lording it over you."

21. Velardeña is a mine in the northern State of Durango where *Porfirista* repression caused the slaughter of many. This *corrido* is another example of the circulation of information due to the rural extension of influence by the Liberal Party.

22. During the recent Latin American dictatorships it was still common, especially in Brazil, to sing popular songs that were apparently innocent, but that contained a hidden political meaning as a means of implicit protest (Puccinelli Orlandi 1992: 120).

23. The third Manuel was the policeman who arrested them.

24. In the States of Morelos and Guerrero they still sing the *Corrido de Prisco Sánchez, Corrido de Lorenzo Caspeta, Corrido del Coronel Rebolledo, Corrido de Pandal, Corrido de Juan Valle, Corrido de Leopoldo Baena*, and the *Corrido de Antonio Pliego*, all of which narrate the sad end of the *pronunciados*, members of an irregular militia that fought with the Liberals against the French invasion and were companions of Porfirio Díaz during the rebellion of Tuxtepec that put him in power. They were all pursued by Díaz himself, once he became president. The ties of these *pronunciados*—now converted into outlaws—with their villages of origin were so strong that they couldn't resist attending the fiesta of the *santo patrono* (village patron saint). This strong link was well known by the government, which took advantage of the situation to set a trap for them. Once arrested, the army hastened to conduct them far from the town in order to *matarlos en caliente* (kill them on the run), a tactic also called *aplicando la ley de fuga* (shooting prisoners in the back because they "tried to run away"). When relatives asked where the prisoners were, they were presented with corpses. Some verses referring to this are found in the *Corrido Anónimo a Porfirio Díaz:*

> Una ley fuga de que infame se ha sabido
> para quitarle la vida
> a todo aquel que ante las leyes mejicanas
> reclamase sus derechos.
> Esto fue causa de la muerte que le dieron
> a García de la Cadena,
> y a otros jefes que con él también se hallaron
> en el Plan de Tuxtepec;
> con la desgracia de no hallar ningún recurso
> ni encontrarse la manera,
> de que podamos libertar a nuestra patria
> de un gobernante tan cruel.

They use the infamous *ley fuga*
to take the lives
of all who reclaim their rights
under the Mexican laws.
This was the reason for his death that they gave
to García de la Cadena,
and to other leaders who seconded him
in the Plan of Tuxtepec;
Unfortunately neither recourse
nor manner was found
to help us free our country
from this cruel governor.

The *ley fuga* refers to persons shot while (supposedly) trying to escape.
25. The content and the central concepts of Zapata's revolution appear frequently, repetitively, and diffused through the *corridos* of the South that narrate the epic of Zapata. I have tried to show that the long struggle of the *campesinos* for their land and their autonomy was an important and necessary step toward the Mexican Revolution.
26. Initially the government had accepted, in the agreements of San Andrés, a relatively generous conception of the autonomy of indigenous pueblos, but later recanted, offering a counterproposal that barely offered a minimalist version of this.

# References

Guardino, Peter. 1996. *Peasants, Politics and the Formation of Mexico's National State: Guerrero 1800–1857*. Stanford, Calif.: Stanford University Press.
Héau. de Giménez, Catalina. 1991. *Así Cantaban la Revolución*. Mexico City: Grijalbo.
Héau Lambert, Catherine. 1997. "El 'Municipio Libre' en México: Una retrospectiva histórica." Paper delivered at the 21st International Congress of the Latin American Studies Association, Chicago, September 26–28.
———, and Gilberto Giménez. 1997. "El Cancionero Insurgente del Movimiento Zapatista en Chiapas: Ensayo de análisis sociocrítico." *Revista Mexicana de Sociología* 59, no. 4: 221–44.
Lafaye, Jacques. 1977. *Quetzalcóatl y Guadalupe*. Mexico City: Fondo de Cultura Económica.
Le Bot, Ivon, and Subcomandante Marcos. 1997. *El Sueño Zapatista*. Mexico City: Plaza y Janés.
Mallon, Florencia E. 1995. *Peasant and Nation: The Making of Postcolonial Mexico and Peru*. Berkeley: University of California Press.
Marx, Karl (N.d.) [reprint date 1852]. *El dieciocho Brumario de Luis Bonaparte*. Moscow: Progress Publishers.
Messner, Johannes. 1952. *Social Ethics*. London: B. Herder Book Co.
Moore, Barrington, Jr. 1996. *La injusticia: Bases Sociales de la Obediencia y la Rebelión*. Mexico City: Universidad Nacional Autónoma de México.
Ortiz Peralta, Rina. 1993. "Inexistentes por Decreto: Disposiciones Legislativas Sobre los Pueblos de Indios en el Siglo XIX: El Caso de Hidalgo." In *Indio, Nación y Comunidad*, edited by Antonio Escobar. Mexico City: Centro de Estudios Mexicanos y Centro-Americanos/Centro de Investigación y de Estudios Superiores en Antropología Social (CEMCA/CIESAS).
Puccinelli Orlandi, Eni. 1992. *As Formas do Silêncio*. Campinas, Brazil: Editora da Universidade Estadual de Campinas (UNICAMP).
Scott, James C. 1990. *Domination and the Arts of Resistance: Hidden Transcripts* New Haven and London: Yale University Press.
Thompson, E. P. 1979. *Tradición, Revuelta y Conciencia de Clase*. Barcelona: Editorial Crítica (Grupo Editorial Grijalbo).

# Contributors

**Susan Eva Eckstein,** professor of sociology at Boston University and former president of the Latin American Studies Association, is the author of *Back from the Future: Cuba under Castro,* as well as *The Poverty of Revolution: The State and the Urban Poor in Mexico* (also in two Spanish editions), and *The Impact of Revolution: A Comparative Analysis of Mexico and Bolivia.* In addition, she is the editor of *Power and Popular Protest: Latin American Social Movements* (also in a Spanish edition) and the author of more than sixty articles on Latin American social, economic, and political developments. With Timothy P. Wickham-Crowley she is co-editor and co-contributor to the forthcoming collection, *What Justice? Whose Justice? Fighting for Fairness in Latin America.* She is currently working on a book on Cuban-American transnational ties.

**Timothy P. Wickham-Crowley** is associate professor of sociology at Georgetown University and an executive member of the Center for Latin American Studies there. He is the author of *Exploring Revolution* and of *Guerrillas and Revolution in Latin America,* as well as several articles on related issues. In recent years he has been working on the explanation of different trajectories in comparative historical development within the Americas since the conquest.

**Mark S. Anner** is a Ph.D. candidate in government at Cornell University and earlier received his Master's degree in Latin American Studies from Stanford. In the late 1980s and 1990s he lived in Central America, where he worked with unions and a labor research center. He is the author of several articles in English and Spanish on labor and free trade zones in Central America. Presently he is conducting research on transnational labor responses to industrial restructuring in the Latin American apparel and auto industries.

**Susan A. Berger** is associate professor of political science at Fordham University. She is the author of *Political and Agrarian Development in Guatemala* and of numerous articles on Guatemalan politics. She is currently working on a book on gender politics in Guatemala.

**Donna L. Chollett** is associate professor of anthropology and coordinator of Latin American Area Studies at the University of Minnesota, Morris. She has conducted research on agrarian issues in Mexico since 1984. Her interests include political economy of agrarian systems, economic restructuring, trade policy, land reform, social movements, and community organization. Her current research addresses changes in the Mexican sugar sector and the effects of sugar-mill closings on cane growers and mill workers.

**Alcira Dueñas** is associate professor of history at the *Universidad de Nariño* in Pasto, Colombia. Her scholarly papers delivered at conferences in the United States and Latin America have been based on her doctoral and postdoctoral research on the cultural history of subordinated groups in colonial Peru. She has recently completed two essays related to that work, "Extirpating and Fabricating the Colonized's Imaginary: The Colonial Educational Project for Andean Elites," and "Constructing Women from their Fragmented Bodies: Medical Discourses and Practices in Late Colonial Peru." She is also completing a book-length study from her ongoing research concerning Andean intellectual work and political culture in the eighteenth century.

**Patricia M. Fernández-Kelly** holds a joint position in the Office of Population Research and the Department of Sociology at Princeton University. She has conducted extensive research on economic internationalization, women's employment in export-processing zones, and migration. Her pioneer research focused on Mexico's *maquiladora* program, and with filmmaker Lorraine Gray she coproduced the Emmy Award–winning documentary *The Global Assembly Line*. She is the author of *For We Are Sold, I and My People: Women and Industry in Mexico's Frontier* and the editor with June Nash of *Women, Men, and the International Division of Labor*. Two of her latest projects examine the conditions surrounding fifty African-American families living in poverty in West Baltimore and the remaking of the Cuban-American working class in Hialeah, Florida.

**Nora Haenn** is assistant professor of anthropology at Arizona State University. She is the author of various articles examining the intersection of environment and power. Most recently, she is working on a book that explores how conservation builds on the tropes and structures of development with ambiguous results for environmental protection.

**Catherine Héau** is professor of nineteenth-century Mexican history at the *Escuela Nacional de Antropología e Historia* in Mexico City. She studies popular culture during the *Porfiriato* and the Mexican Revolution, especially the subject of Mexican *corridos*. She is the author of *Así cantaban la revolución* and of *Cien años de canto y amor por la tierra*, as well as several articles related to revolutionary and contemporary Zapatism in Mexico.

**Nora Claudia Lustig** is the president of the *Universidad de las Américas*, Puebla, Mexico. Previously she was the senior advisor and chief of the

Poverty and Inequality Unit at the Inter-American Development Bank. She was also a senior fellow in the Foreign Policy Studies Program at the Brookings Institution, where she authored *Mexico: The Remaking of an Economy*, one of the many books and articles she has authored or edited, the most recent edited work being *Shielding the Poor: Social Protection in the Developing World*. She was first the codirector and later the director of the World Bank's World Development Report 2000–2001, *Attacking Poverty*. She cofounded and was also president (1998–1999) of the Latin American and Caribbean Economic Association (LACEA). She has been professor of economics with the Center of Economic Studies at *El Colegio de México* in Mexico City, a visiting research scholar at the Massachusetts Institute of Technology in 1982, and a visiting professor at the University of California, Berkeley in 1984.

**Martin Medina** is professor of environmental studies and director of *Ecoparque* at *El Colegio de la Frontera Norte* in Tijuana, Mexico. He has collaborated with governmental, academic, and international organizations in development projects in Asia, Africa, and Latin America. In 2001 he was a finalist for the World Bank's Global Development Network Research Award for his work on scavenger cooperatives in Asia and Latin America. He has written twenty-five publications on waste management and environmental issues.

**Amalia Pallares,** assistant professor of political science and Latin American studies at the University of Illinois, Chicago, is the author of "From Peasant Struggles to Indian Resistance in the Ecuadorian Andes." She has published articles on indigenous politics in Ecuador and Latino politics in the United States. She is currently working on a comparative project on regionalism and political culture in Latin America.

**Mario Pecheny** is assistant professor of methodology in political science and research fellow at the Gino Germani Institute, in the School of Social Sciences at the University of Buenos Aires and the National Council of Scientific and Technical Investigations, CONICET. He is the author of *La Construction de L'avortement et du Sida en Tant que Questions Politiques: le Cas de L'Argentine* and coauthor of *Gays y Lesbianas: Formación de la Identidad y Derechos Humanos* and of *Discriminación: Una Asignatura Pendiente*, as well as several articles on related issues. He currently works on health and human rights issues.

**Alejandro Portes** is professor of sociology at Princeton University and director of the Center for Migration and Development there at the Woodrow Wilson School of Public Affairs. He formerly taught at Johns Hopkins University, where he held the John Dewey Chair in Arts and Sciences; Duke University; and the University of Texas, Austin. He was elected and served as president of the American Sociological Association for 1998–1999, was elected in 2000 to the National Academy of Sciences, and is the recipient of many other academic honors. Born in Havana and educated in Cuba, Argentina, and the United States, Portes is the author of some two hundred articles and chapters on national development, international migration, Latin American and Caribbean urbanization, and economic sociology. His recent books include *City on the Edge: The Transformation of Miami* (dual winner of the Robert Park and the Anthony Leeds awards for best books on urban matters in sociology and anthropology, respectively), *The New Second Generation*, *The Urban Caribbean*, and *Immigrant America—A Portrait* (designated a Centennial Publication by the University of California Press). His current research is on the adaptation process of the immigrant second generation and the rise of transnational immigrant communities in the United States. His latest book, coauthored with Rubén G. Rumbaut, is *Legacies: The Story of the Immigrant Second Generation*.

**Jaime Ros** is professor of economics and fellow of the Helen Kellogg Institute for International Studies at the University of Notre Dame. His major research interests are development economics, structuralist macroeconomics, and the economic problems of the Mexican economy. His most recent book is *Development Theory and the Economics of Growth*. He has edited/written four other books and two monographs, and is also author of over fifty articles in scholarly journals. Formerly he was editor of *Economía Mexicana* and associate editor of *El Trimestre Económico*. Current projects include an edited book with Amitava Dutt on development economics and structuralist macroeconomics, as well as a comparative study with Roberto Frenkel on the effects of macroeconomic volatility in Mexico and Argentina.

**Judith Morganroth Schneider** is associate professor of French and Spanish and chairs the Department of Modern Languages and Linguistics at the University of Maryland, Baltimore County. Focusing on intercultural issues in the works of Jewish authors in the diaspora, she has published essays on contemporary Latin American writers, including Marcos Aguinis, Nora Glickman, Isaac Goldemberg, Rosa Nissan, and Alicia Steimberg, as well as on the modern French Jewish writers, Liliane Atlan, Albert Cohen, and Max Jacob.

**Cynthia A. Wood** is an economist and associate professor of interdisciplinary studies at Appalachian State University. Her work has appeared in *Feminist Economics* and in *Nepantla: Views from South*. Her research interests include gender and development, Latin American economics, and postcolonial feminist theory.

# Index